Trauma Transformed

Empowering the Powerless: A Social Work Series

Edited by Marian Bussey
and Judith Bula Wise

Trauma
Transformed

An Empowerment Response

COLUMBIA UNIVERSITY PRESS   NEW YORK

Columbia University Press
Publishers Since 1893

New York   Chichester, West Sussex
Copyright © 2007 Columbia University Press
All rights reserved

Library of Congress Cataloging-in-Publication Data

Trauma transformed : an empowerment response / edited by Marian Bussey and Judith
Bula Wise.
p. ; cm. — (Empowering the powerless)
Includes bibliographical references and index.
ISBN 978-0-231-13832-1 (cloth : alk. paper) — ISBN 978-0-231-13833-8 (pbk. : alk. paper)
1. Psychic trauma — Treatment. 2. Post-traumatic stress disorder—Treatment. 3. Psychic
trauma—Patients—Psychology. 4. Post-traumatic stress disorder—Patients—Psychology.
5. Resilience (Personality trait) I. Bussey, Marian C. II. Wise, Judith Bula. III. Title.
IV. Series.
[DNLM: 1. Stress Disorders, Post-Traumatic—therapy. 2. Adaptation, Psychological.
3. Survivors—psychology. WM 170 T77746 2007]

RC552.T7T7366 2007
616.85'21—dc22

2007024756

Casebound editions of Columbia University Press books are printed on permanent and
durable acid-free paper.

Printed in the United States of America

c 10 9 8 7 6 5 4 3 2 1
p 10 9 8 7 6 5 4 3 2 1

We wish to dedicate this work
to those who have survived trauma and,
with special recognition and the deepest of gratitude,
to those whose stories grace these pages.

Contents

Series Editor's Note

Trauma Transformed: An Empowerment Response is the seventh book in the social work series Empowering the Powerless, published by Columbia University Press. Traumatic life events represent losses of the severest kind: the historical trauma of the Holocaust, slavery, and massacres of American Indians; the war trauma experienced by genocide survivors and veterans; the trauma of a natural disaster or of an unnatural disaster; the sexual trauma experienced by victims of rape, abuse, and incest; bullying, assault, or murder; and the trauma of losing one's child. While these and other traumatic events are experienced as disastrous and overwhelming, they can also provide opportunities for transformation—for growth and mastery. In editing this collection, Marian Bussey and Judith Bula Wise invited seasoned practitioners and academics to share their experiences and expertise. Bussey and Wise augment the compelling chapters of their contributors with a masterful introduction and conclusion. They have created an exceptional book about trauma, about the processes of transformation from victim to survivor, and about hope, courage, resilience, and finding meaning in the suffering.

I present the series' seventh book, *Trauma Transformed: An Empowerment Response,* with special appreciation and respect for the editors' accomplishments. Having read several drafts of the manuscript, I know firsthand how much time and energy they devoted to this project. I thank Professors Bussey and Wise for their gift to the empowerment series and to the profession's literature. I invite the readers to marvel at that gift.

Alex Gitterman

Acknowledgments

Many lives have come together to shape these pages for their intended purpose and message. First, we extend our deep gratitude to the individuals, families, groups, and organizations whose stories inform and enlighten. You are the guiding light in this volume, facing unasked-for and unimaginable trials, courageously living with and through them, and reshaping—transforming—them into your messages of hope, strength, and resilience. Because of you, others who face trauma in their lives may find sources of comfort and direction that were unknown to you. This gift is immeasurable. To simply acknowledge you is truly inadequate. This book is dedicated to you, individually and collectively.

To each contributing author, our deep thanks for so generously offering your wisdom and experience and for rewarding us as editors with your insight, commitment, and timely submissions. Your compassion and selfless giving, your efforts to alleviate suffering and restore hope, shine through your work. It is a privilege to know you and to have worked with you on this project.

We extend our deep gratitude to Dr. Alex Gitterman. Your attention to the "soul" in these pages and your amazing skill and wise guidance as series editor are constant sources of inspiration. We greatly appreciate the work of Lauren Dockett, senior executive editor at Columbia University Press. Thank you for guiding this manuscript along its way through the stages of development from a loose stack of pages to a coherent, bound volume.

We are grateful to our colleagues at the University of Denver Graduate School of Social Work for the privilege to serve as the program developer and first coordinator (Judith Wise) and as the present coordinator (Marian Bussey) of the Trauma Response Certificate Program. It is your vision and foresight that inspired the earliest stages of thought that are at the root of this volume. To our students, many thanks for your helpful feedback in shaping the early years of the program.

To Amy Pickett, who read drafts and offered useful suggestions, many thanks for giving hours of your time to this work. We know that such hours are not easily available in your busy schedule, and we appreciate the adjustments you made to enhance and strengthen the manuscript.

Judith Wise: To Marian, coeditor, yes, but also treasured colleague and friend, thank you for your unwavering enthusiasm from the moment we first spoke of our ideas for this book to these finishing touches. Our writing and editing these works about transformation have run parallel to the transforming and deepening of my professional respect and admiration for you and of our personal friendship. To Chip go the greatest of thanks for your constant love and support, your flexibility and interest, and your care and feeding. In your warmhearted and generous way, you have contributed more to this work than words can express.

Marian Bussey: It is a pleasure to reflect on the process of writing and editing this book, and so much of that pleasure has been getting to know the keen insight and wonderful vision of my coeditor, Judith Wise. Thank you, Judy, for the hours we've spent talking, reading and rereading, and discovering much about ourselves just as we've discovered more about this trauma work to which we are both committed. I thank my family, who are truly the crucible from which my ideas have emerged, and I thank Luke, whose honesty, support, and love have made this work possible.

Contributors

Marian Bussey, Ph.D.
Associate Professor
University of Denver Graduate School of Social Work

Diane B. Byington, Ph.D.
Private Practitioner, Mind-Body Approaches
Niwot, Colorado

Jean East, Ph.D.
Associate Professor
University of Denver Graduate School of Social Work

Eliana Gil, Ph.D.
Director, Children's Corner
Multicultural Clinical Center
Springfield, Virginia

Laura Kaplan, Ph.D.
Assistant Professor
University of Northern Iowa

Joycee Kennedy, M.S.W.
Clinical Social Worker Emerita
The Empowerment Program
Denver, Colorado

Sue Kenney, M.S.W.
Director
Project WISE (Women's Initiative in Service and Empowerment)
Denver, Colorado

Andrew Malekoff, M.S.W.
Executive Director/CEO
North Shore Child and Family Guidance Center
Roslyn Heights, New York

Susan Manning, Ph.D.
Professor
University of Denver Graduate School of Social Work

Carol J. McCarthy, M.S.W.
Clinical Social Worker
Boulder, Colorado

Faye Mishna, Ph.D.
Associate Professor
Margaret and Wallace McCain Family Chair in Child and Family
University of Toronto Faculty of Social Work

Jane Parker, M.S.W.
Associate Dean
Tulane University School of Social Work

Lynn Parker, Ph.D.
Associate Professor
University of Denver Graduate School of Social Work

Jaime Rall, M.S.W.
Program Director
Colorado Citizens Campaign
Denver, Colorado

Mel Singer, M.S.W.
Private Practitioner
Denver VA Hospital Mental Health Clinic (Retired)
Denver, Colorado

Kay M. Stevenson, Ph.D.
Domestic Relief Program Administrator
Lutheran Family Services of Colorado
Denver, Colorado

Judith Bula Wise, Ph.D.
Professor Emerita
University of Denver Graduate School of Social Work

Maria Yellow Horse Brave Heart, Ph.D.
Associate Professor
Columbia University School of Social Work

Michael Zakour, Ph.D.
Associate Professor
Tulane University School of Social Work

Trauma Transformed

Introduction:
Empowerment as a Response to Trauma

JUDITH BULA WISE

The stories at the heart of this book are from the lives of people who have moved forward with their lives with resilience, courage, and hope following horrific and traumatic experiences. Trauma changes the course of a person's life. Following traumatic experiences, each survivor faces the question of how to fit those events, whether a one-time occurrence or an ongoing situation, into new understandings of life's meaning and purpose.

Salome (all names and some details of client lives in the case examples have been changed to respect confidentiality) experiences each day the reminders of the historical trauma of the massacres of her American Indian ancestors. The Wilsons are survivors of torture, flight, refugee camps, and resettlement. Tay is an adolescent survivor of childhood incest. Frank was a batterer; Joan, his wife, ended their marriage, and Frank now attends a program to understand why he did what he did so that he will never again behave in that way. Beth lives each day facing direct and indirect acts of discrimination against her because of her sexual orientation. Amory, a war veteran, confronts daily memories of atrocities that are unimaginable to those who have never experienced war. Claire lives with memories of being sexually assaulted by a male participant in her day-treatment program, while those she thought were her friends stood by watching. Four-and-a-half-year-old Nicolas reshapes his understanding of safety and acceptance after a vicious dog attack to his head and face. These people, along with the others described in these pages, give us a glimpse of the enormous courage required to survive oppression, discrimination, and terror while being robbed of one's previously known life.

These narratives do not end, however, with mere survival. Through the strength of their own resilience and the empowering support of others, these survivors speak about their change, of what transformed their lives after surviving a traumatic event or after living for years in the midst of ongoing trauma. They acknowledge those helpers who supported them through the confusion, those who created buffers of safety, who offered understanding and respect, sandwiches and water, Kleenex and cleansing. They speak of these advocates of compassion, literally those who "suffer with," as ones who encouraged them to remember and to grieve, not to avoid or deny what happened. These are the people who helped the survivors find their footing again in relationships, in restoring familiar routines for each day, in trusting the simple pleasures. They were there when anger, despair, confusion in thought and speech, and even deeper despair, fear, and countless repetitions of the survivor's trauma story drove others away. These helpers are the authors of the chapters that follow or they are the ones who are described by the authors.

The idea for this book grew from the simultaneous work on two writing projects. The first was a program proposal for the Trauma Response Certificate Program at the University of Denver, and the second was a book, *Empowerment Practice with Families in Distress* (Wise 2005). Weaving back and forth between these two projects, the possibility of a book on trauma response for the Empowerment Series emerged. Without question, the empowerment framework, in thought and practice, has much to offer as a response to trauma.

As *Empowerment Practice with Families in Distress* went to press, the certificate program proposal completed its evaluation process at the various levels of academic review. The words from conversations with trauma specialists over two decades are central to the content of that proposal. These are individuals who work tirelessly to help colleagues and students understand that a person's *response* to trauma takes the form of a recognizable process, geared toward healing and restoration of functioning that is similar to or that even reaches beyond the level of functioning before the trauma. They insist that most often, a trauma response is not a "disorder," regardless of the widespread use of several diagnoses bearing that designation. It is to these empowering thinkers that credit is due for the use of the term *trauma response* in the program's name.[1] Their clarifying perspectives sharpened my three and a half decades of curiosity about the helping process in various roles as practitioner, researcher, educator, administrator, and supervisor.

Definitions of Key Terms

Each chapter in this volume provides an illustration of how trauma transforms through resilience and empowerment. Definitions of *trauma, transformation, resilience,* and *empowerment* serve as a background for the work presented by the contributing authors. Volumes written on each of these terms are readily available to those who wish to read further in a particular area. Though the following definitions are by no means exhaustive, they have been carefully selected because of their relevance to this present work.

Trauma is a universal experience. It is no respecter of rich or poor, of profession or occupation, of country of origin or family of origin, of talent or personal purpose. "In short, anyone can be traumatized, from the most well-adjusted to the most troubled" (Everstine and Everstine 1993:7). Experiences of trauma affect not only the individual's emotional well-being but also "the systems of attachment and meaning that link individual and community" (Herman 1997:51).

Trauma is defined using eight general dimensions and six specific distinctions. The eight general dimensions identified are threat to life or limb; severe physical harm or injury, including sexual abuse; receipt of intentional injury or harm; exposure to the grotesque; violent, sudden loss of a loved one; witnessing or learning of violence to a loved one; learning of exposure to a noxious agent; and causing death or severe harm to another (Wilson and Sigman 2000). The more direct the exposure and the longer and earlier the onset, the greater the risk for emotional damage (van der Kolk, McFarlane, and Weisaeth 1996).

The six specific distinctions that clarify the definitions of *trauma* that are used in the chapters to follow are physical trauma, psychological trauma, social trauma, historical trauma, ongoing trauma, and vicarious or secondary trauma. *Physical trauma* refers to a "serious and critical bodily injury, wound, or shock . . . that resulted from an external source." External sources may include, as in the story of Nicolas, the attack of an angry dog. They also may include such events as airline and auto accidents, physical and/or sexual assaults by strangers, the violence of one's own family members, natural disasters, and terrorist attacks. *Psychological trauma* refers to any critical incident that causes people to experience unusually strong emotional reactions that involve physiological changes and that have the potential to affect their ability to function at work, at home with family members, or in other areas of their lives (van der Kolk et al. 1996). This category of trauma includes repeated verbal and emotional abuse as well as neglect. Recent studies in brain research provide evidence of the physiological change of decreased blood flow in the parietal lobe of the brain following trauma (Hipskind and Henderson 2002).

Social trauma refers to any social condition that perpetuates forms of oppression against vulnerable populations—war, hate crimes, discrimination in education or employment, poverty, homelessness, physical and verbal violence, addictions—and the social institutions that either do not address the condition or blame those who are affected. *Historical trauma*—such as the massacre of American Indian/Native American tribes; the institution of slavery for African Americans; the Holocaust for Jews; hate crimes against lesbians, gays, bisexual, and transgendered people; and the internment of Japanese Americans in concentration camps—plays a particularly devastating role in cross-generational trauma recovery for many people in these groups. *Ongoing trauma* refers to forms of trauma that, instead of being identified with a single event, continue day after day. Examples of ongoing trauma include poverty, chronic illness, addiction, and all forms of prejudice and discrimination because of ethnicity, age, gender, sexual orientation, religion/spiritual beliefs, differing ability, and language. The overlap among these various definitions of trauma offers the reminder that multiple forms of trauma may be experienced simultaneously.

Vicarious trauma (VT) or secondary traumatic stress (STS) is the stress experienced by the helpers (family, friends, professionals) as a result of their empathy while assisting and caring for survivors who have been directly affected by the devastating forces of traumatic events or ongoing trauma. "Trauma is contagious" (Herman 1997:140). Another term used to describe secondary trauma is *compassion fatigue*—that is, "the process of attending to the traumatic experiences and expression may be traumatic itself" (Figley 1999:9). These helpers may experience a variety of responses—intense fear, recollections and re-experiencing of the traumatic event, a sense of helplessness, avoidance, numbing, detachment, sleep disturbances, difficulty concentrating, startle responses, and irritability— all of which are similar to the responses of those with the immediate, or primary, experience of the trauma (Figley 1999:12). Sensing isolation from supporters is also noted as another response by helpers who are suffering from secondary traumatic stress. STS, which "can emerge suddenly and without much warning," is different from burnout, "which emerges gradually and is a result of emotional exhaustion" (17). Empathy and exposure are at the heart of compassion fatigue, rendering trauma workers at high risk for developing the behaviors mentioned above. "Unresolved trauma of the worker will be activated by reports of similar trauma in clients" (21) and may present the necessity of an ethical decision on the part of the worker to remove himself or herself from the helping role if the impairment from reactivated past trauma interferes with providing the best possible service to the client (Bula 2000).

Self-care for trauma workers through balancing the workload with a variety of clients who are at different steps in the recovery process, through engaging in diverse work-related activities with colleagues, and through individualized relaxation routines is a necessity (Pearlman 1999:62). Many agencies contribute to the ongoing care of their trauma workers through VT groups, in which helpers can safely report their experiences and receive support from others. The development of strengths in self and other, the ability to create life-affirming connections, ongoing use of creativity and communication, the ability to confront one's own fears of death, and personal psychological and spiritual maturity have been identified as requirements for trauma workers (Serlin and Cannon 2004:319–320).

Any discussion of "trauma" is incomplete until the diagnoses of post-traumatic stress disorder (PTSD) and acute stress disorder (ASD) have been addressed. As briefly mentioned earlier, there is a specific constellation of behaviors that must be present before a diagnosis of PTSD or ASD is applied. Using these specifications reveals that PTSD is a rare condition, affecting an estimated 8 percent to 10 percent of the people who experience trauma (Naparstek 2004).

The diagnosis of PTSD requires exposure to an extreme stressor and a set of symptoms that last for at least one month. Experiencing, witnessing, or confronting an event or events involving actual or threatened death or serious injury, or a threat to the physical integrity of self or others, plus a response that involves intense fear, helplessness, and/or horror are characteristics of extreme stressors (American Psychiatric Association 1994:427–429). Examples of extreme stressors include serious accident or natural disaster, rape or criminal assault, combat exposure, child sexual or physical abuse or severe neglect, hostage/imprisonment/torture/displacement as a refugee, witness of a traumatic event, and sudden unexpected death of a loved one. Three main types of symptoms occur for a person with PTSD: (1) re-experience of the traumatic event through intrusive memories, flashbacks, nightmares, and/or triggers; (2) avoidance and emotional numbing, evidenced by such behaviors as loss of interest, detachment from others, and restricted emotions; and (3) increased arousal indicated by sleep difficulties, irritability, outbursts of anger, difficulty concentrating, hypervigilance, and exaggerated startle responses (Foa et al. 1999:69).

When the symptoms last one to three months, the condition is referred to as "acute PTSD." If symptoms last longer than three months, it is described as "chronic PTSD." Usually the symptoms begin immediately following a traumatic event, but sometimes they can appear months and even years later. "Delayed PTSD," as this is called, is most likely to occur on the anniversary of the original event, if or when another trauma is experienced (Foa et al.1999:71), or, as sometimes happens in cases of child abuse, when the survivor's children reach the age the survivor was when he or she suffered the original abuse.

Acute stress disorder (ASD) is the diagnostic term used "when symptoms last for less than one month, but are more severe than what most people have. This is too brief to be considered PTSD but increases the risk of later developing PTSD" (Foa et al. 1999:70). Factors that affect the likelihood that a person will develop PTSD are the severity of the trauma, how long it lasted, how close the person was to the traumatic event, how dangerous it seemed, how many times traumatization occurred, whether the trauma was inflicted by other people, and whether the person gets negative reactions from friends and family members (Foa et al. 1999:71).

Trauma response (Everstine and Everstine 1993) is the term proposed for all post-trauma behaviors that do not fit the constellation of symptoms required to arrive at a diagnosis of post-traumatic stress disorder or acute stress disorder. " 'Response' is used to connote the nonpathological aspects of what the DSM calls 'disorder.' . . . When the reaction to trauma is envisaged as part of a restorative process and not as abnormal behavior, a new incentive to helping the victim recover is gained. It is a simpler task to aid a natural process than to cure a disorder" (12–14). An essential task, then, is a carefully rendered differential assessment to determine whether the appropriate descriptor is "disorder" or "response," for the interventions chosen for one may not be effective with the other.

Transformation is change, change that involves being strengthened, rather than destroyed, by trauma. Several times during the work on this book I have been asked the question, Why is it that some people move through their trauma and go on with their lives with a sense of growth and meaning and others get stuck, remaining bitter and angry long after the traumatic event?

To answer this question, it is essential to set aside any categorizing of people's responses into an either/or: either moving on with growth and meaning or staying stuck with bitterness and anger. In fact, the fullness of a post-trauma response involves both. Healing from trauma is a process, one that takes months, sometimes years, sometimes decades. It is a "creative process, a process that ultimately embraces life while unflinchingly staring death in the eye" (Knafo 2004:585). Once the numbness of the initial shock has subsided, enormous fear is usually noticeable through exaggerated startle responses, intrusive memories and flashbacks, fear that may appear irrational to those who have not experienced the same or a similar trauma. Often a major loss is experienced as part of the traumatic experience, therefore initiating all of the well-known stages of response to loss: denial, anger, bargaining, sadness and/or depression, acceptance (Kübler-Ross 1969). Inherent in every post-trauma healing process is the person's telling and retelling and retelling and retelling (something that may get interpreted as "stuck") of "The Story" with all of its appropriate, though usually horrific, emotional content. Being in an environment that feels safe enough for expressions of anger, confusion, fear, and sadness to be released is one of the most crucial aspects in the process of trauma transformation. Those responding to the trauma of others, the helpers, watch for the signs of shock, for multiple retellings of the story, for fury at the oppressors and victimizers, for deep despair and sadness during which survivors may question their own reasons for living, and the helpers also watch for meaning-making and transformation unique to each person's history, ethnicity and culture, age, gender, sexual orientation, language, and religious or spiritual beliefs.

"Suffering ceases to be suffering *at the moment* it finds a meaning" (Frankl 1969:23; emphasis mine). I have chosen to emphasize "at the moment" because the suffering, as defined by the individual, must be allowed its due time. To impose a timeline on the act of finding meaning is to do a grave injustice to both the person and the process of healing during the months and years of a post-trauma experience. The process cannot be rushed. It cannot automatically respond to anyone else's idea of what is a socially acceptable length of time to suffer before moving on. The person is not a victim because he or she is suffering. Facing daily reminders of the trauma that never leave is an act of courage. The survivor's suffering is an all too understandable, natural, emotionally fitting response to life-shattering events and painful ongoing experiences.

To repeat intentionally, for survivors to face their memories and to tell their stories takes enormous courage. They do go on to find meanings, such as stronger bonds with those they love, such as a rearranging of priorities about what is truly most important to them, such as never again taking freedom from violence for granted. The wish, and even the insistence, to be heard, to be believed and respected through all parts of their healing, to be surrounded by supporting family members, groups, and their community keep many survivors moving forward, strong and resilient.

Resilience is defined as "the capacity to rebound from adversity strengthened and more resourceful. It is an active process of endurance, self-righting, and growth in response to crisis and challenge. . . . Resilience entails more than merely surviving, getting through, or escaping. . . . The qualities of resilience enable people to heal from painful wounds, take charge of their lives, and go on to live fully and love well" (Walsh 1998:4). Emphasis is placed on returning "to a level of functioning equal to or greater than before the crisis" (Boss 2006:48), functioning that has been strengthened as a result of the integration and depth of meaning-making that has come from having weathered the trauma. Bonanno (2004), after an extensive review of the research on resilience, made three important observations: (1) there are multiple and sometimes unexpected pathways to resilience; (2) resilience is more common than we thought; and (3) resiliency is more than recovery—i.e., more than the absence of pathology. Walsh (1998) also recognized this last point, viewing resilience as ongoing healthy functioning with aspects of creativity and growth as well as positive outlooks and emotions. She identified key processes in family resilience: making meaning of adversity, positive outlook, transcendence and spirituality, flexibility, connectedness, social and economic resources, clarity, open emotional expression, and collaborative problem solving (133).

> They [survivors of trauma] possess a special sort of wisdom, aware of the greatest threats and deepest gifts of human existence. Life is simultaneously terrifying and wonderful. Their traumatic experience was undeniably

agonizing, and yet, having successfully struggled to rebuild their inner world, survivors emerge profoundly and gratefully aware of the extraordinary value of life in the face of the ever-present possibility of loss.

(Janoff-Bulman 1999:320)

Empowerment is defined as "a process of increasing personal, interpersonal, or political power so that individuals can take action to improve their life situations" (Gutierrez 1990:149). In recent decades, the term *empowerment* has been used and overused to such an extent that the risk of its becoming pointless is a real one. The pervasiveness of empowerment thinking in nearly every aspect of human growth and activity speaks to its wide acceptance. This same pervasiveness can also be viewed as contributing to its potential demise (Weissberg 1999). If the term is so inclusive that it can be applied anywhere, anytime, in nearly every situation, then what unique meaning can be derived from it? Both acceptance and criticism are extensive. The former is grounded in a history of use that has withstood the test of more than a century of application and expanding breadth and depth. The latter—the criticism, conscientious critiques, and lessons learned from those earlier applications—challenges us to be held accountable for the ways in which we use this concept today, being mindful of what empowerment can and cannot do (Wise 2005).

Empowerment is a word with *power* as its base. With this in mind, any use of the word must encompass both the lighter and the darker sides of power. Human relationship dynamics of power over and power under immediately raise those realities to the level of abuses of power and powerlessness experienced by those who suffer, often through traumatic events and circumstances, as a consequence of such abuses. Concepts of power *with* (Wise 2005) or "power as life" (Purvis 1993), on the other hand, provide clear connections with empowerment thought and practice.

Empowerment practice is practice that occurs simultaneously at the personal, interpersonal, and social/community levels, including political action. The chapters of this volume are organized into three parts, each reflecting one of these levels: Part I, Transforming Trauma at the Personal Level; Part II, Transforming Trauma at the Interpersonal Level; and Part III, Transforming Trauma at the Social/Community/Political Levels. Even though a narrative may begin with a story at the personal level, the interpersonal and social/community/political levels will be evident in the response to the trauma. Likewise, with the narratives that begin at the interpersonal and social/community/political levels; the responses to the trauma describe all three levels of interaction.

To provide a structure for each chapter, one inclusive enough for the areas of expertise of the contributing authors yet specific enough to be useful to readers, we asked each author to organize the chapter according to the following guidelines: (1) provide a case illustration; (2) include background information about the particular trauma that will help readers understand its prevalence, social context, and supporting research and knowledge; (3) provide a practice section that shows how helping professionals responded to the trauma presented in the case illustration; (4) offer reflections on the principles of empowerment practice; (5) address the reality of vicarious trauma as experienced in this work; (6) explain how the trauma was transformed and provide recommendations. The principles of empowerment for reflection in the fourth section are (1) building on strengths while diminishing oppressions; (2) enacting multicultural respect (on the basis of the multicultural variables of ethnicity, age, gender, sexual orientation, socioeconomic class, religious/spiritual beliefs, differing abilities, and language); (3) working from an awareness of specific needs; (4) assisting clients—individuals, groups, families, organizations, communities—as they empower themselves; (5) integrating the support needed from others; (6) equalizing power differentials; and (7) using cooperative roles (Lee 2001; Wise 2005). No single recommendation for use of the empowerment principles was imposed. The creative application of each contributor's understanding of these terms gives a glimpse of the widely diverse potentials for strengthening practice represented by the contributors to this volume.

Practitioners in the helping professions will find this book useful for understanding a wide variety of trauma experiences and for learning how the contributors have responded to those experiences. The sections on vicarious, or secondary, trauma speak to all those who work in areas of trauma response, offering strategies for strengthening one's sense of self in order to remain effective in the face of the challenges inherent in trauma work. The volume is appropriate as a text for undergraduate or graduate level courses, both in the classroom and in field practice or internship settings. Excerpts can be useful in both individual and group work, for example, for those recovering from trauma. Hearing the stories of others who have faced and survived and transformed their own experiences of trauma serves as an inspiration for us all.

Note

1. The Trauma Response Certificate Program welcomed its first cohort of eighteen students in 2003. Following my retirement, the program continued to grow under the leadership of Ann Petrila, M.S.W., Nicki Dayley, M.S.W., and Marian Bussey, Ph.D., who now serves as the coordinator of the program. Forty students were accepted for the fall 2006 term.

References

American Psychiatric Association. 1994. *Diagnostic and Statistical Manual of Mental Disorders (DSM-IV)*. 4th ed. Washington, D.C.: Author.

Bonanno, G. A. 2004. "Loss, Trauma, and Human Resilience: Have We Underestimated the Human Capacity to Thrive After Extremely Aversive Events?" *American Psychologist* 59 (1): 20–28.

Boss, P. 2006. *Loss, Trauma, and Resilience*. New York: Norton.

Bula, J. F. 2000. "Differential Use of Self by Therapists Following Their Own Trauma Experiences." In M. Baldwin, ed., *The Use of Self in Therapy*, 213–241. 2nd ed. New York: Haworth.

Everstine, D. S., and L. Everstine. 1993. *The Trauma Response: Treatment for Emotional Injury*. New York: Norton.

Figley, C. R. 1999. "Compassion Fatigue: Toward a New Understanding of the Costs of Caring." In B. H. Stamm, ed., *Secondary Traumatic Stress: Self-Care Issues for Clinicians, Researchers, and Educators*, 3–28. 2nd ed. Baltimore: Sidran.

Foa, E. B., J. R. T. Davidson, A. Frances, and R. Ross. 1999. "Expert Consensus Treatment for Posttraumatic Stress Disorder: A Guide for Patients and Families." *Journal of Clinical Psychiatry* 60 (Suppl. 16): 69–76.

Frankl, V. E. 1969. *The Will to Meaning*. Cleveland: New American Library.

Gutierrez, L. M. 1990. "Working with Women of Color: An Empowerment Perspective." *Social Work* 35:149–153.

Herman, J. L. 1997. *Trauma and Recovery*. 2nd ed. New York: Basic Books.

Hipskind, S. G., and T. Henderson. 2002. "Next Generation High Resolution SPECT: Examples of Images and Types of Disorders." Denver: Brain Matters.

Janoff-Bulman, R. 1999. "Rebuilding Shattered Assumptions After Traumatic Life Events: Coping Processes and Outcomes." In C. R. Snyder, ed., *Coping: The Psychology of What Works*, 305–323. New York: Oxford University Press.

Knafo, D. 2004. "Creative and Clinical Transformations of Trauma: Private Pain in the Public Domain." In D. Knafo, ed., *Living with Terror,*

Working with Trauma: A Clinician's Handbook, 565–580. Lanham, Md.: Jason Aronson.

Kübler-Ross, E. 1969. *On Death and Dying*. New York: Macmillan.

Lee, J. A. B. 2001. *The Empowerment Approach to Social Work Practice: Building the Beloved Community*. 2nd ed. New York: Columbia University Press.

Naparstek, B. 2004. *Invisible Heroes: Survivors of Trauma and How They Heal*. New York: Bantam.

Pearlman, L. 1999. "Self-Care for Trauma Therapists: Ameliorating Vicarious Traumatization." In B. H. Stamm, ed., *Secondary Traumatic Stress: Self-Care Issues for Clinicians, Researchers, and Educators*, 51–64. 2nd ed. Baltimore: Sidran.

Purvis, S. B. 1993. *The Power of the Cross: Foundations for a Christian Feminist Ethic of Community*. Nashville: Abingdon.

Serlin, I., and J. T. Cannon. 2004. "A Humanistic Approach to the Psychology of Trauma." In D. Knafo, ed., *Living with Terror, Working with Trauma: A Clinician's Handbook*, 313–330. New York: Jason Aronson.

van der Kolk, B., A. C. McFarlane, and L. Weisaeth, eds. 1996. *Traumatic Stress: The Effects of Overwhelming Experience on Mind, Body, and Society*. New York: Guilford.

Walsh, F. 1998. *Strengthening Family Resilience*. New York: Guilford.

Weissberg, R. 1999. *The Politics of Empowerment*. Westport, Conn.: Praeger.

Wilson, J., and M. Sigman. 2000. "Theoretical Perspectives of Traumatic Stress and Debriefings." In B. Raphael and J. Wilson, eds., *Psychological Debriefing: Theory, Practice, and Evidence*, 58–69. Cambridge, U.K.: Cambridge University Press.

Wise, J. B. 2005. *Empowerment Practice with Families in Distress*. New York: Columbia University Press.

Part 1

Transforming Trauma at the
Personal Level

1

Nicolas Puts Back the Pieces
Transforming a Childhood Trauma

ELIANA GIL

Four-and-a-half-year-old Nicolas was outside in his yard playing with the family dog, Rocky, a pit bull, as he did most weekdays before dinner, while Dora, his mother, was cooking in the kitchen. Suddenly a neighbor started pounding on the door and yelling for Dora to hurry outside. She rushed out to find Nicolas being brutally attacked by Rocky. Later she learned that Nicolas had been trying to ride Rocky when the dog grabbed him by the face and shook him with great force until Nicolas fell to the ground. Dora rushed at the animal, screaming and using a stick to scare him away. Nicolas lay in a pool of blood, unresponsive and limp. Parts of his face seemed to be torn away. One of his eyes appeared to be full of blood. Dora did not want to touch him or move him for fear of doing more harm. The neighbor, when she witnessed the attack from her window next door, had called an ambulance. The ambulance arrived promptly and Nicolas was rushed to the hospital.

An emergency room evaluation resulted in immediate surgery for Nicolas. The damage to his face was extensive. His ear had been torn off, his tear ducts had been severed, part of his scalp had been ripped from the front of his forehead, and he had teeth marks and scratches on his upper neck and arms. The surgery was long but remarkably successful. Nicolas was in the hospital for a three-week recovery period.

One week before Nicolas's discharge from the hospital, the pediatric social worker called our mental health services agency to arrange for counseling services. She reported that everyone on the staff at the hospital had fallen in love with this child and that his personality was sweet, affable, and engaging. The social worker's greatest concern was that Nicolas's mother had appeared to the nursing staff to be "self-centered and insensitive." Compared to typical responses from other parents in similar situations, who ask, "Is my child safe?" and "How will he or she cope with this?" Dora's response seemed to come from her own experiences, ones that blocked her ability to empathize with Nicolas. Her biggest concern was whether Nicolas's physical appearance would return to normal. She seemed to focus excessively on his looks, making statements like "He used to be the most beautiful child in the world. Oh, my God, why have you done this to me and taken away his beauty?" The staff encouraged her to stop calling Nicolas derogatory names such as carita comida *or* carita pisada, *which in her native Spanish mean "eaten face" or "stepped-on face."*

The social worker described Nicolas's physical progress as nothing short of miraculous. "His wounds are healing well, he has very minimal deformity of any kind, and the most visible problem is that he tears a lot because of the separated tear ducts." She noted that Nicolas had experienced nightmares and, from time to time, stared into space. He was quiet and pensive after visits with his mother. He had no other visitors during his stay in the hospital.

Understanding Physical Trauma from Dog Attack

Each year approximately four million people in the United States are bitten by dogs. An estimated 800,000 of these people receive medical treatment. On average, slightly more than one dozen fatalities related to dog bites occur each year in this country. Most of the victims are children. Five- to nine-year-old boys constitute the largest group of child victims of dog bites. Pit bulls, like Nicolas's dog, have a higher attack rate and are considered to be among the most aggressive dogs (*Morbidity and Mortality Weekly Report* 2003; Presutti 2001).

Specific characteristics of traumatized children include intrusive flashbacks or memories of the trauma; repetitive behaviors; trauma-specific fears; and changed attitudes about caretakers, environmental safety, or the future (Terr 1991). "Even though traumatized children are at risk of developing symptoms of post-traumatic stress disorder, these risks can increase with such variables as lack of social support; man-made traumas versus natural disasters; traumas that involve human aggression; life-threatening traumas; parental distress that hinders the ability to parent; degree to which children perceive parents being in danger; lack of parent-child communication about the trauma; prior trauma or emotional disturbance; and significant, firsthand exposure to the trauma" (Schaefer 1994:299). Parental distress hindering the ability to parent is especially relevant in Dora's response to Nicolas's trauma.

Family members who witness traumatic events and respond with a sense of victimization are often overlooked in spite of the fact that simply learning about the event carries traumatic potential (Figley 1999). In Nicolas's case, both his neighbor (who witnessed the dog attack) and his mother, Dora (who was present during and after the attack), were susceptible to reactions and responses of secondary trauma. Dora's words, "Oh, my God, why have you done this to me?" indicated the strong connection she felt between what had happened to Nicolas and her own sense of being directly traumatized. Other responses of family members suffering from secondary traumatic stress include confusion, irritability, and avoidance, all of which I noted in my sessions with Dora.

Responding to Nicolas and Dora: Intake Session with Dora (Nicolas's Mother)

Dora, 34 years old and from South America, spoke mostly Spanish and was dressed in an artsy way with flowing scarves, large hoop earrings, and extremely high heels. She appeared to enjoy taking care of her appearance. She was candid and spoke with spirited hand and facial gestures, expressing joy and relief at being able to communicate with me in her native tongue. I am also bicultural and bilingual, from Ecuador, a neighbor country of Dora's.

She referred to Nicolas as "a little angel" and told me that unfortunately I would no longer be meeting her "perfect child," but a different version, a deformed version, of her child. She noted that everyone who had met him had something to say about how beautiful he was. "I'm not exaggerating," she said. "People would want to take his picture, and several artists wanted to paint his portrait."

After Nicolas's release from the hospital, Dora stated, "This chapter is over; he is now another child, not my beautiful son of the past." Dora had difficulty finding solace in the fact that Nicolas's recovery was going well.

From her response, I wondered what role physical beauty had played in her life and why Nicolas's appearance seemed to be critically important to her.

I invited Dora to tell me her thoughts and feelings about the accident. She spoke repeatedly about the loss of her child's beauty. Her hurried and repetitious speech, exaggerated emotional affect, and reports of intrusive flashbacks about seeing her son covered in blood were all symptoms of post-traumatic stress. Staying with Dora's focus on loss, I wondered about other losses she had experienced in her life and made a note to ask about her immigration to the United States and the possible loss of contact with extended family members. I was also curious about Nicolas's father and wondered if his absence represented another loss for Dora and Nicolas. For now, though, she insisted on speaking about the changes in her life now that her child was "deformed."

I asked Dora if she understood why her son had been referred to me. She responded that Nicolas did not need therapy, that she was the one who needed help with her suffering and despair. I agreed that both she and her son had been traumatized by this terrible dog attack. I also told her that I was glad to hear that she felt that her son was doing well enough that he would not need therapy. I informed her that I would initially be doing an assessment to determine how he was coping. Dora was very pleased when I gave her the name of my Spanish-speaking colleague, Angela, who would help her with the pain she was suffering. I gave her some forms to fill out and told her that after my assessment, I would give her some feedback about my impression of Nicolas.

Dora was experiencing vicarious traumatization. She felt she had been attacked, mauled, ripped apart, and left destroyed. This event had triggered many emotions and concerns in her. In particular, Dora's investment in her child's physical appearance was obviously causing her great distress. It became increasingly clear that she would be unable to focus on his needs until she explored her own fears and despair. "It's a tragedy," she said, "of monumental proportions that I might never recover from."

Dora spoke of attending church but right now feeling uncomfortable going because people at church would "ask questions." I offered that she could visit the hospital chapel, could speak with the hospital chaplain, or explore other churches where she would not see people she knew, if seeing familiar people was difficult at this time. I also encouraged her to speak with Angela, her therapist, about how to respond to difficult or challenging questions from others. "Religion and spirituality offer comfort and meaning beyond comprehension in the face of adversity" (Walsh 1998).

The shock of post-trauma experience typically interferes with a person's ability to hear and comprehend what is being said. Visual and auditory distortions, as well as confusion in thought processes, are common as one tries to make sense of what has happened. Dora had difficulty listening to what I said to her, looking away and forgetting our conversations. The more I was able to understand her sense of being injured and her acute sense of disempowerment in this situation, the more empathic I became in my responses to her.

My concern for Dora prompted me to call the social worker at the hospital and ask more about Dora's initial reactions and behaviors. The social worker noted that Dora had looked almost "frozen" throughout the surgery and later became agitated and almost manic. During Nicolas's recovery from surgery, Dora's behaviors calmed down except for her rapid speech patterns. I asked if others had visited the hospital or had been with Dora during Nicolas's hospitalization. No family or friends had visited.

Initial Session with Nicolas

Having heard Dora's disparaging comments about the change in Nicolas's appearance, I expected Nicolas to appear with a fairly mangled face. Instead, when Dora introduced me to her child, I could not believe how good he looked. He had scars in various stages of healing around his ear, forehead, and eyes and some faint scratch marks on his face, but given the extent of the attack he had endured, he looked quite good.

I had instructed Dora to refrain from making disparaging remarks in front of Nicolas, explaining that a young child could be extremely sensitive to his mother's disapproval or hopelessness. Even so, she whispered to me, "Finally you can see what I've been telling you." Nicolas continued playing in the waiting room while I invited Dora into my office and explained the resilience of children and how they may not be as interested in their looks.

I asked Dora about her childhood. "When did you first become interested in how you look?"

"I remember my father telling me I had '*cara do chivo*,' a goat's face, and I would always go to the mirror and see if I looked like a goat or not."

"So your father was someone who talked about looks."

"Yes," she said softly. "He was always disappointed that none of us girls looked like our mother. She died in a car crash when we were little."

"How old were you when your mother died?"

"I was five."

Unresolved trauma can be retriggered much later, and it is not uncommon for parents to remember their own childhood traumas when their children reach an age similar to the parent's age when the original trauma was experienced. I wondered whether Nicolas's accident had triggered memories of Dora's own mother's accident when she was about the same age as her son.

"My dad said we looked like we came from an orphanage, and sometimes my sister and I actually wondered ourselves."

This was one of my earliest hints of Dora's childhood suffering and the importance of physical beauty in her life. Learning even this minimal information about her background allowed me to perceive her with more patience and empathy. I encouraged Dora to speak with her therapist about the impact her father's comments had had on her when she was a child, and I repeated the importance of her refraining from making negative remarks about Nicolas. I then invited her to sit in the waiting room while I spoke with Nicolas in my office.

I took Nicolas into the office and showed him around. "What did your mom tell you about coming here to see me?"

"Because the dog hurt my face," he replied.

"Yes, Nicolas, you're here because of the dog biting you and to see how you're doing after the dog attack and your stay at the hospital."

"I have to go back to the hospital because my eye cries all the time."

"How do you feel about going back to the hospital?"

"They are nice for me." Spontaneously he added, "My mommy thinks I look ugly and she wants me to look good like before."

"What do you think about what your mom says about your looks?"

"She doesn't like me now."

"Oh. She doesn't like the scars on your face. How does that make you feel?"

"Sad," said Nicolas in a small voice. "My mom is pretty and wants a pretty boy, not ugly."

"That must be hard for you, Nicolas, to think that your mom doesn't like you now. Was it different before the accident?"

"Oh, yes. My mom said I was the handsomest boy in the world."

"How did you like it when your mom said that?"

"Good, it was good."

Nicolas grabbed a boy doll with bangs and asked if he could comb its hair. "My hair is going to get long and I can hide my scratches," he commented. "Mami will like that." He combed the doll's hair, making the bangs cover its forehead. He then put a clean shirt on the doll and sent him "outside to play." Nicolas asked about other toys in the room and went through a bin of puppets to discover a dog puppet that looked like his. He said he would bring a picture of his dog next time.

Play therapy has been well documented as a helpful strategy with young children in general (Bratton, Ray, and Rhine 2005; Kottman 2001; O'Connor and Braverman 1997; O'Connor and Schaefer 1994; Schaefer, McCormick, and Ohnogi 2005) and with traumatized children specifically (Boyd Webb 2006; Deblinger and Heflin 1996; Gil 2006; James 1989; Shelby and Felix 2005). Trauma variables, such as dissociation in children, have received special attention (Shirar 1996; Silberg 1996). "Several therapeutic elements are at work in the play process, namely, the miniaturization of experiences by the use of the small play objects, the active control and domination of events that are possible in play, and the piecemeal assimilation of a traumatic event by repetitiously playing out that event" (Ekstein 1966, as cited in Schaefer 1994:302).

The potential benefits of diagnostic play include its provision of knowledge about children's perceptions of themselves and their family roles. The child's perception of others can be projected onto play material, the child's compulsion to repeat the trauma symbolically may be present, the child's conflicts and coping strategies may be revealed, and the child's perceptions of the world and his or her family dynamics may emerge. This type of diagnostic play can also assist in differential diagnosis (Marvasti 1994).

Later Sessions with Nicolas

During the next four visits, Nicolas and I got better acquainted as I conducted an Extended Play-Based Developmental Assessment (Gil 2006). He functioned well above his developmental age (Greenspan 1981) in the domains of physical functioning, pattern of relationships, affect, overall mood, and thematic expression. From his play, it was clear that he had some expectable fears and anxieties. Nicolas was a respectful child. I complimented his mother on how polite he was, yet no matter what positive things I said about Nicolas, she focused exclusively on his looks.

In play therapy, Nicolas continued to play with the boy doll, and he also played in the sandbox. He placed miniatures in the sandbox and made a village scenario with houses and fences, streetcars, trees, and a fenced area for sheep. Within two weeks he replaced the sheep with dogs of various sizes and breeds. Eventually he used the pit bull and always put a little house over it.

"Tell me about the world you've made in the sandbox today, Nicolas." He told me about Sandy's house. Sandy was the neighbor who had alerted Dora to the dog attack and called the ambulance. He talked about Sandy and how much he liked going to her house to play with her son, Teddy. He told me that Teddy was his best friend and that he "doesn't even see my scratches. I like it when nobody talks about my scars or the accident."

When Nicolas finally talked about the dogs in the sandbox, he mentioned Rocky, and his eyes welled up. "My mom is going to kill him because she says he's *loco* and we can't keep him because he bites." Nicolas went on to say, "I told her I bothered Rocky and that he didn't want me to get on his back and I did and that's why he got mad." Tears rolled down his face, and he said he missed Rocky and didn't want him to die. I made a mental note to speak to Dora about the dog. Nicolas found a puppet of a large, fluffy, gray dog in the puppet bin and clutched it when he began to cry about Rocky.

In subsequent sessions, Nicolas used this dog puppet routinely. At times the Rocky puppet would attack another puppet, and Nicolas used loud barks, grunts, and other noises during the attacks. Afterward, the Rocky puppet would hide, afraid that he would "get in trouble" for attacking the other puppets. After one of these attacks, the Rocky puppet had an ambulance come to pick up the injured puppet and he stuffed the puppet in the toy ambulance and took it to the play hospital. Once at the toy hospital, the Rocky puppet placed gauze around the injured puppet, placed a vomit tray next to its mouth, and had nurses come take care of the injured puppet. Nicolas made moaning noises for the hurt puppet.

In another session, Nicolas took the Rocky puppet to the hospital instead of the injured puppet. He spent nearly thirty minutes with Rocky in surgery and the doctors trying to help him stay alive. Nicolas looked up at me, tears in his eyes, and said, "Rocky might not make it."

"Oh," I responded, "Rocky may not live."

Two weeks later, the Rocky puppet died. This coincided with the actual dog Rocky being put to sleep. Dora told me that the dog had attacked two of her friends in the past, but she'd never thought he would turn on anyone in the family. She had concluded that it was not safe to keep him. She could not forgive Rocky for ruining her life. "It's better he's gone and can't bite anyone else."

Dora told me that Nicolas was extremely upset at first about Rocky, but later seemed to understand that it was best for Rocky to be put to sleep because he had bitten other people and it was important that she protect other children from being hurt by him. Nicolas cried and cried, but his mother surprised him with a tiny new puppy, which Nicolas embraced immediately. I reinforced Dora's empathy toward Nicolas and praised her for making an effort to help him recover from his loss.

After Rocky was put to sleep, Nicolas came to his next session asking for a real burial for the Rocky puppet. In his real life, the veterinarian had disposed of Rocky's remains and Nicolas was sad that he could not go to Rocky's funeral. Nicolas had attended an aunt's funeral six months before the dog attack and seemed responsive to the process of listening to people talk warmly about his family member. Ordinarily, I might want to do some kind of symbolic ritual burial, but in this case Nicolas seemed to need the closure of actually burying Rocky the puppet. I asked Nicolas if he wanted to invite his mother or his friend Teddy to Rocky's funeral. He asked if just the two of us could bury Rocky and later Teddy and his mom could visit and bring flowers. Of course I agreed to his wishes. Shovel in hand, we went outdoors and found a small patch of land where Nicolas helped me dig a hole. We placed the puppet in the hole. Nicolas placed flowers in the hole, as well as Rocky's dog bone and name tag, which he had made during one of our sessions. I then filled the hole with dirt and Nicolas said a prayer: "Dear Rocky, you were my friend. We played and I gave you treats. You wagged your tail when you saw me. You liked me no matter what I did and how I looked. I will remember you a lot. I like Pepsi, my new puppy, but not as much as you. I love you, and P.S. I'm sorry I bothered you and got you mad. I wish you could learn not to bite when you're mad." With this statement, Nicolas had shifted blame away from himself as causing Rocky to bite him to a more realistic view that Rocky didn't have to bite if he was mad. The play therapy sessions had allowed Nicolas to deal with his sense of responsibility for Rocky's attack and to obtain some closure by saying good-bye to Rocky while, together, we explored Nicolas's perceptions of the attack.

In a subsequent session Nicolas mentioned the day of the dog attack. I asked him what he remembered about the accident. He had told me that he sometimes had nightmares about it and, most recently, when Rocky was put to sleep. I asked him to draw a picture of a nightmare, a directive strategy, since I wanted to bring the dream into the session.

Art-making is both a spontaneous and an invited process that can help clinicians understand a client's internalized work. Art can be used in the beginning phase (assessment) to get to know the person in a way that reaches beyond what he or she might be able or willing to say; in the middle phase to achieve treatment goals; and in the ending phase to review what has occurred over the course of treatment by looking at art products in the order in which they were made (Rubin 2005:128). Patients with medical concerns or who are experiencing medical procedures, as did Nicolas, have been found to be especially responsive to art-making (Rubin 2005).

Nicolas drew his picture of his nightmare carefully and precisely with great concentration (figure 1.1). When he had completed the drawing, I asked him to tell me something about the picture. He pointed out that the lines at the bottom and top of the drawing were strings and that they were tied down to sticks. The strings, he said, "are holding things down." He said that the figure was a face "looking sideways." Pointing to the darkest shape, he said, "That's the ear." He also pointed to an eye, a mouth, and hair. Small dashes of red color had been placed around the eye, head, and ear.

"What's happening in this picture, Nicolas? What's going on with the face?"

"The parts are falling off," he said, "and they need to be tied down. These are knots. Teddy taught me to make knots."

"Oh," I said, "the strings are keeping the parts of the face from falling off."

"Yeah."

"How do you feel looking at your drawing?"

"Scared," he said. "It's like my nightmare."

"Like your nightmare," I repeated, "except you're not sleeping. You're drawing the nightmare, but you're not having it right now."

"Right." His voice was slightly louder this time.

"What would you like to do now that you're looking at this scary nightmare?"

"I want to put it here," he said, pointing to the back of the easel. I placed the picture where Nicolas had indicated. We then played a game of Mankala, and at the end of the session, I reminded him of his drawing of the nightmare.

"Would you like to take it home with you?"

"Heck no," he responded. "You keep it here. It's too scary."

"I'll keep it here for you. Maybe we'll look at it again some other time."

"Maybe not!" And with that he ran in front of me to leave the room.

The following session I put a new set of paints with brushes out for Nicolas. He went right to them. "What should I paint?"

"Anything you want," I said, but he insisted that I should tell him what to paint.

"Well, how about a picture of you?"

"Okay."

Nicolas spent quite a bit of time making a red circle on the top of the head (the dark circle to the left of the face), and he drew that section with more intensity than the rest of the picture. When he had finished, I said, "Tell me a little about your picture" (figure 1.2). Pointing to the red circle, I asked, "What's this?"

"That's my brain trying to fall out." He handed me the picture, saying, "You keep this," and he ran toward the door.

Looking at the picture clearly produced some anxiety in Nicolas. "Okay, I'll keep this here." He disappeared down the hallway to his wait- ing mother.

Nicolas processed his fears in symbolic form through his paintings. When I consulted with the art therapy supervisor, we decided that offer- ing Nicolas some clay would be helpful. We believed that because his physical integrity seemed to be distressing him, the chances were good that he would find a way to work out this concern with the clay. Our hunch turned out to be accurate. When Nicolas and I sat down with the clay, he molded some wormy-looking objects, flattened them, then molded them into balls. He pushed the balls together and announced, "I'm gonna make me!" He made a fairly large oval and added more and more clay and water. When I told him it was time to go, he asked if I could "save his face" for next time (intriguing language), and then he told me he had an idea: we could make the parts of the face and then stick them on. I was struck with the simultaneous simplicity and complexity of the work he had designed for himself. He left skipping and smiling.

When he returned for his next session, we took the wet towel off the clay, and he was happy to see that his "face" was intact. "I'm gonna make the parts now. I want to make the mouth." Nicolas rolled the clay into two little worms. He shaped these lips into many different expressions. "Now I want to make the ears," and he made two large ears, shaping the hole of the ears with a pencil. I showed Nicolas how to press small amounts of clay into a garlic press to make the hair—"spaghetti hair," he called it.

He directed me to work on the head, making it larger and figuring out a way to make it stand. "Okay," I said, "here comes the head." Our time was up, so I placed a wet paper towel and plastic on the head, the hair, the lips, and the ears, and told him we would finish the project the next week.

When Nicolas returned, he made more hair and used it to cover the head and forehead of the sculpture. He carefully placed the lips so that they were "sad," and we attached the ears to the head. I showed him how he might want to make the eyes with a pencil and he did a masterful job. He made tears come down the face with the sharp point of the pencil. He finished by adding more hair and announced, "It's a good and sad face and the parts are glued on." Nicolas tested the glue by pulling on the ears and mouth until he was satisfied that the glue was strong and that there was no way the parts could fall off. He instructed me to keep the face in a safe place (figure 1.3).

The following session, Nicolas asked for the colored clay, and he made a little sculpture of a person. He made a small tree and placed the person next to the tree. When I asked about it, he explained, "This is me and I'm outside playing." This was a good prognostic sign, as he had been less likely to play outside since the accident. He had instinctively drawn a "picture of health" (Malchiodi 1998:165), an indication that there had been a "successful activation of creative energy," which releases healing properties (McNiff, cited in Estrella 2005:196; figure 1.4).

Collateral Work with Dora

During the four-month period that I worked with Nicolas, my coworker, Angela, met with Dora. Initially, Dora showed clear symptoms of having been secondarily traumatized herself. She was self-absorbed, unable to focus on Nicolas's needs, and had begun the natural and necessary step in trauma recovery of repetitive retelling of the story of the dog attack. Angela guided Dora to empathize with Nicolas even though she continued to find it difficult to invite physical closeness with him.

Angela learned that Dora's family history included the abrupt loss of her mother, with feelings of abandonment, harsh emotional abuse from her father, and neglect. Angela recognized that it was highly likely that Dora had experienced the retriggering of some of these memories from her childhood with the recent traumatic experience with Nicolas.

Dora's grandmother, Rosalinda, had recently come to the United States to help Dora with Nicolas. When Angela learned of Nicolas's strong attachment to his great-grandmother, Rosalinda was invited to come to the family therapy sessions. During one of the sessions, Dora told her grandmother that she felt resentful that she was clearly nurturing and sensitive to Nicolas in a way she had not been with Dora when she was small. Rosalinda talked about the difficulties of sharing caretaking responsibilities with Dora's father after her own daughter had died. Dora softened as she listened to her grandmother's description of the pressure she felt to provide caretaking to her grandchildren while she greatly mourned the death of her daughter. Rosalinda also talked about a conflicted relationship with Dora's father and how she confronted him about his harsh manner with all his children. In these sessions with Angela, Dora and Rosalinda began to repair their relationship, an important one for both of them that carried over to Dora's relationship with Nicolas.

Angela and I scheduled joint family sessions to observe and encourage positive mother-child interactions. A traditional approach for the first few meetings was not useful. When we met with Dora and Nicolas, Dora dominated the session, could not engage in meaningful play with Nicolas, fought for both therapists' attention, and seemed resentful when either of us interacted with Nicolas. We found it much more effective to use filial therapy (Guerney 2003; van Fleet 1992, 2005) with Nicolas and Dora. The goal of filial therapy is to take full advantage "of the power of the parent-child bond to build therapeutic rapport" by "giving parents the skills of the play therapist." This is viewed as "the ideal way for parents to relate more positively and appropriately to their children and, at the same time, provide an effective therapy for them" (Guerney 2003:100).

Dora, with Angela's support, observed Nicolas and me in nondirective play. "I've never seen him act like that," Dora told her therapist, pointing out that Nicolas had a smile on his face. "Of course if I just got to play with whatever I wanted, I would like that too!" Angela told her that she would get a chance to do just that, to go into the session with Nicolas and play with whatever she wanted.

I invited Dora into the play session, and she selected Mankala, a game that Nicolas also loved. Nicolas was very happy to see his mother's choice of games, and he immediately pulled up two chairs and a small table. Nicolas showed his mother how to play and he won the first two games. Dora told Nicolas that she remembered playing this game when she was a child. She complimented him on how well he played. Over the next two months, Dora and Nicolas continued with these sessions. Angela and I coached Dora about following Nicolas's lead, about reflective listening, and about observing and commenting on Nicolas's play.

It was evident that Dora was comfortable in the play therapy session. Nicolas noticed and seemed to enjoy being observed. Dora would ask for feedback on how she did, giving Angela and me an opportunity to reinforce her positive or neutral interactions with Nicolas. For his part, Nicolas blossomed in his mother's presence and truly enjoyed these times with her in the playroom. When Nicolas showed his mother how to use the clay or how to make a scenario in the sand, for example, he was visibly happy and excited. Over time, Dora became more playful with her son.

Dora kept all her therapy appointments with Angela. I continued to confer with Angela to collaborate on our treatment efforts. Although Dora did not fully realign her perceptions of Nicolas, she became more sensitive to him and more disposed to seeing him realistically. Eventually she admitted that Nicolas's scars were barely noticeable. She was initially receptive to attending a group for adults abused as children but did not actually attend these groups when they were available.

Nicolas, one of the most resilient children I have ever met, went on to excel in school, eliciting positive responses from his teacher and peers, and he appeared to make a full adjustment post-trauma. He hardly ever referred to his scars, and the anxiety he had expressed earlier about physical disintegration seemed to disappear.

Reflections on the Empowerment Principles

The seven empowerment principles are visible in this work with Nicolas and his mother: building on strengths while diminishing oppressions, multicultural respect, awareness of needs, assisting Nicolas and Dora as they empowered themselves, integrating support needed from others, equalizing power differentials, and using cooperative roles (Wise 2005).

The work with Nicolas represents significant trust in individual capacities and capabilities to address painful events, gather internal and external resources, and process and overcome them. Both Nicolas and Dora brought such capabilities and strengths to this work. Nicolas's winning personality was recognized immediately by hospital staff. Dora's inherent capacities related to protection and nurturing were visible in her attention, though reportedly "frozen" in expression, to Nicolas during and after

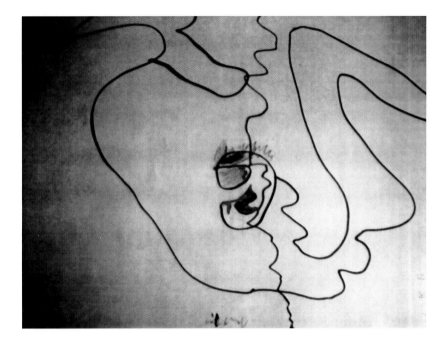

Figure 1.1

Figure 1.2

Figure 1.3

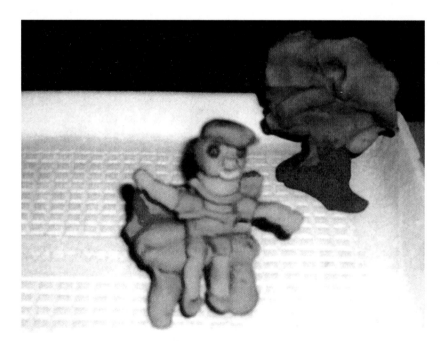

Figure 1.4

surgery. She took action to have the dog, Rocky, put to sleep and, later, presented Nicolas with his new puppy. Dora also voiced her fears and grieving. She faced the death of her dreams for her "beautiful" child and, in her own way, linked her questions about how Nicolas would cope with this tragedy with her own concerns about how to cope. Other strengths were the family bond, Dora's religious beliefs, and an ongoing belief on the part of the therapists that Dora and Nicolas were survivors, that they could come through this experience together. Over time, the oppressive forces of the confusion and uncertainty following the dog attack were replaced by a remarkable physical and emotional recovery on Nicolas's part and, for Dora, the ability to experience her competence as a parent.

Multicultural respect occurred in identifying the similarity in our backgrounds (both from South America), in using Dora's native language, in being attentive to Dora's and Nicolas's differing levels of acculturation, and in referring Dora to a Spanish-speaking therapist. Awareness of their needs occurred on both an individual basis and on a mother-son relational basis. I came to understand how Nicolas had experienced this stressful, frightening event through his drawing, painting, and clay sculpture. And I learned about how he had coped with other stressful times in his life. His network of helpers responded to his needs for safety and support and to give the puppet, "Rocky," a special burial. We responded to Dora's need to be heard in terms of her own trauma by reaching for an understanding of the earlier traumas in her life. Dora's need for a therapist of her own was evident quite early in our interactions with her. Nicolas needed their mother-son connection to be one where he felt continued love and caring from his mother. Dora's initially frantic need for her son's beauty to be restored eventually softened as his wounds healed and she could see that the damage was much less severe than she had originally thought.

Assisting Nicolas and Dora as they empowered themselves was most evident in the play sessions. The need for an integration of support from others was most apparent when learning that Nicolas had had no visitors during his hospital stay except his mother. Angela became a support person for Dora. The grandmother, Rosalinda, became a significant source of support for both Dora and Nicolas. Other supports were encouraged—the hospital chaplain, Dora's church, and the groups for adults who had been abused as children—but were not utilized.

Equalizing power differentials is a significant contribution of filial therapy and was seen in the play sessions between Dora and Nicolas. Providing a Spanish-speaking therapist for Dora likely had equalizing effects.

And, finally, the use of cooperative roles with the hospital social worker, with other hospital staff, with Angela, and with Dora in the play sessions all contributed to building a network of safety and nurturing for Nicolas's recovery. I felt that my primary role was to establish emotional contact with Nicolas and give him many ways to show or tell what he was experiencing. In addition, I was there to witness his reality, provide safety and unconditional acceptance, and reflect back to him what I heard him say or saw him do. Most of what we did together in the sessions came out of mutual discovery, a collaborative experience that seemed to have a grounding effect on this young child.

In addition to the empowerment frame of reference, Greenspan's (1997) principles of developmental play therapy also guided the therapeutic approach. Meeting the child at his/her developmental level; harnessing core developmental processes such as self-regulation, boundaries, communication, and representation of internal experience; aiming to effect changes to negotiate the developmental levels the child has not mastered fully; and promoting the child's self-sufficiency and assertiveness are all evident as well in this work with Nicolas and his mother.

Vicarious Trauma

Lack of empathy is one of the signs that secondary trauma may have been activated. Hearing that Dora, while she was trying to manage overwhelming shock at the hospital emergency room, was perceived as "self-centered and insensitive" was one of the first indications to me that some of the professional medical staff were experiencing vicarious trauma. Hospital emergency staff constantly confront horrifying and traumatizing realities. It is understandable that they experience vicarious trauma.

I found that I also initially bought into these perceptions of Dora. My overriding emotion was to protect Nicolas, yet by maintaining a protective stance I fueled the perception of the mother as harsh and insensitive. I felt irritated when she did not seem to listen to much of what I said to her, looking away and seeming to forget our conversations. Of course, these are predictable behaviors in any post-trauma situation when numbness, an inward focus, confusion, and cognitive distortions are paramount. I had to process my own responses and deepen my understanding of her acute sense of disempowerment in this situation. Parents typically perceive protection as one of their primary duties toward their children. When children are injured, the parents often feel the injury as well. The more I was able to understand Dora's sense of being injured, the more empathic I became in my responses to her.

Conclusion and Recommendations

"The most important and frequent remedies for people suffering from traumatic and post-traumatic stress are *personal*, rather than clinical or medical" (Figley 1999:10). Fortunately, Nicolas experienced a loving and accepting atmosphere before his acute traumatic incident when the pet he was extremely attached to attacked him. He also had a number of intrusive medical procedures that could, in and of themselves, be stressful. Child life specialists and volunteers are present in most hospitals to help distract children through various play techniques during stressful medical procedures. Successful management of medical procedures also occurs through a combination of verbal, i.e., explaining in advance using language appropriate to the child's developmental stage what is about to occur, and nonverbal, i.e., distracting play, expressive therapies (Councill 2003).

Nicolas's physical injuries healed well, but he did have to cope with post-trauma anxiety, as exhibited in nightmares, intrusive flashbacks, and some emotionality. He also had to cope with his mother's negativity about the change in his looks, something that he interpreted temporarily as a loss of his mother's love. As Dora gained insight into her own painful childhood, acknowledged her father's verbal abuse, reconnected with her maternal grandmother, and had more positive and playful experiences with Nicolas, she was able to adjust her view of Nicolas as damaged.

Nicolas used symbolic play and metaphors, stories, and reenactments to display his preoccupations in ways that he could neither process cognitively nor articulate verbally. He externalized and specified his fears through his drawings. He used clay to elicit and mobilize his internal concerns. Van der Kolk (2003) emphasizes that physical activity—a child taking action on his own behalf during treatment, for example—plays an important role in disengaging the child from trauma helplessness. Nicolas's creation of a clay head allowed him to feel empowered and gave him a mastery experience.

There are areas in the work with Nicolas that I would approach differently in retrospect. First, I would be more active in processing my countertransference individually and with my colleagues (Gil and Rubin 2005; Pearlman 1999) by recognizing that such behaviors are often caused by the secondary, or vicarious, trauma experienced in light of the shock of an event as violent as this one, especially when it happens to a young child.

Second, I would broaden my use of Nicolas's family system and would, for example, include Rosalinda in family play therapy sessions. I would focus more on increasing family resilience (Walsh 1998), especially hope, and I would have some parent-child sessions focused on post-trauma play, such as, with Nicolas's permission, allowing his mother to witness some of his post-trauma work such as Rocky's funeral.

The absence of male role models in Nicolas's life was noted, yet with the inquiries about Nicolas's father or a male mentor to spend quality time with Nicolas, Dora became defensive and suspicious, stating that she didn't need help from a man in order to raise her son. It seemed apparent that Dora had had complex relationships with men in her life, similar to the relationship with her father, but she was unwilling to discuss this in depth.

The transformation of Nicolas's trauma came about through his ability to access internal resources, to externalize his worries, to shrink the problem, manage it physically, transform it by molding it with his hands, and in the end achieve a sense of mastery and personal control (Gil 2006). By doing this work, he discharged and contained his anxiety, found concrete ways to represent and manage it, and ended his sessions feeling more confident and reassured that he was intact. He tolerated his fears and overcame the sense that these feelings were dangerous and overwhelming. Participating with Nicolas as he did his work, and with all those who cared for him and supported him, was an experience grounded in resiliency, creativity, and inherent motivations to heal what is injured. It was a transforming experience for us all.

References

Boyd Webb, N., ed. 2006. *Working with Traumatized Youth in Child Welfare.* New York: Guilford.

Bratton, S. C., D. Ray, and T. Rhine. 2005. "The Efficacy of Play Therapy with Children: A Meta-analytic Review of Treatment Outcomes." *Professional Psychology: Research and Practice* 36 (4): 376–390.

Councill, T. 2003. "Medical Art Therapy with Children." In C. A. Malchiodi, ed., *Handbook of Art Therapy*, 207–219. New York: Guilford.

Deblinger, E., and A. H. Heflin. 1996. *Treating Sexually Abused Children and Their Nonoffending Parents: A Cognitive Behavioral Approach.* Thousand Oaks, Calif.: Sage.

Ekstein, R. 1966. *Children of Time and Space, of Action and Impulse.* New York: Appleton-Century-Crofts.

Estrella, K. 2005. "Expressive Therapy: An Integrated Arts Approach." In C. A. Malchiodi, ed., *Expressive Therapies,* 183–209. New York: Guilford.

Figley, C. R. 1999. "Compassion Fatigue: Toward a New Understanding of the Costs of Caring." In B. H. Stamm, ed., *Secondary Traumatic Stress: Self-Care Issues for Clinicians, Researchers, and Educators,* 3–28. 2nd ed. Baltimore: Sidran.

Gil, E. 2006. *Helping Abused Children: Integrating Directive and Nondirective Approaches.* New York: Guilford.

Gil, E., and L. Rubin. 2005. "Countertransference Play: Informing and Enhancing Therapist Self-Awareness Through Play." *International Journal of Play Therapy,* 14 (2): 87–102.

Greenspan, S.I. 1981. *The Clinical Interview of the Child.* New York: McGraw Hill.

——. 1997. *Developmentally Based Psychotherapy.* Madison, Conn.: International Universities Press.

Guerney, L. 2003. "Filial Play Therapy." In C. E. Schaefer, ed., *Foundations of Play Therapy,* 99–142. New York: John Wiley.

James, B. 1989. *Treating Traumatized Children: New Insights and Creative Interventions.* Lexington, Mass.: Lexington Books.

Kottman, T. 2001. *Play Therapy: Basics and Beyond.* Alexandria, Va.: American Counseling Association.

Malchiodi, C. A. 1998. "Art Making and Illness: Drawing a Picture of Health." In C. A. Malchiodi, *The Art Therapy Sourcebook,* 165–194. Los Angeles: Lowell House.

Marvasti, J. A. 1994. "Play Diagnosis and Play Therapy with Child Victims of Incest." In K. J. O'Connor and C. E. Schaefer, eds., *Handbook of Play Therapy.* Vol. 2, *Advances and Innovations,* 319–348. New York: John Wiley.

"Nonfatal Dog Bite–Related Injuries Treated in Hospital Emergency Departments. United States, 2001." 2003. *Morbidity and Mortality Weekly Report.*

O'Connor, K. J., and L. M. Braverman, eds. 1997. *Play Therapy Theory and Practice: A Comparative Presentation.* New York: John Wiley.

O'Connor, K. J., and C. E. Schaefer, eds. 1994. *Handbook of Play Therapy.* Vol. 2, *Advances and Innovations.* New York: John Wiley.

Pearlman, L. A. 1999. "Self-Care for Trauma Therapists: Ameliorating Vicarious Traumatization." In B. Hudnall Stamm, ed., *Secondary Traumatic Stress: Self-Care Issues for Clinicians, Researchers, and Educators,* 51–63. 2nd ed. Baltimore: Sidran.

Presutti, D. O. 2001. "Prevention and Treatment of Dog Bites." *American Family Physician* 63 (8): 1567–1573.

Rubin, J. A. 2005. *Artful Therapy*. New York: John Wiley.

Schaefer, C. E. 1994. "Play Therapy for Psychic Trauma in Children." In K. J. O'Connor and C. E. Schaefer, eds., *Handbook of Play Therapy*, Vol. 2, *Advances and Innovations*, 297–318. New York: John Wiley.

Schaefer, C., J. McCormick, and A. Ohnogi, eds. 2005. *International Handbook of Play Therapy: Advances in Assessment, Theory, Research, and Practice*. New York: Jason Aronson.

Shelby, J., and E. D. Felix. 2005. "Posttraumatic Play Therapy: The Need for an Integrated Model of Directive and Nondirective Approaches." In L. A. Reddy, T. M. Files-Hall, and C. E. Schaefer, eds., *Empirically Based Play Interventions for Children*, 79–104. Washington, D.C.: American Psychological Association.

Shirar, L. 1996. *Dissociative Children: Bridging the Inner and Outer Worlds*. New York: Norton.

Silberg, J. L., ed. 1996. *The Dissociative Child: Diagnosis, Treatment, and Management*. Lutherville, Md.: Sidran.

Terr, L. 1991. "Childhood Traumas: An Outline and Overview." *American Journal of Psychiatry* 148:10–20.

van der Kolk, B. 2003. "The Neurobiology of Childhood Trauma and Abuse." *Child and Adolescent Psychiatric Clinics of North America* 12:293–317.

van Fleet, R. 1992. "Using Filial Therapy to Strengthen Families with Chronically Ill Children." In L. Vande Creek, S. Knapp, and T. L. Jackson, eds., *Innovations in Clinical Practice: A Sourcebook*, 87–97. Sarasota, Fla.: Professional Resource Press.

——. 2005. *Filial Therapy: Strengthening Parent-Child Relationships Through Play*. 2nd ed. Sarasota, Fla.: Professional Resource Press.

Walsh, F. 1998. *Strengthening Family Resilience*. New York: Guilford.

Wise, J. B. 2005. *Empowerment Practice with Families in Distress*. New York: Columbia University Press.

2

Transforming Trauma Responses to Sexual Abuse in Adolescents

CAROL J. MCCARTHY AND JOYCEE KENNEDY

A young girl's struggle to find grace: A 13-year-old girl, whom we will refer to as Tay, was evaluated in a university children's hospital emergency room for a medical emergency. Her teacher, Sarah, accompanied her because of concerns about Tay's deteriorating health. For the last two months, Tay had struggled with stomach pains and insomnia. The previous week, she had experienced abdominal cramps and headaches, and she was currently in a great deal of pain. Irene, a hospital social worker, listened carefully to the story, empathized with Tay, and validated her experience. She reassured Tay that she would be well cared for, and introduced her to the team of medical professionals who would be evaluating her.

The social worker called Tay's family to inform them of the emergency. Tay's younger brother answered the phone and reported that neither parent was home. Irene told the boy that his sister was at the hospital for some tests and that while she was probably fine, it was important for their parents to know. The boy said he thought his parents would be home soon, that they cleaned homes for a living and were working. When he gave Irene his dad's cell phone number, he told her that his parents were Vietnamese and spoke very little English. Tay's father never answered his cell phone. Unknown to anyone in the hospital room, this phone contact with Tay's brother would be the last communication with Tay's family of origin for the next five years.

As Tay met with medical staff, Sarah gave Irene background information from her perspective as a teacher. Sarah reported that Tay had always been reticent and shy. Sarah told Irene that she had not visited Tay's home, but believed she lived with a 10-year-old brother and her parents. Sarah thought the family had immigrated when Tay was 5 or 6. She mentioned there might be other relatives living in the United States. Sarah described Tay as being respected by her classmates and having several friends she spent time with at school.

After about an hour or so, the lead doctor of the team came into the room and sat down with Irene and Sarah. He said that he was admitting Tay for an emergency therapeutic abortion. The fetus looked to be between two and three months old, was badly malformed, could not survive, and was creating a risk to the life of the girl. Irene said that she would call the county child protection team right away to try to locate the parents. She let the doctor know that she would recommend that the Department of Human Services secure temporary custody of Tay, as well as emergency Medicaid. Irene asked if she could see Tay before the surgery. The doctor recommended against this, as Tay had confided in the doctor that she suspected she was pregnant, and she was ready for the procedure. Sarah and Irene developed a short-term plan of support for Tay. Sarah left temporarily to be with her own family, then came back to the hospital that evening. Irene left the hospital to go home while Tay was in surgery. She kept in touch with the child protection team and Sarah by cell phone. Both women were back at the hospital in Tay's room with the doctor when Tay woke up, and they stayed the night at the hospital.

Tay awakened the next morning uncomfortably, yet with surprisingly trusting eyes. She understood what she had gone through because of her meeting with the doctor. She knew the county had temporary custody of her. Once she was sitting up, she looked at Irene and said, "You will never see my family again because my dad is the father of the baby." She began to cry.

Understanding Adolescents and Traumatic Stress

Traumatic stress is an open wound among many adolescents. According to government statistics, 906,000 children and adolescents were determined to have been victims of child abuse and neglect in the United States in 2003. Of those, roughly 90,000 were sexually abused (U.S. Department of

Health and Human Services 2005). These numbers reflect only those cases in which action was taken following reports to child protective services, a small percentage by most estimates.

Post-traumatic stress disorder (PTSD) is often an appropriate diagnosis for adolescents who have experienced sexual trauma. This was certainly true for Tay, as she struggled with all three categories of symptoms for PTSD, including re-experiencing, avoidance, and hyperarousal. However, PTSD can occur along with other diagnoses, such as depression, anxiety, and substance abuse (McFarlane 2001). Tay was challenged by depression, and she abused illegal substances (when she was on the run from her group home).

The trajectory of development for a young person who is violated sexually is affected across biological, social, developmental, and academic functioning. The combination of adolescence and trauma raises complex issues. Adolescents in general already deal with increased levels of stress, and trauma further complicates an already difficult developmental stage (Arrington and Wilson 2000; Rubin 1999).

The transition from childhood to adolescence involves major changes, among them an increased desire for autonomy, emphasis on peer relationships (including sexual ones), increased self-focus, concern with identity issues, and increased ability for abstract thinking (Arrington and Wilson 2000; Baer 1999). Added to this already complex developmental stage are issues of socioeconomics and race and ethnicity (Arrington and Wilson 2000), as well as developing awareness of sexual orientation. Adolescents of color deal with the additional stress of experiencing racism, discrimination, and prejudice (Arrington and Wilson 2000).

When sexual abuse occurs within a young person's immediate family, foster care placement is an option, whether temporarily or permanently. Though the immediate concern of safety from the perpetrator may be taken care of by this action, it is not enough in and of itself. There are environmentally mediated risks to children in our systems of care that have not been adequately addressed. Unlike adult sexual abuse survivors, children and adolescents have developmental needs that require adult facilitation. Basic care, education, and consistent support through the developmental stage of adolescence are some of those needs. When families are not functioning in the role of supporting and satisfying the individual's complex developmental needs, it is essential that someone else fill that role. It is not enough simply to meet basic physical needs.

Responding to Adolescents Who Face the
Traumatic Stress of Incest

Partnering with Tay to tolerate the traumatic stress of incest, as well as the grief of losing a baby and her own birth family, was the mission of a multi-agency team of professionals and surrogate parents for the next five years. The team experienced the privilege of supporting this remarkable young woman. As Tay's story of courage, resilience, and strength unfolded from her endurance of ongoing child abuse for many years, she shared her survival skills: how she cleaned while listening to music; how she set her alarm early in the morning to do her homework; how she protected her mother and her brother from her violent, alcoholic father; how she made breakfast for her brother when her mom was too beaten down to get up.

Her initial placement after hospitalization was in a girls' group home with about ten other teenagers. The group home parents were kind, flexible, and patient. With so many demands from other children, however, the parents were unable to provide the extraordinary level of individualized nurturing and care that Tay needed. She ran away several times from this placement and abused street drugs. She was hospitalized by her ongoing mental health social worker for being self-destructive and a suicide risk. Her caseworker from the county department of human services continued to work with her, finding another foster family. The parental team in this new home was very structured and was raising several adopted children besides Tay. Tay did not want to be adopted. She wished to keep her legal Vietnamese roots. Tay knew she needed a different home.

When young people are removed from their homes, numerous systems often become involved in their care, among them the education system, child protective services, mental health services, and judicial services. Collaboration among these agencies is crucial. From a systems perspective, this is a challenge in the best of circumstances, as different agencies are responsible for different aspects of a young person's care. Our systems of care often are not collaborative enough or comprehensive enough to provide developmental protection, and are not diversified enough to be effective in the treatment of the young people they were designed to serve (McMillen et al. 2005; Rutter 2005).

It is easy for a young person's needs to be lost, skewed, or narrowed by involved professionals. "Cyclical institutionalization" occurs with our young people who are entrenched in the various systems of care. When an adolescent is moved from shelter to foster home, then from psychiatric hospital to residential treatment center, then perhaps to a detention facility and then to a foster home, that young person is likely to lack ongoing, harmonious, committed relationships with significant others, including peers. Consistency with a caseworker or probation officer is helpful, but such professional roles do not negate the need for a personal relationship with a healthy, functional person on a human level throughout the series of placements. The absence of such a relationship can also lead to a lack of cohesion in the youth's social group (e.g., family, school, and community), as well as a lack of relationship built on the reciprocity of respectful communication (Rutter 2005).

Throughout her time of contact with the agency, Tay worked in trauma- and grief-focused individual psychotherapy. Additionally, her therapist searched for her relatives in the state. During placement instability, her teacher, Sarah, gave her daily support at school. Tay's grades plummeted to a perfect straight F average. After securing an array of special consents, a Vietnamese colleague who worked in a local mental health center was able to learn through the Vietnamese community network the whereabouts of Tay's maternal grand- mother. Tay's therapist, as well as the colleague, who agreed to be a language interpreter, went door-to-door for several days in a large apartment complex to locate the grandmother. The team was successful, and the grandmother agreed to meet for a lunch at a local Vietnamese restaurant.

Tay was thrilled to be united with her grandmother, who behaved happily and excitedly to see Tay. But, for the long term, the losses would stay in place. The interpreter was invaluable, since it was unclear how much Vietnamese Tay remembered and her grandmother spoke no English. Tay's grandmother reported that Tay's mother, father, and brother had returned to Vietnam and were doing well. When the incest allegations were explained to the grandmother, the grandmother said the allegations were false, as the behavior was taboo in her culture. She also stated she would not be able to meet with Tay again and would have to say good-bye. Tay did not seem surprised. The two hugged and parted after lunch, not to see each other again for at least another five years.

Tay continued to experience bouts of depression, loss of concentration, and failing grades. Eventually, a new foster home was found for her. She was able to successfully live there for four years. She accomplished feeling protected, safe, comfortable, and harmonious with her foster parents. She developed a sense of cohesion and belonging in the family. Key characteristics of her foster parents were her dad's gentle playfulness and her mom's quietness. Both of her new parents were white and usually accepted one to two other foster children into their home. The couple had no birth children. The father was a retired U.S. Air Force major, and Tay's foster mom was a full-time college student.

Tay's community of adult supporters did not change throughout high school. Her middle school teacher visited her at high school regularly. Her mental health social worker and her caseworker saw her weekly in her home. Her medical doctors from the hospital made an effort to continue seeing her annually. The team provided classic components of trauma-focused treatment, including safe, harmonious relationships, education about traumatic stress dynamics (such as giving Tay readings and showing her films about trauma responses), help with emotional regulation (medical help with a thyroid dysregulation, medication for depression), relaxation techniques, feelings-identification exercises, and help with existential meaning in a Vietnamese context through the Vietnamese interpreter. Tay responded to this structure in positive ways by participating consistently and maintaining communication with her treatment providers. Her ability to verbalize her needs increased as her self-destructive behaviors simultaneously decreased. She partnered with her therapist in her process of acquiring stability and healing.

Tay remained in long-term foster care until she graduated with a B average from high school. She had grown into an engaging, beautiful, resilient young woman. Tay obtained a full-time job and leased an apartment with a friend. Although the county terminated parental rights because the family had vanished, Tay did not want to be adopted by an American family. Her narrative work with her therapist ended when she moved into her own apartment. After she had saved money from working, she resolved to return to Vietnam to find her birth family. She needed to recognize her multi-shaped heritage. She believed she would come back to the United States, as it was her home.

Even in a stable, long-term placement, the issues related to a lack of cohesion in the treatment and the social groups are not often addressed. A study of older adolescents in the foster care system showed that they have a much higher rate of psychiatric challenges than nonclinical populations, including three times the rate of major depressive disorders and twice the rate of PTSD as working-class youths of the same age (McMillen et al. 2005). Long-term out-of-home placements occur because of highly stressful situations in a young person's life, including child abuse and neglect, mental illness, and destructive behavior toward self and/or others. For long-term placement to occur, these stressful situations tend to be ongoing and complicated on an individual, familial, and systemic basis.

From a mental health perspective, accurate diagnosis, comprehensive collaborative treatment plans, and expert levels of case management are needed to adequately serve these youths. Their mental health needs are a part of the picture, as are all of the issues involved in raising an adolescent, often without a specific person (such as a parent) to oversee the situation. Add to this mix the complications of overburdened workers and agencies, fiscal challenges, and unequal access to resources that result from institutionalized racism and classism, and the challenges may seem overwhelming. Resolving these issues is critical, however, not just for the young people involved but also for our society as a whole. Social workers are uniquely positioned in their mission as change agents, as well as keepers of the broader bio-psycho-socio-economic picture, as they provide complex assistance to families in which trauma has occurred.

Empowering Relationships

A strengths perspective was effectively utilized in working with Tay, beginning with the first interview in the hospital emergency room. Bell (2003) identified three assumptions of such a perspective: clients have inherent strengths individually and within their communities, and they are more likely to act on these strengths when they are fully supported and affirmed; clients are experts of their own experiences; and the therapist is a collaborator in partnership with the client. Another powerful model of strength-based treatment comes from the Stone Center's relational-cultural model (Jordan 2003), which places connection at the center of human growth and development: "We believe that human beings grow through and toward connection" (Jordan and Walker 2004:2).

Tay was isolated within her family through the sexual violation by her father. Her needs were not seen or met by other adults around her until that fateful day in the emergency room. The empathy, concern, and care she received from all of the helping professionals clearly mitigated some of the suffering she had experienced within her family. These adults responded appropriately to her situation, and that response allowed her to experience a form of relational competence (Jordan and Walker 2004).

> When we are hurt, misunderstood, or violated in some way, when we attempt to represent our experience to the injuring person and are not responded to, we learn to suppress our experience and disconnect from both our own feelings and the other person. If, on the other hand, we are able to express our feelings and the other person responds with care, showing that we have had an effect, then we feel that we are effective in relationships with others, that we matter, that we can participate in growth-fostering

and healthy relationships. Ultimately, we feel anchored in community and we experience relational competence.

(Jordan and Walker 2004:2)

Asian Americans exist simultaneously in at least two social worlds: "the collectively-based social world of their Asian identified families, religions, and communities, and the individual-based social order of the larger American society" (Ino and Glicken 1999:525). Added stress on the family system may occur when immigrant and refugee backgrounds are present, as further disruptions and destabilization of family relationships are likely under such circumstances (Segal 2000).

Within many Asian cultures, social order and harmony are issues of primary importance (Tsukuda 1999). This is in contrast to a Western view of mental health, in which the restoration of vitality and effectiveness of an independent individual is paramount. The self in Asian cultures is inextricably linked to the effect of individual behavior on the family. In this way, family provides a sense of identity, including broad extended family. Stoicism is highly valued, as is tolerance of hardship (Ino and Glicken 1999).

This collective sense of psychosocial well-being maintains family as the vehicle for sustaining social harmony. It has its roots in Buddhism, Taoism, and Confucianism, philosophies and practices that see the individual as an integral part of the cosmos in harmony with nature. Individual behavior has effects upon oneself, one's extended family, the larger community, and even one's next lifetime. The view of family is not confined to living relatives. Ancestor worship is a key component. Elder respect is critical (Ino and Glicken 1999).

Creating social harmony is the goal of a successful family (Ino and Glicken 1999) and is achieved through highly structured family systems, with the eldest male given the position of authority to govern the family. Abiding by his rule is expected, while he is meant to use care toward his family (Tsukuda 1999). Tay's father held a position of unquestioned power in her family. From a Western perspective, Tay's ostracism from her family upon the discovery of incest is horrifying. Such expulsion from the family is not unheard of in East Asian cultures, however. Seeking outside help defies the authority of the father, as he may be viewed as losing face in the larger community (Tsukuda 1999). His competence as patriarch is irrelevant from the viewpoint of such family structures; that is not at issue. The way to reestablish social order is to expel the destabilizing, nonconforming member. Tay's lack of surprise at her family's disappearance illustrates her understanding of this concept.

Those who treat individuals of East Asian descent must recognize their bicultural identity. Treatment issues must incorporate the concept of the collective self. Significant loss threatens collective identity (Ino and Glicken 1999), which clearly occurred in Tay's situation. Her initial acceptance of the loss of her family, followed by a period of turbulence and self-destructive behavior, points to the activation of these issues. One way she resolved this issue for herself, aside from the powerful meeting with her grandmother, is evident in Tay's need to reconnect with her family as an adult. In cases of severe dysfunction, such as sexual abuse, the client may experience relief that authorities have stepped in, as that intervention models appropriate action in returning harmony to the larger group (Ino and Glicken 1999).

Tay entered treatment in the context of a medical emergency. Once the true nature of the emergency became apparent, medical interventions were paramount, including the bureaucratic tasks of obtaining temporary custody and emergency Medicaid. Once the immediate medical emergency was dealt with, Tay's ongoing emotional and physical safety became the focus. Since her family removed themselves from the crisis by leaving the country, there was no question that Tay would need an appropriate living situation through the child protection system. Mental health treatment also became a priority.

Facilitating the establishment of a safe living situation is crucial in situations such as Tay's. It is part of an empowerment model; in Tay's case it allowed her to give feedback to her providers in order to have her needs met. The helplessness that adolescents often feel when they lose autonomy through being raised by "the system" creates unique challenges for them. Tay's team of professionals worked to meet her needs and to create a safe physical and emotional environment.

Placements for adolescents can be a challenge. Tay had never been involved in the child protection or mental health systems before the discovery of her pregnancy. Moving from a family context to a group home or foster home setting is an enormous transition under the best of circumstances. For many adolescents, incorporating some level of work with the family to provide structure, healing, and possible reunification is a huge part of the treatment planning and collaboration between agencies. In Tay's case, this was not an option. She was a 13-year-old girl without family contact.

Tay's caseworker and therapist collaborated to address placement issues so that an appropriate placement could be found for Tay. She was eventually matched with foster parents who could allow her to regain her previous level of functioning, such as academic achievement, while she pursued mental health treatment.

Dealing with Tay's trauma response directly and respectfully was clearly shown by her therapist. Education about the dynamics and challenges of traumatic experiences is another aspect of an empowerment approach. Effective treatment begins with addressing symptoms of the trauma, such as nightmares, somatic complaints, sleep problems, and concentration problems. Once the client moves out of an emergency-response phase, treatment can move to focus more on relational issues (Avery, Massat, and Lundy 2000).

Tay's family disappeared at a highly vulnerable time. The incest was revealed, creating physical safety for Tay, but she literally lost all connection to her immediate and extended family. Because the source of stress in this situation was the family itself, the support and love provided by a healthy family needed to be created through other connections in Tay's world (Wise 2005). The work with Tay involved achieving consistency through the relationships she did have, including those with her teacher, the clinical social worker, the caseworker, and the medical providers who supported her through the initial crisis. A concerted effort was made to weave these threads together to provide a network of support and a sense of a community for Tay. Because of fiscal constraints and current models of short-term care that are in place, providing such consistency can be a challenge.

Integration of support was also generated with Tay by the search for her grandmother. The use of an interpreter of Vietnamese descent allowed better communication among the grandmother, Tay, and the therapist. Even if Tay had been able to interpret the conversation, it would not have been appropriate to use her in such a way. In such a situation, a perception of a power shift away from the grandmother to Tay may have occurred (Segal 2000), which would ultimately have been disempowering for both of them. A dual role for Tay as both client and interpreter would have jeopardized her situation.

Trauma, particularly when it is created by people in positions of trust, disrupts an individual's experience of being in relationship (Jordan 2004a). "The survival skills of the incest survivor—dissociation, hypervigilance, isolation, and lack of trust—all take a person out of connection" (Jordan 2004a:37). The level of care by Tay's treatment team, and the creation of an environment in which her voice could be heard and her needs expressed, helped to mitigate some of these challenges for her.

Within an empowerment model, equalizing power differentials between the client and worker, as well as between family members, is essential (Wise 2005). In East Asian cultures, authority figures may be perceived as having wisdom (Ino and Glicken 1999). Respect toward cultural beliefs and responsiveness within the therapeutic context while preserving appropriate boundaries promote mutuality in the work (Jordan and Walker 2004). Power differentials can be mitigated by home or community visits as well (Rose 2000), a model used throughout the work with Tay. Seeing Tay outside of an agency setting showed the clinician's interest in all aspects of her life.

Policies within agencies can support or diffuse the power differential between clients and workers, such as agencies' not allowing home visits (Rose 2000). "Managed care and increasing expectations for quick, clear fixes only add to the burden that many therapists feel" (Jordan 2004b:18). In relationships that are inherently empowering, meaning exists between all members of the partnership. Earning trust is a key factor as well (Rose 2000).

Traditionally, mental health treatment models have involved myths: therapists are expert; change in the relationship happens only to the client, while the therapist remains unaffected; the therapist has the power and is not vulnerable or emotionally responsive (Jordan 2004b). An empowerment approach dissolves such myths. The clinician is not an impassive, unemotional, unaffected person in a specific role. Therapists are seen as collaborators in partnership with the client. Tay was an expert on her own life. Her treatment providers respected her as such and allowed themselves to be guided and changed by Tay's needs while creating a safe structure in which she could heal and grow.

Cooperative roles in empowerment practice refer to the multiple and interchangeable roles in which therapists and clients find themselves. No specific role is appropriate throughout the relationship. Context, areas of expertise, and needs in a particular moment inform what role is appropriate to the circumstance (Wise 2005). In Tay's situation, the use of cooperative roles began with the respect shown to her in the emergency room. Tay confided in the doctor before speaking to her teacher or the hospital social worker. The teacher and the social worker honored Tay's request not to see her before her procedure. Tay led the way in terms of what she needed as the expert of her own experience. She was educated and guided throughout her treatment, and she also educated and guided her treatment team.

Vicarious Traumatic Stress

Tay's story evoked powerful feelings among the professionals involved in her life. The process of connecting with someone empathically creates the possibility of secondary trauma symptoms in supporters of trauma survivors (Geller, Madsen, and Ohrenstein 2004). Workers' affective and cognitive states, as well as their view of the world and their relationships, are affected by vicarious trauma. Continued exposure without intervention may have a negative effect upon the worker's ability to connect empathically with clients, sometimes resulting in not believing clients or emotionally distancing themselves from clients to avoid personal feelings (Regehr and Cadell 1999).

Factors that promote resilience in coping with vicarious trauma include: having a sense of competence about one's ability to cope regardless of the specific method involved; having an objective motivation for doing work in the area of trauma, rather than feeling a need to give back because of past support received oneself or attempting to work out one's own trauma through others; the perspective that one's own traumas have been personally resolved; witnessing or experiencing positive role models in coping with extreme stress or hardship in the past; and having buffering personal beliefs about the world without regard to the specific belief (Bell 2003).

Awareness of one's own level of stress is crucial in coping with vicarious trauma. It may be helpful to seek outside support from people who are not involved in the same kind of work. Personal treatment, consultation, debriefing, and involvement in violence prevention are recommended (Regehr and Cadell 1999). On an agency level, Geller, Madsen, and Ohrenstein (2004) have developed a protocol with clear structure and time constraints to allow expression and containment simultaneously. This strategy creates a safe environment in which to talk about thoughts and feelings evoked in the work, and the structure helps to avoid the loss of details during the parallel process of getting caught up in crisis mode. An added component includes a structure for feedback and conceptualization by the direct clinician, as well as colleagues who are not directly involved in the clinical work with that particular family.

The treatment team working in partnership with Tay shared the same practice standards and ethics. While the professionals were deeply moved by Tay's life situation, they also possessed a high degree of resilience. They did not allow their own feelings and needs to get in the way of guiding interventions that were appropriate to the situation. They supported each other by focusing on Tay's needs as they progressed through the course of their work together. Her teacher, caseworker, and therapist worked in partnership to achieve the same goals for Tay while managing their own feelings and reactions.

Conclusion and Recommendations

Being part of a community or family by some definition, in which each individual is understood and accepted, is a key component of recovery from trauma. In some ways, recovery from trauma can be likened to recovery from a broken limb: a cast is used to provide support and stability until such time as the limb is strong enough to function on its own; at that point the cast can be removed (Kennedy and McCarthy 1998). In trauma work, issues of safety are the first priority, followed by alleviation of intense trauma symptoms, and then attention to relational issues (Avery et al. 2000). To extend the broken limb analogy, after initial healing, rehabilitation to regain range of motion, flexibility, and functioning may be the next step. Increased support may be added as needed, and some degree of lifetime attention may be needed. The limb may become sore, and it is more susceptible to future injury (Kennedy and McCarthy 1998).

The same is true for adolescent trauma survivors. A type of cast was created for Tay by handling the medical emergency first. Reinforcements were added to her team for stability purposes, beginning with child protective services and a safe, nurturing living environment. At the outset, the "cast" gave her little freedom of choice or range of motion. A clinical social worker was added to support her with further stabilization in her placements. This worker was also available to support Tay throughout adjustments and crises related to her placement. Once Tay had gained stability in her living situation, her therapist was available to support her through deeper levels of healing. Increased services and supports were added when Tay's ability to regulate her feelings and behaviors was challenged. Such supports were reduced when she stabilized.

The very structure of current systems of care creates a challenging environment for workers involved with abused youth in placement. Two overarching goals, which will involve changes in ideology, are recommended. First, long-term significant connections with young people should be facilitated. Young people who have been traumatized by abuse need to be protected from having additional losses created by a crisis-oriented system.

Sometimes caregivers within the system are seeking to resolve personal issues through child rearing. It is critical that caregivers be carefully screened in this regard. Caregivers need to provide extraordinary or uncommon care. Loving, caring, supportive, dependable relationships represent the most important protective factor in a child's development.

Second, direct services to traumatized youth and families should be provided only through interagency teams, since short-term, single-provider, sequential service is not as effective in trauma recovery. Resource teams need to include the young person, the caregivers, medical doctors, psychiatrists, human service workers, ongoing therapists, teachers, probation officers, appropriate family members, and other supportive people in the young person's life. There is more work to be done than can be accomplished by one caregiver and/or therapist.

On a national level, there are three barriers that need to be overcome. First of all, high turnover is often the norm among treatment providers throughout the systems involved with an individual adolescent. For example, to have three therapists, three homes, and three human service workers helping one child in one year is contraindicated, and may in fact be harmful, resulting in the child's increased distrust of support, confusion about developmental tasks that need to be accomplished, and exacerbated traumatic symptoms.

The second national barrier is the inability of youth and families to easily access needed multi-expertise teams. If a young person does not have needed academic help, for example, her mental health may be affected, or if a youth's thyroid or sleep pattern becomes irregular, he may struggle with developmental tasks.

The third barrier has to do with inadequately designed leadership roles within agencies. Leaders often are reactive and not committed to families for the developmental long haul, a serious concern with a managed-care philosophy. Fiscal constraints may be at the root of this problem, which results in managers' inability to provide the necessary support for caregivers. The voices of caregivers—both professional and familial—need to be heard.

Social workers are uniquely positioned to handle such challenges because of the range of perspectives across the field. Social workers work with individuals in the context of the systems within which they live and identify. Considerations include intrapsychic mechanisms, developmental challenges, family systems, gender, race, ethnicity, socioeconomic status, and sexual orientation, in addition to interactions with systems such as education, human services, and criminal justice. Social work skills of advocacy are essential while maintaining a relational model of respect and mutuality throughout the process of communicating with all parties involved.

In the face of budget cuts, managed care, and other external forces, respect for the power of relationship is essential. Referring again to the Stone Center's relational-cultural model of development:

> Mutual empathy—the interplay of affecting and being affected, of mutual responsiveness and care—lies at the heart of growth-fostering relationships and human development. Thus, relationships are viewed as being an essential part of people's lives, perhaps the primary source of healing and growth

(Jordan 2003:23)

The process of respectful listening, consistency, and caring is crucial in a therapeutic relationship. It is within this process that healing occurs.

References

Arrington, E. G., and M. N. Wilson. 2000. "A Re-examination of Risk and Resilience During Adolescence: Incorporating Culture and Diversity." *Journal of Child and Family Studies* 9 (2): 221–230.

Avery, L., C. R. Massat, and M. Lundy. 2000. "Posttraumatic Stress and Mental Health Functioning of Sexually Abused Children." *Child and Adolescent Social Work Journal* 17 (1): 19–34.

Baer, J. 1999. "Adolescent Development and the Junior High School Environment." *Social Work in Education* 21 (4): 238–248.

Bell, H. 2003. "Strengths and Secondary Trauma in Family Violence Work." *Social Work* 48 (4): 513–522.

Geller, J. A., L. H. Madsen, and L. Ohrenstein. 2004. "Secondary Trauma: A Team Approach." *Clinical Social Work Journal* 32 (4): 415–430.

Ino, S. M., and M. D. Glicken. 1999. "Treating Asian American Clients in Crisis: A Collectivist Approach." *Smith College Studies in Social Work* 69 (3): 525–540.

Jordan, J. V. 2003. "Relational-Cultural Therapy." In M. Kopala and M.A. Keitel, eds., *Handbook of Counseling Women*, 22–30. Thousand Oaks, Calif.: Sage.

——. 2004a. "Relational Resilience." In J. V. Jordan, M. Walker, and L. M. Hartling, eds., *The Complexity of Connection: Writings from the Stone Center's Jean Baker Miller Training Institute*, 28–46. New York: Guilford.

——. 2004b. "Toward Competence and Connection." In J. V. Jordan, M. Walker, and L. M. Hartling, eds., *The Complexity of Connection: Writings from the Stone Center's Jean Baker Miller Training Institute*, 11–27. New York: Guilford.

Jordan, J. V., and M. Walker. 2004. Introduction to J. V. Jordan, M. Walker, and M. Hartling, eds., *The Complexity of Connection: Writings from the Stone Center's Jean Baker Miller Training Institute*, 1–10. New York: Guilford.

Kennedy, J., and C. J. McCarthy. 1998. *Bridging Worlds: Understanding and Facilitating Adolescent Recovery from the Trauma of Abuse.* Binghamton, N.Y.: Haworth.

McFarlane, A. 2001. "Dual Diagnosis and Treatment of PTSD." In J. P. Wilson, M. J. Friedman, and J. D. Lundy, eds., *Treating Psychological Trauma and PTSD*, 237–254. New York: Guilford.

McMillen, J. C., B. T. Zima, L. D. Scott, W. F. Auslander, M. R. Munson, M. T. Ollie, and E. L. Spitznagel. 2005. "Prevalence of Psychiatric Disorder Among Older Youth in the Foster Care System." *Journal of the American Academy of Child and Adolescent Psychiatry* 44 (1): 88–95.

Regehr, C., and S. Cadell. 1999. "Secondary Trauma in Sexual Assault Crisis Work: Implications for Therapists and Therapy." *Canadian Social Work* 1 (1): 56–63.

Rose, S. M. 2000. "Reflections on Empowerment-Based Practice." *Social Work* 45 (5): 403–412.

Rubin, S. E. 1999. "Trauma in Adolescence: Psychoanalytic Perspectives." In M. Sugar, ed., *Trauma and Adolescence*, 3–24. Madison, Conn.: International Society for Adolescent Psychiatry.

Rutter, M. 2005. "Environmentally Mediated Risks for Psychopathology: Research Strategies and Findings." *Journal of the American Academy of Child and Adolescent Psychiatry* 44 (1): 3–18.

Segal, U. A. 2000. "Exploring Child Abuse." *Journal of Multicultural Social Work* 8 (3/4): 159–191.

Tsukuda, G. 1999. "Commentary on the Paper by Ino and Glicken: Treating Asian American Clients in Crisis: A Collectivist Approach." *Smith College Studies in Social Work* 69 (3): 541–546.

U.S. Department of Health and Human Services, Administration on Children, Youth, and Families. 2005. *Child Maltreatment.* Washington, D.C.: U.S. Government Printing Office.

Wise, J. B. 2005. *Empowerment Practice with Families in Distress.* New York: Columbia University Press.

3

Transforming Trauma Responses to Women with Serious and Persistent Psychiatric Disability

SUSAN MANNING

I (the author) was working with a local mental health center (MHC) on a project about strengths-based case management. The project stressed the importance of consumer participation, and I had gotten to know many of the consumers who were receiving services there, including Claire, a woman in her early fifties. Claire had lived with schizophrenia for most of her adult life and had been hospitalized many times. She received day treatment services at the center.

As a result of sharing several friendly conversations, Claire and I developed a caring connection with each other. One day she seemed very distressed and quiet. I asked her what was wrong. She began to cry and said she was afraid to talk about it. After reassurance, she revealed that a male consumer at the MHC had sexually assaulted her. She related that he pushed her up against the wall, placing his hands all over her breasts and hips, thighs and belly. He was saying "filthy things" about her and about women in general. She was able to pull away, and she ran down the hall. Other consumers nearby (male and female) observed the trauma but did not intervene. I immediately asked to whom she had reported this assault and, with agitation, she said, "NO ONE, and I don't want you to tell on me."

She then revealed that the incident was not uncommon for women at this MHC and other institutions where she was a client. She stated that it was easier on her to keep it secret. If she reported it, there would be nothing the staff could do. The perpetrator would deny it, and then retaliate later. She would not hear of filing a report to the police and seemed afraid that the staff would be angry with her if she were to do that. She was deeply afraid of calling attention to herself and provoking retaliation from staff and other consumers. She noted that she spent a lot of time in the sewing room as a way to stay safe because the male consumers "were not interested in sewing and never came in there."

Understanding Trauma of Women with Serious Mental Illness

The experience of trauma is always complex and often unpredictable because of the unique qualities and histories of individuals and groups. A woman's authenticity combines with other factors—the degree of resilience she possesses, the level of support that is available in her environment, and the cognitive perceptions that she uses to interpret and resolve the trauma. In addition, levels of oppression in a woman's life have a profound impact on the experience and resolution of trauma. Working with women with serious and persistent psychiatric conditions requires consideration of all these dimensions and must take into account their histories and their experience with institutional care. For purposes of this chapter, serious and persistent psychiatric conditions include schizophrenia, schizo-affective disorders, bipolar disorders, major depression, and other serious disorders. These women have particular vulnerabilities and strengths with respect to trauma and their responses to it.

Victimization of women with serious mental conditions is often covert and multidimensional. Important dimensions include the nature and scope of the crimes, the experience of trauma within the context of a woman's persistent psychiatric condition, and the nature of institutional settings. Each of these dimensions has implications for the experience of the trauma and opportunities for successful resolution. For purposes of brevity, the term *women* shall refer to women with serious psychiatric disability.

NATURE AND SCOPE OF VICTIMIZATION IN THE MENTAL HEALTH SYSTEM

The victimization of individuals with serious psychiatric disability is "a pervasive problem that has received scant attention" (Dailey et al.

2000:377). The prevalence of incidents such as rape and sexual assault, and of simple and aggravated assault, is much higher for this group than for the general population (Dailey et al. 2000; Hiday et al. 1999). Women who suffer from schizophrenia or bipolar conditions are at a higher risk of rape (Darves-Bornoz et al. 1995). Further, women with a history of victimization (e.g., childhood sexual abuse) are more likely to be victimized again (Darves-Bornoz et al. 1995; Lipschitz et al. 1996).

One study of 234 individuals with serious psychiatric disabilities examines the nature and scope of victimization of this group (Marley and Buila 2001). Women experienced a higher average number of crimes than men. They also were significantly more likely than men to report "the experience of childhood and adulthood sexual abuse by known and unknown perpetrators and to have been raped or threatened with rape by known or unknown perpetrators" (118). The rates of victimization are "substantially higher" than those experienced in the general population (118).

Crimes identified by women as most traumatic were rape by a known perpetrator (17 percent), adult sexual abuse by a known perpetrator (12.4 percent), rape by an unknown perpetrator (10 percent), childhood sexual abuse by a known perpetrator (7 percent), and unwanted sexual activity (6.2 percent). More than half of the women indicated "abuse by a known perpetrator" as the most traumatic (Marley and Buila 2001:120). The most commonly identified known perpetrators of rape and adulthood sexual abuse were family members, friends and recent acquaintances. Service providers were named most often as the perpetrators in the category of unwanted sexual activity. For women, the crime selected as most traumatic had often occurred more than once in their lives; for some, it had happened six or more times.

The evidence suggests that women who are psychiatric survivors are, in fact, more vulnerable to sexual exploitation and abuse. The functional impairments of mental illness increase the vulnerability to victimization, and it is further exacerbated by the women's typical living situations, in impoverished areas with higher crime rates (Dailey et al. 2000). The perpetrators are often people that they know and rely on for support, services, protection, and friendship.

The trauma of victimization extends over a lifetime. Co-occurring disorders (e.g., serious psychiatric disability and substance abuse) increase the likelihood of victimization and add to the burden of managing a difficult condition while trying to live a life. Understanding the nature of serious psychiatric disability, then, is important to understanding responses to trauma.

THE NATURE OF LIVING WITH A SERIOUS AND PERSISTENT PSYCHIATRIC CONDITION

Claire must manage the circumstances of living with the complicated and sometimes debilitating effects of her condition. These effects are complex, and they affect every area of her life and environment—employment and economic status, sense of self in relation to others, and societal and institutional oppression. The nature of her condition is such that there are cumulative effects over time that traumatize and re-traumatize.

POVERTY

First, Claire is poor. The quality of life related to socioeconomic status for psychiatric survivors is, by their own evaluation, substantially lower than that of other groups who are poor (Lehman, Ward, and Linn 1982; Rosenfeld 1992). Typically, psychiatric survivors live in poverty, are unemployed or underemployed, and are sometimes homeless (Bachrach 1987; Belcher 1989). Chronic poverty promotes serious barriers to Claire's access to resources and support.

STIGMA

Living with a serious psychiatric condition means a lifetime of stigma. The labels associated with diagnosis convey an expectation that Claire is different from those who are normal; people with mental illness are perceived as crazy, weird, or unusual, and potentially dangerous (Boltz 1992; Manning and Suire 1996).

Living with stigma promotes internalized oppression (Manning 1998), disempowerment, and isolation from community. Claire internalized these external stereotypes and societal norms, which led to feelings of shame, less belief in her ability to perform, and constant fear of rejection by others (Boltz 1992). Individuals "find it hard to trust their own strengths and identify normal responses to their environment" (Manning 1998:93). Claire's personal power was diminished, while the power of professionals and others in her life was inflated. Others in her community withdrew from her, increasing social isolation.

SENSE OF SELF

Claire was living with a condition that promoted further disempowerment because of the profound loss of self that occurred (Estroff 1982, 1989). Estroff describes a "narrative of loss" that begins with the loss of a personal history—in this case, how Claire was known before her condition developed and was diagnosed. After diagnosis, who she was before was lost to the people who became central in her life (primarily providers and caregivers). Others' reactions to her, as well as the condition itself, changed Claire's sense of self (Estroff 1982, 1989).

In addition, Claire experienced the loss of familiar roles and her social place. Her involvement in community, employment, and family was substantially affected, particularly during the first years after diagnosis, partly because of her frequent hospitalizations and changes in living situations. Life became a restricted environment of narrowed social support networks, poverty, and financial dependence. Claire found herself in an institutional atmosphere that felt threatening to her safety and well-being (Estroff 1993, 1995).

INSTITUTIONAL OPPRESSION

Claire also may have experienced her primary institutions, ones that were necessary for treatment and care, as oppressive and disempowering (Rose 2000). Institutional care (hospitals, clinics, and community mental health centers) does not facilitate the normal adult activities that are required for Claire and others to have "dignified lives in the community" (Davidson et al. 2001:376).

Institutional care, founded on the medical model, relies on "the language of pathology and deficit" (Saleebey 1992:3). Diagnostic labels carried assumptions about Claire's capacity and competence, creating stigma from providers in relation to her. "The professionalized paradigm of diagnosis and treatment is a form of ownership of the power to define the reality of the other, to control and contain the other's meaning by interpretation of their experience" (Rose 2000:404). Rose states that this paradigm promotes an "inherently reproduced domination" (2000:404). The socialization of mental health professionals as experts with power over the resources necessary for Claire's care and basic needs leads to the unintended but ongoing loss of Claire's personal power. Professionals usually support the rights of clients conceptually, but in actual practice they do not always honor those rights through concrete actions (Wilk 1994). Claire's interpretation of meaning is particularly important to her response to trauma.

LEARNED HELPLESSNESS

Claire's tenure in institutional care led to unintended results that were negative. Compliance was rewarded; self-determination and autonomous behavior were discouraged. "Motivation and independence have been educated out of individuals in the mental health system. . . . They are educated to follow the decisions and instructions of many other people, not to follow their own instincts" (Deegan 1992:14). This unintended oppression of individuality leads to the development of learned helplessness, a "central attitudinal barrier" (Deegan 1992:14). Contemporary models of care based on strengths and empowerment do diminish the unintended effects of institutional care. However, the underlying assumptions of regressive professional attitudes may remain in effect, even within a model of recovery.

CUMULATIVE ADVERSITY

Trauma accumulates when associated with lifelong conditions (Alonzo 2000). Claire experienced a cumulative burden of adversity—poverty, stigma, oppression, learned helplessness, and more. She had less access to health and dental care. Outside of her program at the MHC, she may have lived in almost total social isolation. The lack of financial resources affected her ability to participate in the recreational and cultural events that add to quality of life. Finally, she experienced serious exacerbations of her illness resulting in frequent hospitalizations, sometimes against her will. Because of her condition, she may have suffered profound losses such as miscarriage, abortion, the loss of custody of her children, loss of love partners, loss of reproductive choice, or loss of family support. All of these losses could have precipitated mild to severe post-traumatic stress. Over time, this "accumulated burden of adversity" (Turner and Lloyd 1995) could promote in Claire "the fright and overwhelming dread of the loss of social control and life; the breakdown of social situation, of continuity of life, and of future expectations; and the assault on [her] social identity across many life domains" (Alonzo 2000:1477).

WOMEN'S RESPONSES TO TRAUMA

The ability to sort out what Claire actually had experienced was crucial, in order for helping professionals to respond in a productive manner. The following discussion about Claire's response is organized according to Herman's (1992) framework of terror, disconnection, and captivity.

TERROR

The sexual assault represented a threat to Claire's bodily integrity and her "ordinary adaptations to life" (Herman 1992:33). In that instant she faced her helplessness. It is unlikely that this particular event was the first occurrence, nor could she trust that it would be the last. The physical aspects of the attack and her perception that she could not influence the outcome or the likelihood of being attacked again increased her terror. "Traumatic reactions occur when action is of no avail. When neither resistance nor escape is possible, the human system of self-defense becomes overwhelmed and disorganized" (Herman 1992:34). Claire's long-standing history with psychiatric institutions intensified her sense of powerlessness. Further, her perception of the culture of the institution—that male aggressive and assaulting behavior was tolerated, or even condoned, by her peers—reinforced the experience of helplessness.

Stress as a trigger for psychiatric deterioration is well documented. The potential for the trauma to precipitate further disorganization of emotions, cognitive functions, and memory is elevated for Claire and others like her who suffer with schizophrenia. Claire communicated hyperarousal via her "persistent expectation of danger" (Herman 1992:35) and her perception that the only safe place to be was in the sewing room. She experienced generalized anxiety and difficulty sleeping, behavior that staff members interpreted as manifestations of her psychiatric disorder.

The trauma experience, often "encoded in the form of vivid sensations and images" (Herman 1992:38) was likely to have been especially frightening and disconcerting to Claire, since her symptoms included hallucinations. She might have experienced the traumatic event and the sequelae as decompensation, a spiraling into psychosis. The absence of information about what to expect in regard to responses to trauma increased the potential for Claire to misinterpret the meaning of her symptoms.

Claire's use of constriction, staying in the sewing room when she felt totally powerless, was a coping strategy. The constriction helped her to substitute numbing and detachment for the terror, rage, and psychic and physical pain she felt. This numbing and detachment were evident in Claire's response to the assault. She did not cry out to other consumers nearby for help, nor did she go to staff or the authorities after the incident occurred. She went to the sewing room, her place of safety.

The constriction also affected Claire's ability to plan for the future. Her involvement in the day treatment program became more restricted, and she missed out on opportunities for socialization, activities, and "success-ful coping that might mitigate the effect of the traumatic experience" (Herman 1992:47). This withdrawal was particularly significant for Claire, since the nature of her condition already precipitated social isolation and withdrawal under normal circumstances.

Constriction dominated her subsequent behavior. She appeared to be her normal self, resuming her usual schedule and activity. On the inside, however, she felt numb and alienated. These constraints have been described as "negative symptoms . . . not easily recognized and their origins in a traumatic event are often lost" (Herman 1992:49). Claire was viewed as a woman who loved to be in the sewing room, often alone, usually on the fringe of any activity, but not behaving unusually. Her visible actions did not alert the staff to be concerned about her.

DISCONNECTION

A breach of "the attachments of family, friendship, love, and community" (Herman 1992:51) and a common response to a traumatic event, discon-nection damages the development of the self that is maintained through relationships with others. The trust and belief that Claire established about her place in relation to others and her sense of being a part of a commu-nity were shattered. Claire has spent most of her adult life in the shelter or shadow of a mental institution. At the time of the assault, she was spend-ing all day, five days a week, in the day treatment program. She was attached to the institution, to the people who provided services, and to other clients, as her family and her home.

Claire's assault in the institution that she experienced as her greatest support, and in front of people she interacted with as her community every day, damaged her "faith and sense of community" because of the "betrayal of important relationships" (Herman 1992:55). The perceived indifference of other clients gave her the message that her well-being was not important. The breach of trust she felt with the people with whom she shared her life promoted a withdrawal from the very relationships that she needed in order to heal. She was not able to recognize or understand that those who surrounded her also shared the experience of learned helpless-ness and internalized oppression from years as psychiatric survivors.

As Claire's sense of connection with significant others was affected, she lost "her basic sense of self" (Herman 1992:52), which had already been somewhat tenuous. The invasion of her physical body, the emotionally abusive comments about her person, and the subsequent humiliation that she experienced violated Claire's sense of autonomy as a person. Her fear and helplessness in the face of the attack and the reluctance of others to assist her resulted in a feeling of shame and doubt about her response. "Traumatic events, by definition, thwart initiative and overwhelm individual competence. No matter how brave and resourceful the victim may have been, her actions were insufficient to ward off disaster. In the aftermath of traumatic events, as survivors review and judge their own conduct, feelings of guilt and inferiority are practically universal" (Herman 1992:53). Claire's immediate concern about the staff being angry with her conveyed some of her sense of shame and guilt about what had happened to her.

Finally, women who have lived with psychiatric conditions before an assault experience more severe and complex post-traumatic stress reactions (Herman 1992). Claire's own vulnerability from accumulated adversity reduced her resilience and ability to obviate the effects of the assault.

CAPTIVITY

Some aspects of institutional care can be interpreted as similar to captivity, though not in the traditional sense of prison, concentration camps, and domestic abuse. "Prolonged, repeated trauma . . . occurs only in circumstances of captivity. When a victim is free to escape, she will not be abused a second time; repeated trauma occurs only when the victim is a prisoner, unable to flee, and under the control of the perpetrator" (Herman 1992:74). Claire was a captive in the sense that she had little choice to go elsewhere. Psychiatric clients sometimes experience the institution as their only option for treatment. Services are usually provided according to a person's geographic or community location. Claire had only Social Security benefits and Medicaid for payment, and no transportation options beyond the bus. Clients like Claire, who have learned to manage their mental illness through treatment and medications, value the opportunity to participate in the available programs and would not choose to drop out of treatment or leave their "communities." Changing to another treatment facility would not necessarily preclude the possibility that traumatic events could happen in the new setting.

The characteristics of clients that institutions promote are not those that are the most useful in response to trauma and oppression. Adaptation is rewarded, and passive behaviors are reinforced, since social control mechanisms are necessary when working with large numbers of people who experience varying degrees of emotional and behavioral disruption. Claire was adamant about not telling the staff or reporting the assault to the police. She was afraid of causing a problem or disruption, in terms of both the staff reactions to her and her standing and future safety with the other clients.

As the research cited earlier suggests (Marley and Buila 2001), Claire had good reason for her lack of trust. Caregivers do not always provide a safe environment, nor are they always trustworthy. Women with mental illness selected rape and adult sexual abuse by a known perpetrator as the most traumatic crimes. Since a good part of the social system for women with mental illness is associated with their treatment community, it is likely that many of the perpetrators were men they knew—those they considered friends or protectors. Also, service providers themselves were most often the perpetrators of unwanted sexual activity.

Claire was also acutely aware of differences in the distribution of power in the institution. The role delineations in institutions are based on a medical model of care (professionals are experts and clients are recipients) and therefore reinforce the difference in "status and self-esteem, and thus a difference in power" (Manning 1998:90). Experiences of the psychiatric survivor such as "involuntary hospitalizations, electroconvulsive treatments (ECT), forced medications, lack of control over treatment planning, and the absence of informed consent from years of treatment in institutions" reinforce a loss of control over life choices (91). As described by one consumer, "They [the clients] tend to be totally intimidated by the [mental health] system . . . [which wants] to break their will to change their behavior" (Manning, Zibalese-Crawford, and Downey 1994:44). Claire's experience was intricately connected to the institution where she receives care. It follows, then, that the response to her trauma and the promotion of her empowerment must also be linked, in part, to her mental health institution and program.

Response to Trauma: Empowerment for Women with Mental Illness

The stages of trauma recovery—safety, remembrance and mourning, and reconnection (Herman 1992)—combined with an empowerment approach create a framework for a helpful response to trauma for Claire. The fundamental experiences of trauma are disempowerment and disconnection

(Herman 1992). Thus, the recovery process for Claire had to be based on creating opportunities for her self-determination and helping her connect to others, a process that could happen only within the context of relationships. Empowerment is "a relational expression, not a technique or instrument. In empowering relationships, meaning [is] restored to each person; earned trust [is] built into explicit acknowledgment of the purpose of the practice; interactions [are] explored for their links to social structures and their interests; and clients' lives [are] envisioned simultaneously as unique in terms of meaning, but collective . . . in terms of patterns of domination" (Rose 2000:412). Empowerment for Claire, then, was embedded in relationships (Herman 1992).

For Claire to be empowered, she had to be "the author and arbitrator of her own recovery" (Herman 1992:133). Caregivers, instead of controlling what they thought was best, needed to help restore control to Claire herself. Empowerment includes "the freedom to choose; the ability to make things happen; and to move on with living enhanced by well-being" (Wise 2005:24). The voices of consumers with psychiatric disability who identified choice, respect, involvement, contribution, and information/education as other critical variables of empowerment are integrated into the following discussion of empowerment practice as it related to Claire's experience (Manning et al. 1994). Safety was the starting point for the resolution of trauma and the beginning of empowerment for Claire.

SAFETY

Safety, as the first step, had to be addressed immediately. Establishing safety for Claire rested on several key tasks that coincided with empowerment principles (identified in parentheses). These key tasks were naming the trauma (working from an awareness of specific need); establishing a partnership (using cooperative roles); working from a holistic, strengths-based assessment and intervention plan (building on strengths while diminishing oppressive factors); and demonstrating multicultural respect (as indicated in the language of the empowerment principles). Safety for Claire included physical, psychological, and emotional aspects. Safety, like the other stages of trauma response (mourning and remembrance and reconnection), is not linear and does not necessarily become resolved according to particular timelines or stages. The process is dynamic. It was anticipated that Claire might return to issues of safety or mourning or reconnection throughout her process.

NAMING THE TRAUMA

Empowerment does not happen in an environment of secrecy and avoidance. Workers must start the process by asking the right questions. Claire first named the trauma with me because, even though I was in an active participatory role at the MHC at the time, I was outside of the formal mental health system. I consistently conveyed my interest in her life and her experience. I did not have authority over her; we had a *mutual*, reciprocal relationship. She listened to my stories just as I listened to hers. She experienced my *respect* for her, as I inquired about her life and paid close attention to her narrative. Thus, she experienced the *equalizing of power differences and cooperative roles* in our relationship, which was crucial to her empowerment (Lee 1994; Wise 2005).

Naming the trauma had to move beyond the two of us to the larger mental health center community. If Claire had continued to feel she wanted to remain quiet about the assault, an ethical and legal dilemma would have developed. On the one hand, her right to privacy and self-determination and my professional duty to protect her confidentiality were paramount. On the other hand, she had suffered emotional and psychiatric injury, and both she and other clients were at further risk of assault. In addition, Claire's well-being, her best interests from an ethical perspective, depended on open discussion of what had happened and on her participation in the resolution.

Time and opportunity for Claire to explore the dilemma and participate in the decision were crucial. If she continued to feel afraid to participate in the decision about disclosure, it was my professional responsibility to report the incident for her. Social workers who possess confidential information have a duty to warn others if doing so will prevent harm to other potential victims (Reamer 1995). Disclosure in this case was necessary in order to prevent foreseeable harm to Claire and other women in the program (NASW 1996). In addition, disclosure was the first step toward group determination of the ethical standards for community membership; disclosure is a step toward taking responsibility for the "conscience of community" (Green 1987; Manning 2003). Leadership through disclosure helps the community create norms that protect and respect women.

Claire had an undisclosed history of trauma as part of her experience in the mental health system, as do most psychiatric survivors. More than half of psychiatric inpatients and 40 to 60 percent of outpatients report previous physical and/or sexual abuse (Herman 1992). Thus the process had to include the assessment of past victimization experiences. By naming the problem and opening discussion about the past, I conveyed the intent to advocate for Claire's protection and to promote change in the system. Both strategies emphasized collaboration toward her safety.

ESTABLISHING A PARTNERSHIP

The ideal metaphor for the worker/client relationship in Claire's situation was partnership, a sharing of power, a mutuality to strengthen her response to trauma. Her helpers brought clinical knowledge about trauma and mental illness and a commitment to her empowerment and well-being. Claire brought her experiential knowledge, strengths, and coping skills, as well as a willingness to take control over her life decisions and to contribute to the well-being of others.

In partnership, the social worker had a personal commitment to Claire that went beyond her role in the agency, funding issues, and needs assessment. The worker was literally the human link between Claire and the mental health system (Freund 1993). Supporting her to risk reporting what had happened to those in the institution and, with their help and support, to the authorities confronted learned helplessness and provided other avenues to pursue justice.

Similarly, a partnership respected Claire's interpretation of the meaning of the traumatic event. Claire's voice, conveyed through storytelling about her trauma, became "an expression of her individuality in the face of negative social stereotypes . . . an act of self-validation . . . a metaphor for protest" (Kaufmann and Campbell 1995:7). The goal was to understand something about Claire's life according to what was meaningful to her, not according to the framework of a theory.

The partnership approach implied respect for Claire's self-determination and choice, which is essential to the process of recovery. As she made choices, she enacted her own attitudes, values, and beliefs. These, in turn, reaffirmed her sense of self and her authenticity in relation to others. As she became more self-determined, her self-efficacy was enhanced and her self-confidence improved. This process increased her sense of personal power. Claire's internal motivation had to be trusted.

I offered ongoing support to Claire during the days following her report of the assault. Hypervigilance, an exaggerated startle response, suspicion of others in the program, and expressions of fear, shame, and guilt were some of the trauma responses that I noticed.

Building on her strength in telling me about the incident, I hoped the connection between us could serve as the foundation for a partnership to take the next step. One afternoon she asked, "What if he does that to Cheryl?" Cheryl was one of Claire's friends in the program. I invited Claire to say more about her concern for Cheryl, and as we spoke, it became evident that, with the assurance of strict confidentiality, Claire might be able to do for others what she felt she could not do just for herself—that is, report the incident to her MHC social worker. Assuring her that her safety was the highest priority, I offered to assist her in considering a plan to "have a conversation" with her social worker.

With the assurance of confidentiality for her safety, her concern about possible assaults on her friends, a strengthened sense of herself in viewing her responses as coping skills, plus calling on the partnership between us, I offered to accompany Claire to the appointment with her social worker. Claire felt the support of her social worker and was able to describe the incident but hesitated to reveal the name of the man who had assaulted her. She was fearful that the social worker might take action right away and then "he will know it was me who told you."

The social worker was very understanding of Claire's hesitation, acknowledging the risks involved, and said she did not want Claire to feel pressured to reveal his name. She explained that an investigation based on observation would take place and that Claire would be included in decisions about the timing of any action taken. The worker spontaneously offered the possibility that any observation of inappropriate behavior by the "man in question" could begin a procedure to remove him from the program. This possibility appeared to be a great relief to Claire, and it energized and empowered her to want to go further in working with her social worker.

WORKING FROM A STRENGTHS-BASED ASSESSMENT AND PLAN

"[People] . . . have different abilities to comprehend information and a different sense of readiness to move forward than they would if no recent traumatic event had been experienced" (Wise 2005:52). This was especially relevant for Claire. Her coping strategies were intertwined with symptoms of her psychiatric condition and, if they had been interpreted only as symptoms, the opportunity to help resolve the acute trauma could have been missed (Alonzo 2000).

The first task was to "establish the survivor's safety" (Herman 1992:159). Claire and her providers had to evaluate her *perception* of safety in all domains of her life. Staff may have assumed her safety, but this may not have been Claire's interpretation. She did not feel safe in the program, and she isolated herself from others while there. She had to commute to the program from her apartment, and likely felt frightened about walking or taking the bus alone. A significant part of her support system was at the mental health center; support from neighbors or friends seemed minimal or nonexistent. A detailed plan that established her sense of safety and future protection was essential. The plan needed to be concrete and include the structures and assigned responsibilities necessary to carry it out, such as identifying key people, staff, and clients who would accompany her home and partner with her during the program.

The assessment had to be *based on strengths*. This required a fundamental shift in thinking for both Claire and some of her providers, because of the deficit ideology and the language of pathology that prevail in mental health systems (Manning 1998). Claire's journey was one of hope, belief in self, and learning to be self-determined. Practitioners using this strengths-based, contextual view saw Claire as a whole human being and took into account her past and present lack of access to resources and opportunities (Rose 1992). This shift emphasized the importance of Claire's being informed about choices and supported in pursuing choices for herself. The directions chosen were predicated on the knowledge that she brought to the helping process about what she wanted and needed. Her ability to know what was best for her was respected (Jones 1992; Manning 1998). Ultimately she was supported in defining her own reality about the traumatic event.

Providers, in "letting go" of the role of expert, made a place for the diversity of skills and knowledge that Claire brought to the relationship. "The guiding principle of recovery is to restore power and control to the survivor" (Herman 1992:159). Women who have been abused possess resourcefulness and strengths that they have mustered under extraordinary circumstances (Humphreys, Sharps, and Campbell 2005). Claire brought a lifetime of coping with intolerable losses, dislocations, and distress. She had developed unique capacities to cope and to survive; capacities that were identified and mobilized. Her experience was used to help others, which, in turn, enhanced her empowerment (Manning et al. 1994).

Labeling trauma-related behaviors as a "disorder" when those behaviors do not meet the *DSM* criteria for post-traumatic stress disorder has been challenged in favor of "trauma response" (Everstine and Everstine 1993) or "post-traumatic stress response" (Wise 2005). In light of these recommendations, Claire's behaviors were viewed as coping skills necessary to respond to the trauma—behaviors that were useful in promoting a healing process. Helping Claire understand her behaviors as normal under the circumstances enhanced her understanding of what to expect and provided her with a different view of herself; she began to trust her own strengths and capacities (Manning 1998).

A strengths-based assessment and intervention plan does not discount the need for clinical expertise. The "excessive respect for the abstract notion of 'choice' can lead to the perpetuation of neglect or to an increase in the risk of neglect and other harms" (Linhorst et al. 2002:431). Working *with* Claire about *her perceptions* of her capacities and providing clear feedback about clinical perceptions provided her with important information that helped her manage her psychiatric condition and the effects of the assault. This clinical activity was empowering. Abandoning her to be "on her own" would not have met the definition of empowerment.

DEMONSTRATING MULTICULTURAL RESPECT

Because of the potential for misdiagnosis and misinterpretation of symptoms, as well as possible clinician bias, multicultural respect is an important component of strengths-based assessment. Systematic patterns of misinterpretation of symptoms and diagnosis have sometimes resulted from clinician bias, leading to "women, the elderly, members of racial and ethnic minority groups, the poor, and the mentally retarded" being viewed as more pathological than other groups (Good 1997:239).

Research on social class demonstrates consistent findings of worker bias (Lopez 1989). Women with psychiatric conditions typically live in poverty, and in Claire's case, access to sufficient resources was essential to her safety and healing. A worker who lacked such awareness might not have considered what was necessary in order for Claire to have, for example, safe passage to and from the program via public transportation.

Claire's experience of trauma had to be understood within her cultural, ethnic, racial, economic, and spiritual framework. The major question to ask was, "What was meaningful to Claire's interpretation of what had occurred?" Multicultural respect included awareness about the multiple oppressions that Claire experienced. Women with different ethnic, racial, economic, or religious diversities face additional oppression that affects the experience of trauma. Claire's gender, her status as a psychiatric client, and her differences from the dominant group(s) within her environment all added layers of complexity that needed to be explored and understood in order for the plan to be effective.

Claire's ethnicity is European American, but if she were a woman of color a worker's lack of understanding of the presence and history of trauma stemming from racist incidents could cause further bias (Bryant-Davis and Ocampo 2005). Racist experiences parallel the trauma of rape and/or domestic violence and must be considered in the process of assessment as historical traumas that may exacerbate the present experience. The experience of racist incidents for women of color increases the risk factors for other forms of trauma. Mounting evidence "suggests that members of minority subcultures are at particularly high risk for error in psychiatric diagnosis and assessment" (Good 1997:237), putting women of minority communities at risk for ineffective or inappropriate care. Cross-cultural research provides evidence that the definition of "normality," the presentation of symptoms, and patterns of illness are different across cultures (Good 1997). The experience of a psychiatric condition is culture-bound and requires awareness from the responder and the ability to assess through the cultural lens of the woman who has been traumatized.

Finally, respect was critical to Claire's empowerment (Manning et al. 1994). Specifically, "being listened to" and "being heard" were central to experiencing respect from providers of care (95). A relevant assessment required her "disclosure" (Good 1997:240), particularly in regard to cultural rules, roles, and traditions, previous experiences with discrimination and oppressive authority, and the cultural knowledge that she brought to the therapeutic experience, which promoted understanding and healing. Also, Claire's sense of self and self-respect were crucial to empowerment (Manning et al. 1994). Exploring with Claire her involvement in self-care and wellness activities and the promotion of her authenticity by living and expressing her personal values was important in her healing from trauma and in promoting her sense of personal empowerment.

REMEMBRANCE AND MOURNING

The second stage of the trauma response process involves mourning and remembering (Herman 1992). Claire had to tell her story of the assault in detail and in depth many times over in an effort to understand and integrate the meaning of her experience and be able to move forward in her life. This process was one of balance, in which Claire and her workers had a heightened sense of the intrusion of symptoms and the use of constriction as a strategy to avoid symptoms. Claire needed constant information about the nature of this process and her experience of it in order to sort out what was related to the trauma and what was a feature of her psychiatric condition. It was important for her to know that she did not have to respond within a particular time frame and that the unfolding of the process was within her control. Remembrance and mourning required commitment and opportunities for grieving and transforming the trauma.

COMMITMENT TO THE WORK

The commitment to engage in painful and difficult stories is not easy. A gifted and committed psychiatric nurse described this well:

> The pain which my clients have experienced as a result of their illnesses is overwhelming. The losses they have suffered are nearly unspeakable. Sometimes it's been hard for me to endure one more tragic story, to hear about one more loss. At times my urge has been to rush in and try to fix things, which would feel better than being still and hearing the pain. But such things can't be fixed, and trying to do so is disrespect for the person's pain. . . . Sometimes all you can do is just be there.

> (Jones 1992:14)

Each person, client, and worker, each with her own lived experience, demonstrated the commitment required from both Claire and her workers.

After Claire's report of the incident with her social worker and her sense of a trusting connection there, I continued to stay in touch with her in a supportive role. From both Claire and her social worker, I later learned that Claire eventually did have the courage to report the name of the person who had assaulted her. Her worker let her know how important her report was, for Claire was not the first person toward whom he had been aggressive and assaultive. Claire's report added to the evidence needed to begin procedures to have him removed from the program. Later, at a time that would not place any participant at risk, the perpetrator was confronted by his clinician and the administrator of the program with his behavior and was required to leave the program.

STRATEGIES FOR REMEMBERING

Timing is important to grieving and remembering. Claire's ability to tell her story was compromised by the trauma she had experienced. The "numbing, confusion at the cognitive and emotional levels, and distortions in time and space" that are normal coping mechanisms after trauma occurs had interfered with the more abstract interpretations necessary for independent action and goal direction. The first step in Claire's process was awareness. Thus the clinician's ability to collaborate with Claire in an assessment of "readiness" for more autonomy and thus more self-determination was critical (Wise 2005:54).

An associated factor with increased empowerment is the risk that accompanies enhanced personal power (Wise 2005). Claire was aware that she might risk further abuse from the male client(s) if she revealed the assault and that she might risk disapproval from agency staff as she confronted the culture of the system. The development of support to provide partnership with Claire as she went through this process was essential.

Support and opportunity for remembrance are connected to involvement in meaningful structures. Living with a psychiatric disability made it difficult for Claire to create and maintain meaningful structures in her life. Meaningful structures—i.e., "another person, buildings, rituals, pastimes, activities, and so forth" (Jones 1992:10)—provide opportunities for remembrance, sharing emotions, skill building, information sharing, and the development of relationships—all necessary ingredients for healing and for support. "The key word is 'meaningful'" (Jones 1992:10). Claire used such structures to tell her story, to reconstruct her experience, and eventually to integrate the incident into her life.

Empowering structures have to be possible and must be meaningful (Jones, in Manning 1998). *Possible* means that the structures had to fit with Claire's ability to participate, whether through an individual narrative of her story through artwork or journaling or one with other women who had experienced similar trauma. The range of activities had to be relevant to Claire's level of functioning. This process "demonstrates the strengths-based perspective—building on strengths and providing opportunities to develop skills to continue to grow" (Manning 1998:102).

Meaningful structures enhanced Claire's ability to cope with and eventually resolve the trauma. Meaningful structures had a purpose. They were real and relevant to her life rather than contrived activities experienced as busywork. Claire's empowerment involved purposeful and relevant information that facilitated her power to cope with and transform the trauma (Manning 1998). Skill building was accomplished through linkages to others who added to Claire's understanding of trauma and development of successful coping skills. Structures that promoted learning (informational sessions about sexual assault), structures that promoted grieving (loss group with other women), structures that focused on the improvement of her health (relaxation or meditation experiences, exercise or massage), and structures that facilitated relationships and having fun (extending her interest in sewing to community activities with others who enjoyed sewing) were some of the meaningful structures that Claire put in place in her life.

Finally, mourning and remembrance required some specialized help that is not always available within a mental health system. Referral to a rape awareness program and a sexual assault support group provided Claire with the specialized clinical attention that she needed and the support of women who had experienced something similar. Psychiatric clients who suffer from past abuse and current trauma are seldom referred to specialized services for help (Rubin and Panzano 2002:457). Agency staff need to develop increased awareness of "the more complicated picture of these individuals," which can help to increase accuracy in recognition of individual needs.

RECONNECTION

Part of the transformation of Claire's trauma was reconnection to a future. "She can establish an agenda. She can recover some of her aspirations . . . or for the first time she can discover her own ambitions" (Herman 1992:197). Part of Claire's reconnection occurred when she realized that she could make a difference through connecting to others, learning to take power and using the collective for political action.

CONNECTION TO OTHERS

Trauma destroys the connections between self and community (Herman 1992). The "strongest antidote" to Claire's traumatic experience was a feeling of connection to others—a sense of belonging, the "discovery that one is not alone" (215). Belonging and involvement and a sense of community promoted her sense of empowerment (Manning et al. 1994). With community, Claire no longer perceived that she was facing her perpetrator alone or living a shameful secret. Her sense of trust was reestablished, and the betrayal that she had experienced was healed.

The invitation to participate is the "cornerstone of empowerment" (Townsend 1998:154). For Claire, who lived with a psychiatric condition that promoted withdrawal and a paucity of relationships, the value of friendships was paramount in helping her to heal from trauma. Participation, according to Townsend (1998), was invited by "guiding people to discover their individual talents, and by creating opportunities for participation in organizing as well as carrying out activities" (154). This kind of invitation recognized Claire as an "active agent," rather than as "passive client" (155).

LEARNING TO TAKE POWER

Claire learned to take power by making conscious choices to take risks and face danger. Her ability to affect her environment was important, since her trauma took place in the institution. Helping Claire to change her environment to one of support, participation, and capacity building, rather than expecting her to adapt (Rose 1991, 1992), was an empowering choice. With support, Claire addressed and overcame the social pressures of imposed restrictions within the client/staff agency culture by revealing the trauma.

At a later date, a group was initiated and developed collaboratively by Claire, staff, and other clients in the day treatment program to heighten awareness among women about sexual harassment and assault. This type of structure is a reconnection to the future and an opportunity for the creation of new relationships (Herman 1992). Claire understood that she was not the only one who had been traumatized and that there continued to be risk. Other women, then, benefited from prevention activities and education. The opportunity to participate in a collective experience enhanced the possibility of consciousness raising and political action to change the system (Parsons, Gutierrez, and Cox 1998). An important product of this action was that it communicated a willingness on the part of staff to address underlying and hidden traumatic events in an open manner that included action and redress. Thus the agency culture was changed.

USING THE COLLECTIVE FOR POLITICAL ACTION

Claire's experience of exclusion and living in social isolation resulted in a lack of support. What was needed was the experience of "inclusion . . . a feeling of belonging, of having a niche or a meaningful role to play in the life of a community" (Davidson et al. 2001:379). Her life was not limited to the institutional community mental health program. Thus, helping her develop connections to her external community as a citizen was also important. Political actions, such as in rape awareness education or policy development, connected Claire to other citizens with similar concerns and promoted her capacities as a citizen who could effect change.

Identifying a traumatic event embedded in institutional programs and initiating action in response was supportive of the risk-taking necessary for "transformative change . . . necessary to transform *what is* to empowerment" (Townsend 1998:157). In Claire's community experience, the group members together assessed the nature of the risks and the size of the challenge. In partnership, the community group (clients and staff) with Claire initiated the development of internal agency policies that protected against victimization of any members, both staff and clients, changing the culture at the agency to protection and empowerment. Claire and others were empowered through their ability to make a contribution (Manning et al. 1994).

Vicarious Trauma for Workers

The risk of vicarious trauma was present for people working with Claire in the therapeutic and relational process. As Jones (1992) so poignantly described, the experience of helping Claire was an experience of sharing the loss, grief, and devastating traumas associated with serious and persistent mental illness. In addition, the nature of Claire's condition required an understanding of the long-term process of recovery. There was no quick fix, and change sometimes happened only in small steps over long periods of time.

Helpers needed adequate support systems for their own experience, both in the mental health system and in their social environment. The use of groups was as empowering for staff as it was for clients. Group supervision, team meetings, support groups, and men's and women's groups in the community provided avenues for expression of feelings, perspectives, and strategies for healing.

The culture of the mental health agency played an important role. In such an environment the opportunity for and encouragement of feedback about unethical or dangerous practices on the part of clients or staff is crucial (Manning 2003). Staff who are unable to comment on agency policies and practices find themselves experiencing a moral alienation that contributes to burnout and secondary trauma (Manning 2003). Just as Claire felt empowered to address her trauma, so were staff empowered to address the injustices that happened at an organizational level. Formal structures developed as part of the organizational design that gave permission for feedback and action (e.g., ethics committees, annual ethics audits), and routine policy discussions facilitated feedback (Manning 2003; Reamer 2001).

Finally, the intensity of the traumatic experiences that Claire and other women had endured promoted moral disengagement, which could have led to dehumanizing behaviors on the part of workers (Bandura 2002). Workers might have distanced themselves from the nature of the trauma and abuse that was occurring so that they would not be required to respond to it. Distancing could have taken place by avoiding places or people where they would be confronted with information about what was taking place. Structures that helped create opportunities to discuss volatile or potentially disruptive findings gave workers permission to identify problem areas and work on constructive solutions with others (Manning 2003).

Conclusion and Recommendations

The experience of women with serious psychiatric disorders and trauma is complex and multidimensional. Their vulnerability, grounded in past and present history and combined with their relationship to institutions, creates unique challenges for healing from trauma. Social workers, to be effective, must examine their own attitudes and beliefs about partnership and the relational aspects of recovery. More specifically, providers must set aside the role of expert, use cooperative roles to equalize power differentials, and make a place for the wealth of skills and knowledge that these women bring to the relationship and to the process of their own recovery from trauma.

Women like Claire, with the accumulated burden of adversity that they have experienced, also bring tremendous resources, skills, and strengths that can be mobilized for their own recovery. Every stage of the work must be based on those strengths. Both initial and ongoing assessments must be founded upon strengths and must integrate culturally sensitive practice. Throughout the work, it is important for Claire to be informed about choices and supported in pursuing choices for herself in every aspect of her recovery.

Working with trauma in the mental health system also implies working toward change of the institution(s) where women are served. The culture and policies that are meant to protect may, in reality, be inadequate or oppressive. Agency staff can benefit from increased awareness about the complexity of circumstances faced by these individuals. Such awareness adds to the practitioner's ability to accurately recognize and identify unique individual needs. Recovery that empowers survivors of serious and persistent mental illness must be viewed as holistic and must involve a process that encompasses the individual, the interpersonal, and the institutional.

References

Alonzo, A. 2000. "The Experience of Chronic Illness and Post-traumatic Stress Disorder: The Consequences of Cumulative Adversity." *Social Science and Medicine* 50:1475–1484.

Bachrach, L. 1987. "The Homeless Mentally Ill." In W. Menninger and G. Hannah, eds., *The Chronic Mental Patients*, 65–92. Washington, D.C.: American Psychiatric Press.

Bandura, A. 2002. "Selective Moral Disengagement in the Exercise of Moral Agency." *Journal of Moral Education* 31:101–119.

Belcher, J. 1989. "On Becoming Homeless: A Study of Chronically Mentally Ill Persons." *Journal of Community Psychology* 17:173–184.

Boltz, S. 1992. *Creating Partnerships with Self-Help: Differences in the Self-Help and Professional Roles.* Center for Self-Help Research, Working Paper Series. Berkeley, Calif.: Center for Self-Help Research.

Bryant-Davis, T., and C. Ocampo. 2005. "Racist Incident-Based Trauma." *Counseling Psychologist* 33:479–500.

Dailey, W., M. Chinman, L. Davidson, L. Garner, E. Vavrousek-Jakuba, S. Essock, K. Marcus, and J. Tebes. 2000. "How Are We Doing? A Statewide Survey of Community Adjustment Among People with Serious Mental Illness Receiving Intensive Outpatient Services." *Community Mental Health Journal* 36:363–382.

Darves-Bornoz, J., T. Lemperiere, A. Degiovanni, and P. Gaillard. 1995. "Sexual Victimization in Women with Schizophrenia and Bipolar Disorder." *Social Psychiatry and Psychiatric Epidemiology* 30:78–84.

Davidson, L., D. Stayner, C. Nickou, T. Styron, M. Rowe, and M. Chinman. 2001. "'Simply to Be Let In': Inclusion as a Basis for Recovery." *Psychiatric Rehabilitation Journal* 24:375–388.

Deegan, P. 1992. "The Independent Living Movement and People with Psychiatric Disabilities: Taking Back Control Over Our Own Lives." *Psychosocial Rehabilitation Journal* 15:3–19.

Estroff, S. 1982. *Making It Crazy.* Berkeley: University of California Press.

——. 1989. "Self, Identity, and Subjective Experiences of Schizophrenia: In Search of the Subject." *Schizophrenia Bulletin* 15:189–196.

——. 1993. "Identity, Disability, and Schizophrenia: The Problem of Chronicity." In S. Lindenbaum and M. Lock, eds., *Knowledge, Power, and Practice: The Anthropology of Medicine and Everyday Life*, 247–286. Berkeley: University of California Press.

——. 1995. "Commentary on 'The Experiences of Long-Stay Inpatients Returning to the Community.'" *Psychiatry* 58:133–135.

Everstine, D. S., and L. Everstine. 1993. *The Trauma Response: Treatment for Emotional Injury*. New York: Norton.

Freund, P. 1993. "Professional Role(s) in the Empowerment Process: 'Working with' Mental Health Consumers." *Psychosocial Rehabilitation Journal* 16:65–71.

Good, B.1997. "Studying Mental Illness in Context: Local, Global, or Universal?" *Ethos* 25:230–248.

Green, T. 1987. "The Conscience of Leadership." In L. Sheive and M. Schoenheit, eds., *Leadership: Examining the Elusive*. Alexandria, Va.: Association for Supervision and Curriculum Development.

Herman, J. 1992. *Trauma and Recovery*. New York: Basic.

Hiday, V., M. Swartz, J. Swanson, R. Borum, and H. Wagner. 1999. "Criminal Victimization of Persons with Severe Mental Illness." *Psychiatric Services* 50:62–68.

Humphreys, J., P. Sharpts, and J. Campbell. 2005. "What We Know and What We Still Need to Learn." *Journal of Interpersonal Violence* 20:182–187.

Jones, L. 1992. *A Matter of Community II*. Denver: CHARG Resource Center.

Kaufman, C., and J. Campbell. 1995. "Voice in the Mental Health Consumer Movement: An Examination of Services Research by and for Consumers." Paper presented to the American Sociological Association Conference.

Lee, J. A. B. 1994. *The Empowerment Approach to Social Work Practice*. New York: Columbia University Press.

Lehman, A., N. Ward, and L. Linn. 1982. "Chronic Mental Patients: The Quality of Life Issue." *American Journal of Psychiatry* 139:1271–1276.

Linhorst, C., G. Hamilton, E. Young, and A. Eckert. 2002. "Opportunities and Barriers to Empowering People with Severe Mental Illness Through Participation in Treatment Planning." *Social Work* 47:425–434.

Lipschitz, D., M. Kaplan, J. Sorkenn, G. Faedda, P. Chorney, and G. Asnis. 1996. "Prevalence and Characteristics of Physical and Sexual Abuse Among Psychiatric Outpatients." *Psychiatric Services* 47:189–191.

Lopez, S. 1989. "Patient Variable Biases in Clinical Judgment: Conceptual Overview and Methodological Considerations." *Psychological Bulletin* 106:184–203.

Manning, S. 1998. "Empowerment in Mental Health Programs: Listening to the Voices." In L. Gutierrez, R. Parsons, and E. Cox, eds., *Empowerment in Social Work Practice: A Sourcebook*, 89–109. Pacific Grove, Calif.: Brooks/Cole.

———. 2003. *Ethical Leadership in Human Services: A Multi-Dimensional Approach.* Boston: Allyn and Bacon.

Manning, S., and B. Suire. 1996. "Bridges and Roadblocks: Consumers as Employees in Mental Health." *Psychiatric Services* 47:939–943.

Manning, S., M. Zibalese-Crawford, and E. Downey. 1994. *Colorado Mental Health Consumer and Family Development Project: Program Evaluation.* Denver: University of Denver, Graduate School of Social Work.

Marley, J., and S. Buila. 2001. "Crimes Against People with Mental Illness: Types, Perpetrators, and Influencing Factors." *Social Work* 46:115–124.

National Association of Social Workers (NASW). 1996. *Code of Ethics.* Washington, D.C.: Author.

Parsons, R., L. Gutierrez, and E. Cox. 1998. "A Model for Empowerment Practice." In L. Gutierrez, R. Parsons, and E. Cox, eds., *Empowerment in Social Work Practice: A Sourcebook.* Pacific Grove, Calif.: Brooks/Cole.

Reamer, F. 1995. *Social Work Values and Ethics.* New York: Columbia University Press.

———. 2001. *The Social Work Ethics Audit: A Risk Management Tool.* Washington, D.C.: NASW Press.

Rose, S. 1991. "Strategies of Mental Health Programming: A Client-Driven Model of Case Management." In C. Hudson and A. Cox, eds., *Dimensions of Mental Health Policy,* 138–154. New York: Praeger.

———. 1992. "Case Management: An Advocacy/Empowerment Design." In S. Rose, ed., *Case Management and Social Work Practice,* 271–297. New York: Longman.

———. 2000. "Reflections on Empowerment-Based Practice." *Social Work* 45:403–412.

Rosenfeld, S. 1992. "Factors Contributing to the Subjective Quality of Life of the Chronic Mentally Ill." *Journal of Health and Social Behavior* 33:299–315.

Rubin, W., and P. Panzano. 2002. "Identifying Meaningful Subgroups of Adults with Severe Mental Illness." *Psychiatric Services* 53:452–457.

Saleebey, D. 1992. "Introduction: Power in the People." In D. Saleebey, ed., *The Strengths Perspective in Social Work Practice,* 3–17. New York: Longman.

Townsend, E. 1998. *Good Intentions Overruled.* Toronto: University of Toronto Press.

Turner, R., and D. Lloyd. 1995. "Lifetime Traumas and Mental Health: The Significance of Cumulative Adversity." *Journal of Health and Social Behavior* 36:360–376.

Wilk, R. 1994. "Are the Rights of People with Mental Illness Still Important?" *Social Work* 39:167–175.

Wise, J. 2005. *Empowerment Practice with Families in Distress.* New York: Columbia University Press.

4

Transforming Childhood Physical and Verbal Abuse
Mind-Body Approaches to Trauma Treatment

DIANE B. BYINGTON

Erma, a divorced woman in her mid-fifties, sat on my sofa, one knee over the other, both feet shaking. Her arms were rigidly crossed over her breasts. In a taut, low voice she told me about being hit repeatedly by her father as a child, and the time he yelled at her and pushed her down the basement stairs, sending her to the hospital with a broken leg. These memories had recently surfaced, and now she found it nearly impossible to force herself to walk past the closed basement door in her own home, safe though she was from the man who was long dead. She kept remembering the experience, and part of her was con-vinced that someone would suddenly appear at the door and push her down the stairs, even though another part of her knew that her security system would sound the alarm if a stranger tried to enter her house. She was at a loss as to how to handle the extreme fear that gripped her when she attempted to walk down the hall, past the basement door. She could feel herself freeze and numb out even as she spoke to me about the feelings. Could I help?

The precipitating event apparently had occurred two months previously when she fell while walking the dog and landed with her leg under her in a similar position as when she had fallen during the original trauma. No physi-cal harm was done during the recent fall, but over the course of several weeks, the memories of the assault by her father had surfaced, and she felt overwhelmed by her intense anger and fear. Most of the time these feelings were under control, except when she had to walk down the hallway from her living room to her bedroom, which was several times daily.

She had come to consult with me because instead of fading away, these feelings were becoming more intense. Her anger was becoming so extreme that she was having difficulty relating to her longtime boyfriend, or even her female friends. As she put it, "I am afraid of what I might do if I let myself get angry. I might become an abuser just like my father. I am very afraid of my anger." Consequently, she had isolated herself from her support system. She was finding it difficult to sleep, and she awakened several times each night with nightmares about the assault. She experienced difficulty concentrating at work, and startled easily. She was so hypervigilant that she found it difficult to go anywhere other than her living room. She camped out in her living room most of the time and made her way swiftly to her bedroom only to sleep. She lived alone, so no one had observed what she described as her "bizarre" behavior.

The most distressing part of the entire situation for Erma was the hyperarousal she experienced much of the time. She reported ongoing shortness of breath, hypervigilance, tight muscles, and difficulty concentrating. As she described it, "I feel like I am about to jump out of my skin." She couldn't eat, couldn't sleep, couldn't stop thinking obsessively about the memories, cried for several hours each day, and was "ready to snap anyone's head off if they ask me about it."

Understanding Adult Memories of Childhood Trauma

Being yelled at (verbally abused) and pushed down a flight of stairs (physically abused) by a person of trust is surely a trauma with both physical and psychological impact. In Erma's case, the trauma had occurred more than forty years previously, but she was feeling its physical and psychological effects anew since the details of the memory had surfaced unexpectedly. Not only was Erma experiencing psychological distress manifested through extreme fear and anger, but she also began to have pain in her leg where it had been broken when she was a child. Over the years, her body had stored the memory of her childhood trauma (Rothschild 2000).

To understand how traumas of childhood physical and verbal abuse become events that affect emotional functioning across the life span, we need to understand three interrelated responses: (1) the physiological response to a traumatic event; (2) the submerging of the experience into a place in the person's memory where it is not available to conscious thought but still exerts influence on a day-to-day basis; and (3) the retriggering of memories of the original event with physiological responses similar to those at the time of the original event. The following discussion offers further understanding of Erma's response to the retriggering of memories of her childhood trauma and the re-experiencing of physical and emotional sensations equal to the trauma of that childhood event.

As stated in the preface, recent advances in brain research identify structural changes in the brain following trauma (Hipskind and Henderson 2002). Such a response is not surprising given the cascade of events that occur in the brain when we are faced with a life-threatening traumatic event. Such a threat activates the brain's limbic system (specifically, the amygdala and the hippocampus, thought of as the more primitive, preverbal parts of the brain) and the sympathetic nervous system and releases hormones that prepare the body for fight or flight. The physical manifestations of this response involve tensing muscles, heightening peripheral vision, reducing digestive enzymes, and a host of other physiological responses that increase the chances of survival by enabling the person to move rapidly to either fight or flee. Hormones released by the adrenal glands, such as epinephrine, norepinephrine, and cortisol, help the organism mobilize the energy required to deal with the threat, in ways that range from increased respiration and heart rate to enhanced immune function. Normally, the organism will be prepared for fight or flight, but a third response is possible: freezing. Freezing also has survival value, such as when a cat stops playing with a bird that no longer moves. The freeze response has the effect of numbing the organism so that it feels less pain when death is inevitable. Clearly, though, freezing has less survival potential than either fight or flight.

Once the traumatic incident is over and/or the fight-or-flight response has been successful, the release of cortisol will halt the alarm reaction and the production of other stress hormones, bringing the organism back to homeostasis. In people with post-traumatic stress disorder (PTSD), the adrenal glands do not release enough cortisol to halt the alarm reactions. Thus a continuing alarm reaction occurs, manifesting as hyperarousal— the state of high anxiety and physiological tension shown in feelings and actions such as hypervigilance, exaggerated startle response, and difficulty concentrating (Yehuda et al. 1990). Physical reserves are accessed to escape a predator or to fight an assailant, but they are not meant to be a long-term response. All of these reactions are instantaneous, instinctual responses to perceived threats and are not under our conscious control. We cannot override them to make informed, logical decisions at the moment, and we cannot convince our limbic system not to react the way these early, primitive survival reactions dictate.

The limbic system is also involved in remembered trauma. The amygdala aids in the processing of highly charged memories, whereas the hippocampus puts our memories into perspective with regard to time and space. During a traumatic threat, however, the activity of the hippocampus often becomes suppressed, so it is not able to process and store an event (Nadel and Jacobs 1998; van der Kolk 1994). Thus stored traumatic memories are not specific to the time and space in which they first occurred, and they can continue to invade the person's present life.

The autonomic nervous system works to counterbalance the sympathetic nervous system by calming the organism, slowing the heartbeat, relaxing muscles, increasing digestion, and stopping the stress response. If PTSD is to be relieved, hyperarousal must be moderated before it wears the person down to numbness.

Traumatic events leave distinctive footprints on the brain. Those who suffer from acute and chronic PTSD experience exaggerated sensitivity and heightened reactivity in the parts of the brain that process emotions, sensations, and images. Consequently, trauma survivors are more responsive to sensations, emotions, and perceptual cues than those who have not been exposed to trauma (Naparstek 2004). On the other hand, the part of the thinking brain that translates personal experience into language, Broca's area, becomes temporarily less active after a traumatic event. Thus, trauma survivors are acutely aware of danger signals in the form of nonverbal cues in their environments, but they are not able to talk about these cues and process them as they would normal cues. Instead, they react— quickly and extremely—to anything their limbic system perceives as a threat, including memories and perceptions. Only when a person is sufficiently calm can he or she focus on ideas and words.

Responses to Adult Memory Trauma Using Mind-Body Approaches

Trauma has been recognized as a multifaceted problem that disrupts functioning on a systemic level involving both the body and the mind (Damasio 1994; van der Kolk 1994). "Mind-body medicine" has been defined as "an approach that sees the mind—our thoughts and emotions—as having a central impact on the body's health" (Goleman and Gurin 1993:5). In Erma's case, the use of mind-body techniques helped to calm her physical and emotional arousal and to increase her sense of empowerment as she struggled to heal from the aftereffects of the trauma of remembering the abuse she had suffered as a child.

Treatment strategies that are considered to be in the mind-body realm include relaxation practices, guided imagery, biofeedback, and meditation (Finger and Arnold 2002). These techniques, discussed in more detail below, are used primarily for stress reduction. In addition, social support, prayer, hypnosis, healing/therapeutic touch, exercise, journaling, energy therapies, and expressive arts may also be employed to integrate the mind (including emotions and spirituality) with the body (Davis, Eshelman, and McKay 2000; Phillips 2000).

I had worked with Erma for several months on two occasions during the past two years for both physical and emotional problems. She lived with several chronic ailments, including dermatitis and inflammatory bowel syndrome. In addition, she experienced very volatile emotional reactions to what for other people would be small events. Our previous sessions had involved her learning to adjust to these difficult circumstances, developing and using her support system, learning to take less responsibility for how situations turned out, and integrating relaxation techniques into her daily life. Our relationship was strong. I had suspected that some form of trauma had been part of her life, but until now she had had no concrete memories of anything other than a loving childhood.

Regular talking interventions are unlikely to be effective when the trauma survivor is in a state of hyperarousal. The person literally cannot focus her attention on what others are saying. When a trauma survivor is in this state, it is important to provide safety (Herman 1992), which helps decrease the arousal level. In the past, Erma had responded very well to guided imagery and relaxation/breathing. These techniques enabled her to feel more in control and helped her to calm herself. It seemed to me that the same techniques, along with others more specific to dealing with trauma, might be useful again.

My diagnosis at the time of this most recent contact was that Erma was suffering from acute post-traumatic stress disorder. Until recently, the memories of falling down the stairs and the angry look on her father's face when he yelled at her and then pushed her had not been accessible to her. She had remembered that at some time in her childhood she had broken her leg, but the details were foggy, as were many memories of her childhood.

STAGES OF TRAUMA TREATMENT

Judith Herman (1992) has identified three stages for trauma treatment as establishment of safety, remembrance and mourning, and reconnection with ordinary life. My model for trauma treatment also contains three intertwining stages, ones that echo some parts of Herman's stages yet also integrate more fully the awareness of mind-body connections. Each stage will now be briefly defined, then discussed in greater detail, including application to the work with Erma.

In Stage 1, shortly after the traumatic event, the person may be held hostage to hyperarousal and other reactions to trauma, including dissociation, flashbacks, or emotional numbing. The person is helped to feel safe and to calm the hyperarousal by learning techniques for self-soothing. In Stage 2, the survivor continues to use calming and soothing techniques while delving deeper into the trauma and using body-based treatment techniques. Stage 3 involves recognizing how trauma changes a person, making meaning of the experience, and integrating the changed self into a new way of being, often in a different, more authentic direction. The survivor may emerge stronger and more resilient than before the trauma.

STAGE 1: CALMING AROUSAL LEVEL

This stage is discussed as calming arousal level although it also deals with other symptoms. Techniques used at this point are also helpful in calming a generalized stress response. When arousal level is extremely high, there is no point in trying to emotionally process the trauma. The emotions associated with the traumatic experience are triggered by the slightest stress, and it feels as if there is no safety anywhere. In this stage survivors learn that they can control a high arousal level, flashbacks, intrusive memories, dissociation, or whatever other symptom is most alarming at the time.

Slow and steady breathing is a first step in calming arousal level. Part of the stress response is to hold the breath or to breathe shallowly. Many different breathing techniques have been described in the professional literature, but all involve an emphasis on breathing deeply and slowly from the diaphragm (Hendricks 1995; Lewis 2004). Teaching survivors to notice and change their breathing patterns in this way is the first step in helping them to calm themselves. Audio CDs are useful when an individual is first learning this technique (e.g., Byington 2004; Weil 1999).

Second is the safe place meditation. Many survivors have no memory of ever having felt entirely safe in their lives, so this exercise may introduce the physical awareness of safety. The survivor imagines a place where she feels absolutely safe, and she focuses on experiencing sensory perceptions as she imagines herself there. For example, if the safe place is a beach, the person can be instructed to hear the waves, feel the ocean breeze, taste the salty air, feel the sand beneath her feet, and watch seagulls overhead. This technique for calming is widely used for teaching people to calm and self-soothe.

Experiencing a dual awareness of past and present is a third technique that is useful for calming arousal levels and stress responses. This exercise gently reminds the person that, as vivid as the flashback experience is, it is not happening now. Slowly the person's awareness returns to the present moment, with physical sensations providing the grounding for separating past from present experience. Even when a survivor is re-experiencing the trauma, he can be taught to feel his back against a chair, his feet on the ground, his breath moving in and out.

The fourth technique for calming is the use of relaxation exercises. By definition, a person cannot be tense and relaxed at the same time. Because it may be difficult to access the exercises when arousal level is high, it is helpful to practice them at times other than when they are needed to calm arousal level, so that when needed they can be more readily available. Muscle relaxation helps to move a person out of hyperarousal. Relaxation exercises include progressive relaxation, release-only relaxation, and auto-genics (Davis et al. 2000). Progressive relaxation involves tightening mus-cles before relaxing them, and release-only relaxation involves focusing on various parts of the body in order to consciously relax them. Autogenics relaxes the body by imagining that it is, for example, warm and heavy.

These Stage 1 techniques for lowering arousal level work to calm and regulate overtaxed emotional responses. They are most effective when they are practiced regularly, during times of relative calm, so that when arousal level is highest, they are immediately at hand. In addition, after the person has learned these techniques she can access them directly, without the presence of a therapist or coach; thus the survivor is empowered to be more in control of her reactions. Since trauma wreaks havoc with one's sense of control, reestablishing it in some form is crucial for recovery.

Erma and I worked together for approximately six months. For Stage 1, I helped her to identify a safe place in her home and to remember what it was like to feel safe. We used a form of systematic desensitization (Wolpe

1958) to help her stay relaxed while repeatedly imagining that she was walking past the basement door. We worked with her breathing and with a dual awareness to help her control her arousal level. When she felt thoroughly relaxed through the use of relaxation techniques, she walked past the basement door and was able to stay relaxed.

STAGE 2: HEALING AND INTEGRATION

Recovery cannot be said to be complete until the trauma no longer feels like a fresh wound but instead resembles a scar—not forgotten, but no longer a constant source of pain. All treatment methods involve moving into and through the trauma. Not all treatment methods require that the trauma be remembered in detail, but many do.

Once arousal has been moderated and the person can identify a sense of safety, it is important to process the trauma. This task involves moving memories from implicit to explicit memory storage, extinguishing the post-traumatic psychological and physiological reactions, and creating new associations and meaning for the experience. Numerous researchers have suggested that traumatic memories have been dysfunctionally stored in memory, possibly because of inadequate hippocampal functioning (Gunnar and Barr 1998; Shalev, Bonnie, and Eth 1996; Shapiro 2001; van der Kolk 1996b). Traumatic memories tend to be dissociated and stored initially as sensory fragments that have no linguistic components, or as implicit memory (van der Kolk 1996b). These memories can be thought of as wandering around in the brain without a file for storage. One goal of treatment is to help people weave the sensory fragments together and create a personal narrative that can be talked about and then stored appropriately, in explicit memory.

Traumatic memories are triggered by something that is associated with the trauma, whether or not it can be identified. The trigger could be simple or complex, conscious or unconscious. For Erma, the trigger had two parts. The first was her falling and landing in a way that replicated the position of her fall in the original trauma. The second, which most likely happened while she still felt the physical pain in her leg from the fall, was when she walked past the place of the original trauma, the basement door. Just seeing the door triggered physical and sensory memories of the trauma. Individuals who have PTSD are more resistant to extinction of these strong reactions than other people are (Rothbaum and Davis 2003). Therefore, a goal of treatment is to help survivors extinguish reactions to the triggers or learn to tolerate them without going into a fear reaction.

Finally, a third goal is to help survivors learn different ways of being in the world, especially with respect to how they inhabit their bodies. Trauma tends to dampen somatic experiences, and survivors often have a difficult time identifying physical sensations or emotional states. They tend to ignore or discount intuition, especially as related to safety issues. A person who always feels unsafe will not be able to differentiate times when she is really unsafe from all the other times. Therefore, it is very important that trauma survivors learn to recognize and trust somatic experiences and emotions, as well as their own instincts (Heller 2001; Levine 1997).

A number of excellent mind-body treatments have been developed to help survivors move through this stage of healing, and three of them are described here. Each focuses on one of the goals of this stage more than the others do, so it is important that a therapist or coach who is trained in trauma treatment help the person navigate through all of the goals. Since no single treatment is appropriate for every trauma survivor, it is important that the therapist and the survivor work together to come to agreement about which treatment will be the best choice for the particular situation. The skill level of the therapist is a crucial factor in this second phase of treatment. Therapists who have not been trained in a particular technique have an ethical responsibility to avoid attempting it; they should, instead, refer survivors to more-experienced therapists if and when the need arises.

One of the most carefully researched and well-known treatments is eye movement desensitization and reprocessing (EMDR), developed in the 1990s by Francine Shapiro (2001). It shares some elements with other forms of therapeutic exposure methods that use cognitive-behavioral techniques to reduce the emotional distress of traumatic memories, and it has been shown to have similar success in reducing the symptoms (Briere and Scott 2006). The essence of this therapy is the use of bilateral stimulation—i.e., stimulating both the left and the right hemispheres of the brain—while the individual directs his or her attention to traumatic images. Imagining and feeling into a safe place is the first part of the treatment. Only when the person feels safe is the bilateral stimulation introduced. Some examples of methods used by practitioners are alternately tapping on the person's right knee, then the left knee, the clinician moving her or his fingers smoothly back and forth as the client's eyes follow from side to side, or alternately playing sounds in each ear. The survivor tells the narrative of the traumatic experience while the practitioner monitors the amount of emotional disturbance, and the bilateral stimulation is continued until the disturbance level has been significantly reduced. As the treatment continues, a new understanding of the trauma is generally gained, along with a lower arousal level and less-vivid images.

The goal of this treatment is to eliminate emotional and somatic distress in a very short time, while producing cognitive insights and shifts in self-perception. EMDR theory holds that these techniques change the way memories are stored and therefore reduce arousal level and help the person to react less strongly to the triggers. EMDR is not appropriate for every client. Generally, it should not be used to treat people who are not soothed by the safe place meditation or who have high levels of dissociation. It should be used with caution with people who have schizophrenia, active drug or alcohol addictions, neurological impairment, epilepsy, or possible suicidal tendencies (Shapiro 2001).

A second form of treatment helps the person focus on internal body awareness and kinesthetic sense, both of which are inhibited by trauma. Increasing body awareness is included in many of the developing approaches to trauma treatment (Pesso and Crandell 1991; van der Kolk 2002) and is strongly supported by the therapists who work with it (Naparstek 2004). One of the most well-documented body-based treatments is somatic experiencing (SE), developed by Peter Levine (1997). SE focuses on internal body sensations, the primary method of accessing the effects of trauma. As the person attends to these sensations while being relaxed, physical and emotional feelings surface and can become the focus. This helps the body release from the "freeze" state experienced in the original trauma and return to normal.

A third approach is the use of guided imagery. The efficacy of imagery in the treatment of various conditions is widely supported by research; it has been used to alleviate anxiety and depression (Jacobs 1990; McKinney et al. 1997), to enhance recovery from surgery (Dreher 1998), and to increase immune function (Gruzelier 2002). Although many of the newer body-based therapies use imagery in their protocols, little has been done yet with the use of imagery in treating trauma to help move the trauma survivor through the trauma memories. Bellaruth Naparstek's work (2004) is one exception.

In this approach, the right brain is activated by the use of symbols to process the trauma. "The imagery for this stage goes deeper and deliberately aims to help the survivor reestablish a relationship with the world of feelings; face down unpleasant symptoms; move under them, to the core of the hurt; and reestablish a connection with a broader, more spiritual perspective, big enough to hold and transform the enormity of the pain and loss" (Naparstek 2004:229). The survivor listens to guided imagery scripts or audio CDs repeatedly. These scripts are carefully devised to bypass the thinking (left) brain and go directly to the world of sensations and visual imagery. Symbols are used to process the trauma so the person does not have to access the trauma directly and risk being retraumatized. For example, one guided imagery script takes the person through an imagined landscape that is filled with "crumpled piles of shattered dreams" (Naparstek 2004:253) and moves her through the hurt to a place that is deeper, her spiritual essence. This imagery is designed to be experienced repeatedly, so that the triggers are gradually desensitized and the person is able to understand that she is greater than just the trauma experience.

In the work with Erma in Stage 2, we explored the assault itself. Although she quickly recovered her comfort level in her home and was able to walk past her basement door without intense fear, the sadness and anger about the incident continued for some time. We used EMDR to help reconstruct the incident and to process the emotions. She talked with her mother and brother about the assault, which had never been attributed to her father but had been passed off as an accident. Her mother was very apologetic for failing to protect her daughter, and mother and daughter talked at last about their mutual fear of this man who had terrorized them both. Erma explored her body sensations and became more aware of pains in her leg and back. She began to receive regular massages and to practice yoga.

STAGE 3: MAKING MEANING

Trauma changes a person at all levels: brain functioning is different, emotions may be dulled or brought closer to the surface or both, coping in the world is altered. The trauma survivor must grieve for what she has lost, for the person she was and will never be again, and for the loss of innocence embedded in the trauma experience (Herman 1992). In addition, the survivor must find some larger life meaning from the experience—some way that the person is changed *for the better* and not just for the worse. Trauma survivors often identify ways in which they are better, stronger, or more compassionate as a result of their experience. Trauma sensitizes the right brain, increasing the person's ability to call on imagination, intuition, and emotional-sensory experiences (Naparstek 2004). I think of this stage as "finding the gift" in healing from the trauma.

As Erma moved into Stage 3, her volatile emotions gradually began to subside and her physical symptoms abated somewhat. All was not perfect in her life, however. She remained easily rattled by relatively minor life events and tended to feel bad about herself when someone treated her poorly. Dermatitis and bowel problems continued, but at a decreased level. Her emotions remained more volatile than she wanted them to be, even though she was able to work and love successfully. She continued to have trouble with affect-balancing, especially when she neglected her calming strategies of regular exercise, journaling, and listening to relaxing audiotapes.

Increasingly, though, she reconnected with friends and strengthened her relationship with her partner. She felt more worthy of giving and receiving love. She understood how her father's violence related to her being averse to risk and less assertive in many areas of her life. She was unwilling to forgive her father for how he had hurt her, but she was grateful that she had survived this man's abuse. She was also grateful that she had not continued the cycle of abuse in her life and that her grown sons were gentle and loving men. She wanted to help other survivors of abuse. She wrote her story in the hope that it would help someone else. After six months, she left therapy and was able to cope reasonably well on her own and with a newfound feeling of purpose.

Vicarious Trauma

It is well known in the trauma treatment field that vicarious trauma is a danger for therapists. It is very easy to be affected by the intense emotions of trauma survivors, and the ability to empathize makes this tendency even more problematic. Many practitioners have experienced trauma themselves, and unless the trauma has been resolved, repeatedly listening to other people's trauma can retraumatize them. It is especially difficult to avoid retraumatization when working with clients who have experienced the same sort of trauma as one's own.

Mind-body techniques are very useful for therapists as well as for clients. For example, being aware of emotional and physical responses to what clients tell us is crucial. When we realize we are holding our breath, we may be mimicking what our client is doing. Breathing consciously is therefore helpful for both of us. We need to be aware of how working with a particular client is affecting us physically. In order to be effective, we need to be able to experience a "dual awareness": of both the client's subjective state and our own.

When Erma described her fear of walking past the basement door, I could feel my jaw tightening and my breath becoming shallow. Though her fear was not a major fear of mine, I could empathize, and I needed to unclench my jaw and deepen my breathing in order to separate my experience from hers.

I find that it is helpful to take a few minutes between clients to move around, air out the room, and remember my own physical and emotional experience. I have also found it helpful to meditate regularly, exercise, and use other mind-body techniques to rid myself of fearful emotions that are not mine. Support systems are very important for therapists as well as for clients. Mind-body techniques are far more useful for clients if the therapist is familiar with them and can speak from experience. Just as these methods help clients to heal from trauma, they can help people who work with trauma survivors to sustain their ability to help.

Reflections on the Empowerment Principles

Mind-body approaches for trauma treatment are consistent with the principles of empowerment practice. As relaxation skills are strengthened, for example, the oppressive force of post-trauma-related tensions and anxieties is diminished. These approaches require client and practitioner to work together to reach the goal of cognitive shifts, work that can be done only through mutual cooperation as the practitioner assists the client from a position of equality and from an acute awareness of the client's specific needs. These approaches can be highly effective in changing the survivor's perspectives. The changes, in turn, can have a positive impact on the person's relationships with others. The practitioner's ability to integrate and build the support of those others into the client's response to the trauma helps to maintain the strengthening results gained from the use of the mind-body approaches in the treatment. To illustrate the application of these principles in a more specific sense, each will be discussed in the context of the work with Erma.

BUILDING ON STRENGTHS WHILE DIMINISHING OPPRESSIVE FACTORS

The oppressive force of Erma's memories of her father's abuse was clearly interfering with her ability to function on a day-to-day basis. Her inability to eat, to sleep, and to stop obsessive thoughts of the memories sparked an array of chemical responses in her body. Therefore, her own body took on the role of a type of oppressor, so that Erma in a sense was living with an oppressor within. As mentioned earlier, she was literally taken hostage by these memories and reactions. It became crucial for her to call upon her own strengths and the calming resources within herself to counteract the oppressive force of the memories.

She gained strength through her ability to control her breathing and through her use of dual awareness, both of which contributed to a decrease in her arousal levels. Controlled breathing helped her to stay in the present moment and to recognize the safety of the present in contrast to the threat of the past memories. The use of the mind-body techniques also helped desensitize her to concrete memory triggers so that she could walk past her basement door, for example, without losing a sense of relaxation.

WORKING FROM AN AWARENESS OF SPECIFIC NEED

Erma's specific need was directly related to a felt sense in her body, freezing and numbing out, in response to extreme fear (emotional response) that grew out of the intensity of her memories as experienced in her thinking mind. The body-mind relationship was immediately evident in her presentation of her difficulty. Mind-body forms of treatment—i.e., breathing and relaxation—have a direct relationship to the emotions and thought processes, and they are especially effective with promoting change when directed to the client's specific need.

No single treatment is appropriate for every trauma survivor. Erma and I went through a step-by-step process to determine the treatment choices that would best fit her need. That process included describing options and allowing her to choose the ones that appealed to her. We had the advantage of having worked together before, so we were able to reintroduce the Stage 1 interventions that had been effective in the past. Erma was interested in using EMDR, and that was very helpful for her.

When clients are nervous about EMDR, however, we move on to something else. It is very important that clients' intuition about what might be helpful for them be invited and respected. For example, the most important intervention for one client with very early trauma was for her to purchase a baby doll and spend time daily rocking and singing to it. That activity seemed to allow her to give the doll some of the nurturing she had never received herself, and she was able indirectly to soothe the very raw and traumatized places within herself. Finding the person's best treatment choices involves intuition, inspiration, and sometimes trial and error by both client and therapist.

ASSISTING CLIENTS AS THEY EMPOWER THEMSELVES

Trauma disorients and shocks people, throwing them out of their normal routine. In doing so, it can destroy all sense of trust in self and in one's ability to cope. Many trauma survivors require some assistance from others to regain a sense of going forward with their lives without the fears and memories continuing to overwhelm their daily activities.

Erma's ability to learn how to self-soothe through relaxation techniques was an immediate skill that empowered her in the session and one that she could take with her and use at home. Two central directions for empowerment practice are (1) providing information to clients through an educational or learning experience and (2) helping to enhance coping skills (Lee 2001; Wise 2005). Both were used to assist Erma while she learned and practiced the techniques and went on to use them on her own apart from our sessions.

INTEGRATING SUPPORT FROM OTHERS

An important step in Erma's recovery came when she was able to talk with her mother and brother about her father's assault. Erma became aware that she was not alone in her experience of feeling terrorized by this man. She further learned that it was the numbing and silencing effect of the terror itself that had kept her mother and her from sharing their experiences with each other. Erma was very touched to know that her mother loved her and wished to hear about Erma's experience. Telling each other about their struggles brought them closer than they had been in years.

Also, as Erma moved into Stage 3 of her work, she reconnected with friends for the first time in months and reached out to strengthen her relationship with her partner. These reconnections served to strengthen how she felt about herself in ways that contradicted her earlier needs to isolate herself and to feel overwhelmed by her fears.

EQUALIZING POWER DIFFERENTIALS AND USING
COOPERATIVE ROLES

Trauma and, as in Erma's case, the retriggering of earlier trauma raise a sense of powerlessness in such a way that the person's sense of strength and personal power is displaced. Even while Erma reached out for help from a place of strength, she also came to our first session aware of how powerless she felt in light of her recent memories of the abuse by her father. From this position and from our culture's historical perception of a power hierarchy in helping relationships, it was not unexpected that Erma might perceive the therapist as having greater power than she did to influence the outcome of the healing process. Even though our roles are defined differently by virtue of the purpose of our work together, the strengths we bring as individuals are viewed from a vantage point of equal personal power. Both people's strengths are necessary in equal measure for a helpful and healing outcome.

I communicated this stance to Erma by listening carefully to her story, by involving her in all decisions about which interventions would be helpful, and by respecting her choices and her pacing in moving through the various stages of responding to her traumatizing memories. No action in these approaches proceeded without Erma's agreement to participate and my assurance that she could stop the procedure at any time.

Conclusion and Recommendations

Trauma survivors are never the same people they were before the trauma. Healing is possible, however, and many survivors are able to put the experience behind them and live in the present moment. Some are able to take the next step, to transform themselves into stronger, more sensitive, more resilient people than they were before the trauma experience. Transforming trauma is empowering for those who are just entering the healing process, as well as for those who have taken on the task of helping to heal trauma. Trauma survivors may always be more susceptible to stress reactions and more quick to arousal than they might have been if there had been no trauma (van der Kolk 1996a). Survivors who fare best are those who take charge of their own healing process, who use several different approaches to healing, and who work on themselves on many fronts, either simultaneously or sequentially (Naparstek 2004).

As people gain a more calm perspective about the trauma, they are able to move out of isolation and struggles in relating to others; they become able to rejoin the world. They learn how to respond to questions about the trauma and how to maintain the self-care that is emphasized in treatment. They learn to maintain the gains they made and to redirect their attention away from the trauma and its treatment and toward the next stage in life. This is the final part of the healing process. If it has not occurred before, the person moves from a self-identity as a trauma victim to a trauma survivor.

From my experience of working with many trauma survivors, I believe that healing from trauma nudges people to move in a different direction in their lives, a direction that better suits them after the trauma, even if it did not seem as desirable before the trauma. Part of finding the gift in the healing is finding a meaning that is larger than the trauma itself, even a spiritual perspective about the event. It encompasses the new narrative about the trauma. As people tell the story of their trauma experience, without triggering the previously experienced negative responses, they are able to move beyond it and perceive themselves as no longer limited by the experience. Usually people move more slowly in the world than they did before the trauma. It is not uncommon for them to want to help others who have suffered similar traumas. Trauma survivors often find that their priorities change as they become sensitized to what is really important to them.

References

Briere, J., and C. Scott. 2006. *Principles of Trauma Therapy*. Thousand Oaks, Calif.: Sage.

Byington, D. 2004. *Breathing Meditations*. Audio CD. Niwot, Colo.: Lifetime Wellness.

Damasio, A. R. 1994. *Descartes' Error*. New York: Putnam.

Davis, M., E. R. Eshelman, and M. McKay. 2000. *The Relaxation and Stress Reduction Workbook*. Oakland, Calif.: New Harbinger Publications.

Dreher, H. 1998. "Mind-Body Interventions for Surgery: Evidence and Exigency." *Advances in Mind-Body Medicine* 14:207–222.

Finger, W., and E. M. Arnold. 2002. "Mind-Body Interventions: Applications for Social Work Practice." *Social Work in Health Care* 35 (4): 57–78.

Goleman, D., and J. Gurin, eds. 1993. *Mind-Body Medicine*. Yonkers, N.Y.: Consumer Reports Books.

Gruzelier, J. H. 2002. "A Review of the Impact of Hypnosis, Relaxation, Guided Imagery, and Individual Differences on Aspects of Immunity and Health." *Stress* 5 (2): 147–163.

Gunnar, M. R., and R. G. Barr. 1998. "Stress, Early Brain Development, and Behavior." *Infants and Young Children* 11 (1): 1–14.

Heller, D. P. 2001. *Crash Course: A Self-Healing Guide to Auto Accident and Recovery*. Berkeley, Calif.: North Atlantic Books.

Hendricks, G. 1995. *Conscious Breathing: Breathwork for Health, Stress Release, and Personal Mastery.* New York: Bantam.

Herman, J. L. 1992. *Trauma and Recovery.* New York: Basic Books.

Hipskind, S. G., and T. Henderson. 2002. "Next Generation High Resolution SPECT: Examples of Images and Types of Disorders." Denver: Brain Matters, Inc.

Jacobs, J. B. 1990. "Extended Mutual Imagery in Work with Anxious and Phobic Clients." *Clinical Social Work Journal* 18 (2): 175–185.

Lee, J. A. B. 2001. *The Empowerment Approach to Social Work Practice: Building the Beloved Community.* New York: Columbia University Press.

Levine, P. A. 1997. *Waking the Tiger: Healing Trauma.* Berkeley, Calif.: North Atlantic Books.

Lewis, D. 2004. *Free Your Breath, Free Your Life.* Boston: Shambala.

McKinney, C. H., M. H. Antoni, M. Kumar, and F. C. Tims. 1997. "Effects of Guided Imagery and Music (GIM) Therapy on Mood and Cortisol in Healthy Adults." *Health Psychology* 16 (4): 390–400.

Nadel, L., and W. J. Jacobs. 1998. "Traumatic Memory Is Special." *Current Directions in Psychological Science* 7:154–157.

Naparstek, B. 2004. *Invisible Heroes: Survivors of Trauma and How They Heal.* New York: Bantam.

Pesso, A., and J. Crandell, eds. 1991. *Moving Psychotherapy: Theory and Application of Pesso System/Psychomotor Therapy.* Cambridge, Mass.: Brookline Books.

Phillips, M. 2000. *Finding the Energy to Heal.* New York: Norton.

Rothbaum, B. O., and M. Davis. 2003. "Applying Learning Principles to the Treatment of Post-Trauma Reactions." *Annals of the New York Academy of Sciences* 1008:112–121.

Rothschild, B. 2000. *The Body Remembers: The Psychophysiology of Trauma and Trauma Treatment.* New York: Norton.

Shalev, A. Y., O. Bonnie, and S. Eth. 1996. "Treatment of Posttraumatic Stress Disorder: A Review." *Psychosomatic Medicine* 58:165–182.

Shapiro, F. 2001. *Eye Movement Desensitization and Reprocessing.* New York: Guilford.

van der Kolk, B.A. 1994. "The Body Keeps the Score." *Harvard Review of Psychiatry* 1:253–265.

———. 1996a. "The Complexity of Adaptation to Trauma: Self-Regulation, Stimulus Discrimination, and Characterological Development." In B. A. van der Kolk, A. C. McFarlane, and L. Weisaeth, eds., *Traumatic Stress: The Effects of Overwhelming Experience on Mind, Body, and Society,* 182–213. New York: Guilford.

———. 1996b. "Trauma and Memory." In B. A. van der Kolk, A. C. McFarlane, and L. Weisaeth, eds., *Traumatic Stress: The Effects of Overwhelming Experience on Mind, Body, and Society,* 279–302. New York: Guilford.

——. 2002. "The Assessment and Treatment of Complex PTSD." In R. Yehuda, ed., *Treating Trauma Survivors with PTSD*, 127–156. New York: American Psychiatric Association.

Weil, A. 1999. *Breathing: The Master Key to Self Healing*. Audio CD. Boulder, Colo.: Sounds True.

Wise, J. B. 2005. *Empowerment Practice with Families in Distress*. New York: Columbia University Press.

Wolpe, J. 1958. *Psychotherapy by Reciprocal Inhibition*. Stanford, Calif.: Stanford University Press.

Yehuda, R., S. M. Southwick, G. Nussbaum, V. Wahby, E. L. Giller, Jr., and J. W. Mason. 1990. "Low Urinary Cortisol Excretion in Patients with Posttraumatic Stress Disorder." *Journal of Nervous and Mental Disease* 178:366–369.

Part 2

Transforming Trauma at the
Interpersonal Level

5

Transforming Privilege, Power, and Control in Relationship Trauma

LYNN PARKER

Frank: *I joined the men's group here almost five years ago. I encountered this group of men that began asking me some pretty tough questions. I was very resistant, very angry, yet I showed up every Thursday. I typically just didn't want to hear what they had to say, but what would happen is I would think about the things I heard on the way home, and they would sink in. I also remember on more than one occasion some guys telling me that they were really frightened that I was just going to jump across the room and grab somebody. There's an interesting aspect to that because we have no idea of how we appear to our spouse. I used a lot of verbal abuse and intimidation for a long, long time. That's the way you control someone. It's very clear to me that those few occasions when I abused my wife physically were those occasions when, for whatever reason, she had decided to challenge me and not back off, which she almost always did. At that point, it just became important for me to absolutely be in control of that situation and do whatever was required, including physically abusing her, grabbing her, pushing her down, and even on a few occasions kicking her.*

Understanding Privilege, Power, and Control: Roots of Domestic Abuse in Couples and Families

Issues of privilege, power, and control lie at the roots of this beginning narrative of Frank, a 51-year-old Irish Catholic insurance broker. *Privilege*, as the term is used here, means "an invisible package of unearned assets . . . about which [we] are 'meant' to remain oblivious. . . . Doors open for certain people through no virtues of their own. We usually think of privilege as being a favored state, whether earned or conferred by birth or luck. [Privilege] systematically overempower[s] certain groups" (McIntosh 2004:104, 106–107). In Frank's case, the privilege of being a man living in a patriarchal society conferred the historical "privilege," based upon precolonial law and passed down through generations, of a man's supposed right, even responsibility, to control his spouse's behavior and to use physical force, if necessary, to "keep her in her place," a place of subordination to the man. The subsequent domestic abuse was the trauma that brought him and his wife to therapy.

Almeida and Durkin (1999) define *domestic abuse* as "the patterned and repeated use of coercive and controlling behavior to limit, direct, and shape a partner's thoughts, feelings, and actions" (313). While domestic violence continues to be a crushing problem for families, significant changes have occurred over the past decade. According to the Bureau of Justice Statistics (U.S. Department of Justice 2005), the rate of family violence in this country has dropped by more than half since 1993. Much of the credit for the improvement is due to the people quietly working in this field—social workers, women's crisis centers, police forces, and prosecutors—and to the Violence Against Women Act, passed originally in 1994, reaffirmed in 1998, then reauthorized in 2006. But all of these efforts are part of a larger story. The decline in family violence is part of a whole web of positive, mutually reinforcing social trends. Violent crime overall is down by 55 percent since 1993, and violence by teenagers has dropped an astonishing 71 percent, according to the Department of Justice (2005).

Though progress has been made, violence toward partners remains widespread, occurring throughout the life cycle in our society, as well as in all other patriarchal cultures. Family violence still accounts for approximately one in ten violent victimizations, or 11 percent of all reported and estimated unreported violence.

Forty-nine percent were crimes against spouses, 11% were sons or daughters victimized by a parent, and 41% were crimes against other family members. . . . The majority (73%) of family violence victims were female. Females were 84% of spouse abuse victims and 86% of victims of abuse at the hands of a boyfriend or girlfriend. . . . Most family violence victims were white (74%), and the majority were between the ages of 25 and 54 (65.7%). Most family violence offenders were white (79%), and most were age 30 or older (62%). Nearly a quarter of the murders committed from 1998 to 2002 were against a family member.

(U.S. Department of Justice 2005:1, 8)

Family members experience trauma on many levels. Viewing domestic abuse through an empowerment lens requires consideration at the personal, interpersonal, and social/community levels. Personal violence against oneself includes such actions as suicide attempts, addictions, and self-harming behaviors. At the interpersonal level, the trauma of domestic abuse occurs in hierarchies of power and privilege in spouse abuse, child abuse, elder abuse, control of time resources and money, decision making, and allocation of household and people-care responsibilities. It occurs at the social/community level, outside the family, in job availability, sexism, racism, heterosexism, homophobia, colonization, national/international disasters, war, and genocide.

Privilege and power disparities, though they underlie all relationships, are the issues that people collude to deny. Privileges and access to privileges tend to be awarded to those with greater power, or greater perceived power. If raised for conversation and analysis, they can mean trouble. Consequently, the way in which therapists raise issues of power, privilege, and inequity is of central importance to practice that is based upon empowerment and social justice. More specifically, the empowerment approach calls for a consideration of dynamics related to "power over," "power under," and "power with." The empowerment principle of equalizing power differentials is especially relevant to this discussion and mirrors the emphasis found in the social justice approach to practice.

Power and control may be misused by employing an array of tactics and in multiple contexts. Later in this chapter, four diagrams, the "Power and Control" Wheels (Almeida et al. 1992), will identify such tactics in the private contexts of heterosexual relationships and lesbian and gay relationships and in the public context toward lesbians, gays, and people of color.

These tactics are most often used in concert with one another. In the quote that opens this chapter, for example, Frank admits to verbal abuse, intimidation, physical abuse, grabbing, pushing his wife down, and kicking her. Misuses of power in domestic abuse often include physical, emotional, and economic abuse, threats and intimidation, isolation and entrapment, sexual abuse and exploitation, and control and abuse of children. At the social and/or community level of interaction, similar tactics can be observed in the isolation that occurs through job relocation and language barriers.

Private, intimate violence and social/community violence occur within the larger context of cultural violence, embodied in an implicitly hierarchical, patriarchal structure that establishes certain patterns of subordination and oppression. Within the family, as well as outside it, power is distributed according to hierarchies: "First World" (e.g., United States, Western Europe) countries over "Second World" countries (e.g., Mexico, Central and South America, Africa, Iran); men over women and children; whites over persons of color[1]; heterosexuals over gay men, lesbians, bisexuals, and transgendered people; and people with citizenship status over those without. Because they operate on lower rungs of the hierarchy, women, heterosexuals of color, and gay men, lesbians, and transgendered people of all races are affected by the public violence of oppression in their private lives (Kivel 1998). Undocumented immigrant women, because of the added threat of deportation, are at greater risk for abuse along dimensions of isolation, language barriers, and coercive and controlling behavior.

These hierarchies of power and control radically shape the experiences of people in relationships. Simply put, people (individuals, groups, corporations, countries) who have more power and privilege oppress and abuse those who have less power. Removal or withholding privileges from those perceived to be in the less-powerful position is one form of control, an abusive use of "power over." This is reinforced on the social level (e.g., media, sports, hunting), where male aggression is not only encouraged but often glorified and seen as being akin to male identity.

The preponderance of family violence is directed at women, children, and the elderly. While men are victims of violence, most of it occurs outside the home and disproportionately focuses on black males. In partner abuse, the stronger or more powerful partner tends to be the victimizer of the weaker partner. For example, being out of the labor force or having less education than one's partner renders a person less powerful in the relationship. Major relational decisions tend to be made by the partner who earns more income (Schwartz 1994), and people without economic viability are less able to leave an abusive relationship. Both are risk factors for abuse (Bograd 2005).

Domestic violence occurs about equally in gay and lesbian partnerships. Broader social and cultural dynamics such as heterosexism, homophobia, hate crimes, and the discrimination of sexism, classism, and racism must also be viewed as part of the context. Are both partners out? Do both partners have economic means to leave the relationship? Social and cultural factors deeply affect the organization of couple dynamics and the power and privilege afforded one partner over the other.

"Culture," too, must be deconstructed to distinguish the threads that bind a community in healthy ways apart from the norms of patriarchy. To interiorize the notion of "culture" without attending to the larger sociopolitical context in which it is embedded is analogous to having conversations about internal family processes without descriptions of patriarchy. In both cases, the aspects of power that surround family life and exist within it are obscured.

Responding to Misuses of Privilege, Power, and Control

Treatment for batterers, the battered, and their children must occur within a context that views psychological and interactional dynamics as integral parts of the supporting social and cultural context. Several programs exist currently with models of intervention that respond directly to the abuser's violations of privilege, power, and control and that also view psychological and interactional dynamics as essential elements in the treatment context.[2] One program using empowerment as a fundamental element, the Cultural Context Model, is the main focus of this section.

My relationship to this program came from two independent research studies. For the first, I interviewed prominent feminist social workers and family therapists nationally regarding how they address issues of power and privilege in therapeutic sessions with couples. One of those interviewed was Rhea Almeida, who founded the Cultural Context Model. The second study (Parker 2003) concentrated on this unique model, selected because of its unambiguous political approach, with issues of social justice central to its therapeutic program structure. I entered the program as an experienced clinician and an independent researcher interested in learning more about it. Program participants and staff were generous in sharing their experiences with me.

The Cultural Context Model, at the Institute for Family Services (IFS) in Somerset, New Jersey,[3] embraces a transformative approach to healing trauma. Empowerment and accountability in public contexts are fundamental to the model. The seven principles of empowerment practice used as guidelines in this book are embraced in every aspect of this treatment model. Just how a family services program goes about practically addressing issues of power and privilege with all clients is the focus of this discussion. The model is multifaceted and community-based, situating "issues of race, gender, class, and sexual orientation in culturally diverse groups at the core of therapeutic intervention" (Almeida et al. 1998:414). The structure of the program runs counter to that of most therapeutic programs, which limit the experience of change to the interior boundary of individual and family life. As the name suggests, people and problems are considered in context, thereby diverging from Western patriarchal views of the solitary, rugged individual or even of families as isolated, self-sustaining, and thus self-correcting systems. The Cultural Context Model breaks through perceived barriers around the nuclear family by creating a community that directly links families to one another. Within this multifamily or community milieu, clients are helped to examine gender, class, and other systemic patterns that contribute to their dilemmas. The walls of the therapy room are further extended by inviting other significant people into the therapeutic process, including community and religious leaders. The model focuses on dismantling traditional rules of privacy and access to power and social opportunity through the use of open dialogues that focus on principles of empowerment and on maintaining accountability over time.

How does this program operate practically? IFS is a nonprofit agency that serves about two hundred clients per year. The center is located in a lower-middle-class community and on a bus line, serving a very diverse clientele, who are self-referred or referred or mandated to treatment by others. The diversity is not due so much to the location of the institute as it is to program philosophy, which does not separate people by race, sexual orientation, class (via fee structure), or presenting problem. Also, the program's reputation for successful work with domestic violence garners referrals from a wide socioeconomic base from other therapists, organizations, and the court system across the state and beyond. Fees are determined on a sliding scale according to ability to pay and are adjusted to allow multiple members of a family to participate in the therapeutic program. Approximately 30 percent of clients pay near the lower end of the fee scale and 10 percent at the high end. Sixty percent of the clients use some form of insurance. IFS does not participate with managed care, which Almeida considers to be a "subversive system of care—oppressive to providers and consequently to clients" (Almeida 1997).

DISMANTLING RULES OF PRIVACY AND PRIVILEGE

The program at IFS based upon the Cultural Context Model is structured to disrupt power hierarchies (in the language of empowerment practice, to equalize power differentials) in five domains: between therapists and clients, between therapists, between clients, between family members, and in society.

BETWEEN THERAPISTS AND CLIENTS

A team, rather than a single therapist, conducts most of the therapy. Frank, for example, was assigned a volunteer sponsor, who ensured that he was integrated into and supported by the larger IFS community. The sponsor was present as a resource during Frank's initial intake sessions. Both of these structural components aim, in the terms of the empowerment principles, to equalize power differentials and therefore reduce dependency between clients and therapists. Therapeutic influence and accountability (i.e., responsibility and answerability) for maintaining change are expanded through the use of these teams, which include lay sponsors as well as therapists.

> Frank: *When I began coming to the group here, slowly I realized that I had a lot in common with these other men. I realized that these sponsors are there for a purpose, that they are much further down the road than I am. I could relate to them, not all of them, but there were some that had a history very similar to mine. Stan, for example, he was my sponsor. It was clear that we were very similar, but the difference was that he was now proceeding along this road to really changing, and I was just starting.*

BETWEEN THERAPISTS

Team members hold each other accountable for sexism, racism, and homophobia by observing sessions from behind a one-way mirror or on a television monitor. All clinical staff members are trained in this approach and accordingly "sign on" for a clinical environment that rigorously lives its principles. Program philosophy and empowerment practice require that power differentials be equalized. That is, the transformation and liberation of clients, those with less power and privilege, are dependent upon the continuing transformation and openness of clinical staff, those with more power and privilege. Clinical staff members are coached just as the clients are, with gentle and good-natured reminders, when they fall back into dominant or patriarchal thinking or behaviors. There is no assumption that staff members are less immersed in dominant-culture behavior than clients are. That said, Almeida (1997) acknowledges that the therapists who have the most difficulty accepting training in this model are white heterosexual men. Many of these men in our culture, who have been accustomed to holding positions of greater power and privilege, understandably resist accepting a program that asks them to decrease "power over" in favor of "power with" and that also asks them to share their privileged positions with others. In this case it means accepting training from an Asian Indian woman and other team members, some of whom are lay sponsors. It also means having their therapeutic work observed and critiqued for sexism, racism, and homophobia as well as working as a team member ("power with") rather than being *the* expert.

BETWEEN CLIENTS

Therapy is primarily conducted within same-gender groups, or what IFS calls "culture circles," rather than via individual, couples, or family counseling. The culture circles expand traditional therapeutic paradigms to include other, nonrelated people in the change process. There are women's, men's, adolescents', couples', and community culture circles, all of which include people of mixed ages, social classes, races, and sexual orientations. The groups are also varied with respect to the problems that bring clients to therapy—e.g., domestic violence, relationship issues, depression, parenting. Grouping clients by presenting problem or diagnostic category, although intended to create community through shared experience, tends to compartmentalize a person's sense of identity, emphasizing his/her experience around pathology. In contrast, the multi-problem and solution context empowers alternate, more-liberating life stories. Organizing the groups by gender facilitates the examination of the different ways in which dominant patriarchal discourses and practices affect women and men. It also honors the different pace at which women and men develop critical consciousness (Freire 1978), empowerment, and accountability (Hernandez, Almeida, and Dolan-Del Vecchio 2005). The culture circle structure dismantles notions of what is "private" in personal and family life from what could benefit from being more public. It also levels power hierarchies between diverse client populations, thus liberating the perspectives of traditionally subjugated groups (Figuera-McDonough, Netting, and Nichols-Casebolt 2001).

People like Frank, who have abused power in their intimate relationships, often advocate for couples counseling so they can monitor what their partner relates. Though they may present some resistance to the group format initially, all those whom I interviewed later proclaimed the value of the treatment format.

> Frank: *Of course there's a lot of holding accountable in this program, a lot of challenging that I just think is extremely difficult one-on-one with a therapist. I had a lot of therapy, but the individual therapy Joan and I had, it's just not the same thing. I'm not sure what it takes for most of us men, but probably for most of us some kind of a crisis to get us here in the first place, and then breaking down these barriers and getting right down to the very essence of what is really going on inside you. How could you do these things? And then finally realizing how absolutely terrible and unacceptable that kind of behavior really is. You would think that you would know that, but it's not necessarily so. I spent some months of being very guarded and trying to be very much in control; but at some point men just start to really get in touch with the terrible things that they've done. And, it just very quickly came upon me that this behavior was absolutely wrong, it was totally unacceptable. It just could never happen again. It might sound kind of simple, but for guys that are in this program, it's not simple because their whole life has been this course of rigidly trying to be in control. It's not an easy thing to let that go or even to see how absolutely wrong it is.*

BETWEEN FAMILY MEMBERS

The institute uses many tools to help clients identify issues of power and privilege in their families, in their work arenas, and in society at large. After Frank's initial intake session, for example, he joined a same-gender, six-to-eight-week, socio-education orientation group. Consciousness-raising is a core intervention to help clients examine how intersecting issues of race, gender, class, and sexual orientation in culturally diverse groups dominate family life (Bricker-Jenkins, Hooyman, and Gottlieb

1991; Gutierrez and Lewis 1999; Martin-Baro 1994; Parsons, Gutierrez, and Cox 1998; Wise 2005). Intersecting issues of power, privilege, and oppression are central to the issues that bring people to counseling and, thus, are central to healing both person and context (Almeida et al.1998). In the socio-education orientation groups, and in the culture circles, Frank's groups examined the many factors that contributed to the problems for which they came to therapy, including broader social issues. They were given power and control wheels that helped them identify the misuse and abuse of power within four different contexts: two publicly toward people of color and toward lesbians and gays; and two privately in heterosexual relationships and in lesbian and gay relationships (figures 5.1–5.4).

These tools help to educate clients about what constitutes power and control issues. Documentaries and vignettes from such films as *Killing Us Softly, Dialogues with Madwomen, Pocahontas, Joy Luck Club, Monsoon Wedding,* and *Torch Song Trilogy* are used to address the intersections of power, privilege, and oppression in families and society. Family genograms (McGoldrick and Gerson 1985) are constructed to explore multigenerational legacies, gendered and racial norms, and immigration patterns across time.

> Rual (a 15-year-old Cuban student): *They teach us about male privilege— like what is expected of different genders. It's kind of like a class. You learn a lot about life. They don't only teach you about your problems, they teach you about racism, family problems, and even sexism. And, they teach you what you have to know when you get older—like chauvinism and abusiveness.*

IN SOCIETY

The sponsorship program and IFS's active advocacy projects aim to dismantle power, privilege, and oppression on a societal level. Clients eagerly relate their wish to "give back" what they learn at IFS. Several male clients, for example, established the first National Organization of Men Against Sexism (NOMAS) group in New Jersey. Frank was pivotal in this effort. He and other clients also speak at schools and churches on violence prevention, sexism, and domestic violence. Many serve as sponsors to newer IFS clients. The sponsors are unpaid support persons who contribute to the healing process within and outside the therapeutic encounter and serve as mentors to those struggling with issues of equity and nonviolence in

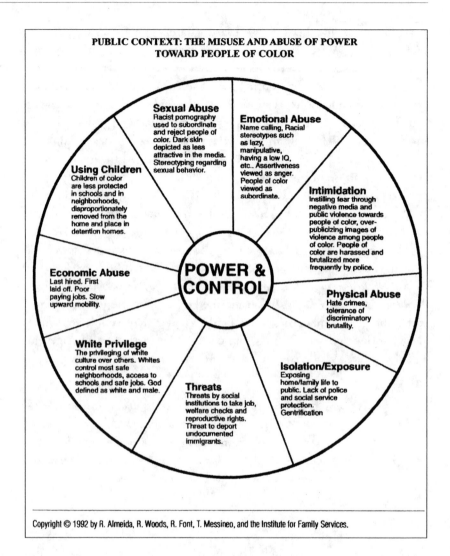

Figure 5.1

relationships. They offer expanded notions of masculinity (e.g., nurturing, gentleness, and empathy) and femininity (e.g., financial viability and empowerment), including respect for women, children, people of color, sexual minorities, and others who are different from themselves. A sponsor may also serve as a resource for a client of the same cultural or religious background or provide needed and missing information about a particular culture circle topic.

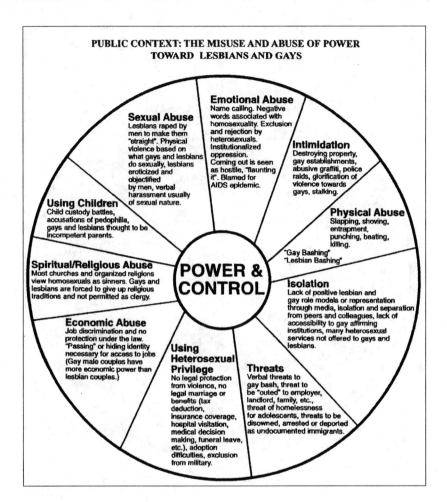

Figure 5.2

Frank: *Someone asked me, "When you're at work and you're angry at someone at work, what do you do about it?" The answer is, "Not much." What they meant was, "You don't say the things to colleagues at work that you do to your wife. Do you? No!" They were trying to convey to me that my behavior was a choice, and I didn't think that it was. I thought that I was being provoked and that I had to react—that my reaction was legitimate. But they were saying, "So someone really pisses you off at work, do you walk up and get in their face? And, if they come back at you, are you willing to throw them against the wall? No! But you do that with your wife. So it's a choice." That was the point they were making, that abusive controlling behavior is a choice. But I didn't*

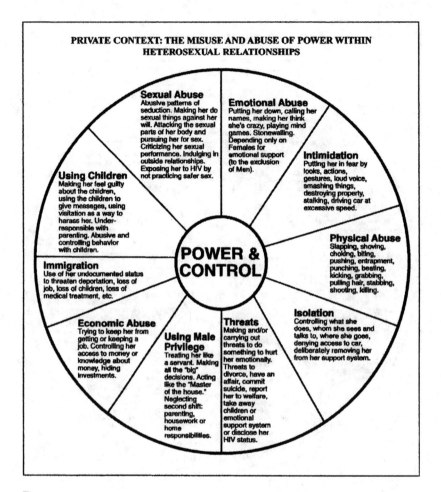

Figure 5.3

know that. I was driving home from group one night to this motel. Somebody just cut me off and pulled right in front of me. I was furious! I was ready to climb out of my car at the stoplight and yank that door open, and yank that guy right out on the street. Then I saw how big the guy was, and I didn't do a thing. At that moment I realized what it was like to be a bully, and that I was one. You have to be real careful who you pick on. You're not going to pick on a big guy. It's a very humbling, even humiliating, thing to see that in yourself, but I think we need to.

The structure, organization, and social justice framework of the therapy at IFS—i.e., culture circles, sponsors, and socio-education—suggest to

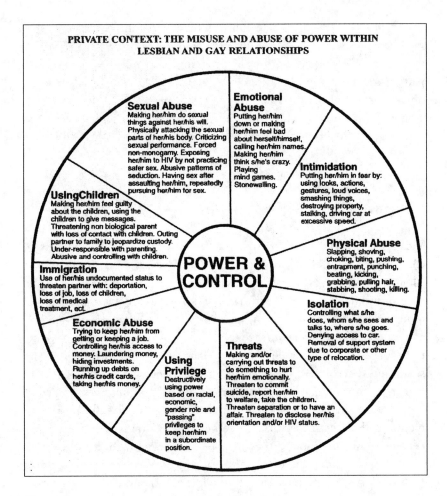

Figure 5.4

clients that (a) issues related to power, privilege, and oppression are central to all relationships, not just overtly battering relationships, (b) problems have social roots, and (c) problems are better solved in a community, particularly one that shares a critical consciousness. Likewise, broader social values that isolate family life from community life are problematic. The elevation of privacy and autonomy perpetuates male rites of passage that are often organized around themes of violence and devaluation of women.

Most therapy occurs by way of the culture circles, which vary in size and range up to twenty people per group. The groups often occur simultaneously and are therefore convenient for family members. This group treatment structure also allows staff members to work as teams with each of the groups. Teams include full-time and part-time therapeutic staff members plus students in training and sponsors. Sponsors are IFS volunteers who have graduated from the program, or people who are asked to participate in a session because of a unique perspective or skill they can offer—e.g., a police officer, a clergyperson, a person of a particular race, ethnicity, or religion. This structure reflects that of the empowerment approach and its principles of integrating the support of others and using cooperative roles.

Vicarious Trauma

Vicarious, or secondary, trauma has been described as "a process of change resulting from empathic engagement with trauma survivors. . . . Anyone who engages empathically with trauma survivors is vulnerable to vicarious traumatization" (Pearlman 1999). At IFS, there is a great deal of change related to empathic engagement with the survivors of violence, and clinicians often acknowledge a sense of vulnerability in doing this work, yet the experience of secondary *trauma*, with the signs and symptoms that the staff member is truly experiencing a trauma, is seldom reported. Instead, the empathic *responses* of the clinical staff are so supported at every stage by every member of the team for all clinical staff members that those responses become "positive transformations, deep personal transformation(s) that include personal growth, a deeper connection with both individuals and the human experience" (Pearlman 1999:51). Just as the empowerment principle of responding from an awareness of specific needs is essential for effective intervention with clients, so too "understanding and responding to one's own needs is the essence of an effective self-care strategy for client and therapist alike" (Pearlman 1999:53).

Team members plan, conduct, and then rehash all sessions together. There is group support at each level so that no one bears the burden of or responsibility for the work alone. Mary, a client whose husband had made serious threats to kill her as well as her therapists, described the support she felt when the entire team from IFS accompanied her to the police station to ask for a restraining order. As she told me this, I thought she must be exaggerating, that maybe it *felt* like the whole team went. I could not imagine they all actually went, as the group ends around ten o'clock at night. However, when I discussed this with the team, they told me that in fact they all did go. Since Mary's husband was a friend of many of the officers, they decided that a large presence of therapists would make a statement. The team action resulted in the police officers' decisive and positive response. They called a judge at home who then came to the station and gave Mary a restraining order. Mary, who had not been taken seriously by the same police officers in the past, felt empowered by the collective action, which clearly prompted the police to be accountable for protecting Mary and staff members at IFS from her very dangerous husband.

Mary's situation would understandably be terrifying to therapists. It was a situation ripe for vicarious trauma, particularly for therapists who worked solo. In fact, Mary's previous individual therapist dropped her as a client when threatened by the husband. It was the team of therapists and sponsors plus the group therapeutic format that provided a context of safety for all, therapists and clients alike. In turn, that team engendered a team response from the police force as well.

These uses of the team are key components in the prevention of the potentially debilitating and numbing effects of secondary trauma. "Finding forums in which to recall and name the rewards of doing trauma therapy is essential. It renews our sense of the meaning of this work, revitalizes our connections with others . . . and reminds us of the importance of an awareness of all aspects of life" (Pearlman and Saakvitne 1995).

The sense of social mission along with a belief that what they are doing is valuable and successful (Bell 2003) buffers the gravity of the work. It was mentioned earlier that issues of social justice are central to the therapeutic program structure at IFS. Working for social justice has been found to be one of the key activities engaged in by trauma therapists to help balance the effects of trauma work (Follette, Polusny, and Milbeck 1994; Pearlman and MacIan, 1995).

Reflections on Empowerment Principles

The program at IFS is guided by two overarching principles: empowerment and accountability. The seven principles of empowerment practice are embedded in these two principles of the Cultural Context Model. Parallels between these two approaches are evident and are highlighted here with the idea that, when combined, they can be used to strengthen interactions for effectively working with clients.

First, all therapeutic interventions aim to empower or liberate clients by developing their critical consciousness, a goal similar to building on strengths and diminishing oppression as well as enacting multicultural respect in the empowerment model of practice. IFS maintains that personal and social liberation occurs when groups of people decipher mechanisms of power, privilege, oppression, and dehumanization (Freire 1978; Martin-Baro 1994), understand how power relationships shape perceptions and experiences, and identify how they can assume a role in social change (Gutierrez and Lewis 1999).

A second principle involves the liberation or empowerment of women, or those with less power and privilege, and depends on the accountability of men, or those who hold more power and privilege (Almeida 2003). Women and subjugated others will go unheard (Weick 2000; Wise 2005) unless those who dominate and/or wield power take responsibility for change, actions that are also consistent with the empowerment principles of building on strength while simultaneously diminishing oppression. Power and equity disparities between genders, races, and sexual orientations, for example, need to be redressed in order to equalize power differentials. In most therapies, there is no expectation for holding clients with more power and privilege accountable for maintaining attitudinal and behavioral changes over time. At IFS, however, the group structure, sponsors, and team approach require this accountability, consistent with the empowerment principle of integrating support from others. The goal is to take pressure off those with less social power—i.e., women—to do all the changing and accommodating. Instead, the onus for change is placed on those with more power to change the oppressive social structure.

When Frank and his wife, Joan, came voluntarily to the program, they each entered their respective culture circle, male and female.

Frank: *What happened was, she was going here, I was going here. I'm not sure what Joan was hearing, but she was certainly getting a crash course in education of power control issues and gender issues and what was going on in our relationship. So that on that particular date, we were in the backyard and had a power struggle that ended with me pushing her down and kicking her. It was literally a turf battle: "This is my space, this is my garden." There was a great deal of separateness in our relationship, which was really a logical consequence of the imbalance that we had, but she had enough courage and information at that point to dash into the house and call the police. That was really an act of courage on her part, and I'm sure that she got that from the couple of months here in the program, making it very clear and rehearsing. "If this ever happens again, this is what you have to do. We'll all support you, we've been through this." And it worked. It wasn't such a happy time for me. I'm hauled away in handcuffs to the local police department. Still thinking, "How could this be happening to me?" That really constituted a crisis that, I think, for a lot of us is really necessary. And Joan filed a complaint in municipal court, and I was found guilty of a misdemeanor. The judge asked Joan if she had anything to say and she asked the judge not to give me any kind of jail sentence. Instead she encouraged him to mandate this treatment process. So he did that and gave me a fine. In my case, I'm sure that I would have continued to participate even without being mandated, but I'm a very strong advocate of mandating effective programs, and I wish more judges would. In fact, recently the people at the institute were invited to talk at the municipal court judges' conference recently in central New Jersey, and they invited me along to represent what I had gone through.*

Frank's and Joan's therapies eventually resulted in Joan's filing for divorce. Part of that process included Frank's process of accountability and reparations for the harm he had caused Joan and their children. Frank regretted that his behavior led to divorce. Joan still, after seven years, holds a restraining order against him, something that Frank now understands and supports.

Others have written about the value of witnesses in the therapeutic context. Examples are reflecting teams (Hoffman 1992) and "definitional ceremonies" using outsider witnesses (White 1999). Different at IFS is the return of the witnesses the next week and the next. This practice affords an ongoing community that can challenge misuses of power and privilege directly and thus empower those with less power and privilege. Even more critical for women, it holds participants, clients *and* staff, accountable over time to change the balance of power and privilege between women and men, and with persons of various class, racial, and sexual orientation locations. This goal reflects the empowerment principles of equalizing power differentials, enacting multicultural respect, and assisting clients as they empower themselves.

What do clients say about their experience of the program at IFS? Four themes emerged from their answers: (1)"Therapy was such a different thing than I had thought," (2)"Breaking down barriers," (3)"Public forum, collective memory," and (4)"No secrets."

THEME 1: "THERAPY WAS SUCH A DIFFERENT THING THAN I HAD
THOUGHT"

Several clients said the therapy they received was different than what
they had expected. Some talked about their initial resistance to the same-
gender culture circle format. Stan, a 34-year-old German construction
worker, came with his wife to the program because their arguments
were becoming more intense and frequent. He was also unhappy with
their sex life.

> Stan: *Therapy was such a different thing than I had thought. I thought we
> would be in couples sessions. . . . So, when you're put in with a bunch of
> men and you only have a short period of time to talk, I always wondered
> what was happening with her. We weren't having couples sessions. It was
> hard at first because things people said in the group were going against
> all the roles I grew up with in my household—the role of the male, the
> husband, the son—it challenged all those fundamental ideas. But I look
> back and I think it was for the best. I concentrate on what's going on with
> me first and not as a couple. I tell this to the men that come here, not to
> get all excited and angry about things because you're uncomfortable with
> confiding in men.*

Stan describes his reaction to and initial discomfort with not being
able to control what his wife was saying in the women's group and
being required to share intimately with other men. The structure is
designed to encourage people to take responsibility for their own
emotional life by requiring that they deconstruct their interpersonal
issues first in the context of the culture circles. Partners go to same-
gender culture circles first to expand their view of themselves and the
situations. When couples counseling is held, it is done within the context of the men's, women's, or couples' circles. Many men stressed how
intimacy with other men taught them skills for being more intimate
with their partners.

Women learn, "I'm not crazy, my situation is." This provides easy
access for an empowerment-focused clinician to build on strength while
diminishing the oppressive, "crazy-making" forces of violent behaviors.
This connection seemed more available to the women because they are
part of the larger IFS community where "crazy-making" issues of power
and privilege are directly and specifically tackled, though separately, by
both genders.

THEME 2: "BREAKING DOWN BARRIERS"

Many clients said that the diverse—i.e., intergenerational, interracial, mixed problem, sexual orientation, and social class—culture circles helped to break down barriers between people who were different from each other and often otherwise would have no contact. This brings to life the empowerment principle of enacting multicultural respect. They were surprised by the commonalities they found. William, a 31-year-old African American psychology student, shared that initially he wanted to be in a black men's group, but he then came to appreciate the value of the diverse men's culture circle.

> William: *The program helps us to draw connections between men of color, men of different classes, and men at different places on the power and control wheel. It helps to bring us together and to see the ways we use power and control in our own lives. The society through the media tells us that we're all separate, and there really aren't many similarities between us. The program here breaks down a lot of the differences that we otherwise might put up as walls between us to keep us from communicating with each other, and coming to terms with the way we use power and control in our lives. . . . I was one who bought into that separation. Then sitting right next to me in the group was a white male cop who physically abused his wife! And then, on the other side sits a white man who is three times my age who sexually abused his daughter! I would say to myself, "What am I doing here because that's not my background. I haven't used my power in those ways." So, early on I was putting up walls and saying, "Well, I'm not really sure this is for me because of the obvious differences." Over time I've realized it is all connected. The ways in which we men use power in our workplace and family life crosses culture and profession and race and age, which I otherwise probably wouldn't have seen. . . . If I say, "Well, I'm not a child molester, I'm not a rapist, I'm not a woman abuser," then the things I'm doing are kind of small as opposed to, "Wow, I'm doing almost exactly what he's doing, just to a lesser degree." Now that goes hand in hand with breaking down those barriers. I'm able to see myself in them and say, "Maybe I do need to be here. Maybe there is some work that I need to do."*

When university police used racial profiling to stop and harass William, IFS clients and staff community members supported William financially and emotionally to take legal action, which he did and won. In his men's circle, William also had many opportunities to give older white men advice, breaking traditional racial and social mores, experiences that would not have been afforded him in a more traditional therapeutic setting or in a black men's group. This also provides a vivid illustration of what it can mean to enact multicultural respect within an empowerment frame of practice.

THEME 3: "PUBLIC FORUM, COLLECTIVE MEMORY"

Clients spoke often about the value of the "public forum" offered through the culture circles, the sponsorship program, and advocacy work, the ways in which this program integrates support from others and uses cooperative roles. Men who initially resisted the culture circle format seemed to become its greatest proponents. These structural elements afford what clients call a "collective memory." For example, clients remember for each other a partner's past misdeeds or commitments made regarding behavioral changes.

Beth, a 42-year-old Irish accountant, for example, wanted to reunite with her husband. He was out of the home because of inappropriate behavior toward their 8-year-old daughter and his involvement with sex clubs, which had cost the family more than $90,000 during the last ten years. The women's culture circle provided a "collective memory" for Beth. They pointed out to her that even though there had been significant improvements in her husband's behavior, he had recently violated boundaries with their daughter. The feedback provided by way of the culture circles and sponsors served a powerful accountability function. When the heat of the moment has passed out of memory for clients, as it often does in cases of abuse, it is still alive in memories of culture circle members, who are committed to empowering silenced voices and holding each other accountable.

Beth's two daughters and her husband attended the children's circle, where they revealed the boundary violations by the father.

Beth: *Knowing that it would get back to both of us, our daughter knew her dad would then be held accountable and that was important to her. So, she's now seeing the safety net of bringing the problem here. She didn't have to say to him, "Daddy, that doesn't feel good when you say that." You know what? She's nine years old. She's not going to say that. But knowing that it would be taken care of is a tremendous benefit! My husband then is held accountable in a public way. It's brought into the men's circle and they say, "What the hell are you doing putting her in that position?" He is put on the spot of publicly having to acknowledge, "Well, I did that." And, he is unlikely to do it again. The truth is that we have been in therapy for nine of our twelve years and no real change occurred until we came here.*

Having several family members participate in the various culture circles seems to be the rule rather than an exception. Clients are encouraged by the structure of the therapy to go public to the culture circles. Issues are aired in a context where clarity can be gained outside the turmoil of the relational moment. Clients learn to be responsible, to maintain a sense of self, and to manage reactivity to others while being emotionally present with significant others. When relationship or family work is deemed appropriate, it is available in the context of a public forum within the men's, women's, or couples' culture circles. This helps break down isolation and secrecy surrounding family life and dilemmas and to garner resources and support for less-reactive responses and behaviors.

THEME 4: "NO SECRETS"

Several clients related that secrecy contributed to their problems—that affairs, pornography, and private psychotherapies left "real" problems unchallenged and therefore intact. If both partners and/or family members are being treated by IFS, there is agreement upfront that secrets are not kept between people or culture circles under the guise of confidentiality. If threats of violence are made or boundaries are violated, the team knows immediately and can respond. This is different from group-oriented domestic violence therapy, where partners tend to be seen by different treatment providers who are then limited by not knowing the full story from both partners (Stith 2000). The therapists are careful to discern whether revealing information would put someone at risk. Partners are seen in different centers, though by the same treatment team, to ensure both safety and accountability. Several women clients, some with current restraining orders against their partners, claimed to feel physically and psychologically safer because the IFS team was treating their partner. They related their feelings of safety to the knowledge that their partner was being held accountable for his behavior by the men's circle and treatment team. Both partners knew that if violent behavior occurred, the treatment team would be informed and take action.

For whom does this program work? Clients say the therapeutic program offered at IFS "works when you work it." They say it is not an easy or brief therapy. A 27-year-old African American female student described it this way:

> Anna: *I think the people for whom it wouldn't work are people who are invested in finding some instant cure, or some biomedical approach. You know, throw a couple of pills at you and say, "See you in six months." If you think you're going to go to brief counseling, or something that is totally removed from a community atmosphere, or that is not going to address all aspects of your being—people who are into that don't want to work that hard. I mean it's a lot of work! So, you've got to be ready to confront what you've been taught since you were a fetus and to look at the world differently. And we have plenty of people who come in and know it's not for them right from the jump because they're not ready.*

The program does not work for everyone. Not all clients who come to the program stay with it. Those who do and are successful challenge fundamental belief systems in the public context of the culture circles.

Conclusion and Recommendations

What can we—particularly those of us who wish to empower oppressed people and to right an unequal social structure—learn from these clients? First, we must structure therapeutic work so that issues of power, privilege, and oppression are integral to each step of the therapeutic process. Second, we must find ways to engage and hold those with more power and privilege accountable to change the unequal power structure.

When a client or therapist steps into IFS, he or she has stepped into another therapeutic world—one where men, people of light skin, heterosexuals, and members of the middle class are not automatically granted the loudest voice. Instead, they are asked to systematically examine their privilege and its consequences for others. Rather than allowing the onus for change to rest on the shoulders of those who have the least power to effect change, the Culture Context Model places responsibility directly on the shoulders of those who have more power to make changes. This shift is empowering to women and others with less social power—the people who, in most therapeutic settings, carry most of the responsibility for change.

This model conveys the message that problems, particularly problems centered in trauma, are better solved in communities of empowerment and answerability than in isolation. The culture circles and sponsors help to break down traditional rules of privacy that serve to maintain positions of power and privilege and, therefore, inequality in relationships and society. As the clients say, "This is not a brief therapy." Instead, it is a resocialization.

Notes

1. "Of color" refers to blacks, Latinas/os (i.e., Chicanas, Puerto Ricans, Cubans), American Indians, Asian Americans (i.e., Koreans, Japanese, Chinese, Vietnamese, Filipinos, and Indians), and those of mixed heritage who appear to be or identify with being "of color."

2. Four such programs are: (1) Family Group Conferencing to address family violence (Pennell and Burford 2000); (2) AMEND—Abusive Men Exploring New Directions (Ewing, Lindsey, and Pomerantz 1984; Lindsey, McBride, and Platt 1993); (3) the Duluth Model: Education Groups for Men Who Batter (Pence and Paymar 1993); and (4) the Cultural Context Model at the Institute for Family Services (IFS) in Somerset, New Jersey (Almeida et al. 1998).

3. Portions of this discussion were published previously in Parker 2003.

References

Almeida, R. 1997. Personal communication.

——. 2003. "Breaking Ties That Bind: Creating Collectives of Liberation." In T. J. Goodrich and L. Silverstein, eds., *Feminist Family Therapy: Empowerment and Social Location*, 293–306. Washington, D. C.: American Psychological Association Press.

Almeida, R., and T. Durkin. 1999. "The Cultural Context Model: Therapy for Couples with Domestic Violence." *Journal of Marriage and Family Therapy* 25:5–32.

Almeida, R., R. Woods, R. Font, and T. Messineo. 1992. "CCM Power and Control Wheels: Public and Private Contexts." Somerset, N. J.: Institute for Family Services.

Almeida, R., R. Woods, T. Messineo, and R. Font. 1998. "The Cultural Context Model: An Overview." In Monica McGoldrick, ed., *Revisioning Family Therapy: Race, Culture, and Gender in Clinical Practice*, 414–431. New York: Guilford.

Bell, H. 2003. "Strengths and Secondary Trauma in Family Violence Work." *Social Work* 48:513–522.

Bograd, M. 2005. "Strengthening Domestic Violence Theories: Intersections of Race, Class, Sexual Orientation, and Gender." In N. Sokoloff and C. Pratt, eds., *Domestic Violence at the Margins: Readings on Race, Class, Gender, and Culture*, 25–38. New Brunswick, N. J.: Rutgers University Press.

Bricker-Jenkins, M., N. Hooyman, and N. Gottlieb, eds. 1991. *Feminist Social Work Practice*. Newbury Park, Calif.: Sage.

Ewing, W., M. Lindsey, and J. Pomerantz. 1984. *Battering: An AMEND Manual for Helpers*. Denver: Loretto Heights.

Figuera-McDonough, J., F. E. Netting, and A. Nichols-Casebolt. 2001. "Subjugated Knowledge in Gender-Integrated Social Work Education: Call for a Dialogue." *Affilia* 16:411–431.

Follette, V. M., M. M. Polusny, and K. Milbeck. 1994. "Mental Health and Law Enforcement Professionals: Trauma History, Psychological Symptoms, and Impact of Providing Services to Child Sexual Abuse Survivors." *Professional Psychology: Research and Practice* 25 (3): 275–282.

Freire, P. 1978. *Education for a Critical Consciousness*. New York: Seabury.

Gutierrez, L., and E. Lewis. 1999. *Empowering Women of Color*. New York: Columbia University Press.

Hernandez, P., R. Almeida, and K. Dolan-Del Vecchio. 2005. "Critical Consciousness, Accountability, and Empowerment: Key Processes for Helping Families Heal." *Family Process* 44:105–119.

Hoffman, L. 1992. "A Reflective Stance for Family Therapy." In S. McNamee and K. Gergan, eds., *Therapy as Social Construction*, 7–24. London: Sage.

Kivel, P. 1998. *Men's Work: How to Stop the Violence That Tears Our Lives Apart*. New York: Hazelden Ballantine.

Lindsey, M., R. McBride, and C. Platt. 1993. *AMEND: Breaking the Cycle*. Littleton, Colo.: Gylantic.

Martin-Baro, I. 1994. *Writings for a Liberation Psychology*. Cambridge, Mass.: Harvard University Press.

McGoldrick, M., and R. Gerson. 1985. *Genograms in Family Assessment*. New York: Norton.

McIntosh, P. 2004. "White Privilege: Unpacking the Invisible Knapsack." In M. H. Andersen and P. H. Collins, eds., *Race, Class, and Gender: An Anthology*, 103–108. 5th ed. Belmont, Calif.: Wadsworth/Thomson Learning.

Parker, L. 2003. "A Social Justice Model for Clinical Social Work." *Affilia* 18: 272–288.

Parsons, R., L. Gutierrez, and E. Cox. 1998. *Empowerment in Social Work Practice: A Sourcebook*. Pacific Grove, Calif.: Brooks/Cole.

Pearlman, L. A. 1999. "Self-Care for Trauma Therapists: Ameliorating Vicarious Traumatization." In B. H. Stamm, ed., *Secondary Traumatic Stress: Self-Care*

Issues for Clinicians, Researchers, and Educators, 51–64. 2nd ed. Baltimore: Sidran.

Pearlman, L. A., and P. MacIan. 1995. "Vicarious Traumatization: An Empirical Study of the Effects of Trauma Work on Trauma Therapists." *Professional Psychology: Research and Practice* 26(6): 558–565.

Pearlman, L. A., and K. W. Saakvitne. 1995. *Trauma and the Therapist: Counter-transference and Vicarious Traumatization in Psychotherapy with Incest Survivors.* New York: Norton.

Pence, E., and M. Paymar. 1993. *Education Groups for Men Who Batter: The Duluth Model.* New York: Springer.

Pennell, J., and G. Burford. 2000. "Family Group Decision-Making and Family Violence." In G. Burford and J. Hudson, eds., *Family Group Conferencing: New Directions in Community-Centered Child and Family Practice,* 171–192. New York: Aldine de Gruyter.

Schwartz, P. 1994. *Peer Marriage: How Love Between Equals Really Works.* New York: Macmillan.

Stith, S. 2000. "Prevalence and Cost of Domestic Violence." *AAMFT Clinical Update* 2(3): 1–8.

U.S. Department of Justice. 2005. "Rates of Family Violence." Washington, D.C.: Bureau of Justice Statistics.

Weick, A. 2000. "Hidden Voices." *Social Work* 45:395–402.

White, M. 1999. "Reflecting-Team Work as Definitional Ceremony Revisited." *Gecko* 2:55–82.

Wise, J. B. 2005. *Empowerment Practice with Families in Distress.* New York: Columbia University Press.

6

Bullying and Victimization
Transforming Trauma Through Empowerment

FAYE MISHNA

*Erin is a bright and talented 11-year-old girl in the fifth grade who recently trans-
ferred to her current school. She was born in Canada shortly after her parents had
emigrated from China, and she lives with them and her older brother in a large
Canadian urban center. At her previous school, Erin had been physically bullied;
other students would shove and hit her, sometimes leaving her with bruises. Erin
had come to expect and even accept being victimized by peers. After transferring to
her current school, she felt relief because the bullying she anticipated did not occur.
Rather, she thought, "Oh, wow, nothing bad is happening." However, something
else was troubling her in the new school: "There is a group of people I know and I
thought that they were my friends. But they tell secrets in front of me. And they'll
say, 'Could you go away?' and I would. I didn't think it was my business. But now
I remember the tone of voice that they used and they meant it meanly."*

Note: All names and identifying information have been disguised. The author acknowledges funding
support by the Social Sciences and Humanities Research Council of Canada (SSHRC), the Margaret
and Wallace McCain Family Chair in Child and Family, and Bell Canada. The information was gathered for a pilot and a full study conducted by the author with co-investigators Dr. Debra Pepler and
Dr. Judith Wiener (Mishna 2004; Mishna et al. 2005; Mishna et al. 2006).

Erin often dreaded going to school, but for the most part she forced herself to attend. When discussing how she felt when she was excluded or told to go away, she said, "It makes me really sad. I think it's my fault. Now when I make a mistake I feel like I have to punish myself so I hit myself. And I think that could be related to the bullying." When upset with herself Erin would hit her head with a book or pinch herself so hard that she drew blood. Feeling that she was to blame and that there must be something about her that caused others to bully her, Erin also felt considerable self-loathing and shame.

For a while Erin did not discuss these experiences and feelings with anyone. She felt confused about how to deal with this situation, since some of the same children she considered to be her friends were the ones who were excluding her. Erin's school is renowned for its all-around excellence, but one teacher expressed concern that the school's reputation as "nice" lessened teachers' and parents' vigilance with respect to bullying. He believed that the bullying within the school "is just as much. It's much more covert. I think because the majority of our bullying is not physical, most parents don't perceive that we have a bullying problem. In fact, many of them may have the same attitude that I heard from teachers when I first arrived, saying, 'Oh, our kids are nice to each other; there is no bullying.'" Clearly struggling with issues related to her exclusion, Erin was willing to see a school social worker to have help coping with her feelings and this problem.

Understanding the Trauma of Bullying

Bullying is a form of aggression that unfolds within the context of a relationship, in which there is an imbalance of power between the child who bullies and the child who is victimized (Olweus 1991; Pepler et al. 2004). This power imbalance may be the result of such variables as size, strength, age, social status, or knowledge of a child's vulnerabilities. Bullying occurs largely within the context of the peer group (Salmivalli 1999). It may be direct (e.g., name-calling) or indirect (e.g., gossip) and covers a wide range of behaviors, from social exclusion to physical assaults (Hanish and Guerra 2000), as well as emotional intimidation, which may stir up strong and overwhelming feelings in the victimized child. With the passing of time and continued harassment, the inequality of power becomes increasingly entrenched, resulting in progressively limited options for the child who is victimized (Pepler et al. 2004).

Many children and adolescents who are bullied experience this form of victimization as traumatic. *Psychological trauma* refers to any critical incident (including repeated verbal and emotional abuse and neglect) that causes people to experience unusually strong emotional reactions that produce physiological changes and that have the potential to affect their ability to function at work, at home, and in other areas of their lives (van der Kolk, McFarlane, and Weisaeth 1996). Stolorow and Atwood (1992) emphasize the relational context in which trauma occurs: "Pain is not pathology. It is the absence of adequate attunement and responsiveness to the child's painful emotional reactions that renders them unendurable and thus a source of traumatic states and psychology" (54). This conceptualization pertains both to dramatic and discrete traumatic events and to more subtle forms of injury.

Precisely because of the gravity of bullying, a sizable body of research has been developed in an effort to understand and address its potentially devastating effects. Bullying is reported to be pervasive in many countries (Olweus 1994) and is a predictable, accepted, and often unspoken, albeit painful, part of childhood. Both children who bully and children who are victimized are at risk of developing social, emotional, academic, and psychiatric problems that may persist into adulthood (Nansel et al. 2001; O'Connell, Pepler, and Craig 1999; Olweus 1993).

Boys are victimized more often than girls (Atlas and Pepler 1998), and they tend to be involved in physical or direct forms of victimization, whereas girls are more likely to be involved in indirect forms of bullying and social exclusion, or relational bullying (Crick and Grotpeter 1996; Owens, Shute, and Slee 2000). Bullying is more prevalent among younger children, occurs among preschool youngsters, and takes different forms at different ages (Nansel et al. 2001; O'Connell et al. 1999).

Children who bully tend to be stronger than their peers, aggressive, and impulsive (Baldry and Farrington 2005; Olweus 1993). They may be somewhat unpopular, but unlike victimized children, they may be popular with certain children (Olweus 1997) who might endorse their bullying behaviors (Nansel et al. 2001). Children who are victimized tend to lack friends and to be rejected by peers (Olweus 1994). Many victimized children, labeled "passive" or "submissive victims," cry easily and are anxious, withdrawn, and physically weak. Approximately 10 to 20 percent of victimized children, who both bully and are victimized, are depicted as "provocative" or "aggressive victims" (Olweus 1978). The families of children who bully have a high degree of conflict, which may include violence, a lack of warmth, or excessive permissiveness (Baldry and Farrington 2005; Olweus 1994).

Peer relations are critical for children's development and are predictors of adult adjustment (Hartup 1992). Observational research studies, entailing videotaping students on the school playground and in classrooms, found that in both locations peers were involved in 85 percent of the bullying episodes (Atlas and Pepler 1998; O'Connell et al. 1999). Despite most children's stated opposition to bullying and support for the victim, in practice peers are reluctant to help the victimized child (O'Connell et al. 1999).

Ecological and societal contexts must also be considered. The attitudes of parents, teachers, and school administrators may contribute to children's victimization, as may teacher and student tolerance of victimization (Twemlow, Fonagy, and Sacco 2003). In schools, factors that foster victimization include a lack of clear rules regarding aggression, little or low principal involvement with students, weak staff cohesion, minimal teacher and student involvement in decision making, and inadequate supervision (Atlas and Pepler 1998). Socioeconomic conditions and attitudes toward violence contribute to the prevalence of bullying (Brinson, Kottler, and Fisher 2004; O'Connell et al. 1999; Salmivalli 1999). The extent of victimization that occurs among children mirrors both the violence in society and the institutionalization of bullying itself (Atlas and Pepler 1998; Twemlow et al. 2003).

Children who are victimized are at risk for internalizing problems such as anxiety and depression (Olweus 1993; Pellegrini 1998), report feeling afraid in school, avoid school more frequently (Slee 1994), and may also experience academic difficulties (Clarke and Kiselica 1997). Childhood aggression often continues into adolescence, and childhood bullying behavior may progress into adolescent delinquency or gang activity (O'Connell et al. 1999). Olweus (1997) found that boys in grades 6–9 who bullied were roughly four times more likely to be convicted of a crime by age 24 than boys who were victimized or who were not involved in bullying. Children who bully are more likely to be unhappy at school (Nansel et al. 2001) and to be depressed as youth and as adults (Slee 1995). Children who both bully and are victimized are the most severely rejected and have particularly serious adjustment problems (Pellegrini 1998).

Incidents considered to be ordinary or common by some can be experienced by others as traumatic. Various factors contribute to this difference in perception. One such factor is the repetition of a traumatizing experience, which can seriously erode an individual's sense of trust and sense of self and other and can interfere with adjustment (Janson and Hazler 2004).

Due to the seemingly minor nature of indirect and non-physical forms of bullying, adults very often underestimate the potential damage for the victimized child. This lack of validation or recognition of the child's pain further damages the child and can increase the likelihood that the child might feel traumatized (Stolorow and Atwood 1992). Bystanders may also experience significant levels of distress that can have detrimental long-term effects (Janson and Hazler 2004).

The enormous influence of the interpersonal context within a school, such as the school's tolerance of and ability to handle social aggression, must be recognized (Twemlow et al. 2003). A lack of connectedness among students and between students and teachers can lead to detrimental outcomes including violence (Twemlow, Fonagy, and Sacco 2002). As an extreme example, analysis of the Columbine tragedy revealed that one factor, among the multiple factors and conditions that may have contributed to the killing rampage by Eric Harris and Dylan Klebold, was their chronic victimization by popular school athletes (Greenfield and Juonen 1999). The horrific violence at Columbine represents an extreme reaction, which clearly does not occur in the majority of schools. Nevertheless, when bullying is prevalent, the students who are victimized feel a great deal of suffering (Aronson 2004).

Bullying is a complex phenomenon. Hence a systemic ecological framework, which shows how the dynamics extend beyond the children who bully or who are victimized, is necessary to understand this behavior. Individual characteristics, social interactions, familial factors, and ecological and cultural conditions all interact to contribute to social behavioral patterns (Atlas and Pepler 1998). Interventions must therefore target more than the children who are directly involved.

Responding to Bullying

Erin and her mother each described their relationship as close, and Erin expressed feeling supported by her mother. She said, however, that in the past her mother didn't always believe her when she told her about being bullied, for example about "being chased around the schoolyard by this kid waving his fists and saying 'I'm going to hurt you.'" Erin explained that her mother "thought it was happening so often that she was thinking, 'Is Erin really telling me the truth because this is happening so often?'" Erin exclaimed, "And of course I was!" She stated, "To assume that it is true is much better than to assume that it's not true.

*When my mom doesn't believe me, it's sort of hard because then you have no
support. So when you have no support in dealing with the issue, it is not going
to stop. Although kids can do something, children cannot always deal with this
kind of situation. I mean, we just can't on our own. It is not as if we were born
with some sort of sense of what to do here, what to do there. So we need help in
that situation.*" Erin's mother had no idea that Erin was being excluded at her
current school and explained that when she first heard, she had worried that "*it
was something worse. I thought somebody was pushing her or hitting her or
something like that.*" She felt relieved to hear that her daughter was only being
socially excluded because "*this is what kids do.*" Her mother corroborated Erin's
view that in the past she did not always believe Erin's accounts of being bullied,
which she attributed to her daughter's tendency to be "*dramatic.*"

Surprised that Erin reported being bullied, her teacher observed, "*It never
occurred to me that Erin would be bullied because she can stand up for herself
and is liked and well adjusted.*" Furthermore, Erin was a solid student, which
was at odds with the teacher's assumption that bullying "*would affect your
concentration and grades.*"

Interventions to address bullying, typically school-based, have had
mixed success. Reasons for this variable effectiveness include inconsistent
institutional and societal commitment, prohibitive time and personnel
demands, and teacher and school variables (Kallestad and Olweus 2003).

There is consensus that interventions must encompass all levels, including the school, the classroom and peers, parents, and the individual children involved in bullying, and that the interventions must be supported
by broader structural initiatives (Olweus 1993). Effective programs involve
identifying and intervening with students considered at risk; providing
education to all students on skills, strategies, nonviolent problem solving,
and information to foster a positive social and learning environment; and
developing interventions that promote a safer, more caring, and responsive climate (Twemlow and Cohen 2003). Twemlow and Cohen add that
"at the end of the day all violence prevention programs come down to relationships: our ability to listen to ourselves, to recognize others' experience and use this information to solve problems, to learn and be creative
together" (121).

RESPONDING TO ERIN

Several features of Erin's experience of bullying leave her vulnerable to
feeling traumatized: the repetitive nature of her exclusion, not having been

previously believed by her mother, the lack of awareness by both her mother and her teacher of her current exclusion, and her mother's lack of appreciation for the seriousness of relational bullying.

The social worker responded in several ways. First, she appreciated the seriousness of indirect bullying. Relational aggression has only recently been recognized as a distinct form of bullying, and it has been used to describe the ways in which girls tend to bully (Crick and Grotpeter 1996). There is evidence of the potentially severe effects of relational bullying (Owens et al. 2000). Nevertheless, both children and adults often either do not consider indirect or relational aggression as bullying or view it as less serious (Mishna, Pepler, and Wiener 2006), which can lead to overlooking the damage of this form of bullying.

Erin was subjected to repeated exclusion and victimization by peers that she considered friends, and she was negatively affected by this behavior. A definition of bullying that encompassed social exclusion allowed Erin to realize that she had the right not to be treated in such a manner. The social worker validated and helped Erin articulate her responses.

In addition to working with Erin, the social worker responded by providing information for Erin and her parents and teacher on the potentially devastating impact of bullying behaviors that are not obvious or that do not appear to be serious (Craig, Henderson, and Murphy 2000). This education can also occur with the whole class or school, and the social worker planned how to do that in this case. With Erin's permission, she provided information about the seriousness of exclusion and indirect bullying to Erin's parents, in order to help them take the events seriously and respond appropriately. Similarly, the social worker needed to work with the teacher to increase her understanding of the complexity of bullying. It appeared that the teacher's assumptions about characteristics that victims would display—for example, that they would not be well adjusted or well liked—might have been one factor that prevented her from recognizing that Erin was bullied and that it was having a detrimental effect on her.

Erin considered the children who bullied her to be friends. Having or desiring a friendship with the child who bullies may inhibit the victimized child's ability to disclose (Mishna 2004). The social worker therefore had to balance her recognition that this behavior constitutes bullying with an understanding that Erin might be afraid of acknowledging to herself or disclosing to others this problematic behavior, for fear of losing the friendship. Despite her newfound awareness that she should not be excluded by her friends, Erin was faced with the very real dilemma of how to act on that recognition, since the potential loss of her friends may have seemed too big a risk. Children in grades three and four are more likely to ask a teacher for help when they do not care about maintaining a friendship with the child who was the aggressor (Newman, Murray, and Lussier 2001). If children do want to continue the friendship, they find it hard to protect themselves; Mishna (2004) found that one girl could not use her teacher's advice to stay away from a boy who physically bullied her "because we've been a little bit friends for a year."

By and large, friendship is depicted as positive and as a source of protection for victimized children (Grotpeter and Crick 1996). Having friendships can ameliorate the negative effects of victimization and decrease the likelihood that a child will continue to be bullied (Hanish and Guerra 2000). Nevertheless, it must be recognized that "dyadic friendships can either diminish or reinforce the peer victimized child's vulnerabilities" (Crick and Nelson 2002:599). Children's friendships are foundational for the acquisition of skills and competencies (Newcomb and Bagwell 1995) and may serve as prototypes for later relationships, such as those with romantic partners (Laursen and Bukowski 1997). Without information to the contrary, adults might believe that leaving children to their own devices in navigating friendship fosters growth. Social workers have an important role to play in working with adults to intervene, in order to help children deal with bullying within friendships. For instance, Erin clearly needed support to reject being bullied as part of her friendships.

Erin was displaying negative effects of being bullied, such as dreading school and wanting to avoid it despite being a strong student; she was also blaming and hurting herself. Without support and interventions by trusted adults, Erin's behavior could have potentially escalated into sustained self-harming behavior and school avoidance, resulting in deterioration of her grades. Erin clearly had many protective factors, including individual characteristics as well as her positive relationships with her parents and her teacher, upon which it was necessary to build (Baldry and Farrington 2005).

Even after recognizing that she was being bullied, Erin did not tell her parents or teacher. Often, reported bullying underestimates the problem, precisely because many children do not admit to being victimized (Hanish and Guerra 2000). Even if the children do report it, sometimes adults doubt children's feelings or do not view incidents as bullying, even though the child was upset or felt bullied (Mishna 2004; Mishna et al. 2005). The adult's conclusion shapes his or her response (Craig et al. 2000). Doubting a child's perspective may contribute to his or her lack of disclosure to teachers (Mishna et al. 2006). "The victims internalize the implied message that the adults have discounted their worth as individuals, and they carry this message forward into adulthood" (Clarke and Kiselica 1997:316).

It is critical that adults listen to and validate the child's experience of victimization. Failure to do so can lead to the child's feeling traumatized (Stolorow and Atwood 1992), to doubting his or her own feelings and views, and to not telling adults about the victimization. Erin articulated that she and other children needed to be believed and helped by adults with bullying situations, and she clearly stated the danger when this does not occur. Her ability to recognize the need for adult help was a protective factor, but it did not negate her vulnerability if adults did not listen or did not believe her account.

Recognizing that children are reluctant to volunteer information about their involvement in bullying, the social worker must take responsibility for looking for clues of bullying involvement and asking direct questions. For instance, it was important that the social worker be alert to whether Erin's victimization entailed racial bullying, since research has shown that disparagement of a person's race is among the most typical forms of bullying (Nansel et al. 2001). For example, the social worker might determine whether Erin's peers made derogatory comments regarding her race when they told her to go away.

It is imperative also to become informed about new forms of victimization, such as cyber bullying (Smith 2004). Communication technologies are changing how individuals interact and learn. The Internet has created a new world of social communications, particularly for young people whose use of e-mail, Web sites, instant messaging, Web cams, chat rooms, text messaging, and social networking sites is exploding worldwide. These electronic communication tools can also be used as a method through which children and youth are bullied by their peers.

Vicarious Traumatization in Responding to Bullying

Vicarious traumatization refers to "the transformation that occurs within the therapist (or other trauma workers) as a result of empathic engagement with clients' trauma experiences and their sequelae" (Pearlman and MacIan 1995:558) and can lead to therapeutic impasses. The prevalence of bullying suggests that a sizable percentage of adults may have had experiences with bullying (Kallestad and Olweus 2003; Mishna et al. 2005; Mishna et al. 2006). Hence, practitioners who work with children and adolescents involved in bullying and other forms of school violence must deal with feelings of their own that may be raised when working with the children, parents, and educators, to respond effectively and to prevent the work from being compromised.

Erin's social worker had many years of experience working with children and adolescents who experienced sexual and physical abuse, death and school bullying and violence. She was thoughtful, caring, and conscientious about continuing her own professional development. She found work with Erin to be rewarding and noted Erin's ability to articulate her concerns and reflect upon herself and her interactions. After several sessions, the social worker began to feel decidedly impatient with Erin's dilemma about how to respond to the friends who sometimes excluded her yet at other times were welcoming. Rather than exploring Erin's responses, as she typically would, the social worker advised Erin to end these friendships because they "obviously are not friends." Erin accused the social worker of not understanding, and the result was an impasse in the therapy. After reflection and consultation, the social worker realized that Erin's experiences touched on her own experiences of being excluded and rejected by several "friends" when she was in middle school. The social worker had suffered with low self-esteem after that and as a result of her shame had never mentioned the incidents to anyone. Until now, the social worker had not even considered those experiences particularly significant, but exploring Erin's intense pain had triggered her memory of these long-ago experiences that she'd thought she'd forgotten. This recognition allowed the social worker to separate her own feelings from Erin's and thus to repair the impasse.

Reflections on the Seven Empowerment Principles

BUILDING ON STRENGTHS WHILE DIMINISHING OPPRESSIONS

To build on children's strengths or protective factors and to diminish oppressions and risk factors (Baldry and Farrington 2005), it is necessary to include social relations at all levels—peers, parents, teachers, and school administrators. Preventive interventions are required that provide information and support to the entire school population, rather than to just the children who are involved in bullying, with the aim of preventing bullying and the negative consequences and potential trauma for children who might otherwise be victimized (Elinoff, Cafouleas, and Sassu 2004).

Erin expanded her understanding of what constitutes bullying behavior, which helped her to feel she had "rights." Reinforcing this newfound strength requires the significant adults in Erin's life to (1)listen to and validate her experiences and feelings, (2)help her deal with her feelings and find ways to respond effectively to peers, including friends, when they exclude her, and (3)provide education and strategies to peers regarding bullying behavior.

Erin believed it was her fault that she was excluded. It was critical to help her attribute her exclusion to factors other than herself, in order to prevent further erosion of her self-esteem (Twemlow and Cohen 2003). After reading the definition of bullying, Erin realized she should not be excluded, which demonstrated her receptiveness to altering her attributions about the bullying behavior. She needed support on a variety of levels to transform this initial shift in thinking from "there must be something wrong with me" to "I should not be treated this way." Such support was empowering, preventing further erosion of her self-esteem, and mediating the experience of exclusion so that it no longer needed to become traumatic. Erin could then develop effective coping behaviors in response to bullying treatment by her peers.

The manner in which a school manages social aggression is critical in preventing psychosocial and academic problems for the children who are involved (Twemlow and Cohen 2003). Erin, for instance, needed her school and teacher to respond to the seriousness of social exclusion and the right of each child to be listened to and treated well. Otherwise, her shift in thinking about her exclusion might not be sustained, which could put her at risk to feel traumatized and to deteriorate in her social, emotional, and academic functioning.

ENACTING MULTICULTURAL RESPECT

Among the reasons for the variable outcomes of school-wide programs is inadequate adaptation of programs to each school's particular characteristics and culture (Astor et al. 2005). The increasing diversity of student populations demands that interventions incorporate strategies to work with culturally diverse groups (Brinson et al. 2004). Groups that are at increased risk for victimization include students who identify as lesbian, gay, bisexual, or transgender (LGBT) (Murdock and Bolch 2005), students who are nonwhite (Smith 2004), and students with exceptionalities, learning disabilities, and conditions that affect their appearance or mobility (Thompson, Whitney, and Smith 1994).

WORKING FROM AN AWARENESS OF SPECIFIC NEEDS

Along with broad-based interventions that target all students and interventions that are tailored to the particular school and students, it is necessary to identify children who are at risk or who are beginning to show signs of problems, in order to prevent escalation (Elinoff et al. 2004; Twemlow and Cohen 2003). Although Erin appeared to be doing well and was articulate, she fit this category. She had been physically bullied in the past and was currently excluded by peers, which was affecting her self-esteem and her attitude toward attending school. Helping Erin cope effectively at this point could prevent escalation of her difficulties. Fortunately, she was receptive to seeing a social worker.

Interventions aimed at bullying must address the dynamics and the attachment issues inherent in friendships and bullying among friends (Mishna 2004; Mishna et al. 2006). It appeared that Erin complied with these children's demands to go away and blamed herself for the situation. Fox and Boulton (2005) suggest that although at times non-assertive behavior is adaptive in response to bullying, at other times this behavior suggests a lack of effective social skills. Hence, it was important to determine whether Erin required assistance to manage interactions with friends, and to determine the skills with which she needed help (Asher, Parker, and Walker 1996).

ASSISTING CLIENTS—INDIVIDUALS, GROUPS, FAMILIES, ORGANIZATIONS, COMMUNITIES—AS THEY EMPOWER THEMSELVES

Programs must be developed in response to the unique needs of each school to ensure that interventions are planned together with schools and communities. The following beliefs underlie successful programs: "The efforts to fit a program to a school should involve grassroots participation, that students and teachers need to be empowered to deal with the problem, that democracy is at the core of a good violence program, and that schools should demonstrate a proactive vision about the violence problem in the school" (Astor et al. 2005:30). Interventions at multiple levels provide support and structure for the involved students and adults to learn and to make changes that are adaptive and empowering.

INTEGRATING THE SUPPORT NEEDED FROM OTHERS

Punitive approaches instituted by schools, for instance metal detectors and "zero tolerance" policies, are at odds with the findings on positive outcomes from programs that foster prosocial skills and provide nurturance and acceptance for students (Twemlow et al. 2002). Despite their reluctance to report bullying, a significant number of students ask for help and often find interventions by parents, teachers, and peers to be effective (Hunter, Boyle, and Warden 2004). When asked how to solve bullying, children advise involving adults (Mishna 2004). Erin clearly recognized her need for adult support. An important role of the social worker would be to assist Erin's parents and teacher in responding to her victimization experiences. Erin would require support from adults and if possible other students as she attempted to rectify the situation.

Most anti-bullying programs encourage victimized children to tell their parents or teachers in order to get help to put an end to the situation (Hunter et al. 2004). Various factors influence how adults respond to bullying incidents and consequently whether they provide the needed support (Craig et al. 2000; Kallestad and Olweus 2003; Mishna et al. 2006). Social workers can help teachers and parents become conscious of their views and attitudes. If a child turns to an adult who does not consider the situation bullying, the adult must respond in a way that does not invalidate the child's perspective. It is essential to ensure that when children do tell, adults respond in such a way that further encourages children to tell.

EQUALIZING POWER DIFFERENTIALS

Bullying results from a power imbalance (Pepler et al. 2004; Smith 2004). Hence, along with interventions that address problem and conflict resolution skills, the school culture must be changed so that bullying behaviors are not supported.

Certain practices in schools, communities, and society represent systemic abuses of power. These must be addressed before school bullying problems can be expected to improve (Twemlow et al. 2003). Smith (2004) writes: "The concern with the 'systematic abuse of power' in schools has a legitimate and important focus on relationships in school (and even on pupil-pupil relationships primarily), but it is also part of a wider set of relationships and issues in schools, communities and societies that we are still grappling with, and will continue to be doing for the foreseeable future" (101–102).

An example of equalizing power differentials within the social worker/client dyad was the realization on the part of the social worker that her attempt to direct Erin to drop her friends stemmed more from her own feelings. She took steps to own those feelings and change the directive stance she had been taking with Erin.

USING COOPERATIVE ROLES

The recognition that support is needed and that many students do not talk to their parents or teachers about victimization has led to the implementation of programs utilizing peer support (Hunter et al. 2004). Peer interventions must include curricula that incorporate activities that foster social cognition, such as perspective taking, problem solving, and conflict resolution (Dill et al. 2004); programs to change students' attitudes that support bullying (Owens et al. 2000); and interventions to reduce bystanders' encouragement of bullying (Salmivalli 1999).

Peer mediation has increasingly been utilized to address bullying, although more research is needed to determine its effectiveness (Smith 2004). Fostering a positive school climate requires both that educators as well as students increase their skills and that teachers make use of bullying incidents as an opportunity to engage the class in a mutual discussion on bullying and roles (Twemlow et al. 2003).

Conclusion and Recommendations

An increased emphasis on human rights and the recognition that individuals' rights are commonly abused seem to be an impetus for the recent focus on victimization among children and adolescents. These rights include "not being harassed or discriminated against by virtue of sex, race, disability, sexual orientation, personality or circumstance" (Smith 1997:254). Bullying is a pervasive form of victimization that can have widespread and lasting repercussions. Bullying can be experienced by children as traumatic as a result of the severity, type, or frequency of the victimization. Regardless of the nature or associated features of the victimization, however, a child can feel traumatized if adults do not intervene appropriately.

The bullying dynamic calls for a perspective that takes into account the inherent complexities involved—the individual and the social and environmental context. Erin's trauma as a result of being bullied by girls she considered her friends was transformed through the work she and the social worker began—work that also included bringing in her mother, the teachers, and eventually the school system. The adult-child relationship in particular empowers children's ability to manage in many areas, and especially in bullying situations.

References

Aronson, E. 2004. "How the Columbine High School Tragedy Could Have Been Prevented." *Journal of Individual Psychology* 60 (4): 355–360.

Asher, S. R., J. G. Parker, and D. Walker. 1996. "Distinguishing Friendship from Acceptance: Implications for Intervention and Assessment." In W. M. Bukowski, A. F. Newcomb, and W. W. Hartup, eds., *The Company They Keep: Friendships in Childhood and Adolescence*, 366–405. Cambridge, U.K.: Cambridge University Press.

Astor, R. A. 1995. "School Violence: A Blueprint for Elementary School Interventions." *Social Work in Education* 19 (2): 101–115.

Astor, R. A., H. A. Meyer, R. Benbenishty, R. Marachi, and M. Rosemond. 2005. "School Safety Interventions: Best Practices and Programs." *Children and Schools* 27 (1): 17–32.

Atlas, R. S., and D. J. Pepler. 1998. "Observations of Bullying in the Classroom." *Journal of Educational Research* 92 (2): 86–99.

Baldry, A. C., and D. P. Farrington. 2005. "Protective Factors as Moderators of Risk Factors in Adolescence Bullying." *Social Psychology of Education* 8:263–284.

Brinson, J. A., J. A. Kottler, and T. A. Fisher. 2004. "Cross-Cultural Conflict Resolution in the Schools: Some Practical Intervention Strategies for Counselors." *Journal of Counseling and Development* 82 (3): 294–301.

Clarke, E. A., and M. S. Kiselica. 1997. "A Systemic Counseling Approach to the Problem of Bullying." *Elementary School Guidance and Counseling* 31:310–325.

Craig, W. M., K. Henderson, and J. G. Murphy. 2000. "Prospective Teachers' Attitudes Toward Bullying and Victimization." *School Psychology International* 21 (1): 5–21.

Crick, N. R., and J. K. Grotpeter. 1996. "Children's Treatment by Peers: Victims of Relational and Overt Aggression." *Development and Psychopathology* 8:367–380.

Crick, N. R., and D. A. Nelson. 2002. "Relational and Physical Victimization Within Friendships: Nobody Told Me There'd Be Friends Like These." *Journal of Abnormal Child Psychology* 30 (6): 599–607.

Dill, E. J., E. M. Vernberg, P. Fonagy, S. W. Twemlow, and B. K. Gamm. 2004. "Negative Affect in Victimized Children: The Roles of Social Withdrawal, Peer Rejection, and Attitudes Toward Bullying." *Journal of Abnormal Child Psychology* 32 (2): 159–173.

Elinoff, M. J., S. M. Cafouleas, and K. A. Sassu. 2004. "Bullying: Consideration for Defining and Intervening in School Settings." *Psychology in the Schools* 41 (8): 887–897.

Fox, C. L., and M. J. Boulton. 2005. "The Social Skills Problems of Victims of Bullying: Self, Peer, and Teacher Perceptions." *British Journal of Educational Psychology* 75:313–328.

Greenfield, P. M., and J. Juonen. 1999. "A Developmental Look at Columbine." *APA Monitor Online* 30 (7).

Grotpeter, J. K., and N. R. Crick. 1996. "Relational Aggression, Overt Aggression, and Friendship." *Child Development* 67:2328–2338.

Hanish, L. D., and N. G. Guerra. 2000. "Children Who Get Victimized at School: What Is Known? What Can Be Done?" *Professional School Counseling* 4 (2): 113–119.

Hartup, W. W. 1992. "Friendships and Their Developmental Significance." In H. McGurk, ed., *Childhood Social Development*, 175–205. Gove, U.K.: Erlbaum.

Hunter, S. C., J. M. E. Boyle, and D. Warden. 2004. "Help Seeking Amongst Child and Adolescent Victims of Peer-Aggression and Bullying: The Influence of School-Stage, Gender, Victimisation, Appraisal, and Emotion." *British Journal of Educational Psychology* 74 (3): 375–390.

Janson, G. R., and R. J. Hazler. 2004. "Trauma Reactions of Bystanders and Victims to Repetitive Abuse Experiences." *Violence and Victims* 19:239–255.

Kallestad, J. H., and D. Olweus. 2003. "Predicting Teachers' and Schools' Implementation of the Olweus Bullying Prevention Program: A Multilevel Study." *Prevention and Treatment* 6 (21) [Article A] Retrieved January 15, 2006, from http://content.apa.org/journals/pre/6/1/21.

Laursen, B., and W. M. Bukowski. 1997. "A Developmental Guide to the Organisation of Close Relationships." *International Journal of Behavioral Development* 21 (4): 747–770.

Mishna, F. 2004. "A Qualitative Study of Bullying from Multiple Perspectives." *Children and Schools* 26 (4): 234–247.

Mishna, F., D. J. Pepler, and J. Wiener. 2006. "Factors Associated with Perceptions and Responses to Bullying Situations by Children, Parents, Teachers, and Principals." *Victims and Offenders* 1 (3): 255–288.

Mishna, F., I. Scarcello, D. J. Pepler, and J. Wiener. 2005. "Teachers' Understanding of Bullying." *Canadian Journal of Education* 28 (4): 667–691.

Murdock, T. B., and M. B. Bolch. 2005. "Risk and Protective Factors for Poor School Adjustment in Lesbian, Gay, and Bisexual (LGB) High School Youth: Variable and Person-Centered Analyses." *Psychology in the Schools* 42 (2): 159–172.

Nansel, T. R., M. Overpeck, R. S. Pilla, W. J. Ruan, B. Simons-Morton, and P. Scheidt. 2001. "Bullying Behaviors Among U.S. Youth: Prevalence and Association with Psychosocial Adjustment." *JAMA* 285:2094–2100.

Newcomb, A. F., and C. L. Bagwell. 1995. "Children's Friendship Relations: A Meta-Analytic Review." *Psychological Bulletin* 117 (2): 306–347.

Newman, R. S., B. Murray, and C. Lussier. 2001. "Confrontation with Aggressive Peers at School: Students' Reluctance to Seek Help from the Teacher." *Journal of Educational Psychology* 93 (2): 398–410.

O'Connell, P., D. Pepler, and W. Craig. 1999. "Peer Involvement in Bullying: Insights and Challenges for Intervention." *Journal of Adolescence* 22:437–452.

Olweus, D. 1978. *Aggression in the Schools: Bullies and Whipping Boys.* Washington, D.C.: Hemisphere.

——. 1991. "Bully/Victim Problems Among Schoolchildren: Basic Facts and Effects of a School Based Intervention Program." In D. Pepler and K. Rubin, eds., *The Development and Treatment of Childhood Aggression,* 411–448. Hillsdale, N.J.: Erlbaum.

——. 1993. *Bullying at School: What We Know and What We Can Do.* Oxford, U.K.: Blackwell.

——. 1994. "Annotation: Bullying at School: Basic Facts and Effects of a School Based Intervention Program." *Journal of Child Psychology and Psychiatry and Allied Disciplines* 35 (7): 1171–1190.

——. 1997. "Bully/Victim Problems in School: Facts and Interventions." *European Journal of Psychology of Education* 13 (4): 495–510.

Owens, L., R. Shute, and P. Slee. 2000. "'Guess What I Just Heard!' Indirect Aggression Among Teenage Girls in Australia." *Aggressive Behavior* 26:67–83.

Pearlman, L. A., and P. MacIan. 1995. "Vicarious Traumatization: An Empirical Study of the Effects of Trauma Work on Trauma Therapists." *Professional Psychology: Research and Practice* 26 (6): 558–565.

Pellegrini, A. D. 1998. "Bullies and Victims in School: A Review and Call for Research." *Journal of Applied Developmental Psychology* 19 (2): 165–176.

Pepler, D., W. Craig, A. Yuile, and J. Connolly. 2004. "Girls Who Bully: A Developmental and Relational Perspective." In M. Putallaz and K. L. Bierman, eds.,

Aggression, Antisocial Behavior, and Violence Among Girls: A Developmental Perspective, 90–109. Duke Series in Child Development and Public Policy. New York: Guilford.

Salmivalli, C. 1999. "Participant Role Approach to School Bullying: Implications for Interventions." *Journal of Adolescence* 22:453–459.

Slee, P. 1994. "Situational and Interpersonal Correlates of Anxiety Associated with Peer Victimization." *Child Psychiatry and Human Development* 25 (2): 97–107.

——. 1995. "Bullying in the Playground: The Impact of Interpersonal Violence on Australian Children's Perceptions of Their Play Environment." *Children's Environments* 12 (3): 320–327.

Smith, P. K. 1997. "Bullying in Life-Span Perspective: What Can Studies of School Bullying and Workplace Bullying Learn from Each Other?" *Journal of Community and Applied Social Psychology* 7:249–255.

——. 2004. "Bullying: Recent Developments." *Child and Adolescent Mental Health* 9 (3): 98–103.

Stolorow, R. D., and G. E. Atwood. 1992. *Contexts of Being: The Intersubjective Foundations of Psychological Life*. Hillsdale, N.J.: Analytic Press.

Thompson, D., I. Whitney, and P. K. Smith. 1994. "Bullying of Children with Special Needs in Mainstream Schools." *Support for Learning* 9 (3): 103–106.

Twemlow, S. W., and J. Cohen. 2003. "Guest Editorial: Stopping School Violence." *Journal of Applied Psychoanalytic Studies* 5 (2): 117–123.

Twemlow, S. W., P. Fonagy, and F. C. Sacco. 2002. "Feeling Safe in School." *Smith College Studies in Social Work* 72 (2): 303–326.

——. 2003. "Modifying School Aggression." *Journal of Applied Psychoanalytic Studies* 5 (2): 211–222.

van der Kolk, B. A., A. C. McFarlane, and L. Weisaeth, eds. 1996. *Traumatic Stress: The Effects of Overwhelming Experience on Mind, Body, and Society*. New York: Guilford.

7

Insidious Trauma and the Sexual Minority Client

LAURA KAPLAN

Beth is a 30-year-old woman who has lived with her partner, Cindy, for five years. At first she reports she is happier than she ever remembers being; she has a job that pays enough for her to afford regular bills and yearly vacations; and they have supportive friends. Beth entered counseling because she often feels sad and unsure of herself. She was recently promoted to a supervisory position at work but believes her abilities are inadequate for the job.

Since her job promotion four months ago, Beth has lost fifteen pounds although she has not been dieting. "I just have no appetite; I just don't feel much like eating. Mostly I want to sleep. I can't seem to get enough of that except I must be having sad dreams because even though it looks like my life is going well today, I am worried, feeling like there's nothing ahead for me. I'm worried about Cindy leaving me. For a long time I've felt like things are just not working out so well." Over the last three years or so, when she thought her life was "really together," she still felt sad and more negative than positive about the future. Beth is fearful of being "found out that I don't know what I'm doing at work." She worries that she will not be able to take care of herself or Cindy as they age and about "ending up alone when I'm old." "I just feel pretty useless, and I'm tired of feeling like I'm always struggling to climb a mountain that's got nothing at the top anyway."

The ideas and examples of empowerment practice with the sexual minority client presented here are not in response to a hierarchy of principles and interventions to be followed step by step. As with most things, one size does not fit all. The following discussion, using the case of Beth, is intended to raise awareness about the influence of oppression and other social factors upon the therapeutic relationship and to enhance the reader's ability to transform those influences into empowering practice responses.

Understanding Insidious Trauma and Major Depressive Disorder in the Sexual Minority Population

People who experience trauma do not always present to mental health professionals with symptoms of post-traumatic stress disorder (PTSD) or acute stress disorder (ASD). People frequently continue to live beyond the traumatic incidents and make adaptations in their daily lives. Often the adaptation rather than the trauma is what brings a client in for services. For example, in her narrative, Beth does not disclose a traumatic event; this is not her reason for seeking assistance. She is concerned about feeling hopeless and worried about losing her job and her lover. She speaks about depressive symptoms rather than a specific identifiable stressor in her life. Her complaints may reflect adaptive patterns to living with prolonged trauma. Although the skilled therapist would likely address this possibility, it may be dismissed if it is determined that Beth has no history of physical, sexual, or psychological abuse in her childhood or adult relationships. However, "depression is among the clearest symptomatic responses to trauma" (Fallot and Harris 2002:479).

Trauma commonly underlies many psychosocial problems: depression; fears about social interactions or being in public; social withdrawal; shame; guilt; beliefs that one is not as good as other people; difficulties in making oneself feel safe physically or emotionally; difficulties in developing trust in relationships; experiences of dissociation, numbing, or "spacing out"; difficulties with sleeping or eating; and substance abuse (Broman 2003; Fallot and Harris 2002). Individuals presenting with such symptoms may be diagnosed with mood or anxiety disorders rather than identified as having reactions to trauma, since these disorders are closely associated with trauma.

Beth's concerns about her work, relationship, and daily living activities—experiences that most people have in living day to day—become areas of greater concern for people who are sexual minorities. She worries about what her landlord thinks about renting to her and Cindy. She wonders if as a supervisor she is expected to attend social events, and whether spouses are expected to attend. Is she out at work? Would this be detrimental to her career and work relationships? Do Beth and Cindy need partnership benefits and are these available? Are Beth and Cindy thinking about long-term plans in their relationship, such as having children or purchasing a home? Such thoughts may be stressful to most people. But for lesbian, gay, bisexual, or transgender (LGBT) people who do not have legal rights as a given, there is always the reminder of living in a society that sees you as being less than other citizens and inherently wrong. This is not simply a matter of having to spend more money for legal contracts between partners (no small matter, this can be an expense that is simply out of reach for many people). Whatever brings LGBT clients in for services, trauma must be considered as a factor in their lives.

Trauma is not only seen as an isolated incident. It also includes the societal influences on the trauma experience. It is part of the normal experience of people who are members of oppressed groups, and it is reinforced by the way social institutions treat and react to the victim (Brown 2004). Members of these oppressed groups experience ongoing traumas in trying to live their daily lives. These insidious or

> subthreshhold traumatic stressors . . . include exposure to (a) news that a member of one's group has been the target of bias-based violence or discrimination; (b) negative and stigmatizing images of one's group in media, textbooks, and discourse of peers or coworkers; and (c) various forms of institutionalized racism, heterosexism, and other exclusionary systems of value in which the individual is denied access to material or human resources solely on the basis of group membership.
>
> (Brown 2004:466)

The buildup of these insidious stressors over time can lead to a diagnosis of PTSD. It is not just the violent incident or the natural disaster that results in a trauma response; repeated stressors over time, either individual or ongoing, may result in symptoms of mental health disorders or problems in living. Oppressed groups experience incidents of physical, psychological, social, and historical trauma across their lifetimes.

Mood, anxiety, substance abuse disorders, and comorbidity of these occur at higher prevalence rates among gay men and lesbians than among the heterosexual population (Cochran, Sullivan, and Mays 2003). This higher prevalence of mental health disorders in this population is likely due to the difficulties of being part of a stigmatized group. Research indicates that depression, lack of support, substance abuse, and a history of victimization are linked to suicidal thoughts and behavior in sexual minority youth (Russell and Joyner 2001). The absence of support, repeated victimizations of varying severity, struggles with self-acceptance, and prejudice as reflected in legal, social, and mental health systems increase the risk for mental health disorders.

Research on the prevalence of mental health disorders among populations of sexual minorities is limited. Much of it is based upon small sample sizes, often because of limitations such as having to use existing mental health databases that do not clearly distinguish between sexual orientations, lack of response to surveys by sexual minorities (Cochran et al. 2003:59), and the low number of participants in older age groups (D'Augelli and Grossman 2001:1009). Additionally, there is a risk of bias in that people who are willing to admit in research, or in public, that they are sexual minorities, are more likely to be found in larger cities, where variations in sexual orientation may be more common among the general population and may be protected by law. There is also evidence that members of sexual minority groups are more likely than heterosexual people to use mental health services, including support groups (Cochran et al. 2003).

Heterosexism, the belief that heterosexuality should be the norm for all people, "denies, denigrates, and stigmatizes . . . legitimizes hostility, discrimination, and even violence" (Mallon 2001:64) toward lesbian, gay, bisexual, and transgender people. Homophobia is an irrational fear of people whose intimate relationships are primarily with persons of the same sex.

The National Coalition of Anti-Violence Programs found that between 2003 and 2004 there was a significant increase in reported incidents of anti-LGBT violence, including murder, arson, assaults with weapons, harassment, and incidents perpetrated by organized hate groups. There were also increases in incidents targeting LGBT organizations, victims aged 50 and older, coworkers, employees, tenants, neighbors, relatives, and acquaintances (NCAVP 2005). From extreme violence and murder to verbal harassment, victimization has occurred at an increasing rate over the last thirty years. These forms of trauma, insidious if one identifies with the victim group, overt when they happen to the individual, are part of the daily experience of being a sexual minority today. Repeated exposure to the threat of violence in the form of physical or verbal incidents has an incremental effect, can be traumatic, and can lead to symptoms of post-traumatic stress such as dissociative states, flashbacks, and hypervigilance (Brasham and Miehls 2004; Brown 2004). Individuals who are victimized also have "significantly less efficacy and were more likely to attribute set-backs in their life to societal prejudice, compared with victims of non-bias crimes" (Rose and Mechanic 2002:15).

To view Beth's depressive symptoms as a treatable disease, possibly through cognitive therapeutic interventions, is inherently biased in that it holds the client responsible for changing her thoughts and feeling while denying the social experience that influences the way she feels and thinks about her life (Davison 2005). It is often difficult to separate the effects of insidious stressors (e.g., fears of losing one's job, housing, family, partner, property, or fear of physical harm) from the diagnosis of a mental health disorder seen as a disease solely within the individual. Beth does not have to be a victim of violence herself to feel as though her life is threatened. If her view of herself is that she is a person who is vulnerable to harm and that her life may be threatened, that perception will influence her life experience.

Most of us, in order to be able to live without constant anxiety about threats, develop a belief (or illusion) that we will not come to harm. This protective thinking tells us that the world is not out to get us and that we can live our lives from day to day with some sense of meaning and hope-fulness (Otis and Skinner 1996). When this belief is betrayed, psychosocial ramifications ensue. An extreme act of personal violence is not necessary to change our perceptions about safety and worth. Being followed on a street or when leaving a bar, racist or homophobic slurs yelled from a moving car, and finding your car windshield smashed or in some other way vandalized are all frightening experiences in which the victim under-stands that the perpetrator may at any moment become violent. Having profanities screamed at you or having eggs or beer thrown at you is not uncommon in the experience of LGBT people. At the extreme of this continuum of violence, also too frequently against LGBT people, is mur-der. Since sexual minorities are stigmatized in this society, many incidents go unreported because of the fear of further victimization by authorities or communities once the individual is identified as LGBT. Additionally, vic-tims may believe that the incident was not a reportable offense; victims see no point in reporting it because the perpetrators left the scene and would not be identifiable; or, when the perpetrator was a family member, it was considered a personal rather than a police matter (Herek, Cogan, and Gillis 2002).

The individual is victimized because of her or his identity, cutting to the core of what is integral to people's search for meaning, knowing and accepting oneself. Self-acceptance of one's sexual minority identity involves risk.

Responding to Insidious Trauma with the Sexual Minority Client

In assessing Beth's readiness to change, we first dealt with the presenting issues. It is common for people who identify as sexual minorities to be victims of bias crimes and harassment throughout their lifetimes (Burn, Kadlec, and Rexer 2005; Mallon 2001; Otis and Skinner 1996). Positive attitudes toward sexual minorities are correlated with knowing people who are LGBT, and there is evidence that an effective strategy for overcoming stereotyping is to have personal knowledge about groups that are stereotyped (Burn et al. 2005).

Beth entered counseling to improve her life, to gain confidence in her job, to relieve her worries about the future and her relationship, to sleep better, and to increase satisfaction with her life. Hearing her state these goals and wanting to help her accomplish them is an empowering occurrence. Yet, as a professional dedicated to helping people live full lives, I had to ask the question: Can I expect to help Beth reach her goals when I am aware of the institutional heterosexism that she has to face to reach even simple goals?

First, I asked Beth for more information about her experience of her symptoms—not just duration and severity but specific stories concerning what she believes leads to her feelings and descriptions of the times, places, situations, and with whom she experiences these feelings. She identified feelings of hopelessness, sleeping and eating difficulties, and intimacy concerns. It is difficult to live as a lesbian today. Both feminist and strengths-based perspectives acknowledge that. Next we examined the role of insidious trauma and biases in the context of her stories. Being a lesbian is only one part of Beth's identity. I learned more about how she defines herself from her stories. Some difficulties at work may be attributable to her age, or to being a woman, or to having religious differences or different social interests. It is not helpful to narrowly define issues of oppression or privilege; people experience both in their lives.

What may be normal stressors in the lives of healing professionals may be more traumatic for clients who identify as sexual minorities. Ongoing bias experienced by oppressed populations causes psychosocial distress for individuals. Repeated experiences of bias crimes can result in a diminished ability to cope with stressors over time. Unless we change the situation, or our clients' understanding of their life's context, we are doing them an injustice.

Oppression continues to exist, in part, because the personal remains personal. Unless individuals come forward and speak of their experience, the oppression continues. Empowerment is about speaking up, breaking the silence of the personal trauma in order to change the oppression in the public and private worlds. As professional helpers committed to empowering actions at the personal, interpersonal, and social/community levels, we must break the silence in our own experience.

To deny that heterosexism (or any other oppression) has no effect on our lives serves to reinforce the mentality that maintains the existing oppressive structures. As bell hooks put it, "We can claim our triumph and our pain without shame" (1995:135). Social workers can help clients to see the interconnectedness between the personal and the political as a way to understand the role of societal oppression in the pain and shame of trauma victimization. Using the seven empowerment principles (Lee 2001; Wise 2005) plus interventions at the personal, interpersonal, and social/community levels, I will take a closer look at Beth's situation, heterosexism, and the social worker's role in this case.

Vicarious Trauma

Vicarious trauma, or compassion fatigue, is a risk for the professional who works with sexual minorities, particularly for those who themselves identify as members of oppressed groups. This perspective also makes demands upon the professional. Social workers are expected to assist clients in taking power in their lives. To do so, however, workers must acknowledge their own authority and reevaluate it on personal, professional, interpersonal, and societal levels. Social workers who are experiencing vicarious trauma have the symptoms of PTSD and may cross boundaries with their clients because of their over-identification with client struggles. They may ignore their personal need to resolve problems, or feel helpless with client problems. If clients fail, affected clinicians can become angry with them, give up on them, and disengage from them, or withdraw from their own social and professional lives (James and Gilliland 2005). Agencies should provide staff with supervision, consultation, and referrals to treatment when needed.

Integrating Empowerment Principles with Practice Responses

BUILDING ON STRENGTHS WHILE DIMINISHING OPPRESSIONS

"I just feel pretty useless, and I'm tired of feeling like I'm always struggling to climb a mountain that's got nothing at the top anyway." Beth clearly indicated a belief that things were not working out for her. She could not see her accomplishments; she was aware only of the fear of losing them. Intrinsic to the relationship and a first step to working effectively with her was building trust.

Since she displayed symptoms of depression, I talked with her about a psychiatric consultation. The psychiatrist prescribed medications, and the pharmacological interventions were effective in helping her improve in the areas of sleeping, eating, and energy level as well as increasing her ability to concentrate. In turn, these advances enhanced her readiness for new ways of thinking and acting, and she was better able to cope with her stressors at work and in her relationship. The use of language that built on her strengths while identifying oppressive influences in her daily life helped her to assess her abilities, perceptions, feelings, and goals for change. Using this information, we chose interventions based on several levels of empowerment.

Beth's primary relationships were one focus for empowerment interventions on the interpersonal level at this early stage. To help Beth take control of her life on the interpersonal level, it was important to encourage her to maintain communication with Cindy. I asked Beth to discuss her observations with Cindy, particularly their comfort with the public aspects of their relationship. Open communication, important in any relationship, is particularly crucial for lesbian or gay couples, where individual and couple boundaries, needs, roles, and expectations need to be honestly discussed (Berzon 1997).

Education and information gathering play a significant role in empowering practice. As I worked with Beth and Cindy, I evaluated my own personal beliefs, experiences, and knowledge about heterosexism and its influence on my professional practice. I personally believe that it is important for sexual minorities to be out (disclosure of sexual identity to others) in all aspects of their lives. However, there are risks to this decision, and each person must determine where and when being out is a safe choice.

Some people are out in all of their activities and relationships. Others may feel that it's safe to be out to friends and family but that, because of the type of work they do, it's unsafe to be out to their employers. Teachers and church employees may be out in their social lives but may quite realistically fear the loss of their jobs if employers learn of their sexual orientation. Thus there can be tension between the empowering strategy (being out) and the individual's safety and well-being. How do we empower those without privilege when the best strategies do not enable privilege? This presents a great challenge to professionals working with clients of minority status.

Disclosure of sexual identity is correlated with increased self-esteem and confidence (Barrett and Logan 2002; Berzon 1997). Hostile environments, however, preclude the desire to disclose sexual identity. Full disclosure in all segments of one's life is not always desirable or safe. Coming out is not a dichotomous choice between no disclosure and complete disclosure. Beth, for example, may risk losing her job if she is out at work, but she could be supported if her church community were aware of her sexual identity. Beth and I evaluated this issue, and the choices of where, how, and to whom she can safely disclose, her understanding of safety, and the possible consequences and alternatives to dealing with these issues must be addressed along with Cindy's role in the decision. Here it is helpful for the social worker to understand the risks involved in advising for or against disclosure, including what it means to her or him to have sexual minorities come forward to break their silence. It is not a simple matter, but can be an empowering process for both the client and the professional.

Exploring Beth's comfort in the workplace and community with respect to her relationship with Cindy provided information about how safe she feels in these settings. Is she comfortable talking about how they spent the weekend, holding hands in public, attending work events with Cindy? If Beth feels safe in these behaviors, she can be congratulated on taking risks. If she is unwilling to engage in such behaviors, it is important to acknowledge her strength in maintaining a relationship in the face of such stress. Learning more about what feels safe and not safe to Beth and Cindy in their daily activities is critical to determining their willingness to take risks, and in identifying the influence of oppression in their lives.

Interventions on this interpersonal level may include asking Beth to pay attention to people at work. Do they have photos of partners/spouses in view? Do they discuss their weekend activities? Do they hold hands? Do they bring their partner/spouses to picnics? Early strategies in the counseling relationship often are simple and can include observing and journal writing, as the client notes the observations and her feelings and thoughts with respect to the experience.

ENACTING MULTICULTURAL RESPECT

Sexual minority victims of bias crimes who seek medical, psychological, or legal help are likely to display symptoms of PTSD or depression. The more victimization one experiences, the more likely it is that the person will seek help (Rose and Mechanic 2002). Thus, it is likely that by the time sexual minority clients present for services, they have experienced bias crimes and they are living daily with verbal harassment personally or through media. The vulnerability that results requires great sensitivity on the part of the professional, making respect in attitude and language critical.

Given the oppressive climate in much of our society, an individual may feel safest by not disclosing sexual orientation to anyone; consequently it is quite possible that a client does not present as a member of a sexual minority when entering the helping relationship. Clients often keep some personal information from the professional, at least until trust is developed. The initial language used in encounters tells the client much about the safety and acceptance of the professional. Even seemingly benign questions, such as "Are you married?" rather than "Do you have a special intimate relationship in your life?" clue the client in on values or judgments that preclude feeling safe and accepted. Appropriate and genuine language is important. Cultural consultants can be of great help. Although it may be appropriate to learn resources and information from the client, the social worker/client relationship should not focus on the professional's educational needs.

As professionals, it is always important for us to examine our own prejudices. Sometimes we are not aware of the depth of them until we start listening and talking with people who are members of oppressed groups. Our environment and the oppressive messages we see and hear influence us in our personal lives and in professional practice.

There is evidence that social workers are accepting of sexual minorities overall, and that knowledge about people who are sexual minorities increases this acceptance (Newman, Dannenfeiser, and Benishek 2002). However, even though research with graduate social work students found a high rate of acceptance for sexual minorities in general, some specific responses were of concern. Participants disagreed with statements that gay couples should have the right to adopt children, that it would not be upsetting to learn one's child is gay or lesbian, that homosexuality is normal in humans as in other species, and that lesbians should not be discriminated against in employment because of their sexual orientation. Responses showed agreement with statements that lesbianism is a sin (Newman et al. 2002). These findings illustrate the difference between "talking the talk" and "walking the walk," as well as the interconnectedness between the personal and the public spheres. The social worker who agrees with these responses may be unaware of the impact of this thinking on work with clients. This social worker may encourage a client not to come out at work, to her family, or to her church. And conversely, if the worker believes everyone should be out, she may encourage the client to take risks for which she is not ready, or that may never be safe for her. In either case, the workers must be responsible for examining their own prejudices, and this is where supervision and discussions with consultants who may have different opinions are recommended.

In the process of helping clients, we cannot assume that membership in one specific group defines the extent of their identities. Few of us define ourselves by one characteristic. Treating Beth only as a lesbian rather than having her define her identity and being inclusive of her as female, adult, daughter, partner, limits our ability to help her gain power in her life.

WORKING FROM AN AWARENESS OF SPECIFIC NEEDS

The social work process involves exploring issues and needs with clients on several levels and considering the interrelatedness of personal, interpersonal, and societal factors in their lives. At the same time, the social worker strives continuously to be aware of the personal nature of these issues and their influence on the therapeutic relationship.

Beth's first personal need was to reduce her distressful symptoms. She felt overwhelmed, and moving too quickly in the process could have increased this discomfort. Cognitive strategies enhanced rest and nutrition and helped reduce her feelings of being overwhelmed, of having low energy, and anxiety. As sleep and nutrition patterns stabilized, her needs moved to self-esteem and relational issues. It was here that raising awareness about heterosexism (and other forms of oppression) influenced her feelings about herself, her potential, and her relationships. It was crucial to balance these comments so as not to attribute all of her stressors to her sexual orientation. Beth said she felt like an impostor at work. We looked at how these feelings might be related to societal prejudices about being a woman; how lethargy relates to the physical and mental vigilance needed to maintain her relationship while keeping secrets; and how feelings of failure and hopelessness relate to the energy it takes to maintain her identity and relationships while experiencing oppressive messages that she is bad or not good enough. Placing these messages in the context of the world in which she lives, rather than seeing herself as the source of the negative feelings, can be empowering.

ASSISTING CLIENTS AS THEY EMPOWER THEMSELVES

It is important to honor the coping strategies that people use to survive in a difficult world. Our clients who identify as sexual minorities have overcome much to reach a point where they can self-identify as LGBT. It takes even more courage to come out to other people, particularly those who are part of a system known for its oppression. The mental health system has a history of pathologizing sexual and gender identity. While homosexuality is not a mental health disorder, gender identity issues remain classified as pathologies (APA 2000). Conversion and reparative therapies are used across the country in spite of condemnation by mental health professionals (Appleby, Colon, and Hamilton 2001). Social workers have opportunities to intervene by advocating against these strategies and educating the public about the truth.

Clients who identified as sexual minorities during their youth may also be survivors of an oppressive child welfare system. Reports of severe sexual and physical abuse and constant verbal abuse by other youths and staff members in residential facilities; ongoing verbal abuse, and sexual and physical assault by family members and foster care providers are commonplace (Mallon 2001). Mallon's examination of youths in the child welfare system found that youths (78 percent) and professionals (88 percent) stated that it is not safe for young people to self-identify as lesbian or gay within group care facilities (65). In agency settings, workers may join the verbal harassment or ignore it (98 percent of the study participants reported that verbal harassment occurred daily in group homes), and crimes of sexual and physical assault (52 percent) may occur with no consequences for the perpetrators (72). For many of these youths the streets seemed safer than group, family, or foster homes. One young man confronted staff for not responding to verbal harassment and was told he should expect harassment if he comes out to others. Four individuals reported being raped, and at least one young woman was raped by a male staff member supposedly as a "corrective" to her lesbianism (Mallon 2001).

Amid the challenges, individuals who are minorities are aware of power in some aspects of their lives. There is power in the young person who chooses the streets instead of an abusive child protection system. People who refuse to deny their sexual orientation or gender identity even while protecting it in some settings, and those who seek help despite knowing that the helping system and its professionals may label, diagnose, and attempt to treat them in ways that are oppressive, experience power. Honoring clients for advocating for themselves is key here. Assisting a client in self-empowerment may be more about the social worker's changing the way she or he thinks about client behaviors and choices than it is about teaching the client.

INTEGRATING THE SUPPORT NEEDED FROM OTHERS

Beth reported that she and Cindy had a supportive group of friends. These relationships were reinforced as part of the intervention process. Joint sessions with Beth and Cindy ensured that both of them were communicating while working toward improving their relationship.

On a community level, I provided information on local and national resources. Beth and Cindy were not aware of some of the policies and laws affecting their lives. Knowing resources and understanding how Beth and Cindy could use them was empowering because of the range of choices available to them. Because a person can be fired on the basis of sexual orientation unless there is a state or local law preventing such dismissal, I gave Beth and Cindy information about protective laws concerning discrimination. Information on advocacy and support groups locally and nationally was also empowering for them at the community level. Part of empowerment at the point where the personal level and the community level overlap is to understand that one is not alone. Other people have similar experiences. Validation of this through community advocacy and support groups is integral to the empowerment process.

One of Beth's conflicts was centered around her strong religious faith. Religious support groups and welcoming, or open and affirming, congregations (designations used by religious communities to identify as accepting of sexual minorities) were recommended. Community social groups, events such as music and arts festivals, community centers, support groups such as Parents and Friends of Lesbians and Gays (PFLAG), professional networks such as Gay Lesbian Straight Educators' Network (GLSEN), and advocacy groups such as the National Gay Lesbian Task Force (NGLTF) provided opportunities for support in various realms of Beth's life. It was important that she know what supports and choices were available, but she herself decided which, if any, to use.

EQUALIZING POWER DIFFERENTIALS

Because of the nature of professional knowledge, skill, responsibilities, and ethics, it is not possible to have an equal relationship with our clients. It is possible, and necessary, however, to engage in open discussions about the existing power differentials in helping relationships and to find the best ways to maintain boundaries, care for ourselves, and assist in the empowerment of clients (Kaplan 2001). These boundaries can be particularly difficult to maintain when the professional is a member of the same population as the client.

My personal beliefs about disclosure, oppression, advocacy, religion and spirituality, the mental health systems, and the connections between personal and public issues must not be imposed upon my clients.

Equalizing the power differentials does not mean that the worker and client know everything about each other. It does mean that the worker honestly supports and assists the client in achieving power over her own life, understanding the choices and consequences, and making decisions from an awareness of self and an awareness of social factors at the personal and public levels.

USING COOPERATIVE ROLES

A key feature of using empowerment viewpoints and strategies with clients is open communication about the therapeutic process. Discussion and clarification of roles, labels and diagnoses, treatment plans, purpose of the relationship and strategies, goals of the client, the worker, and the agency/system in which they are located, and the theoretical background are part of the open process of an empowerment perspective. Ongoing reflection with the client about the process and levels of empowerment, her readiness and ability to make changes, and identification of the change actions are integral to the relationship (Wise 2005). In traditional Western helping systems, the professional's knowledge base is often presented as if it is secret. Much of this information can and should be shared with clients. Who would not want to know that, as frightening and risky as it is, being out actually results in very positive experiences? Just as secrets about trauma and identity preclude a satisfactory personal life and help to maintain oppressive social structures, secrets about the therapeutic process can preclude the possibility of leaving clients with tools they can use to continue growth beyond the professional relationship.

Conclusion and Recommendations

Beth's example is a commonplace scenario in mental health. Clients often present with concerns that appear general—unhappiness in several aspects of life, discomfort or feelings of being overwhelmed in work and relationships, a sense of futility in life with no clear causes. An empowerment approach to transforming trauma responses in which we consider personal, interpersonal, and societal/community influences is recommended to help these individuals.

When working with members of oppressed populations, it is critical to understand that these individuals are victimized in ways that may not be overtly discernible in their presentation to the counseling relationship. Bias crimes and incidents, from verbal harassment to violent acts, occur on a daily basis. Heterosexism and homophobia reinforce marginalization, hate, discrimination, silencing, and violence against sexual minorities (Mallon 2001). Living in an environment where one feels, or is, threatened regularly results in long-term psychosocial distress and trauma reactions (Brown 2004; Burn et al. 2005; Herek et al. 2002; Otis and Skinner 1996). Verbal harassment alone sends a message to people that their identity, values, and beliefs are unacceptable. In a society that claims to be diverse and accepting, individuals feel betrayed (Brown 2004). These incidents and crimes can be addressed within the context of the therapeutic relationship. In order to do so, the professional must be continuously self-aware and reflect upon personal beliefs, judgments, and values. The use of empowerment principles can guide social workers to examine their own experiences, feelings, and beliefs and to consider the ways in which these influence the professional-client relationship.

The empowerment perspective has a goal of "leaving trauma survivors more capable of believing themselves and seeing themselves as a source of authority about their life narratives" (Brown 2004:469). Some individuals take risks such as being out in any form, joining a welcoming congregation, or getting married (Brown 2004). Some clients move from empowerment on a personal level, in acknowledging their own identity and experience of survival, to a societal level, taking action with public advocacy movements. The expansive range of possible actions allows this dual-faceted goal of empowerment—i.e., belief in self and seeing self as a source of authority—to be fully realized.

References

American Psychiatric Association (APA). *Diagnostic and Statistical Manual of Mental Disorders, Text Revision (DSM-IV-TR)*. 4th ed. Washington, D.C.: Author.

Appleby, G. A., E. Colon, and J. Hamilton. 2001. *Diversity, Oppression, and Social Functioning: Person-in-Environment Assessment and Intervention*. Boston: Allyn and Bacon.

Barrett, B., and C. Logan. 2002. *Counseling Gay Men and Lesbians: A Practice Primer*. Pacific Grove, Calif.: Brooks/Cole Thomson.

Berzon, B. 1997. *Permanent Partners: Building Gay and Lesbian Relationships That Last*. New York: Dutton.

Brasham, K., and D. Miehls. 2004. *Transforming the Legacy: Couple Therapy with Survivors of Childhood Trauma*. New York: Columbia University Press.

Broman, C. L. 2003. "Sexuality Attitudes: The Impact of Trauma." *Journal of Sex Research* 40 (4): 351–357.

Brown, L. S. 2004. "Feminist Paradigms of Trauma Treatment." *Psychotherapy: Theory, Research, Practice, Training* 41 (4): 464–471.

Burn, S. M., K. Kadlec, and R. Rexer. 2005. "Effects of Subtle Heterosexism on Gays, Lesbians, and Bisexuals." *Journal of Homosexuality* 49 (2): 23–38.

Cochran, S. D., J. G. Sullivan, and V. M. Mays. 2003. "Prevalence of Mental Disorders, Psychological Distress, and Mental Health Services Use Among Lesbian, Gay, and Bisexual Adults in the United States." *Journal of Consulting and Clinical Psychology* 71 (1): 53–61.

D'Augelli, A. R., and A. H. Grossman. 2001. "Disclosure of Sexual Orientation, Victimization, and Mental Health Among Lesbian, Gay, and Bisexual Older Adults." *Journal of Interpersonal Violence* 16 (10): 1008–1027.

Davison, G. C. 2005. "Issues and Nonissues in the Gay-Affirmative Treatment of Patients Who Are Gay, Lesbian, or Bisexual." *Clinical Psychology: Science and Practice* 12 (1): 25–28.

Fallot, R. D., and M. Harris. 2002. "The Trauma Recovery and Empowerment Model (TREM): Conceptual and Practical Issues in a Group Intervention for Women." *Community Mental Health Journal* 38 (6): 475–485.

Herek, G. M., J. C. Cogan, and J. R. Gillis. 2002. "Victim Experiences in Hate Crimes Based on Sexual Orientation." *Journal of Social Issues* 58 (2): 319–339.

hooks, b. 1995. *Killing Rage, Ending Racism*. New York: Holt.

James, R. K., and B. E. Gilliland. 2005. *Crisis Intervention Strategies*. 5th ed. Belmont: Thomson Brooks/Cole.

Kaplan, L. E. 2001. "Dual Relationships: A Call for Open Discourse." *Professional Ethics* 9 (1): 3–29.

Lee, J. 2001. *The Empowerment Approach to Social Work Practice: Building the Beloved Community*. 2nd ed. New York: Columbia University Press.

Mallon, G. P. 2001. "Sticks and Stones Can Break Your Bones: Verbal Harassment and Physical Violence in the Lives of Gay and Lesbian Youths in Child Welfare Settings." In M. E. Swigonski, R. S. Mama, and K. Ward, eds., *From Hate Crimes to Human Rights: A Tribute to Matthew Shepard*, 63–81. New York: Harrington Park.

National Coalition of Anti-Violence Programs. 2005. *Annual Report on Anti-LGBT Hate Violence*. http://www.ncavp.org/media/MediaReleaseDetail.aspx?p=1420;=1492.

National Institute of Mental Health. 2005. *Facts About Post-Traumatic Stress Disorder*. http://www.nimh.nih.gov/publicat/ptsdfacts.cfm.

Newman, B. S., P. L. Dannenfeiser, and L. Benishek. 2002. "Assessing Beginning Social Work and Counseling Students: Acceptance of Lesbians and Gay Men." *Journal of Social Work Education* 38 (2): 273–288.

Otis, M. D., and W. F. Skinner. 1996. "The Prevalence of Victimization and Its Effect on Well-Being Among Lesbian and Gay People." *Journal of Homosexuality* 30 (3): 93–121.

Rose, S. M., and M. B. Mechanic. 2002. "Psychological Distress, Crime Features, and Help-Seeking Behaviors Related to Homophobic Bias Incidents." *American Behavioral Scientist* 46 (1): 14–26.

Russell, S. T., and K. Joyner. 2001. "Adolescent Sexual Orientation and Suicide Risk: Evidence from a National Study." *American Journal of Public Health* 91 (8): 1276–1281.

Wise, J. B. 2005. "Empowerment Then and Now." In *Empowerment Practice with Families in Distress*, 19–55. New York: Columbia University Press.

8

When a Client Dies
Transforming Agency Grief

MARIAN BUSSEY

The daytime staff heard the news as they arrived one weekday morning: a client at this transitional housing shelter for women and children, located in an inner-city neighborhood in a large midwestern city, had been murdered the night before. News of Sonia's shooting was reported in the morning paper, but in a very small item, with no names. Her death might not even have appeared in the paper except that neighbors in the apartment complex were the ones who made the initial calls to the police. Most staff members who had had time to read the paper that morning before work didn't know it was Sonia, but the night staff had gotten the call from the police. As each case manager arrived that morning, the story was told and retold, and everyone asked, "Have you heard . . . ? What do you know . . . ?" Because the paper hadn't given any names, there was still hope that perhaps it wasn't really her; could someone else have taken her ID? And because the shooter was not identified, there was a lot of speculation: was it the ex? Staff who had worked most closely with Sonia knew that she had moved two states away to try to escape his violence. But if it was her ex, how did he track her that far? Was it someone in the complex who'd watched her move in? Someone off the street?

Not knowing was one of the hardest parts. The staff gathered in small groups, in between the times they needed to attend to current clients and to the business of the day, to talk about what might have happened. The director, who had gotten the call from the night staff, had come in earlier than usual that day and was on the phone much of the morning trying to learn more from the police and to offer the agency's willingness to do whatever it could. But as is typical procedure in such an investigation, the police could not give out certain details to anyone, so the period of not knowing stretched on throughout the morning. After lunch, however, the first real report came in. The police could confirm that the shooter was the husband she had tried to escape and that he had stalked her movements and waited until her first night of independence to kill her.

The transition shelter staff were acquainted with the loss of clients to exposure, to illness related to their time spent living outdoors, or to occasional random street violence. But no matter how often they had dealt with the loss of a client, to know that this tragedy had befallen a young woman who was trying to put her life together after leaving an abusive situation brought up tremendous feelings. Many felt shock and a sense of disbelief—"I can't believe it; she was just here Monday and talking about getting her own place." Others moved swiftly into anger—anger at the man she had tried so hard to leave behind; anger at the system that cannot protect women. Some felt guilt—"Why didn't we see it coming? How could we have warned her?" The hardest part was that the social work staff had to keep going for the current clients. They might grieve in private, but they had to keep the shelter running, keep the other residents informed, and help them deal with their feelings. It was this knowledge of social work's double role that led the director to search for a social worker who could help her agency grieve.

Understanding the Dynamics of Agency and Workplace Grief

A body of information does exist about the loss of a client to suicide and the effects of such an event upon therapists and medical personnel (Strom-Gottfried and Mowbray 2006). It is a difficult situation, and particularly hard on new practitioners and student interns in the helping fields. Mental health agencies are aware of the shock to the therapists involved, and many have a protocol for dealing with such critical incidents. Much less has been written about the loss of a client to murder, yet for the vulnerable populations with whom social workers interact, murder and other violent means of death are unfortunately part of their lives.

The reaction to learning about client death, while not the same as being attacked oneself or seeing someone else attacked, is nonetheless a shock, potentially traumatic, and brings up the issue of traumatic loss and bereavement. Neria and Litz (2003) note that the two fields of trauma theory and bereavement studies have recently begun to create a common conceptualization that merges understandings from both. They believe the term *traumatic bereavement* "should be employed to describe the unique experience of losing a significant other due to sudden, violent, or accidental means. . . . Survivors through a traumatic bereavement have to cope with the trauma and any resulting stress in addition to the death and the grieving process" (78). In their experience, violent death, especially by malicious violence, is particularly hard and creates the greatest potential for ongoing post-loss distress. They emphasize that survivors will often experience feelings of intense anxiety, feelings that are almost inevitable upon the universal recognition of our vulnerability and the constant possibility of our own death.

The experience of a violent death at work (whether of a coworker or a client) or even to be in a state of grief over a private violent death, makes necessary a difficult adjustment in a normally professional climate. It is hard to integrate the two worlds. "Before integrating the loss the grieving person must deal with the effects of trauma and the layer of anxiety it places over day-to-day life. Deaths by suicide or homicide complicate grief, leaving survivors feeling victimized and experiencing a measure of self-blame or shame" (Lattanzi-Licht 2002:172). Moreover, in some workplaces, one is expected to compartmentalize grief and carry on with the job. There may be a degree of psychological reassurance, for both the agency and the workers, in carrying on after loss and grief. In those cases, when "workplace norms typically ask us to separate our personal and professional selves, it is easy for grieving employees to feel unacknowledged" (167). Lattanzi-Licht uses the term *disenfranchised grief* for this unacknowledged state. The transitional housing agency avoided disenfranchising their workers' grief by taking the time to call in a specialist in group crisis and debriefing.

The term *traumatic grief*, according to Jacobs (1999), is being proposed as a diagnosis related to the intensity of distress experienced by the bereaved person, whether or not the death was the result of a traumatic event. This definition sets traumatic grief apart from *traumatic bereavement*, in which the trauma is multiplied by the sudden violence of the death. The feelings of shock, denial, anger, guilt, and sorrow that the staff of the transitional housing center were feeling indicate that they were experiencing traumatic bereavement.

One aspect of a workplace or client death is that it involves a community of grievers, the size of the agency or business. The process of mourning, therefore, is similar to that of larger communities that have faced more public or more widespread loss and disaster (Corr 2003). A community tragedy creates the possibility of a serious and shared grief. Corr points out that the grieving a community does after a tragedy goes beyond the emotional qualities—it is also physiological, cognitive, social, and spiritual. It is hard for any community if traumatic losses follow each other, one after another. This realization is important in mental health and other social work settings, where such losses may build up or may even be seasonal (in the case of client suicide). Corr also links trauma and grief in another way, suggesting that the symptoms of PTSD themselves could be seen as a kind of complicated grief process, with profound and ongoing physical and emotional manifestation.

In order for communities or agencies to move through trauma and loss, they need to grieve together. Williams, Zinner, and Ellis (1999) point to the challenge contained within the crisis, describing the first task of healing as "to acknowledge what has happened to the fullest extent possible" and the second task as "to try to restore community equilibrium" (8). That restored equilibrium may happen in many ways, but it will usually require a group experience of the loss and a search for meaning that becomes part of the community or agency's narrative history. A shared loss from a traumatic death may be more bearable when grieved as a community. "A sense of the shared suffering of others, both in one's immediate social network and among those who have experienced a similar loss, is often a great comfort to people" (McBride and Johnson 2005:283).

Responding to Agency and Workplace Grief

Steven was recommended to the transitional housing shelter by colleagues who knew he had done special training in debriefing work during his previous job at an employee assistance program (EAP). His training provided him with the skills to lead a structured group intervention, four hours in length, which moves in phases from introduction to fact-finding to reactions to closure.

After introductions and setting the stage for what was about to occur, Steven began by recapping what he knew from the agency director about the circumstances of the death. He then invited the staff of the shelter to tell him more about Sonia. "You know, I didn't know Sonia. I've just heard about her. Could you tell me something about her?" He found that several staff had very clear impressions of Sonia. Their memories often took the form of small vignettes—something she had said while waiting with a staff person, her interest in finding out more about her newly adopted city. But with the memories and descriptions came the grief. Several staff were crying, and Steven gave them time to do so. Others were still in a kind of shock, voicing their disbelief that someone so young and so close to her first independent goal could be killed. There was anger at the fact that her husband had been able to trace her path and find her, and they also questioned their own role: "What if we hadn't let her transition out so soon?" But even asking that question brought up the answer: she was ready to go; she had told them that, and she was excited to be moving. She had told her primary caseworker, in particular, on the afternoon ride over to the new place, how much she appreciated the help from the homeless shelter and from the community organization that had given her the vouchers to buy her own household belongings. Hearing that story helped the rest of the staff. It had been Sonia's decision, and they had helped her.

At other debriefings (particularly with commercial businesses), Steven sometimes had to work hard to transition the group through the stages of processing, but with a social work staff, the group itself moved readily through the stages. He did pass out the handouts on normal reactions to a traumatic event—because everyone can use a reminder that this experience may produce some powerful emotional swings, a flood of painful thoughts, and distressing somatic changes, particularly with respect to sleep routines.

As the session was heading toward a close, Steven could see staff begin to return to the immediate present and to make concrete offers of support and empathy for each other, especially for Sonia's primary caseworker. This agency worked well as a unit, and they were concerned for each other. They then turned their concern toward the world Sonia had inhabited. Someone suggested making individual donations and an agency donation, and some wondered what she would have wanted a donation to go to. Finally one person named the community agency that had provided concrete household goods and store vouchers, an agency they frequently worked with and that depended on private funding. This gift, they concluded, would embody her spirit and could bring them a sense of closure.

Steven used a structured form of debriefing, or critical incident response, to help the agency process its shock and grief. The practice of formal debriefing after a traumatic event has spread worldwide and evolved over the past two decades since its inception as a method of helping emergency services teams recover after particularly difficult rescues or disasters, yet it is not without controversy. The procedure will be described first, and then the controversy explored.

A recent update by Everly, Lating, and Mitchell (2005) presents the theory behind debriefing as that of crisis intervention and locates the critical incident stress debriefing (CISD) process itself within a more comprehensive critical incident stress management (CISM) system that will include pre-disaster planning, consultation, education, and referrals for individual ongoing therapy if warranted. Debriefing is "designed to mitigate the psychological impact of a traumatic event and accelerate recovery from acute symptoms of distress that may arise in the immediate wake of a crisis or a traumatic event" (227). The participants are usually a small group or a team of people who have experienced a shared traumatic event. The debriefing is offered to everyone in that situation, as a universal intervention, rather than targeting only those who exhibit the most distress, in recognition of the fact that crisis affects us all, whether we react by showing our emotions or by holding them in. It is not therapy and thus does not call for self-disclosure unless a participant wants to respond in that way. In the CISD model, seven phases move the group members through their reactions to a trauma—from cognitive processing, to emotional processing, and back to cognitive integration at the end:

• Introduction (described as crucial): providing the purpose and framework of the meeting, the ground rules, the need for confidentiality, and describing the leader's own role
• Facts: getting a description of the facts surrounding the traumatic event from all participants (unless they choose to pass)
• Thoughts: asking all participants about their first or most prominent thoughts about the event (again, they may pass)
• Reactions: inviting those who wish to describe their reactions (a word more readily understood and responded to than *emotions*) to the trauma
• Symptoms: asking for specific physical, emotional, behavioral, cognitive experiences
• Teaching: normalizing the symptoms that have been put forth by members of the group as part of human reactions to a traumatic event, not as signs of abnormality or weakness; describing possible future predictable symptoms the participants may experience; providing stress-reduction strategies

• Reentry: summarizing, answering questions, providing handouts, and touching on the themes the group has generated (Everly et al. 2005:228–231)

While this approach is not therapy, the authors do offer some cautions about the need for training and sensitivity in doing this work. Clearly it is not undertaken before essential safety and basic needs have been met. Participation should be voluntary. It could have the potential to traumatize someone who had not been as close to the traumatic event as others, so that the need for working with preexisting groups or teams is clear. The goal of the teaching phase is not to suggest that everyone will have ongoing symptoms but to normalize such symptoms in advance for those who will. Finally, since the debriefing providers have had training and can recognize signs of severe distress in people, they should attempt to offer anyone who is exhibiting extreme depression, dissociation, psychotic symptoms, high arousal, or physical pain a different kind of intervention, more individually focused (Everly et al. 2005).

Steven's methods were very similar to the steps described by Lewis (1994) in discussing the practice of debriefing after a "critical incident" in the workplace. He describes some differences between responding to trauma in a workplace where trauma is *unexpected*, such as a bank, a store, or a school, and responding to trauma in a workplace where trauma is *expected*, such as among those who provide emergency services (police officers, firefighters, rescue personnel). With emergency services teams, not every day's work requires a debriefing, but sometimes highly stressful incidents occur that can overwhelm even those who have been trained to handle crisis and disaster. Addressing the crisis is crucial for the organization, because work is one of our most vital roles. Many people spend more time at work than they do with family members, and their work relationships are very important to them. Like Everly et al. (2005), Lewis reminds us that this work is not therapy and that it does not try to draw out any preconceived emotional response from those who are handling the tragedy stoically. He is careful to define the state that survivors of a workplace trauma are in after a critical incident as "Critical Incident Stress," which he tells them is "the body and mind's coping response of a normal person to an abnormal situation . . . . If feelings are shared, understood, and accepted by oneself and others, the recovery from Critical Incident Stress will be more rapid and more thorough" (67).

Part of the effectiveness of the successful debriefing process lies in an emphasis on wellness and normalization, rather than any suggestion that the small group or team is being singled out because of abnormal reactions:

> Debriefing needs to be conducted within a philosophical atmosphere of wellness, increasing rescuers' sense of control, cohesion, communication, commitment and sense of challenge . . . . [It] fosters natural connections among teams and helps rescuers to provide witness to what they have experienced, felt, and need to know . . . . One aspect of debriefing is storytelling, set within limits in order to prevent overload and retraumatization.
>
> (Williams et al. 1999:59)

Using group interventions or debriefings within the first three days after a traumatic event has ended is recommended in the UN standards for disaster response (Hillman 2002) and has been used in countries as widely separated as Israel (Shalev 2002) and Finland (Saari 2005). Shalev found that debriefing increased group cohesion and reduced symptoms of stress after combat exposure. It is "most difficult, if not impossible, to recover from trauma on one's own. As with serious physical injury, psychological wounds require the help of others to heal. The prime element of such help is to first break the wall of mental isolation that often follows exposure to extreme stressors" (Shalev 2002:165). Saari makes a similar point in describing Finland's system of crisis response teams, which help after events as different as a single suicide or the sinking of a ferry. There will be people who, she writes, turn down crisis help out of pride or a sense of stoicism. But she frames the work as a kind of caring, a psychological first aid offered to all. More traditional crisis counseling, provided only to those who seek it from a counseling center, could "abnormalize future symptoms" (134), whereas a universal early intervention normalizes them.

The work that social workers and other mental health professionals do is similar in some ways to both non-emergency workplaces and to emergency services. Human service agencies working with clients at high risk of harm or violent death, including both homicide and suicide, have the most in common with emergency and rescue services and often have crisis plans in place. Agencies that serve clients who are at lower risk of harm may not anticipate such crises. A program such as a transitional housing agency falls somewhere in between; client death is not a constant presence, yet it is always a possibility.

Several other practitioners in the area of crisis intervention or disaster response also present models for prevention or reduction of further distress after disaster (Macy et al. 2004) or workplace trauma (Kleber and Brom 2003) in contrast to the earlier debriefing model of Mitchell and Everly. The community-based post-traumatic stress-management services offered by Macy and colleagues emphasize developing linkages with natural community leaders in order to build local expertise in crisis management. They offer a variety of groups and individual therapy, including orientation sessions, stabilization groups within the first three days, and coping groups. Some elements of the orientation and stabilization groups incorporate phases similar to CISD and add grounding and mindfulness techniques to reduce neurophysiological arousal symptoms. Unlike a critical incident stress debriefing, however, their model requires that participants commit to attending at least three sessions. Kleber and Brom developed interventions for traumatized bank employees who had experienced armed robberies and for survivors of motor vehicle accidents. Their model utilizes several contacts with survivors and offers practical help and information, support, reality testing (by sharing information from others' perspectives), and confrontation (to counteract denial). While these interventions differ in amount of time spent and format (Kleber and Brom's can be either group or individual), they have several elements in common with CISM, suggesting an evolution toward a best clinical practice after crisis.

Several studies have presented neutral or negative findings about the value of debriefing, the most often cited being the work of Rose, Bisson, and Wessely as part of the evidence-based-practice series in medicine of Great Britain's Cochrane Collection (Rose et al. 2001, 2003). Their review of eleven studies concludes that single-session psychological interventions may not help lessen later PTSD, and may even increase later symptoms. A meta-analysis of seven studies (several of which were included in Rose et al.'s review) found similar results (van Emmerik et al. 2002). However, several serious definitional and methodological difficulties can be identified that limit the generalizability of their conclusions.

The first is that most of the single psychological interventions reviewed were not actually group debriefings and bore little relationship to the kind of post-crisis or post-disaster group work described above. The interventions studied were commonly one-on-one sessions held in a hospital setting for individuals who had recently experienced motor vehicle accidents, burns, violence, miscarriage, or normal childbirth. It may be that a one-on-one talk with these clients was not effective in reducing later symptoms of trauma, but that does not have much bearing on group debriefings. So to equate talking to a recent burn victim, one on one, in his or her hospital bed, with a formal debriefing of a related group after something like the sinking of the *Estonia* in Finland (Saari), or a workplace death (Lewis), does not make sense definitionally.

The second difficulty is that while the studies were chosen on the basis of having random assignment to an intervention or a control group (which allows the most accurate conclusions about the value of an intervention), some of the studies were based on a very small sample size, which occasionally resulted in a situation in which the random assignment did not actually produce equivalent groups (which would be the research goal). In several of the burn and motor vehicle accident studies, the sample who received individual psychological interventions turned out to have more serious injuries than the sample who did not. For a more thorough discussion of how the studies chosen for the Cochrane Collection differ from agreed-upon debriefing practices, Myers and Wee (2005) provide much detail. They also present additional studies, not included in the work by Rose et al. (2001, 2003), that did use randomization and also showed benefits for emergency services workers who received debriefing.

This is not to say that CISD has never been misapplied or has not caused harm. There are media reports that people have felt coerced by their employer to attend a debriefing and that it was of little use, or caused them distress. More research is needed on this issue of poorly applied *group* debriefing techniques, especially since that was not the issue with the original Cochrane Review article of individual debriefing sessions that raised an alarm.

Vicarious Trauma: Compassion Fatigue and Compassion Satisfaction

Helping an agency through the process of shock and grief that follows a client death has the potential to stir up many feelings, especially if such situations are a frequent part of the work of a social worker in an EAP or contracting with a crisis response program, and especially if the death was a violent one. There is always the possibility that the ones helping the helpers have themselves experienced a client death at an earlier point in their careers or that they will take on the tremendous load of sorrow that comes with being with people as they mourn. This experience of vicarious trauma (Saakvitne and Pearlman 1996) or compassion fatigue (Figley 1999) has been noted with respect to both the more long-term work with clients who have endured complex trauma because of prolonged or childhood violence and the mental health responders to a crisis or disaster situation (Cunningham 2004). The two terms have developed in tandem during the last thirty years and refer to similar phenomena—the emotional cost to mental health workers in helping clients through extremely difficult times and hearing their stories of hurt and pain. Vicarious trauma refers more to the psychological processes evoked by our clients' devastation and betrayal: "It includes our strong feelings and our defenses against those feelings. Thus vicarious traumatization is our strong reactions of grief, rage, and outrage, which grow as we repeatedly hear about and see people's pain and loss . . . and it is our numbing, our protective shell, and our wish not to know, which follow those reactions" (Saakvitne and Pearlman 1996:41). It is also "an inescapable effect of trauma work. It is not something clients do to us; it is a human consequence of knowing, caring, and facing the reality of trauma" (25).

Compassion fatigue emphasizes the stress involved. Figley uses the equivalent terms *compassion fatigue* and *secondary traumatic stress* as "a syndrome of symptoms nearly identical to PTSD except that exposure to a traumatizing event experienced by one person becomes a traumatizing event for the second person" (11). He agrees with Saakvitne and Pearlman that the response is not an aberration: "It is the natural, predictable, treatable and preventable unwanted consequence of working with suffering people" (4).

Responding to a client death, as with other types of workplace loss or trauma, is more like crisis/disaster work, though it differs from more widespread community disaster in that the social worker providing the debriefing process did not himself live through a shared traumatic event. Steven's situation would be more similar to an outside worker's coming into a traumatized community.

But in addition to the risk of vicarious trauma, this work also has great potential for the other facet of compassion fatigue—compassion satisfaction (Stamm 2005). *Compassion satisfaction* refers to the sense of well-being and pride that comes with doing work with clients who are in emotional pain and seeing that work make a difference. Items on the compassion satisfaction scale refer specifically to the feelings of happiness, pride, satisfaction, success, and invigoration that come with helping others. In fact, Steven expresses a sense of gratitude to be doing the work he does. "I feel privileged to share this time with the staff who are struggling through grief. You watch the process unfold and sometimes you feel a sense of awe at the end—of how they face it, what they reach together." There has been at least one study of the overlap of compassion fatigue and compassion satisfaction among crisis/disaster mental health providers; Myers and Wee (2005) surveyed a group of professionals attending an international disaster mental health providers conference and found that while the risk of compassion fatigue (defined as moderate, high, or very high scores on the measure) was present in 40 percent of the providers, the level of compassion satisfaction (same scoring range) was even higher—89 percent of the group.

Reflections on Empowerment Principles in Responding to Agency Grief

Just as individuals and families can be empowered (Lee 2001; Wise 2005), so can groups brought together by a shared public tragedy. The groups may differ in significant ways from some of the families that social workers serve, and they are often brought together by their workplace ties, but their vulnerability after a sudden and violent death is very real and creates a sense of shared distress. The work of sharing that distress with others creates the empowerment that allows them to find their individual and shared strengths and grieve the loss.

Building on strengths while diminishing oppressions. The crisis intervention model of providing a universal, non-stigmatizing group approach to all those who are affected by a shared trauma sends the message that to struggle with grief and stress after a trauma such as client death is normal and that healing will happen. In a sense the oppression a group like this faces is the oppression of violence in our society and the ways in which current values and policy work against reducing that risk of violence in the lives of clients served by social workers.

Enacting multicultural respect. For the social worker entering a workplace or service agency to help the staff process trauma—in this case a violent death—it is important to remain aware of both the agency's culture and norms and the multiplicity of cultures and norms represented by the people in the group to be served. Steven's experience as a clinical social worker and his knowledge of group process helped him create a safe and accepting atmosphere that let the group know they could open up to the extent they wished to. He was also very aware of the fact that he was a man, the same gender as the person who had killed Sonia, coming into an agency staffed primarily by women. The agency director helped staff feel comfortable with him by attending the debriefing meeting herself and establishing a sense of safety and trust.

Working from an awareness of specific needs. Steven has received formal training in debriefing and follows the structure that has been defined—yet each agency or business is different, and he is able to move flexibly between phases if needed. He also pays attention to the group members, recognizing that some need to express their grief and others need simply to hold it in and listen.

Assisting clients as they empower themselves. When outside crisis intervention or disaster response professionals come to an agency or rescue team or community, they are using the power of the group itself to process the loss, to build a new narrative, and to consider how they will change as a result of the loss.

Integrating the support needed from others. Debriefing or critical incident response encourages support within a preexisting group, often a work group who have established relationships with each other and will continue to do so after the intervention has formally ended. While Steven provided a form of support that the agency appreciated, it was very satisfying for him to see the emotional and pragmatic expressions of support that welled up within the staff itself.

Equalizing power differentials and using cooperative roles. The role of the professional in this case is to set the stage for group processing and then to step back, providing information about reactions to trauma as necessary. Equalizing power differentials is particularly evident in the initial phases of a debriefing group, when the leaders acknowledge their need for the group to inform them about what has happened.

Crisis or post-disaster counseling for workplaces or groups of emergency service professionals involves several levels of client systems—both the agency as a whole, represented by the administrator who sets up the intervention, and the group of workers who attend. The social worker will serve as a resource person for the administrator, providing consultation about common reactions, needs, the natural differences in the ways people deal with grief and death. He or she may be asked for advice and recommendations on anything from appropriateness of time off to types of memorials. A body of information about these issues does exist (Kaul 2003; Lewis 1994), and the social worker can take on the role of educator. In the group session itself, the social worker frames the movement of the group toward the goal of increased understanding and shared grief, attends to the reactions of the group, and helps facilitate the expression of both emotion and cognitive processing. By its nature, crisis debriefing with helping professionals is based on work with the group of people who experienced the crisis, not with individual clients or patients (Lewis 1994). It is meant not to pathologize bereavement but to normalize the strong reactions that many people will have. It should leave the participants feeling more in control, not less: "The major roles of debriefing are to provide clarification and to help rescuers recognize that they are experts concerning the disaster itself, not further victims" (Williams et al. 1999:59).

Conclusion and Recommendations

A sudden and violent client death sends shock waves through the agency of professionals who have worked with him or her. As with a disaster on a larger scale, there is no way to prevent the strong emotions that will follow this tragedy; the only preparation will have been to anticipate beforehand the kinds of help that might be needed in such a situation and to know how to access that help. The transitional housing agency discussed here chose to call in a social worker who was trained in a critical incident stress debriefing model to help them come together as a group to grieve the loss of their client.

The model used draws upon crisis intervention theory and the value of addressing the difficult and varying emotions that will be experienced by the work group, as well as upon the positive value of group interaction itself. There is a tremendous need for information and clarification, as each person knows only certain details about a death or other workplace trauma. And there is a sense of shared bereavement that enfranchises the expression of grief, rather than disenfranchising or forcing it underground.

An agency, particularly a social work agency, may be able to facilitate its own process, using professional staff. But that response means that the facilitator must undertake a dual role; he or she must not only grieve but also take the lead in helping colleagues grieve. As agencies plan for their own responses after a critical incident such as a client suicide or murder, they may want to call upon the services of an outside consultant who is trained in this kind of crisis group work. If so, it is recommended that

- the intervention be held within three days—both to provide information and to address the situation when people's minds and hearts are in the most turmoil

• the intervention be universal yet voluntary (*Universal* means that the agency invites everyone who shares in the experience of the event to attend and backs that invitation up by sending administrators and supervisors as well. *Universal* suggests that strong reactions during this time are not unusual or problematic; they are normal. And since coerced participation is not true participation, attendance at the intervention should be *voluntary*.)

• the intervention follow a structure that is based on experience with the ways people move between emotion and cognition and their needs for closure.

References

Corr, C. 2003. "Loss, Grief, and Trauma in Public Tragedy." In M. Lattanzi-Licht and K. J. Doka, eds., *Living with Grief: Coping with Public Tragedy*, 63–76. New York: Brunner-Routledge.

Cunningham, M. 2004. "Avoiding Vicarious Traumatization: Support, Spirituality, and Self-Care." In N. B. Webb, ed., *Mass Trauma and Violence: Helping Families and Children Cope*, 327–359. New York: Guilford.

Everly, G. S., J. Lating, and J. Mitchell. 2005. "Innovations in Group Crisis Intervention." In A. R. Roberts, ed., *Crisis Intervention Handbook: Assessment, Treatment, and Research*, 221–245. 3rd ed. Oxford: Oxford University Press.

Figley, C. R. 1999. "Compassion Fatigue: Toward a New Understanding of the Costs of Caring." In B. H. Stamm, ed., *Secondary Traumatic Stress: Self-Care Issues for Clinicians, Researchers, and Educators*, 3–28. 2nd ed. Baltimore: Sidran.

Herman, J. 1997. *Trauma and Recovery*. 2nd ed. New York: Basic Books.

Hillman, J. 2002. *Crisis Intervention and Trauma: New Approaches to Evidence-Based Practice*. New York: Kluwer Academic/Plenum.

Jacobs, S. C. 1999. *Traumatic Grief: Diagnosis, Treatment, and Prevention*. Philadelphia: Brunner/Mazel.

Kaul, R. E. 2003. "Workplace Interventions." In M. Lattanzi-Licht and K. J. Doka, eds., *Living with Grief: Coping with Public Tragedy*, 245–261. New York: Brunner-Routledge.

Kleber, R. J., and D. Brom. 2003. *Coping with Trauma: Theory, Prevention, and Treatment*. Lisse, Netherlands: Swets and Zeitlinger.

Lattanzi-Licht, M. 2002. "Grief and the Workplace: Positive Approaches." In K. J. Doka, ed., *Disenfranchised Grief: New Directions, Challenges, and Strategies for Practice*, 167–180. Champaign, Ill.: Research Press.

Lee, J. A. 2001. *The Empowerment Approach to Social Work Practice: Building the Beloved Community*. 2nd ed. New York: Columbia University Press.

Lewis, G. W. 1994. *Critical Incident Stress and Trauma in the Workplace: Recognition . . . Response . . . Recovery*. Levittown, Pa.: Accelerated Development.

Macy, R. D., L. Behar, R. Paulson, J. Delman, L. Schmid, and S. Smith. 2004. "Community-Based, Acute Posttraumatic Stress Management: A Description and Evaluation of a Psychosocial-Intervention Continuum." *Harvard Review of Psychiatry* 12 (1): 217–228.

McBride, J., and E. D. Johnson. 2005. "Crisis Intervention, Brief Therapy, and the Loss of Life." In A. R. Roberts, ed., *Crisis Intervention Handbook: Assessment, Treatment, and Research*, 279–302. 3rd ed. Oxford: Oxford University Press.

Myers, D., and D. F. Wee. 2005. *Disaster Mental Health Services*. New York: Brunner-Routledge.

Neria, Y., and B. T. Litz. 2003. "Bereavement by Traumatic Means: The Complex Synergy of Trauma and Grief." *Journal of Loss and Trauma* 9:73–87.

Rose, S., J. Bisson, and S. Wessely. 2001. "A Systematic Review of Brief Psychological Interventions ('Debriefing') for the Treatment of Immediate Trauma Related Symptoms and the Prevention of Post-Traumatic Stress Disorder (Cochrane Review) update." *Cochrane Library* 3.

——. 2003. "A Systematic Review of Single Psychological Interventions ('Debriefing') Following Trauma. Updating the Cochrane Review and Implications for Good Practice." In R. Orner and U. Schnyder, eds., *Reconstructing Early Intervention After Trauma*, 24–40. Oxford: Oxford University Press.

Saakvitne, K. W., and L. A. Pearlman. 1996. *Transforming the Pain: A Workbook on Vicarious Traumatization*. New York: Norton.

Saari, S. 2005. *A Bolt from the Blue: Coping with Disasters and Acute Traumas*. London: Jessica Kingsley.

Shalev, A. Y. 2002. "Treating Survivors in the Immediate Aftermath of Traumatic Events." In R. Yehuda, ed., *Treating Trauma Survivors with PTSD*, 157–188. Washington, D.C.: American Psychiatric Publishing.

Stamm, B. H. 2002. "Measuring Compassion Satisfaction As Well As Fatigue: Developmental History of the Compassion Satisfaction and Fatigue Test." In C. R. Figley, ed., *Treating Compassion Fatigue*, 107–119. New York: Brunner-Routledge.

Strom-Gottfried, K., and N. D. Mowbray. 2006. "Who Heals the Helper? Facilitating the Social Worker's Grief." *Families in Society* 87 (1): 9–15.

van Emmerik, A. A., J. H. Kamphuis, A. M. Hylsbosch, and P. M. Emmelkamp. 2002. "Single Session Debriefing After Psychological Trauma: A Meta-analysis." *Lancet* 360:766–771.

Williams, M. B., E. S. Zinner, and R. R. Ellis. 1999. "The Connection Between Grief and Trauma: An Overview." In E. S. Zinner and M. B. Williams, eds., *When a Community Weeps: Case Studies in Group Survivorship*, 3–17. Philadelphia: Brunner/Mazel.

Wise, J. B. 2005. *Empowerment Practice with Families in Distress*. New York: Columbia University Press.

Part 3

Transforming Trauma at the Social/
Community/Political Levels

9

The Impact of Historical Trauma
The Example of the Native Community

MARIA YELLOW HORSE BRAVE HEART

As she combed her hair—long, wavy, and dark brown with golden high-lights—Salome looked in the mirror at her triguena *(tan) complexion, almost dark enough to be a full-blooded Indian. Her almond-shaped black-brown eyes surveyed her features. She could not decide whether she had a Taino Indian nose or more of a Lakota nose, like her mom. Her cheekbones were less pronounced than her mom's—more like her dad's. She might be able to pass for a* gitana *(Gypsy) from Spain as much as a Puerto Rican. She began to cry as she thought about her mother's painful boarding school experiences on a South Dakota reservation. Her mother was beaten for speaking Lakota; she had to kneel all day, many times holding her books; she was sexually abused by a priest; and she scrubbed floors and peeled potatoes constantly. Salome felt guilty now, thinking of cutting her hair and how much that would hurt her mother, who had had her own long hair forcibly cut at six years old at the boarding school. Her mother had been angry with her for getting blond highlights. "Are you trying to be like your Spanish great-grandmother?" she had asked in anger. Salome had never met her paternal great-grandmother, who had blond hair and blue eyes and who had migrated to Puerto Rico, where she married a mestizo man who was at least half Taino Indian. Salome glanced at the picture of her parents on her dresser. Her father had talked about boarding school history as well, being a descendant of Carlisle Indian School survivors when Puerto Ricans were sent to Carlisle after Puerto Rico became a colony of the United States. Looking now at the picture of her mostly Taino Indian mestizo father, who had a small amount of African ancestry, she could see traces of "that Spanish woman," as her mother often called her great-grandmother.*

When I first saw Salome, she could not figure out why she felt so sad much of the time, like she was grieving the loss of someone or something. She felt overwhelmed at school, although at sixteen she was doing very well. Salome felt she had to be perfect, and sometimes the pressure was just too much. She was thinking of lying to her parents so she could go to the party and drink, like most of the other kids in her class did. However, she was afraid. She sometimes thought about killing herself—not to die really but to find relief. How could she talk about her own problems with fitting in at school as the only half-Lakota student there when her parents had suffered so much? If she lied and they found out, maybe they would send her to a boarding school too. Salome often had nightmares about being shot at Wounded Knee or being thrown down a flight of stairs at boarding school, even though she never personally experienced either. She recalls her mother sharing family stories about ancestors who survived the Wounded Knee Massacre.

Salome felt she never could be as smart as her older sister, who had light skin, frizzy black hair, and blue eyes. Her sister, too, had to be perfect and was constantly anxious, worried about failing even though she had straight As in school. Salome had nearly a 4.0 average herself. She wanted to go to college—away from home—but how could she abandon her parents? Salome felt that she could not find her place in the world.

Understanding Historical Trauma

Salome's emotions and perceptions are manifestations of intergenerational massive group trauma, passed on to her from her parents. Historical trauma colors her view of the world. *Historical trauma* is cumulative emotional and psychological wounding, over the life span and across generations, emanating from massive group trauma experiences. The reaction to this intergenerational trauma is the *historical trauma response*, which may include self-destructive behavior, substance abuse, suicidal thoughts and gestures, depression, anxiety, low self-esteem, anger, difficulty recognizing and expressing emotions, survivor guilt, intrusive trauma imagery, identification with ancestral pain, fixation to trauma, somatic symptoms, and elevated mortality rates (Brave Heart 1998, 1999a, 1999b, 2003). The historical trauma response is analogous to traits identified among Jewish Holocaust descendants (Danieli 1998), as well as Japanese American World War II internment camp descendants (Nagata 1998). Associated bereavement accompanies historical trauma grief, known as historical unresolved grief. This grief may be considered impaired, delayed, fixated, and/or disenfranchised (Brave Heart 2003).

One of the particularly heinous historically traumatic episodes in Native history is the "boarding school era," which began in 1879 (Brave Heart and DeBruyn 1998; Noriega 1992), with the first national residential school being the Carlisle Indian School in Pennsylvania, although there were some church-run boarding schools in the northeastern United States before this time. Native children, forcibly removed from parents and tribal communities under federal policy and placed in boarding schools operated by the Bureau of Indian Affairs and churches, experienced physical and sexual abuse, starvation, incarceration, punishment for speaking their native languages, separation from family and tribal communities sometimes for years at a time, and emotional deprivation. A significant number of modern American Indian adults, particularly those in midlife, descended from this legacy and survived their own negative boarding school experiences.

To help the reader understand Salome's experience, this chapter will give some background on historical trauma theory and will explain the impact of historical trauma upon American Indians and Alaska Natives, also referred to as Native or Native Peoples. Native Peoples also include other Indigenous populations in the Americas, such as Native Hawaiians and Native Pacific Islanders and Natives or First Nations in Canada.

The chapter will also mention the impact upon other massively traumatized populations and will describe the contributions of historical trauma theory to the helping profession, as well as the ways in which empowerment practice is congruent with historical trauma interventions. Secondary traumatization, a critical issue in historical trauma intervention work, will be examined.

HISTORICAL TRAUMA THEORY DEVELOPMENT

Historical trauma theory emerged from thirty years of clinical practice and observations, coupled with preliminary qualitative and quantitative research (Brave Heart 2003). This theory addresses massive cumulative trauma across generations as well as the life span. The more limited diagnosis of post-traumatic stress disorder (PTSD) is inadequate for capturing the influence and characteristics of Native trauma (Brave Heart 2003; Robin, Chester, and Goldman 1996). The result of the genocide of Natives (Stannard 1992; Thornton 1987) and ongoing oppression, historical trauma is a useful concept that is receiving widespread acceptance in Indian Country, reservations, and communities of American Indians.

Historical trauma theory addresses the hypothesis that Natives may have higher thresholds for clinical responses than the PTSD criteria (APA 1994) because of the pervasiveness of American Indian trauma (Manson et al. 1996). Historical unresolved grief, as a component of the historical trauma response, elucidates the character and prevalence of major and atypical depressions among Northern Plains tribes (Brave Heart 2003; Robin et al. 1996). Literature on Jewish Holocaust survivors and descendants (Yehuda 1999) supports the theoretical constructs that underpin historical trauma theory, specifically the historical trauma response features and their intergenerational transfer. Native-specific literature calls for the development of culturally based trauma theory and interventions (Manson et al. 1996; Robin et al. 1996). The influence of history and the continuing transfer of trauma across generations are germane to developing effective culturally appropriate prevention and intervention strategies for Native Peoples as well as for other massively traumatized populations.

Historical trauma is a major influence upon the high Native mortality rates from alcoholism and alcohol-related conditions, suicide, homicide, and health conditions. These rates are evident in an examination of Indian Health Service statistics for the Aberdeen Area, for example, which includes predominantly Lakota (Teton Sioux) reservations (Brave Heart 2001a, 2003). The Aberdeen Area has the highest overall mortality rate of all Indian Health Service Areas, almost twice the rate for all Indians in the general population. Some Lakota reservations have an age-adjusted mortality rate of 3.6 times the national average (Aberdeen Area Indian Health Service 1999).

Alcoholism death rates are higher for American Indian youth than for youth of all races; further lifetime alcohol use is at 96 percent for Indian males and 92 percent for Indian females by the twelfth grade (Oetting and Beauvais 1989). The age at first involvement with alcohol is younger for Indian youths, and negative consequences are more prevalent and severe (Moran 1999; Oetting, Beauvais, and Edwards 1988). Alcoholism mortality rates for Lakota reservations are almost five times higher than the all-Indian rate and almost 29 times higher than the U.S. all-races rate (Aberdeen Area Indian Health Service 1999). Impaired parenting, resulting from boarding school trauma specifically and historical trauma in general, may be associated with substance abuse risk factors.

Aberdeen Area suicide rates, more than twice those of the general population and 1.5 times the all-Indian rate, are the second highest in the Indian Health Service Areas, exceeded only by those of Alaska. Homicide rates are highest in the Aberdeen Area, at 1.5 times the all-Indian rate and 2.2 times the U.S. all-races rate. This area also has the highest infant mortality rate. For all American Indians, death before age 45 is common, at 24 percent for females and 35 percent for males, compared with the U.S. all-races rate of 10.3 percent (the Euro-American rate is 8.6 percent, and the African American rate is 23.2 percent) (Indian Health Service 1997).

Nearly 50 percent to 67 percent of the reservation population lives below the poverty level. Aberdeen Area has the highest poverty level of all Indian Health Service Areas, at 1.6 times that of the all-Indian rate and 3.8 times that of the general population (Indian Health Service 1997). Shannon County, South Dakota, location of Pine Ridge reservation, is one of the poorest counties in the United States. In 1999 per capita income was $6,286. Of the 12,466 people who live there, 52.3 percent live below the poverty level. Unemployment is 73 percent on some Lakota reservations (BIA Labor Force Report 1998; Indian Health Service 1997). Pine Ridge unemployment soars to 83 percent, and its dropout rate is more than 60 percent from kindergarten through twelfth grades (Oglala Sioux Tribe Education Department 2002).

These conditions indicate high mental health risks and needs and trauma exposure to tragic losses, child physical and sexual abuse and neglect, family and community violence, high rates of alcohol-related accidents, and suicides. The elevated incidence of death exposes surviving community members to frequent traumatic events and the accompanying grief. Additional risk factors for trauma exposure among Natives include oppression, racism, and low socioeconomic status (Brave Heart 2003). These present-day problems are superimposed upon a backdrop of historically traumatic losses across generations.

Native history meets the United Nations definition of genocide (Legters 1988). Lakota history, as one example of Native historical trauma, includes massive traumatic group experiences incorporating the 1890 Wounded Knee Massacre ("Wounded Knee Remembered" 1990), war trauma, prisoner-of-war experiences, starvation, and displacement; the separation of Lakota children from families and their placement in mandatory, often abusive boarding schools (Tanner 1982); and the tuberculosis epidemic, during which more than one-third of the Lakota population died between 1936 and 1941 (Hoxie 1989; Tanner 1982). Cumulative losses across generations, including language, culture, and spirituality, contributed to the partial collapse of family kinship networks and indigenous social structures. This legacy, in concert with the current psychosocial conditions, has contributed to ongoing intergenerational trauma.

Salome's parents carry a legacy of boarding school trauma. Salome's mother is a boarding school survivor and the child of boarding school survivors. For Salome's father, the boarding school legacy is limited to a direct lineal ancestor who attended the Carlisle Indian School, one of a number of Puerto Ricans sent to Carlisle (Brave Heart, Colon, and Armendariz in press).

The negative impact of boarding schools is suggested by the incidence of sexual and physical abuse reported by boarding school survivors (Brave Heart 2003). One effect of the schools was to deprive Native families of a traditional familial milieu in which to raise children with indigenous values and parenting practices. Because of forced early separation from their own parents and being deprived of their parents' affection, boarding school survivor parents may also be emotionally unavailable to their children and may lack parenting skills such as culturally congruent nurturing behaviors and effective disciplinary practices.

Emotional attachment, observed among the Lakota traditionally, plays an important cultural role in addressing historical unresolved grief. The degree of attachment to family is manifested in traditional Lakota mourning practices and is also evident among other Native Peoples. For example, bereaved close relatives cut their hair and sometimes their bodies, acts that serve as external manifestations of grief and symbols of the deep attachment to the lost relative. Detachment from the lost object, a part of the mourning resolution process (Pollock 1989), may be incomplete among Natives who maintain active relationship with ancestor spirits. Traditional Native rituals for grief resolution and burial were outlawed with the 1881 U.S. policy banning the practice of Native ceremonies. Natives were forced to either abandon ceremonies or practice them secretly, thereby impairing traditional mourning resolution. With the rapid progression of massive traumatic losses, Native grief became impaired and unresolved, manifesting in depression (Brave Heart 2001a, 2003).

INTERGENERATIONAL TRANSFER OF TRAUMA

Survivors and descendants of intergenerational massive group trauma carry internal representations of generational trauma, which frame their perceptions of the world and their interactions with others. This phenomenon perpetuates trauma transfer to successive generations (Danieli 1998; Nagata 1998). In one examination of PTSD among offspring of Jewish Holocaust survivors, adult children of survivors had a higher level of cumulative lifetime stress (Yehuda 1999). Holocaust offspring with a parent having chronic PTSD were more likely to develop PTSD in response to their own life span traumatic events. Parental trauma symptoms, rather than the offspring's trauma exposure, are the critical risk factors for children who manifest their own trauma responses.

In addition to Jewish Holocaust and Japanese American internment camp survivors, African American historical trauma has become the focus of more recent literature regarding the legacy of slavery (Cross 1998; Leary 2001). Racism and oppression exacerbate African American PTSD (Allen 1996). Trauma exposure intensifies with lower socioeconomic status and shorter life expectancy, and darker skin color negatively affects socioeconomic status among African Americans (Hughes and Hertel 1990).

Native trauma is not adequately represented nor accurately reflected by the current PTSD nomenclature (Robin et al. 1996), specifically historical trauma. Culture influences symptom presentation. Cultural bias in assessment instruments may exist, and American Indians may have a higher trauma threshold. Hence, PTSD rates may be even higher than the reported 22 percent, compared to those of the general population, which stand at 8 percent (Office of the Surgeon General 2001). Life span trauma exposure for Indian youth is markedly elevated (Brave Heart 2003; Manson et al. 1996).

Salome's depression and trauma response features were examined in terms of Lakota culture, which also influenced her response to her parents' trauma. The Lakota collective ego ideal (Brave Heart 1998), an interdependent and generous person who places the good of the Lakota Nation before self and endures suffering for the good of others, added to Salome's survivor guilt and compensatory fantasies, attempting to undo or make up for the past. Although Lakota ceremonies involve sacrifice through fasting and generosity, the original intent was purity of generosity and love for the Oyate (the People) as well as transcending the physical reality to communicate more closely with the spiritual world. The influence of Catholic guilt and suffering distorted some perceptions of traditional Lakota sacrifice. This distorted notion, with its emphasis on suffering rather than upon joyful generosity and giving, fuels the belief that one's lot in life is to endure pain. Salome, with both Lakota and Catholic influences as well as the legacy of generational boarding school trauma, was predisposed to developing survivor guilt and compensatory fantasies.

Responding to Historical Trauma: Empowerment Treatment with Salome

In Lakota culture, the goal of empowerment is to function as an integral part of creation. To gain power, the Lakota individual must acquire help from the spirits to benefit the extended kinship network or the tribe. One's sense of self is developed in relation to all of creation. Influencing one's environment, a component of empowerment practice, was traditionally accomplished by invoking supernatural help to affect events and the natural world. Historically, massive group traumatic events altered this capacity to influence the government-regulated environment. A return to traditional empowerment has the potential to restore an indigenous healthy sense of self and sphere of influence. Communal goals, a foundation of empowerment practice, can be cultivated, based upon the collectivity inherent in Lakota culture.

THE HISTORICAL TRAUMA AND UNRESOLVED GRIEF INTERVENTION

Individual and family clinical work with Salome and her parents incorporated their historical trauma and principles of culturally congruent assessment and intervention with Native clients. Such principles included, for example, culturally aware methods for developing rapport with this family, learning about and adjusting to their mix of traditional Native and acculturated values for each person, and within each session developing a deeper understanding of how they view their culture, their communication styles, and their skin color issues.

Treatment focused on ameliorating the historical trauma response for Salome and fostering a re-attachment to authentic traditional Native values, which served as protective factors to limit or prevent substance abuse as well as transmission of trauma across generations. For the Lakota, children are sacred spirits returning to earth and parents have a sacred responsibility. Rekindling these values promises to promote improved parenting skills and parent-child relationships. Salome's parents were helped to examine their boarding school trauma and its effect on their relationship with their daughter. Improved parent-child relationships provide another protective factor against substance abuse and the transfer of the historical trauma response.

Helping parents to improve their parenting skills through addressing their historical trauma is one type of group empowerment intervention delivered by the Takini Network, a Native nonprofit organization I founded to help Native Peoples heal from intergenerational massive group trauma (Brave Heart 2001a, 2003). The parenting model incorporates the Historical Trauma and Unresolved Grief Intervention (HTUG), which I developed, and has been recognized as an exemplary model (Center for Mental Health Services 2001). I have used this intervention in my work since 1992. It focuses on ameliorating cumulative intergenerational trauma responses through intensive group experiences (Brave Heart 1998, 2001), which incorporate psychodynamic, cognitive-behavioral, and exposure features. Intervention goals are congruent with empowerment principles: building on strength while simultaneously diminishing oppressive forces, enacting multicultural respect, basing the work on a sensitive awareness of the needs of the participants in the group, and utilizing the support from others. The intervention goals are also consistent with post-trauma treatment: imparting a sense of mastery and control (van der Kolk, McFarlane, and Weisaeth 1996) within a traditional retreat-like setting, a safe milieu.

Participants in the HTUG model are exposed to historical trauma content through the use of audiovisual materials such as documentaries about the Wounded Knee Massacre and boarding schools. This stimulates historically traumatic memories and trauma response features.

The effects of the boarding school legacy on parenting and the resulting transfer of that trauma to Salome was addressed with Salome and her parents. In service of the empowerment principle of working from an awareness of Salome's specific needs, this intervention helped facilitate the release of her unique trauma response features: depression, low self-esteem, guilt, a victim identity, self-destructive behaviors, and compensatory fantasies. Salome and her parents could then openly talk about their experiences and feelings. Framing the trauma in a historical context helped them experience their own life span and family trauma as more understandable, less stigmatizing, and less isolating. They became empowered to face this trauma and its effects.

HTUG clients participate in small- and large-group processing, listening to others who shared similar experiences. This experience provides opportunities for them to be heard by others, which helps to diminish trauma-related thoughts and memories. Traditional Native spiritual practices, such as the purification lodge, prayer, song, and smudging (burning sage and sweetgrass) are included throughout the HTUG intervention. These activities pace the experience of intense emotions so that their release will not overwhelm participants. Although the group HTUG intervention was not available to Salome and her parents due to limited funding to provide the intervention, the principles were incorporated in practice with them. This historical-trauma-focused practice empowered the family by enhancing personal and spiritual strengths. Traditional cultural practices increased their connection to indigenous values and a pre-traumatic past (Brave Heart 1998, 2001a).

Traditional Lakota healing ceremonies and approaches are empowering and afford opportunities for processing and releasing emotions through prayer. The *inipi*, or purification lodge, and the HTUG intervention are ideal for Salome and her family, permitting disclosure, cohesiveness, and bonding, including healthy connection with ancestors. Salome and her parents were encouraged to participate in traditional healing ceremonies. This provided opportunities for role-modeling affect (emotional) tolerance, self-regulation, and trauma mastery. HTUG, through empowerment of participants, accomplishes outcomes equivalent to those of the Phase Oriented Treatment strategies for PTSD (van der Kolk, McFarlane, and van der Hart 1996), utilizing stabilization, which includes education and identification of feelings; deconditioning of traumatic responses and memories; restructuring of traumatic internal systems; reestablishment of safe social connection and efficacy in relationship; and collection of restorative emotional experiences (426). HTUG principles were adapted for individual and family work with Salome and her parents.

Another key component of HTUG is the facilitation of a consolidated positive Lakota identity through transcendent Lakota cultural experiences such as the *oinikage* (purification ceremony), which permits cathartic self-disclosure, ego enhancement, collectivity, reformation of self, transfers expectations of healing, and further models affect tolerance (Brave Heart 1998; Silver and Wilson 1988).

The Historical Trauma and Unresolved Grief Intervention and its integration into parenting skill-building interventions have been delivered in South Dakota and expanded to tribes across the United States. Its effectiveness is promising. Short-term evaluation indicates that it facilitates (a) a beginning resolution of traumatic grief and trauma response features, including a decrease in hopelessness as well as an increase in joy, (b) an increase in positive Native identity, (c) an increase in protective factors and a decrease in risk factors for substance abuse, (d) perceived improved relationships for parents with their children and relatives across generations, and (e) perceived improvement in parenting competence as well as family connections and sensitivity to their children (Brave Heart 2000).

Salome was also encouraged to return to the traditional Lakota concept of the extended kinship network, or *tiospaye* (a collection of related families), which provided an extensive social support system. This intervention exemplified the essential nature of integrating support from others in order to realize empowering practice. The *tiospaye* offers alternative resources if immediate family members are embroiled in conflict and disagreement. Traditionally, the *tiospaye* is expected to embrace the Woope Sakowin—the Seven Laws of generosity, compassion, respect, humility, wisdom, courage, and *wowacintanka* (to develop a great mind)—the capacity to be patient, maintain silence, and observe the natural world (Brave Heart and Kills Straight 1996). By embracing the Seven Laws, Salome's mother's extended kinship network offered her an increased sense of positive identity and support. Connecting Salome with Lakota and other Native families in the urban area as well as her own relatives on her mother's home reservation provided her with additional support.

Since Salome is a culturally mixed individual, intervention with her also attended to the issue of identity and connection with her communities. Multicultural individuals have the right to choose the group with which they identify as well as the right to maintain a multicultural identity (Root 1992). Through multicultural respect for her choice, Salome and I considered a variety of coping skills that she could use to strengthen her connections with others in her cultural communities. Although Salome's phenotype (skin color and features) resembles her ancestors from both ethnic groups, she may still experience some rejection because of being of mixed heritage. We talked about coping with rejection at times by whichever group she chooses to identify with, as well as at other times with invalidation by the general population. Among the Lakota, once an individual is given a Lakota name and has the ears pierced traditionally, an affirmation of the person as a member of the Lakota Nation is symbolized and the promise of protection as a member is given.

Also included is an expectation of loyalty and commitment from the member to the Lakota Nation. Another Lakota tradition includes a sacred rite of adoption. Sitting Bull, for example, in manifesting traditional Lakota compassion and inclusivity, adopted an enemy captive boy as his son and remained loyal to and protective of this son until his assassination in 1890. At the same time, the boy also remained fiercely loyal to his *Hunka* (adoptive) father. Implicitly, then, loyalty to the Lakota Nation may demand a monocultural identity as Lakota from individuals, like Salome, who are mixed, particularly if they have received their Lakota names in a ceremony. However, modern influences from the dominant culture, increasing intermarriage, and activism by multicultural groups also shape choices regarding identity.

Salome had not received her Lakota name and had never visited her mother's reservation because of the distance of her residence from the reservation and the lack of resources for travel. Being phenotypically Lakota and Puerto Rican, Salome was fortunate in that she could be accepted at least superficially in both communities. I used the empowering principle of assisting Salome in her decision about what would be in her best interest, being careful not to assume that it was too difficult to maintain an Indian identity in an urban center or to place a value judgment on the choice Salome made. This approach helped to equalize power differentials that might have been perceived to exist between us.

Within the Latino community, there are many people with Indian ancestry who identify with that heritage. Brave Heart, Colon, and Armendariz (in press) describe Indian identity issues among Puerto Ricans who have significant Indian DNA and phenotype. Native identification is often suppressed with a focus on Spanish and African ancestry. For Salome, choosing to identify as Puerto Rican, like her father, still includes Taino Indian heritage, phenotype, and the ancestral legacy of boarding school at the Carlisle Indian School.

When I left the area where Salome and her parents lived to accept a new position in another area, Salome was expressing much more comfort with her identity and was regarding the multiple sources of her heritage as something unique about her, a strength on which she could build to create her own meanings about who she is. She was especially interested in exploring and learning more about her parents' history in boarding schools. She recognized that her own choices about how to live her life would have an impact on her children, on the generations to come.

Additional trauma intervention techniques for working with PTSD (van der Kolk et al. 1996), particularly group modalities, are highly effective when combined with the focus on historical trauma and culturally adapted for Native clients. Such techniques include group sharing, videotape stimulus material to facilitate retrieval of repressed memories, and cognitive content about the traumatic history as well as education about typical responses to that history. Such retrieval empowers trauma survivors to understand their emotional reactions, and this understanding, in turn, can limit feelings of isolation and fear, congruent with the actions in empowerment practice that strive to build upon strengths while diminishing oppressive forces. Providing opportunities for emotional processing and releasing can bring a sense of relief to survivors as well as the experience of being heard and understood.

Coping with Vicarious Trauma

Working with historical trauma, including life span trauma, can be challenging for providers, particularly Native providers, those from other massively traumatized groups, or clinicians who have trauma histories themselves. Experiences of clinicians and first responders in massive traumatic events, such as the September 11, 2001, attacks, are recounted in Danieli and Dingman (2005). Included in these accounts is literature on Native first responders at Ground Zero whose reservation trauma was exacerbated by the September 11 trauma (Brave Heart et al. 2005). The pain of massive group trauma is so overwhelming that crying with clients may be not only unavoidable but appropriate.

The same is true in working with Native populations where the pain is so massive, generational, and persistent. European American clinicians must struggle with guilt and Native clinicians with triggers of their own generational trauma. Other massive group trauma survivors and their descendants, like American Indian clinicians, must cope with their own trauma and may identify strongly with Native clients. This can be a positive outcome, as empathic attunement is easy to achieve, but objectivity could be clouded by intense emotions. Standard mental health professional education does not adequately prepare clinicians for working with such intense emotional content. Clinicians must modify their approaches and have supervision and specialized trauma training to cope with vicarious traumatization and to maintain their effectiveness.

Conclusion and Recommendations

To date, the Historical Trauma and Unresolved Grief Intervention, a group empowerment model, has been conducted with groups of participants ranging from 18 years to 75 years of age. Community historical trauma workshops across generations have also been successfully conducted. The intervention is effectively adaptable for adolescent groups. A group historical trauma intervention was the primary recommendation for Salome and her parents, an intergenerational HTUG group, an adolescent group for Salome, and an adult one for her parents. A parenting group that incorporated historical boarding school trauma was also strongly recommended for Salome's parents. Family sessions with a focus on empowerment, connecting the family with external social supports and raising their consciousness of historical trauma and the ongoing racism and oppression that impinges upon optimal family functioning were essential with this family.

A further recommendation was connecting Salome and her family with the local Indian center and Puerto Rican community programs. Despite the Catholic boarding school legacy, Salome and her family periodically attended church, which served as an additional community resource for them. Many Natives practice both traditional Native spirituality and Christian religions. The Indian center could refer the family to a traditional Native healer or healing ceremony in the urban area. Salome's father could choose to participate in Caribbean spiritual traditions, such as *spiritismo*.

Family therapy, if used with Native clients, must be attentive to certain cautions. A family therapist, for example, could explore extended-family kinship networks but, in doing so, would need to be aware of indigenous communication patterns and taboos, which limit direct verbal communication in cross-gender interaction between siblings and between a man and his mother-in-law (Brave Heart 2001b). Traditionally, many older Lakota do not express overt emotions or physical affection in front of outsiders, particularly non-Natives, as such behavior is seen as impolite. Family therapy techniques such as sculpting or requiring family members to sit next to one another may violate cultural taboos. Further, asking a family member to directly address another verbally and with direct eye contact may require a Native family to violate norms. Additional details regarding challenges of family sessions also merit attention (Brave Heart 2001b).

Salome benefited from individual sessions in which her experiences were validated. She was empowered to explore her multiple identities and to make her own choice regarding what cultural practices to embrace. Choices for coping were facilitated. Culturally congruent verbal and nonverbal communication styles were noted. Salome was approached with multicultural respect and cognizance of both the Lakota and the Puerto Rican cultures. Exploring her generational history of boarding school trauma facilitated consciousness-raising about historical and sociopolitical factors. Brave Heart (2001b) highlights further issues that arise in empowerment-informed individual therapy. Finally, Salome and her family could benefit from alcohol education and alcohol prevention programs.

Historical trauma theory provides an empowerment framework for intervening with Native clients and communities. The Historical Trauma and Unresolved Grief Intervention affords participants an opportunity to address generational as well as life span trauma. The emphasis on traditional Native culture is congruent with the empowerment principles of building on strengths while diminishing the impact of oppressive forces, enacting multicultural respect, working from an awareness of clients' specific needs, assisting clients in their choices to empower themselves, integrating the support needed from others, equalizing power differentials, and using cooperative roles. The intervention respects indigenous concepts of power, which are defined within the ecological framework of intimate relationships with the spirits and all of creation. Communal goals are part of a foundation for empowerment practice and can be cultivated through the collectivity inherent in Lakota culture. A return to traditional Native empowerment has the potential to restore an indigenous healthy sense of self and sphere of influence.

References

Aberdeen Area Indian Health Service. 1999. *Aberdeen Area Population, Release #34. Indian Health Service Census Population Estimates for Fiscal Years 1998–2007*. Aberdeen, S.D.: Indian Health Service.

Allen, I.M. 1996. "PTSD Among African Americans." In A. J. Marsella, M. J. Friedman, E. T. Gerrity, and R. M. Scurfield, eds., *Ethnocultural Aspects of Posttraumatic Stress Disorder*, 209–238. Washington, D.C.: American Psychological Association.

American Psychiatric Association (APA). 1994. *Diagnostic and Statistical Manual of Mental Disorders* (DSM-IV). 4th ed. Washington, D.C.: Author.

BIA Labor Force Report 1998. Aberdeen, S.D.: Bureau of Indian Affairs.

Brave Heart, M. Y. H. 1998. "The Return to the Sacred Path: Healing the Historical Trauma and Historical Unresolved Grief Response Among the Lakota." *Smith College Studies in Social Work* 68 (3): 287–305.

——. 1999a. "Gender Differences in the Historical Trauma Response Among the Lakota." *Journal of Health and Social Policy* 10 (4): 1–21.

——. 1999b. "Oyate Ptayela: Rebuilding the Lakota Nation Through Addressing Historical Trauma Among Lakota Parents." *Journal of Human Behavior in the Social Environment* 2 (1/2): 109–126.

——. 2000. "Wakiksuyapi: Carrying the Historical Trauma of the Lakota." *Tulane Studies in Social Welfare* 21–22:245–266.

——. 2001a. "Clinical Assessment with American Indians." In R. Fong and S. Furuto, eds., *Culturally Competent Practice: Skills, Interventions, and Evaluations,* 163–177. Boston: Allyn and Bacon.

——. 2001b. "Clinical Interventions with American Indians." In R. Fong and S. Furuto, eds., *Culturally Competent Practice: Skills, Interventions, and Evaluations,* 285–298. Boston: Allyn and Bacon.

——. 2003. "The Historical Trauma Response Among Natives and Its Relationship with Substance Abuse: A Lakota Illustration." *Journal of Psychoactive Drugs* 35 (1): 7–13.

Brave Heart, M. Y. H., E. Colon, and B. A. Armendariz. In press. "Historical Trauma Within the Latino Community." In M. Y. H. Brave Heart, B. Segal, L. M. Debruyn, J. Taylor, and R. Daw, eds., *Multicultural Experiences of Historical Trauma: Roots, Effects, and Healing.* Binghamton, N.Y.: Haworth.

Brave Heart, M. Y. H., and L. M. DeBruyn. 1998. "The American Indian Holocaust: Healing Historical Unresolved Grief." *American Indian and Alaska Native Mental Health Research* 8 (2): 56–78.

——. In press. "The Historical Trauma Response Among Natives: The Lakota Example." In M. Y. H. Brave Heart, B. Segal, L. M. Debruyn, J. Taylor, and R. Daw, eds., *Multicultural Experiences of Historical Trauma: Roots, Effects, and Healing.* Binghamton, N.Y.: Haworth.

Brave Heart, M. Y. H., L. M. Debruyn, D. Crazy Thunder, B. Rodriguez, Jr., and K. Grube. 2005. "This Is Hallowed Ground: Native Voices from Ground Zero." In Y. Danieli and R. Dingman, eds., *On the Ground After September 11: Mental Health Responses and Practical Knowledge Gained on the Third Anniversary.* Binghamton, N. Y.: Haworth.

Brave Heart, M. Y. H., and B. Kills Straight. 1996. "The Takini Network Lakota Parenting Curriculum and Historical Trauma and Unresolved Grief Intervention Curriculum." Unpublished manuscript.

Center for Mental Health Services. 2001. *Lakota Regional Community Action Grant on Historical Trauma.* Community Action Grant, Minority Initiative.

Rockville, Md.: Substance Abuse and Mental Health Services Administration (SAMHSA).

Cross, W. E., Jr. 1998. "Black Psychological Functioning and the Legacy of Slavery." In Y. Danieli, ed., *International Handbook of Multigenerational Legacies of Trauma*, 387. New York: Plenum.

Danieli, Y., ed., 1998. *International Handbook of Multigenerational Legacies of Trauma*. New York: Plenum.

Danieli, Y., and R. Dingman, eds. 2005. *On the Ground After September 11: Mental Health Responses and Practical Knowledge Gained on the Third Anniversary*. Binghamton, N.Y.: Haworth.

Hoxie, F. E. 1989. *A Final Promise: The Campaign to Assimilate the Indians, 1880–1920*. Cambridge: Cambridge University Press.

Hughes, M., and B. R. Hertel. 1990. "The Significance of Color Remains: A Study of Life Chances, Mate Selection, and Ethnic Consciousness Among Black Americans." *Social Forces* 68 (4): 1105–1120.

Indian Health Service. 1997. *Regional Differences in Indian Health*. Washington, D. C.: U. S. Department of Health and Human Services.

Leary, J. D. 2001. "African American Male Violence: Trying to Kill the Part of You That Isn't Loved." PhD. dissertation, Portland State University Graduate School of Social Work.

Legters, L. H. 1988. "The American Genocide." *Policy Studies Journal* 16 (4): 768–777.

Manson, S., J. Beals, T. O'Nell, J. Piasecki, D. Bechtold, E. Keane, and M. Jones. 1996. "Wounded Spirits, Ailing Hearts: PTSD and Related Disorders Among American Indians." In A. J. Marsella, M. J. Friedman, E. T. Gerrity, and R. M. Scurfield, eds., *Ethnocultural Aspects of Posttraumatic Stress Disorder*, 255–283. Washington, D. C.: American Psychological Association.

Moran, J. 1999. "Preventing Alcohol Use Among Urban American Indian Youth: The Seventh Generation Program." *Journal of Human Behavior in the Social Environment* 2 (1–2): 51–67.

Nagata, D. 1998. "Transgenerational Impact of the Japanese-American Internment." In Y. Danieli, ed., *International Handbook of Multigenerational Legacies of Trauma*, 125–140. New York: Plenum.

Noriega, J. 1992. "American Indian Education in the United States: Indoctrination for Subordination to Colonialism." In M. A. Jaimes, ed., *The State of Native America: Genocide, Colonization, and Resistance*, 371–402. Boston: South End Press.

Oetting, E. R., and F. Beauvais. 1989. "Epidemiology and Correlates of Alcohol Use Among Indian Adolescents Living on Reservations." In NIAAA, *Alcohol Use Among U.S. Ethnic Minorities*, 239–267. Research Monograph No. 18. Rockville, Md.: U.S. Public Health Service.

Oetting, E. R., F. Beauvais, and R.W. Edwards. 1988. "Alcohol and Indian Youth: Social and Psychological Correlates and Prevention." *Journal on Drug Issues* 18:87–101.

Office of the Surgeon General. 2001. *Mental Health: Culture, Race, and Ethnicity. A Supplement to Mental Health (1999): A Report of the Surgeon General.* Rockville, Md.: Substance Abuse and Mental Health Services Administration, Center for Mental Health Services.

Oglala Sioux Tribe Education Department. 2002. *Pine Ridge Indian Reservation.* Pine Ridge, S. D.: Author.

Pollock, G. H., ed. 1989. *The Mourning-Liberation Process.* Vol. 1. Madison, Conn.: International Universities Press.

Robin, R. W., B. Chester, and D. Goldman. 1996. "Cumulative Trauma and PTSD in American Indian Communities." In A. J. Marsella, M. J. Friedman, E. T. Gerrity, and R. M. Scurfield, eds., *Ethnocultural Aspects of Posttraumatic Stress Disorder*, 239–253. Washington, D. C.: American Psychological Association.

Root, M. 1992. *Racially Mixed People of America.* Thousand Oaks, Calif.: Sage.

Silver, S. M., and J. P. Wilson. 1988. "Native American Healing and Purification Rituals for War Stress." In J. P. Wilson, Z. Harele, and B. Hahana, eds., *Human Adaptation to Extreme Stress: From the Holocaust to Viet Nam*, 337–355. New York: Plenum.

Stannard, D. 1992. *American Holocaust: Columbus and the Conquest of the New World.* New York: Oxford University Press.

Tanner, H. 1982. "A History of the Dealings of the United States Government with the Sioux." Unpublished manuscript. Prepared for the Black Hills Land Claim by order of the United States Supreme Court. On file at the D'Arcy McNickle Center for the History of the American Indian, Newberry Library, Chicago.

Thornton, R. 1987. *American Indian Holocaust and Survival: A Population History Since 1492.* Norman: University of Oklahoma Press.

van der Kolk, B. A., A. C. McFarlane, and O. van der Hart. 1996. "A General Approach to Treatment of Post-Traumatic Stress Disorder." In B.A. van der Kolk, A. C. McFarlane, and L. Weisaeth, eds., *Traumatic Stress: The Effects of Overwhelming Experience on Mind, Body, and Society*, 417–440. New York: Guilford.

van der Kolk, B. A., A. C. McFarlane, and L. Weisaeth, eds., 1996. *Traumatic Stress: The Effects of Overwhelming Experience on Mind, Body, and Society.* New York: Guilford.

"Wounded Knee Remembered." 1990. *Lakota Times Special Edition*, December.

Yehuda, R., ed. 1999. *Risk Factors for Posttraumatic Stress Disorder.* Washington, D.C.: American Psychiatric.

10

Transforming the Trauma of
September 11, 2001, with Children and
Adolescents Through Group Work

ANDREW MALEKOFF

A group of early-adolescent boys and girls who lost parents in the attack on the World Trade Center prepared for the ending of their group sessions by decorating stones to be placed in a memorial rock garden (Malekoff 2004). The kids in the bereavement group sat together around a rectangular table covered with newspaper. In front of each of them was a smooth oval-shaped stone, roughly double the size of a portable CD player. They decorated the stones with unique designs of paint and glitter, each one a personal remembrance of their moms or dads. As they decorated, the group worker moved from one to another, admiring and asking them about each design. "Mine is painted gold," beamed Mack. "I painted it gold because my dad is like gold to me." A heart framed Jenny's design, "because my mom will always be in my heart." On Seth's stone were two intertwined hands, a small one and a larger one that showed "me and my dad were best friends." Victoria painted a fire hat and said, "My dad is my hero." On some stones they painted, "I will miss you," on others, "I will always love you," and on some a combination of both. Many included a patriotic theme. There were lots of stars and stripes. Each one of them touched a chord in the others as they spoke . . . "He's like gold. . . . She will always

be in my heart. . . . He was my best friend. . . . He's my hero . . . " The
room was enveloped in a warm glow.

After a week or so, when the stones were dry, a memorial ceremony that the
"9/11 bereavement group" planned was held. This was an important ritual for
kids whose moms' and dads' bodies were never recovered or were found only in
parts. During one group meeting Alison revealed that her family couldn't
decide whether to bury her father in a regular-sized casket or a baby casket.
She explained, "All they found was his arm."

The surviving parents and siblings, many of whom also decorated stones in
their groups, participated in a candle-lighting ceremony in which each one
had a chance to choose a spot in the rock garden and place his or her rock
there. If they chose to, they could say a few words. Or they could simply
silently place their stone. Benches surround the rock garden, a sacred place
created by caring group members, a place they will return to for just a look, or
to sit for a while and remember someone dear and to recall their time
together as a group.

In the immediate aftermath of the September 11, 2001, terrorist attack on the United States, several graphic artists joined together to produce a softcover book titled 9/11: *Artists Respond*. It is a collection of art, sequenced to showcase the artists' response to the terror that befell the world. One nine-frame piece, titled *Please Stand By . . .* (Loeb and Campbell 2002), features a girl about eight years old watching a cartoon program on television. By the third and fourth frames, the image on the screen changes to a live feed of the twin towers ablaze. As the little girl stands mesmerized, stuffed animal in hand and face pressed against the screen, the commentator announces, "We interrupt this program to take you live . . . " The little girl turns away and calls, "Mommy . . . " The next three frames begin with her mother dropping a full basket of laundry. Then, with her face twisted in anguish, she embraces her daughter to shield her from the unrelenting images. The final frame is a close-up of the little girl asking, "Mommy, when are the cartoons gonna come back on?" (Gitterman and Malekoff 2002:4)

Understanding Child and Adolescent Survivors of Terrorism

More than three thousand children lost a parent in the 9/11 attacks. More than two-thirds of these children were under seventeen on that day. Millions of others watched the attack on television, most repeatedly (Ahern et al. 2005). To date, there are no studies using a longitudinal design to evaluate the impact that the attacks had on children and adolescents. However, surveys of thousands of New York City children and adolescents, six or more months after the attack, point to higher rates of stress disorder, major depression, generalized anxiety, agoraphobia, separation anxiety, sleeping disorders, numbing, increased arousal, and fears than are evidenced in the general population (Pfefferbaum et al. 2005:311–312).

The terrorist attacks of September 11, 2001 (9/11), demonstrate in the most horrific terms that violence, grief, and trauma know no bounds and have become a fact of life in communities across the United States. The aftermath of 9/11 involves a complex healing and recovery process for those who were directly affected, one that addresses the most basic assumptions about self and community. 9/11 has also had direct and rippling effects on the millions who saw it on television, know about it, and grieve with those who were there. Children and adolescents are particularly vulnerable to the consequences of this devastating life experience.

The troubling impact of the neurobiological and psychosocial consequences of trauma and violence include post-traumatic stress disorders and responses such as impaired cognitive, behavioral, and psychosocial development, dysfunctional thinking and processing, altered attention and concentration, anxiety, depression, dissociation, aggression, violence, suspicion, mistrust, sense of foreshortened future, isolation, and changes in peer and family relationships.

Two years after 9/11, one young person who lost a parent said to a newspaper reporter, "Sometimes it feels like a scab that can't heal" (McCrummen and Smith 2003). The poetry of a thirteen-year-old, who did not lose anyone but who did witness airplanes crashing into the twin towers repeatedly on a television set in middle school, is another graphic illustration of the widespread impact, lingering effects, and lasting imprint that traumatic events can leave in their wake. Just weeks before writing the poem, its author, Darren, was asked if he thought about 9/11 anymore. "No, not really" was his response, one that clearly illustrates, in light of his subsequent poem, the coping function of denial as one stage in the grieving and loss process. Think of a young person you know, someone who *looks okay*, as you read on.

Fate or Fantasy

6:00 am
alarm goes off
wake up
do the usual
shower, brush teeth, drink coffee
get on the train

arrive at Penn Station
Take subway downtown to
    chambers street
Look at watch
Late
it's 8:30
Try to get on every elevator
All used
Wait
5 minutes go by
finally get on elevator
100th floor
it's 8:35
in office

turn on computer
8:37
Put head on my desk
Building shakes
Thought I was asleep

Immediately look out window
See man in mid air
Tumbling
Screaming profanities
People crying

People screaming in shock
Rushing to get to stairs and elevator
Hear cry of children

Take another glance out window
More smoke and debris
People lying on the ground
Fire fighters and police officers every
where
Finally get a feeling
We've been hit
A jet has hit the World Trade Center
Don't have much time
So I jump
Down
And down
100 flights
Look in the windows
Crying faces
People panicking
As I fall and fall it seems like an
    eternity
Above me falling is my brother
He calls to me
What are you doing here
You must realize
Is this fantasy or your true fate
O my god
Sweating
Late for work
it's 9 o'clock
Turn on television
ABC
Lying in bed
Eyes closed
Hear "This just in . . . the North
    tower has
been hit by a jet
plane"
Open eyes and realize
Fate or Fantasy. . . .

These words now haunt me until I
  start
to recover
Years have gone by
Therapy isn't working
Can't take it any more
Jump off of the empire state
  building
While dropping
Hear
Fate or fantasy . . . you choose

once again my worst fear has not yet
ended
But it has just begun.

—Darren Malekoff (2002)

Uncomplicated grief is a normal process of grieving that occurs when an important relationship is lost. Added to the equation in traumatic grief are symptoms of distress and trauma, in which "the usual grief responses of yearning are mixed with frightening memories of the traumatic event. Thus the sadness and longing for the person who died combine with the trauma and may disrupt or derail the usual grief process" (Webb 2004:12). Traumatic grief, therefore, needs to be separated from other forms of grief, in part because it places the individual at increased risk for ongoing mental illness if left untreated (Pfefferbaum et al. 2005).

What has been described as a "clinician friendly" definition of childhood trauma (Scheidlinger and Kahn 2005) is offered by Lenore Terr (1991), who defines it as the emotional fallout of "one sudden external blow or series of blows rendering the young person temporarily helpless and breaking past ordinary coping" (11). Mourning and rebuilding are needed in the resolution of traumatic life events.

Collective trauma is "a blow to tissues of social life that damages the bonds linking people together, and impairs the prevailing sense of communality" (Erikson 1976:154). After trauma, individuals become isolated and lose the capacity to use community supports. They risk experiencing recurrent despair, psychic numbing, and even clinical depression that strip them of the ability to react affectively, to recognize and make use of emotional reactions. Perhaps Judith Herman (1997) said it best in two simple words: "Trauma isolates" (214). In the aftermath of the collective trauma of 9/11, some children and adolescents felt unprotected and on their own, like orphans who felt they must take care of themselves. Herman also reminds us that "the failure to complete the normal process of griev-ing perpetuates the traumatic reaction" (69).

Over the past thirty years, children from around the world and close to home have felt the direct impact of terrorist attacks. In 1974 terrorists launched the Ma'alot massacre in Israel, in which more than one hundred children were captured in a school building, twenty-two were killed, and many more wounded and traumatized (Ayalon 2004). Thirty years later, in 2004, hundreds of children and adults were taken hostage in an elementary school in the Russian town of Beslan (Danieli, Brom, and Sills 2005). On the third day of the standoff between the security forces and the hostage-takers, almost 350 were killed, more than half of them children, and hundreds more suffered trauma. Between these two attacks countless terrorist attacks occurred around the world, including homegrown horrors in the United States that have become branded forever by their locations—Oklahoma City and Columbine.

As each of these situations evolves and becomes part of our collective reality and consciousness, professionals from around the world working with children in the aftermath of trauma are faced with the challenge of sharing knowledge and sharing care to confront this "psychological war-fare against the community" that requires "community-based, culturally congruent interventions, with a public mental health approach, in an ongoing, integrated network of services promoting community and indi-vidual resilience, specialized training, international collaboration, and continued dialogue concerning the role of the media" (Danieli et al. 2005:775–776). It is very important to include the last item, the role of the media, in the equation because of its intrusive impact on young people who live far away from a terrorist attack.

Intrusive thoughts are common in the aftermath of a traumatic event as well. They may surface at any time, and they may be triggered by remind-ers or emerge without any reason at all (Gurwich and Messenbaugh 1995). The media, particularly television, are pervasive triggers of unwelcome reminders, and there is very little chance to screen out disturbing images and rhetoric in the aftermath of a major disaster. Having the means to cope with unwelcome reminders is a critical need for young people in the aftermath of a traumatic event.

A key question raised by trauma experts is how to regenerate a sense of human interdependence and community. Although many social rituals help support mourners through the process of normal bereavement, there is no custom or common ritual that recognizes the mourning that follows traumatic life events. "In the absence of such support," Herman (1997) states, "the potential for pathological grief and severe, persistent depression is extremely high" (70). At a November 11, 2001, meeting in New York City sponsored by the Red Cross, Diane Myers, a psychiatric nurse and trauma specialist, stated, "It is because trauma isolates that we need to reduce isolation and foster social connection to overcome alienation" (Myers 2001). In other words, recovery from trauma must involve restoring a sense of community, which is also one of the key functions of group work.

Empowering Responses with Group Work Activities to Welcome Positive Memories with Child and Adolescent Survivors of 9/11

Among the many innovations in the aftermath of 9/11, group interventions empower young people by encouraging grieving, strengthening individual coping skills, and restoring connections—a sense of community—in the isolating aftermath of disaster. The purpose of this section is to present practice illustrations for group work to empower children and youth in the aftermath of disaster. Nancy Boyd Webb (2005) recommends involving "children and adolescents in selected stress-reduction activities prior to introducing group exercises that may arouse anxiety related to memories of traumatic loss" (367). Such activities are best when they help children calm down and soothe themselves in fun ways. The blending of verbal and nonverbal activities to engage young people and help them heal is illustrated in the following narrative. This exercise helps identify feelings and can be viewed as a first step toward stress reduction and improved coping, both of which are necessary for addressing complicated bereavement.

A group of rough-and-ready, rambunctious, athletic eight- and nine-year-old boys was formed in a local elementary school. All had lost fathers in the World Trade Center. Nothing would work to encourage them to talk. I racked my brain and then decided to try something different. "We're going to try something fun and new." "What?" they asked.

I brought in a large bowl to be filled with water and several Wiffle balls with the name of a different feeling (e.g., angry, sad, frustrated) taped to each ball. The balls were then wrapped in a clear plastic covering to keep them dry and reveal the name of the feeling. I directed each of the group members to take turns, using only one hand to pick up a ball and then hold it (them) down in *the bowl filled with water and to say something about the feeling related to a day of the week. For example, Anger: "On Sunday I got angry when my favorite football team lost," or Nervous: "I got nervous on Sunday when I had to go back to school." I purposely did not start them off talking about the loss, as that would have been too threatening. First I wanted them to understand feelings, to label them.*

After each ball was chosen and held down in the water, I asked them to take a second and third and fourth ball, and so on, never letting go of any of the balls they chose. As they held down several balls in one hand, the water spilled over the side, or they lost their grip on one or more of the balls and it popped up to the surface. One member threw up his hands and said: "Okay, okay, I get it, I get it already, we can't keep down all our feelings at once or they will pop up or spill over." "What does that mean?" I asked them. "Feelings popping up and spilling over?" And the once silent members answered almost in unison, "It means we can't control it, can't keep it in anymore, it can pop up in bad ways . . . you can't hold down what you can't control."

This little game seemed to open them up and they were off and running, or I should say talking. Now that their feelings were out, we could move to the task of how to reduce stress (Toni Kolb Papetti, personal communication 2005).

Group work is indispensable in the aftermath of traumatic events and can serve as a counterforce to bleak outcomes that result from isolation after disaster occurs. It can help to empower individuals by restoring human dignity, building coping skills, helping them to find their voice, and making things happen on personal, interpersonal, and social/community levels (Wise 2005). Most of all, combining healing from trauma and empowerment must involve restoring a sense of community "through a reciprocal process from conceptual understanding to visible action" (Wise 2005:20). What better way is there to accomplish this than through group work, with its dual vision of individual goals and social ends? (Lee 2001). "If trauma isolates, group work connects" (Malekoff 2001).

Competent group work requires the use of both verbal and nonverbal activities. Group work practitioners must, once and for all, learn to relax and to abandon the bizarre belief that the only successful group is the one in which people sit still and speak politely and insightfully (Malekoff 2004). Group work activities are more than "tools," more than programmed content, more than "canned" exercises, and more than a mechanistic means to an end. Middleman (1985) aptly described the "toolness of program more as putty than a hammer, i.e., as a tool that also changes as it is used" (4). In addition to a wealth of available structured resource material (e.g., games and exercises), other activities grow spontaneously out of the living together that the group does.

The illustrations include several groups of young people who lost parents in the World Trade Center. The group members created moving symbols and rituals for remembering, learned skills to cope and soothe themselves in the face of unwelcome reminders, and exercised their voices to make a difference and extend the bonds of belonging beyond themselves (Malekoff 2004).

CREATING A BOARD GAME TO REMEMBER DAD

Activities in groups can have special meaning when they are the group's own creation. One group of preteens struggled with the words to address their experience. One group worker patiently tried various activities and finally decided to go in another direction.

She had an idea and asked, "What kind of games do you like to play?" Freely listing their favorites: Pictionary, Charades, Word Blender, etc., she activated the group to create a board game from scratch. Each of the boxes on the board represented a different feeling. They used an hourglass to keep time. There were game cards in each category of the favorite games they had identified. For example, game cards for Charades might direct the player whose turn it was to act out a time when her or his dad was angry. Everything was about the person who died. The game pieces were handmade clay pieces that represented something memorable about their dads. For example, one group member made a football ("Dad and I watched the NFL on Sundays").

Another made an ice cream cone in remembrance of a special place they went for ice cream "after my soccer games." And another made a sneaker, because "Dad jogged every morning." The group worker told the members that they could take the game pieces home each week but they declined because, as one said, "We want to keep them here because when we come here, that's when we play with our dads" (Toni Kolb Papetti, personal communication 2005).

COGNITIVE-BEHAVIORAL STRATEGIES IN GROUP WORK TO EMPOWER YOUNG PEOPLE TO COPE WITH INTRUSIVE THOUGHTS

Group work can help young people to normalize intrusive thoughts or flashbacks, regulate feelings, soothe and take care of themselves, and calm themselves down in the here and now so that such thoughts don't interfere with attention and concentration; and so that the young people can have a life (van der Kolk 1987). Cognitive behavioral understanding and rehearsal can help in the calming-down, self-soothing, and rebuilding process (Malekoff 2004).

Examples of cognitive-behavioral tools to help young people to calm themselves in the face of intrusive memories and reminders include those that can be used differentially at home and at school. One illustration is a group of pre-adolescent boys and girls who used art supplies to construct a game, one intended to be "played" alone. On a piece of hard cardboard, a circle is drawn and then divided into several slices, like a pie. An activity that one might do to redirect thoughts or provide some self-soothing is described in words or depicted in drawings on each slice. A spinner is added to the center of the pie. If unwelcome reminders spring forth at home, the object is to spin the spinner and see where it lands. The choices might be, for example, play a video game, call a friend, write in a journal, read a book, or take a nap. In the group, the discussion about what choices are available reinforces for members that they are in the same boat and that they are not just survivors/victims but they have something important to offer.

In school, the choices of activities for these purposes need to be more dis-creet, as the group members do not want to face the embarrassment of reach-ing into their book bags and pulling out their spinners. An alternative is to draw the image of a traffic stop sign and paste it on the back of a notebook. In school the choices are different than at home. The stop sign is divided into segments that are more likely to engage one's imagination. Choices might include a safe place or a happy place to travel to in one's mind temporarily. Examples are a park, ice cream parlor, baseball field, or someplace that the family traveled to that evokes a pleasant memory, like a family gathering close to home or a family vacation farther from home. Again, in the group the kids can help one another think about what to include and why.

Two variations of these activities have been referred to as Change the Channel and Safe Place Imagery. Nancy Boyd Webb (2005) offers detailed instructions for presenting activities to cope with intrusive thoughts. For example,

Change the channel: "Imagine that your head is a television set. Lots of pictures are going through your head. But YOU ARE IN CONTROL—you can change the channel if you don't like the station. Pretend that you are watching something scary that makes you feel bad; put your hand up to your ear, and pretend that it is the knob on the TV set. Twist the 'knob' and now put your 'safe place' picture in place of the scary picture. You can do this to help yourself feel calmer whenever you get upset."

(367–368)

These activities—Wiffle Ball Feelings, Creating a Board Game, and Change the Channel—share a common thread in that they offer young people who have suffered a traumatic event, and perhaps a major loss, the opportunity to begin to gain some control and power over their lives.

HELPING YOUNG PEOPLE TO MAKE WAVES:
GIVING VOICE THROUGH GROUP WORK

Group workers tune in to the "near things of individual need and the far things of social reform" (Schwartz 1986). This dual vision was first conceptualized by one of the earliest group work researchers, Wilbur Newstetter (1935). Group workers help group members become active participants in community affairs so that they might make a difference, might one day change the world where others have failed. Understanding the dual vision is especially critical for youth today when so many world-shattering and traumatic events affect our lives. Kids need to learn how to make waves, big waves and gentle waves (Malekoff 2004). A good group can be a great start for this kind of consciousness development and action. For one group, this involved an opportunity to advise the experts.

A colleague who was working with a group of adolescents who had lost their dads in the attack on the World Trade Center asked for their advice (Judy Esposito, personal communication 2004). She told her group, "I was asked to make a presentation at a national conference of bereavement counselors. The meeting is being held in Kansas City. They want to learn about what we're doing in New York that helps. I'd like them to learn from you. What should I tell them? What advice do you have? What do you think helps?" The group members said to tell them:

- Grown-ups need to know that kids have a voice.
- Grown-ups need to listen.
- Groups are important to feel better and not to feel alone.
- Grown-ups need to be patient and to know that grieving takes a long time.
- It is okay to laugh. Laughing doesn't mean you forgot about your lost loved one, or aren't still hurting.
- It is okay to have fun. After all, "That is what our dads would want."

The group members were eager to have a report when the group worker returned and were pleased that their input was accepted and well received.

Group workers can offer opportunities for action that represent triumph over the demoralization of helplessness and despair. Maintaining a dual vision enables group workers to encourage group members, when they appear to be ready and willing, to shift from individual to social goals. A simple act, such as being invited by a professional to advise bereavement counselors, makes a powerful statement to young people. It teaches them that making a difference and taking action can be accomplished through quietly thoughtful means as well as more dramatic, "in-your-face" approaches such as antiwar protest marches. It tells them that we believe they have something valuable to offer. Exercising what one has to offer is one part of what true empowerment is about.

Enlisting the opinions of the young "advisors" was a gentle approach, as is yet another group's creation and public display of a quilt of remembrance adorned with colorful squares, each uniquely devoted to a lost loved one. More turbulent waves may come in the form of participation in public demonstrations related to the war in Iraq or in response to the controversy regarding plans for how the deceased should be memorialized at Ground Zero. Participation in a group can be invaluable in helping young people to think through powerful issues that they feel passionate about and to sort through strong feelings before making a commitment to join an organized movement or taking individual actions for a cause in which they strongly believe. Making waves is an inherently spiritual act, one that leads young people to think and feel deeply. Making waves is an empowering and hopeful act and an antidote to inertia and apathy.

Sights, Sounds, and Smells: The Impact on the Social Worker

Helping youth cope with their losses and grief can stir powerful parallel feelings in the social worker (vicarious traumatization and remembrance). This is particularly true when the social worker is from the same grieving community and has experienced losses of his or her own. On October 28, 2001, in my role as a social worker in a children's mental health agency located about twenty-five miles from Ground Zero, I attended a memorial service at the World Trade Center that drew thousands of mourners. Writing about the experience helped me decompress after weeks of intense activity surrounding the terrorist attack (Malekoff 2002).

> We [a contingent of mental health professionals] were strategically spread out among an ocean of loved ones, our task that day to provide support for grieving family members who sat amid the smoldering ruins, bearing witness to the horror that so viciously intruded into their lives.
>
> As the service drew to an end, I walked several blocks to the Hudson River where we boarded a boat and headed back to the Pier where we would later greet loved ones once more; mothers, fathers, sons, daughters, brothers, sisters, husbands and wives, all of whom would receive urns with the ashes from Ground Zero. It would be about a thirty-minute ride. As we drifted away from Ground Zero, I tried to wrap my mind around what I just came from. The idea of 15,000 mourners at a gravesite for thousands of murder victims in a location less than an hour from my home was hard to absorb.
>
> As we approached the WTC, I thought about the scores of people I met in the previous weeks who escaped and their surreal descriptions of the morning of 9/11, images and sensations that will never leave them; the odor of jet fuel; sweat-drenched firefighters in full gear climbing up stairs and urging everyone else to head down; women bursting from the buildings carrying shoes in hand in order to run faster; people jumping to their deaths rather than being burned alive; and frantic figures scattering from the site holding food trays overhead to avoid the blizzard of debris, running as fast as their legs would carry them past stretch limousines with assorted airplane parts jutting from the hoods.
>
> One woman, an employee of a twin tower based insurance firm, told me that when she exited the building, the first thing she did was look up. Almost immediately she saw the second plane crash into tower two. She said that before she could run to safety she had to find another witness to confirm what she saw. "I thought I was going crazy, hallucinating," she said. The horrifying images of those who escaped are rivaled only by the tyranny of imagination that now plagues the bereaved.
>
> Weeks before the memorial service, we had been receiving calls at the agency. There were calls from businesses, local government, the New York City Fire Department, and local schools and community groups. Working and living in an increasingly diverse community, we learned about the re-awakened terror of immigrants who escaped violent and oppressive regimes for the land of the free and who now said, "I didn't think that this could happen here." We met parents of Muslim faith who feared for their

children's safety, including one mother who dyed her children's hair blond so that "they wouldn't be mistaken for kin of the terrorists."

We also received direct calls from people who escaped and families who lost loved ones. One call was from a parent whose eleven-year-old son Danny refused to eat. His father was missing. Through Danny's story, I learned about the tyranny of imagination. Danny imagined his father to be alive in his office in the World Trade Center and trapped, alone, and starving. If his father couldn't eat, Danny reasoned, then he wouldn't eat.

(29–30)

I knew that my colleagues and I, for years to come, would be helping those like Danny deal with the grief and trauma that had so suddenly and viciously invaded and torn their world apart, shattering any sense of normalcy, safety, and community. Although familiar to mental health professionals before 9/11, the terms *traumatic grief* and *post-traumatic stress* would soon forever become a routine, rather than irregular, part of their lexicon.

Parallels Between Group Work Principles and Empowerment Principles for Children and Youth in the Aftermath of Disaster

Practice principles for group work to empower children and youth in the aftermath of disaster mirror empowerment principles in important ways. These principles empower young people by building individual coping skills and preventing isolation.

PROVIDE PROTECTION, SUPPORT, AND SAFETY

Children and youth need safe places to go, with worthwhile things to do, and opportunities for belonging. And they need relationships with competent adults who understand and care about them. Living through traumatic events can contribute to a pervasive sense of fearfulness, hypervigilance, and despair. Participation in a safe and supportive group can serve as a counterforce to the alienating and numbing aftermath of a traumatic event. Group workers must carefully attend to the structure of the group to ensure a basic level of physical and emotional safety that helps to cultivate a sense of trust and that will enable the worker to mutually identify needs with group members (thus equalizing power differentials) and to assist the youth as they empower themselves. Both hands-on practice savvy and ongoing advocacy are required in order to ensure sound environments for group development. A safe haven is a prerequisite for tapping in to the strengths that group members have to offer after a trauma has occurred.

CREATE GROUPS FOR SURVIVORS THAT REESTABLISH CONNECTIONS AND REBUILD A SENSE OF COMMUNITY

Trauma leads to demoralization, disorientation, and loss of connection. Participation in a supportive group addresses the primary need of trauma survivors to affiliate. Group affiliation can provide mutual support, promote cooperative roles, reduce isolation, integrate support from others, and normalize young (and older) people's responses and reactions to what feels like a surreal situation. When addressed in a group context, these are important steps to rebuilding a sense of community.

OFFER OPPORTUNITIES FOR ACTION THAT REPRESENTS TRIUMPH OVER THE DEMORALIZATION OF HELPLESSNESS AND DESPAIR

"Talking about the trauma is rarely if ever enough," advises noted trauma expert Bessel van der Kolk (1987). He points to the Holocaust memorial in Jerusalem and the Vietnam War Memorial in Washington, D.C., "as good examples of symbols that enable survivors to mourn the dead and establish the historical and cultural meaning of the traumatic events . . . to remind survivors of the ongoing potential for communality and sharing." He goes on to say that this also applies "to survivors of other types of traumas, who may have to build less visible memorials and common symbols to help them mourn and express their shame about their own vulnerability." Examples are writing books or poetry, engaging in social action, volunteering to help other victims, or any of the multitude of creative solutions that individuals can find to confront "even the most desperate plight" (437). Taking action with and on behalf of others can open the door to increasing empathy and multicultural respect among children and youth and help them to empower themselves to make a difference (see "Making Waves" poem at the end of this chapter). Group workers help foster the ability to make waves by taking a cooperative role in the group process and by modeling multicultural respect and social advocacy. Other authors have also shown the importance of using the arts to give voice to young people affected by traumatic events, including drawing (Yedida and Itzhaky 2004), sand play (Carey 2004), music (Loewy and Stewart 2004), and group projects such as murals, metaphoric play, and other creative activities (Haen 2005).

UNDERSTAND THAT TRAUMATIC GRIEF IS A TWO-SIDED COIN THAT INCLUDES BOTH WELCOME REMEMBRANCES AND UNWELCOME REMINDERS

Group work can provide a safe space for young people to grieve their lost loved ones in the aftermath of a disaster. However, without adequate tools to use in coping, some dimensions of remembering can be crushing to one who is traumatically bereaved. The two sides of the "remembering coin" are welcome remembrances of a lost loved one and unwelcome reminders of a loved one who was lost. One side is an empowering experience and involves addressing sadness and longing by gradually welcoming loving memories. The other side is a disempowering experience and involves intermittently succumbing to uninvited and intrusive thoughts and the tyranny of imagination. Developing awareness of specific and individual needs—welcome and unwelcome—is critical to empowering oneself. In the illustrations above, group activities were used to elicit loving memories and to manage the stress of intrusive reminders.

Conclusion and Recommendations

This chapter emphasizes the value of group affiliation as an empowering counterforce to the dissolution of the bonds that link people to one another in the aftermath of collective trauma, and the accompanying disorientation, demoralization, and loss of connection. Group work provides a potent tool for helping young people to grieve and develop coping skills to counter traumatic grief, giving voice and encouraging action, and promoting resilience in the face of the most adverse conditions (Baum 2005; Lee 2001).

Group activities usually originate with group workers' responding on the basis of their knowledge of what works best for what kids in what situations. But this is not always the case. Group workers must be flexible enough to welcome the group's ideas and innovations, as seen earlier when the group created a board game to remember their dads. These are the creative applications, the member- and worker-initiated innovations that can be cultivated and brought to life in the group, contributing to a feeling of empowerment and a growing sense of groupness and rich history of experience together.

Curricula and manuals on group work and individual work with traumatized and bereaved people are plentiful and are great resources, primarily if the group members themselves use them and welcome modification and innovation. This also applies to the use of evidence-based cognitive-behavioral strategies. Think curriculum-informed versus curriculum-driven, so that children and adolescents can be active participants in decision making and problem solving.

Group workers must go beyond being flexible and innovative in the use of activities. They must also find a balance between when to provide clear direction and instructions (i.e., Change the Channel), when to encourage the group to be inventive (i.e., Creating a Board Game to Remember Dad), and when to experiment (i.e., Wiffle Ball Feelings). All offer the opportunity for young people to regain some sense of control and power over their lives.

In the post-9/11 world, there are many opportunities for all three levels of empowerment practice—the personal, the interpersonal, and the social/community. At the personal level are ways of helping young people individually and collectively to transcend trauma, to discover new ways to cope from day to day, and to regenerate community in the isolating aftermath of disaster. At the interpersonal level, offering good group experiences in the aftermath of trauma provides children and youth the opportunity to develop skills for coping with the stress of intrusive and unwelcome reminders and enables them to share memories of loved ones in a supportive environment with others who are "all in the same boat." The good news, as illustrated above and gleaned from studies of children in disaster around the world, is that many of them were found to "maintain an active and positive attitude in the face of adversity" (Rosenfeld et al. 2005). All they need is *a little help from their friends.*

Ways of assisting young people, particularly older adolescents, at the community and sociopolitical level can be seen in an interest to engage in consciousness development (Breton 1992) in response to new post-9/11 realities such as war abroad, civil liberties at home, and the role of the mainstream media (Goodman 2004). In other words, we can help young people to find their voice and make a difference—*make some waves.*

One key to being a good adult partner with adolescents is helping teenagers to make waves (Malekoff 2004). Our young people need to see the potential of changing not only oneself but also one's surroundings so that they may become active participants in community affairs, so that they might make a difference, might change the world one day where we have failed to. It is essential that we help teenagers to make waves, that we become guiding lights leading them toward a sense of meaning and purpose.

Making Waves

what's it like to
  have no voice
  have no say
  have no choice;

what's it like to
  make no waves;

to have
  optical-delusions
  and
  spiritual-
contusions;

  psychic-psorosis
  and
  civic-sclerosis;
to
  make no waves;

to be told
  what's so
to think
  so what;
to hang
  on the

edge
  of a
  terminal
  rut;

skyscraper up
no ground floor
two-way mirror
no back door
elevator out
stairway down
level below
lost and found;

where's my voice
where's my say
where's my choice
where's my wave;

want to make waves
tackle real need
take on the
kingdom of
corporate greed;

sheet rock craters

fists in flight
aimless days
  dreamless nights
decade plus three on
  terra non firma
extra layer of
  rawhide derma;

give me liberty
or
take my breath;

want to make waves

have something to say
  something to say

want to make waves
want to shake things up
want to wake things up
want to wake you up
  want to shake you up:

you primal
dreamers
you silent

screamers	not rants and raves	some waves
you screaming	want to make waves	want to make waves
dreamers;	not psychic caves	want to make
	want to make waves	waves
hear my voice	not nine to five graves	want to get wet
my say	want to make waves	want to make
my choice;	not corporate slaves;	some waves
	want to make waves	want to make waves.
want to make waves	want to make waves	
want to move the earth	want to jump in	
want to make waves	want to make	

—Andy Malekoff ©

References

Ahern, J., S. Galea, H. Resnick, and D. Vlahov. 2005. "Television Watching and Mental Health in the General Population of New York After September 11." In Y. Danieli, D. Brom, and J. Sills, eds., *The Trauma of Terrorism: Sharing Knowledge and Shared Care, An International Handbook*, 109–124. Binghamton, N.Y.: Haworth.

Ayalon, O. 2004. "Children's Responses to Terrorist Attacks." In D. Knafo, ed., *Living with Terror, Working with Trauma*, 171–200. New York: Aronson.

Baum, N.L. 2005. "Building Resilience: A School-Based Intervention for Children Exposed to Ongoing Trauma and Stress." In Y. Danieli, D. Brom, and J. Sills, eds., *The Trauma of Terrorism: Sharing Knowledge and Shared Care, An International Handbook*, 487–498. Binghamton, N.Y.: Haworth.

Breton, M. 1992. "Liberation Theology, Group Work, and the Right of the Poor and Oppressed to Participate in the Life of the Community." In J.A. Garland, ed., *Group Work Reaching Out: People, Places, and Power*, 257–270. Binghamton, N.Y.: Haworth.

Carey, L. 2004. "Sandplay, Art, and Play Therapy to Promote Anxiety Reduction." In N. Boyd Webb, ed., *Mass Trauma and Violence: Helping Families and Children Cope*, 216–233. New York: Guilford.

Danieli, Y., D. Brom, and J. Sills. 2005. "Sharing Knowledge and Shared Care." In Y. Danieli, D. Brom, and J. Sills, eds., *The Trauma of Terrorism: Sharing Knowledge and Shared Care: An International Handbook*, 775–790. Binghamton, N.Y.: Haworth.

Erikson, K. 1976. *Everything in Its Path: Destruction of Community in the Buffalo Creek Flood.* New York: Simon and Schuster.

Esposito, J. 2004. Personal communication.

Gitterman, A., and A. Malekoff. 2002. "Introduction to September 11 Memorial Issue." In A. Gitterman and A. Malekoff, eds., *Reflections: Narratives of Professional Helping* (September 11 Memorial Issue) 8 (3): 4–6.

Goodman, A. 2004. *The Exception to the Rulers: Exposing Oily Politicians, War Profiteers, and the Media Who Love Them.* New York: Hyperion.

Gurwich, R., and A. Messenbaugh. 1995. *Healing After Trauma Skills: A Manual for Professionals, Teachers, and Families Working with Children After Disaster.* Oklahoma City: Department of Pediatrics, University of Oklahoma Health Sciences Center.

Haen, C. 2005. "Rebuilding Security: Group Therapy with Children Affected by September 11." *International Journal of Group Psychotherapy* 55 (3): 391–414.

Herman, J. 1997. *Trauma and Recovery.* 2nd ed. New York: Basic.

Lee, J. A. B. 2001. *The Empowerment Approach to Social Work Practice: Building the Beloved Community.* 2nd ed. New York: Columbia University Press.

Loeb, J., and J. Campbell. 2002. "Please Stand By . . ." In *9–11: Artists Respond.* Vol.1, 28–30. Milwaukie, Ore.: Dark Horse Comics.

Loewy, J., and K. Stewart. 2004. "Music Therapy to Help Traumatized Children and Caregivers." In N. Boyd Webb, ed., *Mass Trauma and Violence: Helping Families and Children Cope,* 191–215. New York: Guilford.

Malekoff, A. 2001. "On Making Connections and Being Flexible: A Group Worker's Diary of the First Ten Days Following September 11th, 2001." *Social Work with Groups* 24 (3/4): 3–10.

——. 2002. "The Longest Day." In A. Gitterman and A. Malekoff, eds., *Reflections: Narratives of Professional Helping* (September 11 Memorial Issue) 8 (3): 28–35.

——. 2004. *Group Work with Adolescents: Principles and Practice.* 2nd ed. New York: Guilford.

McCrummin, S., and J. Smith. 2003. "Trying to Move Beyond the Pain: Two Years Later, Kids of 9/11 Coping in Different Ways." *Newsday,* September 7, 2003.

Middleman, R. 1985. "Integrating the Arts and Activities in Clinical Group Work Practice." Paper presented at the Center for Group Work Studies, March 22, 1985, Barry University School of Social Work, Miami Shores, Florida.

Myers, D. 2001. Red Cross Sponsored Meeting. November 11, 2001. New York, N.Y.

Newstetter, W. 1935. "What Is Social Group Work?" In *Proceedings of the National Conference of Social Work,* 291–299. Chicago: University of Chicago Press.

Papetti, T.K. 2005. Personal communication.

Pfefferbaum, B., E. DeVoe, J. Stuber, M. Schiff, T. Klien, and G. Fairbrother. 2005. "Psychological Impact of Terrorism on Children and Families in the United States." In Y. Danieli, D. Brom, and J. Sills, eds., *The Trauma of Terrorism: Sharing Knowledge and Shared Care, An International Handbook,* 305–318. Binghamton, N.Y.: Haworth.

Rosenfeld, L., J. Caye, O. Ayalon, and M. Lahad. 2005. *When Their World Falls Apart: Helping Families and Children Manage the Effects of Disasters.* Washington, D.C.: NASW Press.

Scheidlinger, S., and R. Kahn. 2005. "In the Aftermath of September 11: Group Interventions with Traumatized Children Revisited." *International Journal of Group Psychotherapy* 55 (3): 335–354.

Schwartz, W. 1986. "The Group Work Tradition and Social Work Practice." In A. Gitterman and L. Shulman, eds., *The Legacy of William Schwartz: Group Practice as Shared Interaction.* Special Issue. *Social Work with Groups* 8 (4): 7–28.

Terr, L. 1991. "Childhood Traumas: An Outline and Overview." *American Journal of Psychiatry* 148:10–20.

van der Kolk, B.A. 1987. *Psychological Trauma.* Washington, D.C.: American Psychiatric Press.

Webb, N.B. 2004. "The Impact of Traumatic Stress and Loss on Children and Families." In N. Boyd Webb, ed., *Mass Trauma and Violence: Helping Families and Children Cope,* 3–22. New York: Guilford.

——. 2005. "Groups for Children Traumatically Bereaved by the Attacks of September 11, 2001." *International Journal for Group Psychotherapy* 55 (3): 355–374.

Wise, J.B. 2005. *Empowerment Practice with Families in Distress.* New York: Columbia University Press.

Yedida, T., and H. Itzhaky. 2004. "A Drawing Technique for Diagnosis and Therapy of Adolescents Suffering Traumatic Stress and Loss." In N. Boyd Webb, ed., *Mass Trauma and Violence: Helping Families and Children Cope,* 283–303. New York: Guilford.

11

Response to Poverty as a Form of Transforming Trauma

JEAN EAST AND SUE KENNEY

Jennifer, the 23-year-old mother of a 9-month-old boy, sought counseling at the suggestion of her mother. Jennifer has lived with Dan, the father of her baby, for four years. Recently, both Jennifer and Dan lost their jobs, and Dan has become verbally abusive and at times severely angry with Jennifer and with others. He refuses to seek psychological help. Both feel the stress of unexpectedly finding themselves as parents and having only the income from Temporary Assistance for Needy Families (TANF) with which to support their family. Jennifer has little personal support except for her mother, who lives out of state, and Dan—and she now feels trapped and dependent on him.

Jennifer's story is one of interpersonal violence. She has never known security as an adult. When she was a baby, her parents separated, and she grew up watching her mother struggle to provide for her. As a child, she was sexually abused by a family friend. That loss of innocence made her feel guilty and dirty about herself, she recalls. She subsequently began a series of relationships early in her teens. In fact, she says she has "always been in a relationship. I don't know how to be with myself."

Now, Jennifer endures the increasing verbal violence of Dan but feels too guilty to end the relationship—she does not want her child to grow up with only one parent, as she did. Jennifer experiences depressive episodes and periodic panic attacks, and she once suffered a rash that was medically unexplained. She feels very disconnected from others and even from herself: "My mind wanders, I feel isolated, I feel stupid and like a loser, and I have no goals. I lost myself—there is no me. I am unable to set goals because I fear I can't meet them."

Jennifer is having difficulty finding work, due to her lack of both education and transportation, and she is hesitant about finding quality child care for her son. The family currently lives downtown in a low-cost apartment that is in disrepair. They never have enough money at the end of the month, but Jennifer admits to buying fast food as a way of rewarding herself without thinking about the financial consequences of her actions. She is afraid, depressed, and unable to focus, which leaves her feeling always disorganized. She knows things are not right in her life: "I feel angry, resentful, sad, and lonely. I don't want to face the truth." But she is willing to try something new. Her hopes for counseling were "to increase my sense of who I am, to release and deal with my issues, to heal the hurt, lessen confusion, and find 'me' again."

* * *

Kim's entire life changed when she lost her stable job and her husband went to prison. She and their teenage son live in public housing and subsist on public assistance. She has some post-secondary education and had a good-paying federal job; however, both a health crisis and layoffs caused her to spend all of her savings. The disruption caused by her husband's imprisonment and her own decreasing sense of self make it difficult for her to become both personally and economically self-sufficient.

Kim was raised in a middle-class family, and she refuses to view herself and her family as the stereotypical black family living in poverty: "I don't see myself as poor, and it's hard to admit that I have nothing." As a result, she often deals with the trauma of poverty by portraying herself as having more economic and psychological stability than she actually does. This portrayal has led her to overspend, borrow money she is unable to repay, and isolate herself from the people who trusted her and have helped her along the way—people she knows she needs in her life. Kim projects a persona of great confidence, leadership ability, and "having it all together." She possesses the strengths of intelligence, vivaciousness, and verbal expertise. However, the reality of her life of poverty, coupled with her desire to be something more than she currently is, have led to instability and an inability to meet her goals of completing her education and securing stable employment. Kim's description of her situation illustrates that link: "I worked for seventeen years in a prestigious career for the government. I was married and had a family. I had it all. Then it fell apart. My job was ended, I was diagnosed with diabetes, my husband was incarcerated, my 401(k) had run out. I felt I was at the lowest of lows. I was injured. I was scared." For Kim, the sense of fear and powerlessness was very traumatic.

These two case examples, which demonstrate both chronic and situational poverty, introduce the complexity of poverty and trauma, which will be explored in this chapter. When we think of poverty in the United States, we often picture a run-down inner-city housing complex, with abandoned cars on the street and children playing with pop bottles as toys. Or we see a rural wooden shack with broken steps and an elderly woman on the front porch. Both of these images are part of the portrait of poverty in the United States. But there is also an aspect of poverty that we do not see—the family who rents a small home or apartment but must visit a food bank each month to get by, or the three families who share a large duplex and do without any "extras" so the bills can be paid. As this chapter is being written, the public is reminded of the ongoing poverty in this country through the images of Hurricane Katrina and its aftermath—again, people who were hidden from our view. Poverty, both seen and unseen, is part of the fabric of this country.

Poverty itself is a complex concept with multiple meanings and associations. It is relative to context and to country, and it can be a sudden event, a situational crisis, or a long-term, persistent problem. In 1965 Miller stated that "poverty is an emotionally charged word that can trip us up if we are not careful" (36). In 2003 Kilty and Segal asked: "Why do we seem to hate the poor? Why do we want to put them out of our awareness?" (3). The emotions associated with poverty are strong; thus poverty as trauma is an important perspective. Certain types of trauma are more prevalent among people in poverty, particularly trauma related to violence. And poverty itself is seen as a form of social trauma, defined in the introduction to this volume as "any social condition that perpetuates forms of oppression against vulnerable populations."

In this chapter we review definitions and theories of poverty, propose considerations for poverty as trauma, and describe a community-based agency known as Project WISE (founded by the authors) as a model of empowerment practice for women experiencing poverty.

Understanding the Scope of Poverty and Its Relation to Trauma

Historically, poverty has been defined as a lack of adequate resources to meet basic needs such as food, clothing, and shelter. Within that broad definition, there have always been individuals and families who were poor, in the United States and around the world. Sachs (2005) makes the distinction between extreme poverty, which is mostly found in developing countries, and moderate and relative poverty. "Moderate poverty generally refers to conditions of life in which basic needs are met, but just barely. Relative poverty is generally construed as a household income level below a given proportion of average national income" (20). The focus of this chapter is the United States and the experience of poverty in the context of a nation of wealth.

Following World War II, there was a general perception that poverty was nearly eradicated in the United States. However, that perception did not last. A striking moment in this country's consciousness about poverty was the 1962 publication of Michael Harrington's book *The Other America*, in which he described the poverty amid the new plenty in the United States. That work is credited with rediscovering poverty in this country, and it set the stage for a decade of programs known as the War on Poverty. Recently, as a result of Hurricane Katrina in 2005, poverty in this country has once again gained notice. Samuelson (2005) describes the effect of the images of people stranded by the hurricane as analogous to Harrington's classic book. This latest rediscovery of poverty is a sharp contrast to a report in 2001, in which a survey conducted by National Public Radio, the Kaiser Family Foundation, and Harvard University's Kennedy School of Government stated: "Americans aren't thinking a lot about the poor these days" (National Public Radio 2001). It is not known if our new consciousness will lead to new solutions, but the existence of moderate and relative poverty in this country can hardly be ignored.

Beyond the broad concepts of poverty, in the 1960s the federal government began measuring poverty, thus providing a quantitative definition relative to a standard of living. The federal poverty level, set by the Social Security Administration, was based on the cost of food for a family, multiplied by three. At that time, food costs represented approximately 33 percent of a family's budget. In the formula, food costs are calculated based on an "economy" food plan, not an adequate food plan for a family. It is significant that "the poverty level was meant to represent 'how much is too little'—a measure of income inadequacy rather than adequacy" (Colorado Fiscal Policy Institute 2002).

The Census Bureau adjusts poverty guidelines each year. According to the census figures of the past decade, the official poverty rate in the United States has fluctuated slightly. Between 1992 and 1994 the rate was

14.5 percent. In 2000 it dropped to a low of 11.3 percent (CLASP 2000). In 2003 the rate rose to 12.5 percent, and in 2004 it was 12.7 percent. In 2005 the poverty threshold for a household of three was $16,090 a year; that is, a family with an income below that figure is classified as poor. Extreme poverty in this country is considered to be an income less than 50 percent of the designated threshold. The official definition of poverty may not be useful, however, in understanding poverty as trauma, other than to indicate the potential number of people who might suffer the consequences of poverty—approximately 38 million in this country in 2004.

Establishing economic guidelines defines poverty levels, but it is also crucial to examine the differential impact of poverty on vulnerable populations. Poverty disproportionately affects children, people of color, and women. In 2004, 12 million children lived in poverty in the United States—a rate of 17 percent. Poverty is especially evident among children of color. For example, 33 percent of black children and 28 percent of Latino children live in poverty (National Center for Children in Poverty 2005). In 2003 the poverty rate (for all ages) was 8 percent for whites, 24 percent for blacks, and 22 percent for Hispanics. In 1978 Diana Pearce coined the phrase "feminization of poverty" to describe the social phenomena of women being disproportionately poor (28). Women have always suffered from poverty in this country (Abramovitz 1996), and that has continued over the past several decades. For example, in 1982, women-headed households had a poverty rate of 40 percent, while the poverty rate in the general population was approximately 13 percent. In 2003, women-headed households had a poverty rate of 35.5 percent, compared to a poverty rate of 12.5 percent for all people. In addition, the poverty rate for all women in 2003 was 12.4 percent, compared to 8.9 percent for men (Cadena and Sallee 2005; Legal Momentum 2004).

In the United States, millions of people face the trauma of poverty every day. From 1964 to the first decade of the twenty-first century, the poverty narrative has taken many forms. Generally the literature on poverty falls into four categories: (1) the demographics of poverty; (2) analysis of the causes of poverty, including the relationship of public policy to poverty; (3) the effects of poverty; and (4) the stories of poverty.

We view poverty as a web—a set of interconnected strands, all of which relate to each other. At the center of the web is a political and economic structure that includes capitalism, the global economy, the tax structure, and the values and belief systems that permeate the market economy culture of the United States. "Any capitalist economy creates winners and losers, and the United States is no exception" (Stevenson and Donovan 1996:67).

More specifically related to economics is the labor market. Poverty generally means an individual or family is not succeeding in the labor market—that is, they are not working, or if they are working, their salary is insufficient to support their basic needs. This problem can be understood in two ways. First, it can be seen as a problem of the individual, where a person's participation in the labor market is limited by his or her lack of human capital skills—the education and job skills necessary to succeed in the labor market. For example, those with only a high school education in 1999 had average annual earnings of $24,572, compared to $45,678 for those with a bachelor's degree (U.S. Census Bureau 2000). But this problem also can be viewed as a problem at the societal level. For example, another cause of failure in the labor market is the "labor glut which keeps many Americans unemployed or underemployed, and suppresses wage levels" (Stricker 2003:23). Whether because of a lack of human capital or an abundance of low-wage workers, the labor market plays a major role in the poverty web.

Another important strand in the web of poverty is the impact of racism and sexism. The statistics illustrating the relationship of race and gender to poverty were presented earlier. The underlying causes of this phenomenon are many and have deep historical roots. It is hard for many analysts to recognize that the structural nature of racism keeps African American, Latino/Latina, and American Indian communities impoverished (Kushnick and Jennings 1999): "The racialization of poverty is strengthened and facilitated by private and public policies that continue to result in residential and educational segregation" (11). The multiple oppressions of race and gender, and their relationship to class, potentially increase the trauma of poverty for many who are poor.

Poverty also can be examined as a result of both economic and social policies. This represents another key strand in the web, particularly as it relates to providing or not providing protection from the fluctuating labor market. Capitalism alone cannot be blamed. Other rich capitalist countries have social policies that help support people who are not succeeding in the labor market. However, U.S. social policies, such as TANF or Medicaid, actually help to maintain poverty by keeping benefits low and access to benefits limited.

Another strand in the poverty web is a lack of resources—particularly a lack of important basic needs supports, such as adequate low-income housing, access to health care and insurance, and affordable child care. Each of these deficiencies contributes to keeping people stuck in poverty.

Finally, the poverty web is held together by strong cultural norms and beliefs. Katz notes: "How we think and speak about poverty and what we do (or don't do) about it emerges as much from a mix of ideology and politics as from the structure of the problem itself" (1989:5). Ideas about personal responsibility, dependency, marriage and family, and cultural norms about the work ethic underlie the poverty discussion and play a critical role in our approach to poverty in this country.

The concept of poverty as a web is complex, and it emphasizes that there is no single cause of poverty. But knowledge of the web is important in responding to the trauma of poverty in an empowering way. Both Jennifer and Kim are caught in the web. Their lack of higher education, their resulting low incomes, family stress, violence, and imprisonment all play a part in their lives. Economic supports created by policies such as TANF do not provide enough income for them to escape poverty. And their difficulty in securing and retaining employment without access to the affordable child care, health insurance, and housing needed to be self-sufficient also contributes to keeping them in poverty.

The new TANF policy emphasizing marriage as an additional measure of success placed further pressure on both Jennifer and Kim when they applied for benefits. Not all relationships are healthy, and the assumption that marriage is part of the solution disempowers women by encouraging possibly unhealthy relationships. Finally, both Jennifer and Kim have reported discrimination based on gender or race, and they feel that, as women, they carry a tremendous burden for child rearing.

One way to approach the trauma of poverty is to examine the relationships between poverty and other potentially traumatic events or conditions. These include health problems, mental health problems, addiction, domestic violence and community violence, early-childhood abuse, discrimination, and lack of access to vital resources such as health care, housing, child care, and education.

For example, low-income women face numerous health problems. Romero et al. (2003) found that 68 percent of low-income women suffered from one of nine chronic health conditions and 63 percent reported that their health problems made daily activities difficult. The link between mental health and income is well established. Low income "is one of the strongest predictors of a mental health disorder," with "those in the lowest socioeconomic group . . . about two-and-a-half times more likely to have a mental health disorder compared to those in the highest socioeconomic group" (Derr, Hill, and Pavetti 2000:3). Specific studies of the low-income population who are using welfare assistance (TANF) have found that depression is particularly prevalent among TANF recipients; 42 percent of long-term welfare recipients suffered from clinical depression, a rate seven times that of the general adult population (Barusch et al. 1999:5).

Interpersonal violence is also associated with poverty. "Socioeconomic status, as measured using some indicator of poverty, is a useful starting point for understanding and controlling violence" (Reiss and Roth 1993:131). Childhood victimization, including both physical and sexual abuse, has been found to be prevalent among low-income women and women on welfare (DeParle 1999; Ingram, Corning, and Schmidt 1996). Studies on mental health and the welfare population have also found high levels of post-traumatic stress disorder (PTSD) and anxiety (Derr et al. 2000). While poverty may not be the cause of many of the circumstances described above, poverty is clearly associated with conditions that can be considered traumatic.

In addition, two important components of psychological trauma—terror and disconnection (Herman 1997)—can be applied to poverty. Terror implies an event in which "the victim is rendered helpless by overwhelming force" (33), resulting in a sense of powerlessness. Disconnection is related to feeling apart from the world, lacking trust and safety in one's day-to-day life. "Traumatic events call into question basic human relationships. They breach the attachments of family, friendship, love and community" (51).

These two components of trauma can be related to the distinction between situational or crisis poverty and long-term poverty. Situational or crisis poverty might be the result of a force beyond one's control, such as a fire that destroys one's home. If the home was the only financial asset and there was no insurance, the family might find itself at another level of poverty. Situational poverty is viewed as more easily overcome because it is assumed that one has other resources, such as job skills or education, which would allow for recovery. While that is possible, it is also possible that situational poverty can evoke the feelings of helplessness and fear that are associated with the more catastrophic events normally linked with terror.

Persistent poverty, on the other hand, can have long-term effects on individuals and families. And while persistent poverty may disrupt one's family and friendships, it is the disconnection from community that can have the most dramatic effect. For example, in research conducted by Profitt (2000) on women survivors and psychological trauma, a respondent stated: "The first feeling to come up for me would be inadequacy because that's what society has made me feel: inadequate. You're poor [and in school] we are the ones that were made fun of; we were the ones that were put down" (72). This sense of not belonging and of being ridiculed is an example of disconnection from one's environment.

Another way poverty can be considered trauma comes from the experience of being poor in the wealthiest nation in the world. It is interesting to note that in the mid-nineteenth century all parts of the world were roughly similar in terms of levels of poverty and wealth. By the twenty-first century, the United States and Canada had far surpassed the remainder of the world in wealth (Sachs 2005). In addition, in the past twenty years in the United States, the gap between the rich and the poor has grown significantly, creating "a pyramid of inequality" (Hays 2003). How does this situation affect people who have little financial stability, when they see the wealth in their community? How do they feel, knowing that they are unable to afford what so many take for granted—such as occasionally ordering a pizza for dinner or buying new clothes? As one woman who found herself in poverty wrote, "If we could we would be somewhere else, believe me!" (Walker 1996:27).

Finally, it is important to remember that poverty may not be the "presenting problem" as one begins trauma work with an individual, family, or community; however, it may be a related factor, and understanding the issues of poverty is crucial. Although the trauma of poverty may be more subtle than other forms of trauma, such as natural disasters or physical assault, its effects, suffered by too many in this country, are no less traumatic nor significant.

Responding to the Trauma of Poverty Through Empowerment

Project WISE (Women's Initiative for Service and Empowerment) was started in 1995 to provide services to women affected by the dynamics of poverty and other related issues. Its mission is to empower low-income women by offering them opportunities to achieve personal, family, and economic goals and attain positive involvement with their community. Project WISE has three main program areas: individual counseling; support and education groups; and a women's leadership program that includes community organizing, leadership development and training, a mentoring program, and a Women's Leadership Council. Participants range from age nineteen to fifty-five; they are 50 percent Latina, 30 percent Anglo, 19 percent African American, and 1 percent Native American.

Services provided by Project WISE are based on a feminist empowerment model (East 1999; Gutierrez 1990). Personal empowerment is a process whereby individuals increase their self-esteem, increase their self-awareness, and explore their cultural identity and spirituality. Empowerment occurs on three levels—personal, interpersonal, and political—and the empowerment model is gender-specific; therefore, a gender lens is considered in the intervention strategies. Within the Project WISE model of services, participants may be involved in counseling, psycho-educational groups, and personal growth activities. The range of services is illustrated in the following examples from the work done with Jennifer.

Jennifer needed several interventions at the personal level—she had become more seriously depressed, was unable to sleep, and was experiencing anxiety in seeking employment. She was evaluated at the public health clinic, and the Project WISE therapist and the psychiatrist were able to discuss an appropriate treatment, including therapy and medication. Subsequently, with her sleep and depression beginning to improve as a result of the treatment, Jennifer began to examine her life experiences and work on changing her behavior patterns.

Jennifer is a responsible parent. She completed her high school education, but she described struggling in school and having some dyslexia. She would like to attend college, but has been scared of school and said she "hides" when it comes to formal education. That tendency to hide became a focus of the sessions with her therapist, and over time she found that she did not have to hide. She began to risk participating in groups and found she could speak out in them.

Interpersonal empowerment is a process of increasing one's power in one's immediate environment, be it family, school, or agencies where one receives services. This component includes increasing knowledge and skills in critical thinking, assertiveness, problem solving, maintaining a healthy system of social and emotional support, and accessing resources. The services that support interpersonal empowerment include counseling, support groups, a mentoring program, advocacy, and specific skills training. Jennifer was paired with a mentor who offered both emotional support and help with her survival issues. Jennifer lacked transportation and was afraid of driving. She also had made a painful decision to separate from

Dan and needed to find housing. Jennifer's mentor patiently helped her reduce her fear of driving and took her to look for an apartment that would be suitable for her and her child. She would get some child support from Dan, and she found a part-time job at a landscaping company. Through these activities, Jennifer's sense of hope increased along with her sense of self.

Community/political empowerment is defined as gaining power in one's community and its institutions and acting on public policy issues on behalf of oneself and others. Community empowerment also includes giving back or making a contribution to the community. In Project WISE, community empowerment is encouraged through a women's community organizing project, policy advocacy and research, and a Women's Leadership Council. A final program, which encompasses all three with program staff on mental health issues and on changing her environment, is the annual Leadership Retreat. Jennifer eventually joined and used her talents on the Women's Leadership Council.

Vicarious Trauma When Responding to Poverty

People have different experiences of poverty and wealth, trauma, and less stressful circumstances. Therefore, they have different experiences of learning and have drawn different conclusions from what they have learned. Most people do not choose to suffer trauma. However, caregivers or those in the helping professions consciously choose to become involved with those who suffer poverty and trauma. But, as Boyd-Franklin (2004) notes, helping professionals "are often unprepared and overwhelmed" by the realities of poverty (37).

Secondhand exposure, multiplied person after person, family after family, can have the effect of traumatizing the caregiver in ways that can be either obvious or subtle. This secondary traumatic stress, or compassion fatigue, can reduce one's effectiveness, rob one of enthusiasm, and shorten one's tenure (Figley 1995). At Project WISE, staff have developed strategies for addressing this traumatization, including:

1. Realizing that they have the vital resources to do this work
2. Detaching from the outcome without personalizing the outcome; trauma is transforming, and one does not know if it will be enriching or diminishing

3. Understanding one's desired personal growth benefits—i.e., being responsible, being useful, and processing one's feelings when not experiencing those benefits

4. Cultivating the interpersonal skill of compassion, appreciating another's pain (but not identifying with it), and practicing being present yet detached

5. Creating a self-care plan

The work can be done without complete attachment to the role as care provider, victim advocate, or therapist, and as a result one can experience a level of freedom that protects oneself from vicarious traumatic stress.

Empowerment Principles and Responding to Poverty

In an empowerment model, it is important to teach both staff and participants the economics of poverty and the links to mental health, class difference, and the oppression resulting from racism and sexism. The principles of empowerment practice outlined by Wise (2005) are very applicable to the practice model of Project WISE and will be defined in the context of responding to poverty.

BUILDING ON STRENGTHS AND DIMINISHING OPPRESSION

In the Project WISE model, and in working with someone who experiences poverty, it is very important to identify and build on strengths at the individual, family, and community levels. Low-income families and neighborhoods are often identified by their numerous problems, such as violence, crime, and poor housing. However, very little is said about the positive aspects, such as families' strength and ability to survive on small incomes, to build social networks and extended-family resources, or to change unhealthy patterns learned in childhood.

Building on strengths helps to diminish the oppression of poverty. When Young (1990) refers to the five faces of oppression as relationships that "delimit people's material lives" (44), including access to resources and opportunities or lack thereof, one cannot help but think of poverty. Poverty is oppressive in so many ways that many people in poverty will not at first believe there is any way out. The work with Jennifer on continuing her education and feeling comfortable in groups took time. That progress was made by building on her own strengths, especially her willingness to examine her life and initiate changes.

Another example of building on strengths and diminishing oppression is a Project WISE effort in a public housing development. This development was created to increase opportunities for low-income families by promoting education and rewarding employment using escrow accounts for personal advancement and homeownership. Many of the residents are attending school, but many drop out because they cannot pass a class, most often math. (The fact that many low-income students with a high school degree are not prepared for college-level courses is a systemic oppression.)

Building on their own strengths and the strengths of their community, residents formed focus groups to discuss their practical needs. With their input, a College Club was started to offer tutoring for residents and others. Some outside tutors were recruited, but the residents also helped each other with class preparation, depending on their strengths and skills. Negotiations with the housing authority made the community center available for the weekly College Club.

At the same time, meetings were held with college officials about the barriers that low-income residents face in trying to pursue an education. While individuals were able to build on their motivation to succeed and enhance their educational opportunities, the potentially oppressive structures of the college were challenged. Many adult students need special preparatory education in order to succeed at the college level. Tutoring offered through the college had been inconsistent (a person never had the same tutor twice), and the time frame was too short for what these adult students needed. Many Project WISE participants know that education is a route out of poverty and that pursuing education can diminish their fear of the future. Having the on-site tutoring at the housing development helped them build their educational strengths.

ENHANCING MULTICULTURAL RESPECT

The families and communities in which the Project WISE participants live are at the intersection of nondominant ethnicity, gender, and socioeconomic status. The target population of the program is low-income women with diversity in race and ethnicity. Accordingly, at Project WISE each relationship is built on multicultural respect—it is a developmental process—not the result of a one-time intervention.

In terms of addressing poverty, the bridge begins across class lines. An example is the mentoring program, which often matches a low-income woman with a middle-class woman. Unlike many programs, where the mentors are trained separately, at Project WISE participants and volunteer mentors are trained together. They receive the same information, and a dialogue is created regarding class assumptions and difference and the mentoring partners' future relationship.

Another program piloted at Project WISE was a series of sessions that addressed the hidden rules of class and economic behaviors that affect those living in poverty (Payne 2001). The stereotypes of class issues and poverty ignited lively discussions and thoughts about how to make changes for the next generation. An example was used about a teenage boy being stopped by the police, the various types of language a teen would use as he was confronted, and the different reactions that each would produce from the police. Mothers began to realize that they had not had that kind of discussion with their children. The significance of stereotypes was heightened as one person made the assumption that the teenage boy in the example was African American. Mothers such as Kim identified with the many times that these assumptions are made in their lives.

Nationally, we are experiencing a massive relocation of families from the Gulf Coast to other U.S. cities as a result of Hurricane Katrina. People living in lifelong poverty now must adapt to other cities and new lives. This situation highlights another link between environment and economic and political circumstances and the resulting trauma. A Project WISE board member and chair of the Department of Anthropology at the Denver Museum of Nature and Science linked poverty and the trauma of relocating during a recent news analysis:

"What is the relationship between economics and cultural preservation and what does this mean for cities? What are we going to learn about human resiliency? What happens when you lose all of your objects that you've imbued with the spirit of your everyday experience? What happens to the power of these objects, the essence of them when they're gone and you're left holding in your hands the hands of your children, your family and the life of your community?"

At Project WISE telling one's story is a part of gaining and using one's voice. As Wise (2005) states, "Multicultural awareness takes on its unique shape through family stories of survival and coping, through the narratives of ancestors, and the history of transitions, crises, rituals and celebrations" (76). Project WISE works toward multicultural respect at every level of the organization.

WORKING FROM AN AWARENESS OF SPECIFIC NEEDS

Awareness of specific needs is particularly important when serving people who are experiencing poverty, because they often face a crisis of resources. A recurring example at Project WISE that links internal and external needs has to do with providing adequate mental health care for issues like depression, substance abuse, and PTSD. In the counseling program, many women experience those conditions and their symptoms. While counseling can help the women develop new understanding and new skills, they also need access to medical evaluations, medications, or possibly hospitalization. Program staff are often very proactive in helping women secure those resources, and they frequently accompany participants to a clinic or hospital to advocate for services.

During the community-organizing process of conducting one-on-one interviews, barriers are identified. They are then tabulated and the related issues are addressed during the monthly educational forums. Through this process, individual and collective needs are made known, they are shared, and actions are taken. For example, it became clear that a policy needed to be changed when child care was about to be eliminated for people attending post-secondary education. As a result, women testified before the local Welfare Reform Board and received an extension permitting child care to continue. Recently, a Welfare Reform Board member stated, "The board has been influenced in policy decisions by the testimonies of Project WISE participants."

ASSISTING CLIENTS AS THEY EMPOWER THEMSELVES

The Project WISE model assumes that staff do not empower women, but rather that the program creates the space and opportunities for women to empower themselves. Many participants who began in counseling found their voice and used that voice with others in small-group settings. Through the process of realizing their strengths, participants who were engaged with child welfare began to advocate for themselves in the child welfare system to get appropriate help for an emotionally unstable child or to effect a change in a welfare regulation. Participants are now speaking for themselves and improving life for others as well. One participant testified before the Welfare Reform Board and a state legislative committee to explain the issues associated with children who have special needs for mental health treatment and how those issues affect a parent's ability to meet welfare requirements. The participant had received counseling at Project WISE, was on the Women's Leadership Council, and was an active participant in the Women's Community Organizing Project. She stated: "I have been given the freedom (and the tools) to find myself. Project WISE changed my perspective and I've been able to change my life and the life my children will lead."

Another participant expressed concern to her mentor about being told by her welfare case manager that she would be unable to continue her post-secondary education. Subsequently, in cooperation with other program participants, she took action to ensure that the welfare department implemented state legislation that allowed people receiving TANF to access post-secondary education or vocational training. She acted on her own power to get what she needed while also benefiting others.

As the foregoing examples indicate, empowerment experienced both personally and in the community becomes an antidote to the helplessness and disconnection that may result from persistent poverty.

INTEGRATING THE SUPPORT NEEDED FROM OTHERS

Women who live in poverty are often isolated, which can add to their trauma (Belle 1990). The Project WISE model addresses that issue by not only supporting women to receive individual services but also encouraging them to engage with other women through groups and leadership development programs. This approach is the cornerstone of integrating support.

Social support and social networks can modify stress and enhance capacity (Hampshire and Healy 2000). Social networks are a crucial component in bringing about individual and family security as well as a healthy involvement in one's community. During research on empowerment practices with three Denver organizations serving women, participants noted Project WISE as providing a "safe place"—one in which stories could be told without judgment or consequences.

Herman (1997) observed that survivors of trauma can reestablish a sense of safety if adequate social support is available. Understanding the importance of social support is at the heart of the Project WISE model: all participants are encouraged to join group activities and build their support networks. When a person has limited resources, a support system is critical in meeting basic needs such as transportation and child care. Even the simple act of getting a ride to an appointment or having someone to watch children for a few hours can relieve a tremendous amount of stress. Program participants help each other with these simple, or not so simple, acts all the time. After becoming involved in Project WISE activities, Kim helped organize residents at the housing development so they could have a support network and not feel so isolated. They now help each other with a variety of activities, including mowing their small area of grass, which they are required to do to avoid being fined.

EQUALIZING POWER

A basis of victimization is an unequal balance of power, which, when taken further, becomes traumatic. This type of victimization occurs within families, systems, and institutions. Often poverty is a resulting partner in the lack of equalizing power. With poverty there may be a lack of education, an accompanying lack of information, and/or the lack of social and psychological expertise to maneuver in the many systems of which people are a part. At Project WISE there is a strong belief in equalizing power as much as possible. This is done through sharing information, strategizing with participants for change, and maintaining contact with those who have acted to change their family or community circumstances. During group activities such as story circles and leadership retreats, staff, mentors, and participants share their stories and what has influenced them in their lives. This "mutual sphere of influence" emphasizes the program as a safe setting in which the players are growing and learning, each on her own journey. Another dimension of equalizing power is developing and sharing leadership and acting on mutual community concerns. Project WISE provides leadership and advocacy training and includes a Women's Leadership Council with representation on the Project WISE board of directors, helping the organization's decision-making process. Kim, who participated on the Women's Leadership Council, also took on the role of consultant when program staff were reviewing a financial education curriculum. She helped the staff critique the stereotypes and language used.

USING COOPERATIVE ROLES

Clearly a link to equalizing power is the existence of cooperative roles. As Wise (2005) states, "In empowering practice, role sharing means that no role works in only one direction" (86). Co-creators and co-investigators are two roles used at Project WISE, where the sharing of roles is implicit in each program area moving toward individual and social change. The counselor offers therapeutic skill and learns from the participant the patterns she needs to be aware of, as well as what is working for the participant to reduce trauma and stress. Mentors note that, in sharing the growth process, they learn and are influenced as much as the mentee.

Participants and residents of public housing are co-investigators with the researcher as they study the success of the self-sufficiency housing program to establish escrow accounts for residents to meet their future housing and educational goals. In addition, each year the leadership retreat is developed, planned, and presented with the participants taking the lead, and the staff co-participating as appropriate. At the two-day retreat, it is often difficult to distinguish between the staff and the participants, due to the collaborative approach and role sharing.

Poverty does not need to be a lifelong condition, and through cooperation it can become less traumatic. Project WISE staff function as collaborators in a circular rather than a hierarchical pattern, each offering expertise from her or his particular stance and each contributing to the empowerment of the other. A Project WISE participant, reflecting on the meaning of the program in her life, stated that one of its unique features was the apparent absence of distinction between staff and participants.

Conclusion and Recommendations

Traumas like war, violent assaults, and natural disasters can have strong psychological and physical effects on people, as many of the chapters in this book demonstrate. However, the trauma from poverty may not be as dramatic. Certainly there is enough evidence, both empirical and anecdotal, to suggest that poverty can have damaging results for some and not for others. When layered with early-childhood abuse and adult mental health problems, poverty becomes an added oppression that can exacerbate a trauma response. Even by itself, however, poverty can cause trauma reactions, particularly a sense of powerlessness, hopelessness, and disconnection from community.

The implications of considering poverty as trauma can be delineated at both a practice level and a policy level. At a practice level, the first important consideration is to recognize the oppression and consequences of poverty on an individual, a family, or a community. For example, an intervention for a school shooting in a middle-class community would be different from one in a low-income community. Practitioners need to recognize the effects of poverty and the likelihood for associated traumas that are a part of the web of poverty.

The second key practice implication is that interventions that conceptualize change at the personal, interpersonal, and community levels are critical. While a social worker may not always be in a setting that combines individual clinical work with community-organizing interventions, the empowerment principles can still be applied. Following the empowerment principles outlined in this book and this chapter can guide practitioners in offering meaningful services that take into account all components of the poverty web.

At the policy level, the possibilities are vast. Poverty and policy are linked at the international, national, and state levels. Nationally, we have seen some of the "hidden" pockets of poverty come to attention. Policies are being set: reauthorization of TANF, continuation of war, and reduction in child care and health care funding. At state levels, decisions are made about levels of funding for capital improvements versus human services. All of these policies need to be analyzed through the lens of social class so that those who suffer poverty are considered.

We put forth the prospect that social policy could be based on a strengths perspective and that an empowerment practice lens in policy and program development could lessen poverty and mitigate the resulting trauma.

References

Abramovitz, M. 1996. *Regulating the Lives of Women: Social Welfare Policy from Colonial Times to the Present.* Rev. ed. Boston: South End Press.

Barusch, A. S., M. J. Taylor, S. H. Abu-Bader, and M. Derr. 1999. *Understanding Families with Multiple Barriers to Self Sufficiency.* Salt Lake City: Social Research Institute, Graduate School of Social Work.

Belle, D. 1990. *Lives in Stress: Women and Depression.* Beverly Hills, Calif.: Sage.

Boyd-Franklin, N. 2004. "Therapy with African-American Inner-City Families." In A. Lieberman and C. Lester, eds., *Social Work Practice with a Difference,* 30–47. Boston: McGraw-Hill.

Cadena, B., and J. Sallee. 2005. "Why Did Poverty Rise in 2004? A Preliminary Analysis of the U.S. Census Bureau's Poverty Report." *Poverty Research*

Insights (Fall 2005): 1–6. Ann Arbor: National Poverty Center, University of Michigan.

CLASP: Center for Law and Social Policy. 2000. *CLASP Update: Census Bureau Release: Latest Poverty and Income Data.* October.

Colorado Fiscal Policy Institute. 2002. *Fact Sheet, Federal Poverty Measures.*

DeParle, J. 1999. "Early Sex Abuse Common among Welfare's Women." *New York Times,* November 28. http://www.newyorktimes.com/library/national/ 112399wis-welfare.html. Retrieved November 1, 2000.

Derr, M. K., H. Hill, and L. Pavetti. 2000. *Addressing Mental Health Problems Among TANF Recipients: A Guide for Program Administrators.* Reference No. 8528–100. Washington, D.C.: Mathematica Policy Research.

East, J. F. 1999. "An Empowerment Practice Model for Low-Income Women." In W. Shera and L. Wells, eds., *Empowerment Practice in Social Work: Developing Richer Conceptual Foundations.* Toronto: Canadian Scholars' Press.

Figley, C., ed. 1995. *Compassion Fatigue: Coping with Secondary Traumatic Stress Disorder in Those Who Treat the Traumatized.* New York: Brunner/Mazel.

Gutierrez, L. 1990. "Working with Women of Color: An Empowerment Perspective." *Social Work* 352:149–153.

Hampshire, A., and K. Healy. 2000. "Social Capital in Practice." Paper presented at the Australian Institute for Family Studies Conference.

Harrington, M. 1962. *The Other America: Poverty in the United States.* New York: Macmillan.

Hays, S. 2003. *Flat Broke with Children: Women in the Age of Welfare Reform.* New York: Oxford University Press.

Herman, J. 1997. *Trauma and Recovery.* 2nd ed. New York: Basic Books.

Ingram, K. M., A. F. Corning, and L. D. Schmidt. 1996. "The Relationship of Victimization Experiences to Psychological Well-being among Homeless Women and Low-Income Housed Women." *Journal of Counseling Psychology* 43:218–228.

Katz, M. 1989. *The Undeserving Poor: From the War on Poverty to the War on Welfare.* New York: Pantheon.

Kilty, K., and E. Segal. 2003. Introduction to K. Kilty and E. Segal, eds., *Rediscovering the Other America: The Continuing Crisis of Poverty and Inequality in the United States,* 1–6. New York: Haworth.

Kushnick, L., and J. Jennings. 1999. "Introduction: Poverty as Race, Power, and Wealth." In L. Kushnick and J. Jennings, eds., *A New Introduction to Poverty: The Role of Race, Power, and Politics,* 1–12. New York: New York University Press.

Legal Momentum. 2004. *Reading Between the Lines: Women's Poverty in the United States,* 2003. New York: Author.

Miller, H. 1965. "The Dimensions of Poverty." In B. Seligman, ed., *Poverty as a Public Issue,* 20–51. New York: Free Press.

National Center for Children in Poverty. 2005. *Who Are America's Poor Children?* New York: Author. September.

National Public Radio Online. 2001. "Talk of the Nation: Poverty in America." May 7. Retrieved from http://www.npr.org/programs/specials/poll/poverty/.

Payne, R. 2001. *A Framework for Understanding Poverty.* Highlands, Tex.: aha! Process.

Pearce, D. 1978. "The Feminization of Poverty: Women, Work, and Welfare." *Urban and Social Change Review* 11 (1–2): 28–36.

Profitt, N. J. 2000. *Women Survivors, Psychological Trauma, and the Politics of Resistance.* New York: Haworth.

Reiss, A. J., and J. A. Roths, eds. 1993. *Understanding and Preventing Violence.* Washington, D.C.: National Academy Press.

Romero, D., W. Chavkin, P. H. Wise, and L. A. Smith. 2003. "Low-Income Mothers' Experience with Poor Health, Hardship, Work, and Violence." *Violence Against Women* 9:1231–1244.

Sachs, J. 2005. *The End of Poverty: How We Can Make It Happen in Our Lifetime.* New York: Penguin.

Samuelson, R. J. 2005. "Poverty . . . Again." *Rocky Mountain News,* September 24.

Stevenson, M. H., and E. Donovan. 1996. "How the U. S. Economy Creates Poverty and Inequality." In D. Dujon and A. Withorn, eds., *For Crying Out Loud: Women's Poverty in the United States,* 65–78. Boston: South End Press.

Stricker, F. 2003. "Staying Poor in the Clinton Boom: Welfare Reform and the Nearby Labor Force." In K. Kilty and E. Segal, eds., *Rediscovering the Other America: The Continuing Crisis of Poverty and Inequality in the United States,* 51–68. New York: Haworth.

U.S. Census Bureau. 2000. "Educational Attainment in the United States (Update)." Washington, D.C.: U.S. Department of Commerce. March.

——. 2003. "Income, Poverty, and Health Insurance Coverage in the United States, 2003." Washington, D.C.: U.S. Department of Commerce.

Walker, L. 1996. "If We Could We Would Be Someplace Else." In D. Dujon and A. Withorn, eds., *For Crying Out Loud: Women's Poverty in the United States,* 65–78. Boston: South End Press.

Wise, J. B. 2005. *Empowerment Practice with Families in Distress.* New York: Columbia University Press.

Young, I. M. 1990. *Justice and the Politics of Difference.* Princeton, N.J.: Princeton University Press.

12

Transforming the Trauma of Torture, Flight, and Resettlement

KAY M. STEVENSON AND JAIME RALL

Peter and Annie Jefferson with their three children, Theresa Davis and her 8-year-old son, and Frederick and Gertrude Wilson with their four children ranging in age from 2 to 15 are just three among the recent influx of refugee families from conflicted and war-torn Liberia. Every member of each of these families has either been tortured or witnessed the torture of their loved ones in traumatic events associated with the civil war in their homeland. They also experienced continued threats to their survival in the refugee camps where they lived before their arrival in the United States.

All the parents and children present with mental health concerns. Most noticeably, Annie appears exhausted, overwhelmed, and depressed. Peter is visibly agitated and anxious. Frederick and Gertrude's 15-year-old daughter complains of emotional distress and physical pain. She has been chronically absent from school. Their 11-year-old daughter has been sent home from school for engaging in several fights with other students. Peter and Annie's youngest child appears to be noticeably withdrawn or detached from classroom activities. Theresa's son has been reported as aggressive and boisterous, and refuses to comply with teacher requests to remain in his seat, raise his hand, or wait in lines.

In addition to Frederick and Gertrude's 15-year-old's complaints of physical pain, Gertrude, Annie, and Peter also have physical health problems, some resulting from their refugee experiences of torture, trauma, and/or deprivation. All of them need long-neglected dental attention.

All the parents worry about how they will survive on limited financial resources. Peter and Frederick express concern about not being able to find employment. Gertrude asks how she will care for her 2-year-old during the day and be home when her other children arrive home from school if she is required to work.

These Liberian families speak English, but their accents sometimes pose communication barriers with those who speak U.S. English dialects. Both the refugee parents and their children are experiencing difficulties understanding and being understood by English-speaking Americans.

All the parents express concerns about the adjustment and progress of their children in American schools. They do not understand the school rules or procedures. They are concerned that their children are not being adequately disciplined at school, and they fear their children will not advance because neither the parents nor the children understand what is required of American students.

Most of the parents voice confusion about how they can adequately discipline their children in America, where traditional forms of Liberian punishment are prohibited. Peter and Annie acknowledge that they discipline their children by beatings with sticks, sometimes after a teacher has raised concerns to the parent about the child's school progress and/or behavior. Their children appear at school with welts and bruises, necessitating notification of child protective services, as required by law.

Understanding the Traumas of Torture, Flight, and Resettlement for Immigrants, Asylees, Refugees, Asylum Seekers, and Undocumented Immigrants

The beginning of the twenty-first century has been called "a time of profound sociopolitical change and upheaval" (Miller and Rasco 2004:5). Uncounted millions have been displaced from their homes because of persecution, oppression, war, political unrest, poverty, social upheavals, and/or natural disasters. In the United States, a nation with a strong tradition of providing refuge to the world's poor and oppressed, the ongoing influx of immigrants seeking a better life within our borders—with or without "legal" documented status—continues to be a hot political topic. Immigration is also of concern to social work practitioners, who are more likely than ever to encounter immigrants in their practice and must therefore be sensitive to the special needs and strengths of this group of people.

Who are these millions of "displaced persons"? Definition of several terms may provide some clarification. *Immigrant* is a general term for any person moving from one country to another and covers a vast variety of motivations for that movement, including but not limited to economic, political, and/or personal motivations. It includes more specific classifications, such as asylees and refugees, asylum seekers, and undocumented immigrants.

An *asylee* or a *refugee* is defined, according to international law, as a person who has left her or his country of origin "owing to a well-founded fear of being persecuted for reasons of race, religion, nationality, or membership of a particular social group or political opinion, . . . and . . . unable, or owing to such fear, is unwilling to avail her/himself of the protection of that country" (UNHCR 1984). This definition is also accepted by the United States Bureau of Citizenship and Immigration Services. Asylees and refugees constitute an important subset of immigrants with special psychosocial and sociopolitical issues. To be granted the protection of asylum in the United States, an immigrant must apply and prove that he or she has "credible fear" of persecution and/or loss of life if he or she should return to the country of origin. This "credible fear" is often based on a history of torture and/or imprisonment. An *asylum seeker* is defined as a person who has applied for but has not yet been granted asylum.

Asylum seekers and refugees differ only in their location upon application for admission. An asylum seeker applies for admission in the United States or at a port of entry, and a refugee applies from outside the United States. All rights and protections that apply to refugees in international conventions and national law also apply to those who are granted asylum. However, there are significant and real differences between refugees and asylum seekers in terms of the conditions under which they arrive, services upon arrival, and legal status as residents.

Refugees arrive in a new country with legal status and practical support. Many come from refugee camps sponsored by international nongovernmental organizations (NGOs), having escaped conflicts within their national borders. Recognized as documented immigrants, refugees are typically sponsored by agencies or individuals in the host country. Sponsors, such as religious organizations and voluntary agencies, or VOLAGS (like Lutheran Family Services in our case study), may provide assistance with housing, food, transportation, and access to health, educational, and social services. Refugees also have legal sanction to seek employment and receive other community-based services.

In contrast to refugees, asylum seekers arrive not yet having gained permanent legal status, and therefore these immigrants lack the practical support that accompanies such status. Some asylum seekers enter this country in possession of temporary status, such as a traveler's or student visa. However, many have escaped from torture and/or detention in their countries of origin without any legal documentation. Once in the host country, asylum seekers begin an often lengthy and complex immigration process to gain asylum and become permanent residents. Upon successful completion of the asylum process, asylees (like refugees) are eligible to work and to receive services through voluntary agencies and other agencies for permanent residents.

In the meantime, asylum seekers are not eligible for many of the services that are available to refugees. An asylum seeker may have to rely on limited services, such as homeless shelters and indigent health care. Asylum seekers with a history of torture may also be able to access limited mental health, social services, legal, and health assistance from one of about thirty-five torture treatment centers in this country.

Many asylum seekers arrive without families, few financial resources, and limited familiarity with American culture and immigration procedures. The uncertainty of their legal status and fear that they may be sent back to countries where they have been persecuted are major stressors for them. In short, although asylum seekers have experienced the same kinds of trauma from persecution and oppression as refugees have, their different legal status upon entering the host country tends to increase other stressors while simultaneously reducing available support.

Although the actual total is probably higher, an estimated 35 million to 38 million people worldwide have been displaced from their homes by civil and interstate war, as well as by various forms of state-sanctioned repression and persecution (UNHCR 2002; United Nations Office for the Coordination of Humanitarian Affairs 2002). Included in this group are approximately 13 million individuals formally recognized as refugees or asylum seekers according to the 1951 UN Convention Relating to the Status of Refugees (UNHCR 1951).

While many asylum seekers arrive without legal documentation such as a passport and a visa, *undocumented immigrant* is the term used to describe an immigrant without documentation who has *not* applied for asylum. Pejoratively referred to as "illegal aliens," these individuals arrive with diverse histories and motivations. They may or may not have experienced internal displacement and persecution, including torture. Like refugees and asylum seekers, they are at risk for trauma associated with flight, fear of detention, discrimination, deprivation, poverty, and the inaccessibility of resources. In this chapter the focus is on the traumas associated with refugees and asylum seekers, keeping in mind that other immigrants may also have experienced such sociopolitical violence without the formal recognition that refugee or asylee status indicates.

All immigrants, regardless of legal status, past persecution, motivation, personal history, or levels of practical support in the new country, share certain challenges. These include the challenges of acculturation (gaining familiarity and comfort with the way things are done in the new host country) and isolation from everything that was formerly familiar. All immigrants must learn how to navigate new communities, including new support networks and bureaucracies. At the same time, they must also learn to negotiate the cultural assumptions and practices of the host country.

The Nature, Dynamics, and Consequences of Torture

To provide effective community interventions for refugee populations, such as the Liberian families in our case study, we must understand the nature, dynamics, and consequences of torture—events that have precipitated the immigration of these individuals, families, and communities to this country. Refugees and asylum seekers have, by definition, been subjected to the trauma of sociopolitical violence in the form of persecution and oppression, and have established a credible fear of losing their lives should they return home. Traumatic experiences in the home country may include war, imprisonment, and, frequently, torture. In fact, the prevalence of torture among refugees may be as high as 35 percent (Jaranson and Popkin 1998). This estimate includes both those who have been tortured themselves and those who have vicariously been traumatized by the torture of a loved one. Other immigrants who are not defined as refugees or asylum seekers may have experienced similarly traumatic events associated with their displacement. Tragically, as late as 1999, torture was being practiced in 132 countries, according to Amnesty International (Piwowarczyk, Moreno, and Grodin 2000). As many as 500,000 survivors of torture now reside in the United States.

The United Nations defines torture as the intentional infliction of severe pain or suffering, whether physical or mental, instigated by or with the consent of persons in authority (UNHCR 1984). This definition incorporates four key elements: (1) the infliction of severe physical and/or psychological pain, (2) a perpetrator and a victim, (3) torture as a purposeful, systematic activity, and (4) deliberate use of torture by governmental or paragovernmental representatives.

"The goal of torture is often to break down political opposition through coercion and humiliation" (Piwowarczyk et al. 2000). Torture is a strategic means of destroying and silencing individuals, families, communities, and organizations. It is used to oppress populations deemed by those in power to be dangerous (Fabri 2001). When torture is perpetrated to control populations, it can be seen in its sociopolitical context. Victims may be activists, leaders, members of minority ethnic or religious groups, or individuals chosen at random to reinforce a general societal climate of terror and mistrust.

Methods of torture vary and are classified as physical, psychological, or sexual. As international bodies have instituted more active monitoring of human rights, torture has become more psychological, thus leaving less physical evidence. The Center for Victims of Torture in Minnesota reports lasting psychological trauma among its clients, inflicted by such methods as sham executions, sexual torture, prolonged arbitrary detention especially with sensory deprivation, disappearance of a loved one, threats against family members, and being forced to witness the torture of others (Jaranson 1995).

The psychological sequelae of torture have been observed to include symptoms associated with the *DSM-IV-TR* category of post-traumatic stress disorder (PTSD). Nearly all clients who present for torture treatment meet the diagnostic criteria for PTSD, showing high rates of avoidance, arousal, and re-experiencing symptoms, as well as other associated symptoms consistent with this diagnosis, such as guilt, low self-esteem, changed identity, and psychosomatic symptoms (Genefke and Vesti 1998).

Psychological sequelae of torture are also consistent with Herman's concept of complex PTSD, which encompasses the special sequelae of trauma involving prolonged captivity, totalitarian control, and repeated interpersonal trauma (Herman 1997). Finally, a separate "torture syndrome" has also been hypothesized, which emphasizes memory impairment, sleep disturbances, anxiety, depression, and a cluster of psychosomatic symptoms, as well as an explicit recognition of the sociopolitical motivations of torture (Elsass 1997; Genefke and Vesti 1998). "Torture syndrome" has not yet been empirically validated (Basoglu et al. 2001).

Regardless of how one characterizes it, torture trauma is unusual among traumatic responses in that it is not simply a *consequence* of the event but rather is the *purpose* of the event. The psychological sequelae of torture are precisely the characteristics that the torturers hope to produce in the oppressed population: terror, helplessness, hopelessness, and the destruction of identities, belief systems, trust, relationships, and communities. Torture trauma is perhaps a most apt, if tragic, illustration of the feminist maxim "The personal is political." Within the context of the refugee community, torture may destroy fundamental human capacities to trust others and to engage in family and community life. Torture survivors may have anxieties about personal safety and difficulties with attachment and bond maintenance, identity and role functioning, and issues related to justice and existential meaning (Silove 1999).

Triple Trauma Paradigm

Immigrants have typically experienced trauma during at least three points in their dislocation. The term frequently used by professionals to describe these events is *triple trauma paradigm*, referring to a cumulative series of events that act as severe stressors to many immigrants. The Liberian families in our case study are illustrative of the triple trauma paradigm, as the examples from their stories will indicate in the discussion to follow. The three points of trauma for a displaced person are: (1) preflight displacement periods of exposure, (2) flight, and (3) resettlement.

PREFLIGHT DISPLACEMENT PERIODS OF EXPOSURE

Usually in the person's own country or region, this type of trauma is characterized by exposure, varying in length and intensity, to various types of violent experiences, which may include imprisonment, torture, abduction, murder, "disappearance" of family members or friends, witnessing or experiencing physical assault, rape, and other forms of sexual violence, the destruction of one's home and property, severe poverty, forced participation in acts of violence, and a persistent state of fear and vulnerability.

Peter and Annie Jefferson and their children chose to stay in their village through the first weeks of violence in their part of the country. On one occasion paramilitary soldiers entered their home, ransacked their belongings, and beat Peter in the presence of his wife and children. Peter also witnessed the torture and death of several members of his extended family, including an uncle and a nephew. When a neighbor reported that soldiers had killed most of the men in a nearby village, the Jeffersons gathered their remaining belongings and escaped under cover of darkness that night.

Theresa Davis and her son, Michael, lived in an urban area near the capital city of Monrovia. Michael, age five, witnessed his mother being dragged from their home, brutally beaten, and taken to jail, where the conditions for her release included providing sexual favors. Michael, terrified for his life and fearful that his mother was dead, hid in the home for four days with little food and water.

Frederick Wilson was an elder in his village. He was regarded as a man of power and influence in the community. When paramilitary soldiers arrived in the village, Frederick's wife, Gertrude, was dragged from their home while Frederick and his children were held at gunpoint. Gertrude was repeatedly raped in the presence of not only her family but the entire village to demonstrate Frederick's incapacity to protect those who trusted him.

FLIGHT

The decision to flee sets into motion a series of profound losses and disruptions, including separation from family members who are unable or unwilling to flee, the abandonment of one's home and other material possessions, the loss of social networks and of social and occupational roles, the loss of familiar cultural norms, and the reality of leaving behind a range of familiar and deeply valued settings, such as a parcel of land attained after years of labor or an ancestral burial ground that represents continuity with one's ancestors. There may also be trauma associated with the journey itself, such as witnessing the death of a loved one or being coerced into prostitution or other acts in order to acquire travel documents and/or transportation (Miller 2004).

Peter and Annie Jefferson and their children escaped under cover of darkness and hid in the forests by day. As their night travels continued, they impressed on their children that the slightest noise could result in the death of the entire family. By the time they reached a refugee camp, their youngest child was near death with dehydration.

In the middle of the night on his fifth day of hiding in their home, young Michael Davis's uncle drove up and coaxed Michael from his hiding place into the car. Theresa was stowed under a blanket in the trunk of the car to avoid detection from authorities as they traveled. Her brother transported the two of them to a remote village, where another friend drove them across the border to a refugee camp. In the camp, Michael became extremely vigilant of his mother, never letting her out of his sight. He began fighting with other boys and continued this behavior once he and his mother relocated to the United States.

Because of his status as an elder, Frederick Wilson was able to barter for false documents to get passage from the country for his family. After the family's escape to a refugee camp, Maria, Frederick and Gertrude's 12-year-old daughter, became extremely withdrawn, refusing to eat or interact with family members or others.

RESETTLEMENT

Immigrants typically encounter a set of profound psychosocial stressors wherever they relocate, including stressors related to multiple losses and changes resulting from the reality of displacement and the challenges of adapting to life in new and unfamiliar settings. These include social isolation and loss of traditional social support networks, uncertainty regarding the well-being of loved ones who were unable or unwilling to make the journey, a lack of income-generating opportunities and a corresponding lack of economic self-sufficiency, discrimination by members of the host society, the loss of valued social roles and a corresponding loss of meaningful role-related activities, and a lack of access to essential health, educational, and economic resources. Strong links have been observed and documented between this constellation of stressors and the development of depression and anxiety (Miller 2004).

When the Wilson family arrived in the United States, 12-year-old Maria had the physical and emotional characteristics of a much younger child, showing few signs of puberty. With the onset of menarche, she began to complain of discomfort and pain, refusing to leave the house despite severe discipline from her father. Figure 12.1 illustrates the psychological effects of political violence and displacement on individuals, families, and communities.

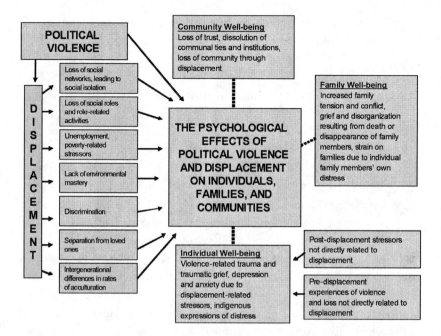

Figure 12.1. The Adverse Effects of Political Violence and Displacement on Individuals, Families, and Communities

The figure describes the far-reaching psychological effects of political violence and displacement not only on individuals but also on entire families and communities. The public rape of Gertrude Wilson painfully illustrates the use of torture to destroy the social networks and social roles of a community leader by an attack not on him directly but on his spouse. This act of torture was intended to impress upon Frederick Wilson and his community his inability to exert leadership, thus reinforcing his lack of environmental mastery. Such acts create dissolution of trust in both the individuals involved and the family's and community's sense of well-being.

Theresa Davis and her son, Michael, found the dislocation of living in a refugee camp a source of discrimination from other refugees because of Theresa's ability to gather needed resources for herself and her son since she was an object of sexual interest among men in the camp. Annie Jefferson's exhaustion and depression, as well as the detachment of her youngest son, illustrate some of the intergenerational issues occurring as a result of the pre-displacement experiences of violence and loss, the dissolution of community ties, the displacement stressors of life in refugee camps, the individual responses to trauma and emotional stress, and the ongoing challenges immigrants face after relocating in a new culture and community.

Responding to and Transforming the Triple Trauma Experience

The Jeffersons, the Davises, and the Wilsons all face numerous psychosocial challenges in the resettlement process. With the assistance of a local voluntary agency, Lutheran Family Services, whose mission it is to resettle refugee families, these families moved into an apartment complex, their caseworker helped enroll their children in neighborhood schools, and ongoing meetings with the caseworker helped them access needed resources, learn to use local transportation, find employment, and manage their money.

Their case manager has myriad questions to consider. Which of their concerns are related to the effects of preflight, flight, and resettlement experiences? How should concerns be prioritized to ensure successful integration of these families into their new homes? Recognizing the potential impact of both torture and trauma in these families, what individual, family-centered, and community resources should be included in an intervention plan?

"Effective interventions are likely to be those that identify and strengthen protective factors—such as the often overlooked resources present in refugee communities—while minimizing the salience of risk factors that may compromise people's well-being" (Rasco and Miller 2004:386). To address the destructive impact of political violence on the social fabric of communities, Rasco and Miller conclude, refugee mental health programs should have two core goals: (1) to help traumatized individuals and families resolve, or at least manage effectively, symptoms of trauma and loss and (2) to enhance the capacity of refugee communities to cope effectively with their many dislocation and resettlement stressors (27). This approach embraces the framework of empowerment practice, which addresses personal, interpersonal, and social/community levels of interaction simultaneously while it also integrates the seven principles of empowerment practice (Lee 2001; Wise 2005), to be discussed in greater depth in a later section.

TRANSFORMATION OF INDIVIDUAL AND FAMILY TRAUMA: PRINCIPLES OF TORTURE TREATMENT

Torture trauma is the result of a deliberate strategy meant to produce terror, powerlessness, and mistrust. Therefore, the most basic principles of interventions for torture trauma emphasize safety, control, and trust, and the need to avoid retraumatization (Behnia 2004; Engstrom and Okamura 2004; Fabri 2001; Hanscom 2001; Ortiz 2001; Rothschild 2000). This is true in legal, medical, social service, and mental health settings, most salient in the last, where a sense of safety is essential to service provision and where it must be addressed as early as the first assessment appointment.

The emphasis on safety and control in trauma treatment agrees with many other trauma intervention models that place safety at the forefront of treatment. This point is made in diverse models for the same reason: trauma of all kinds undermines a sense of safety and security. Everstine and Everstine's model (1993) starts with a stabilization phase, positing that "the victim must recapture a fundamental sense of safety and control before moving on to the more complex, introspective tasks . . . of psychotherapy" (53). Likewise, the first stage of Herman's model is the establishment of safety (1997).

Reestablishing safety, control, and trust for a torture survivor has several components. First, the survivor must always have control over the therapeutic setting: to leave, move, guide conversation, report or not report details of the trauma history, or reconfigure the physical environment. At the same time, the therapist must communicate a consistent commitment to the survivor and a willingness to hear the trauma narrative, so as to avoid reinforcing trauma-induced tendencies toward isolation or silence and to build a trusting relationship.

To create a sense of safety, the therapeutic context must be as different from the torture situation as possible. For example, institutional, clinical settings, face-to-face discussions, and directive questioning techniques may all be reminiscent of torture (Fabri 2001; Piwowarczyk et al. 2000). To confirm the sense of safety, the practitioner must be aware of his or her own reactions to the trauma narrative. Any indications of disbelief, disgust, fear, or voyeurism in response to the history may undermine the survivor's sense of safety (Piwowarczyk et al. 2000).

Finally, the practitioner gives information to the survivor about trauma responses and possible techniques for recovery. The survivors must understand that their psychological responses are normal, and indeed, intended, consequences of torture, rather than an uncontrollable and terrifying "craziness." Education helps to produce a sense of self-control and normalcy. Information about trauma recovery along with education about treatment techniques also creates a sense of control over the recovery process.

Because Theresa Davis had been incarcerated in a dark, subterranean room, a safe environment for her included meeting in a well-lit room above ground. The therapy room on the second floor was filled with plants and cushions, creating a relaxed, unofficial space not at all reminiscent of where she had been held. To help Gertrude Wilson feel in control and safe, her therapist encouraged her to embrace a pillow when revealing her torture story. Work with Michael Davis focused on play activities with sand and music, so different from his recollections of his abandonment and terror of losing his mother. Peter Jefferson and Frederick Wilson were referred to a men's group, where expressions of feelings were not impeded (in their view) by the presence of women.

Vicarious Trauma

Working with survivors of sociopolitical violence and immigration trauma presents many of the same challenges as working with any other traumatized population. The practitioner is likely to experience elements of vicarious trauma, characterized by slow, cumulative, pervasive, and transformative effects on the helper's inner experience and sense of self that occur as a result of engaging empathically and repeatedly with these survivors and with their traumatic narratives (Saakvitne and Pearlman 1996). Practitioners may take on the feelings and attitudes of the victim, rather than assuming the preferred role of "responder," or may evidence other signs and symptoms that echo the primary traumatization of the survivor himself or herself. Examples of such signs and symptoms include intrusive symptoms, avoidance of painful stimuli, and/or hyperarousal (APA 2000). Intentional physical, psychological, emotional, and spiritual self-care is required to offset these effects.

Within these broad definitions, vicarious trauma experiences that result from working with refugees and immigrants may pose some unique challenges for the practitioner. First, the traumatic narratives to which the practitioner is exposed present story after story of egregious and *deliberate* harm by one human being to another. Stories of sexual torture may be particularly challenging in this respect. Practitioners may themselves be challenged by the same hopelessness and mistrust of other human beings that the torture was meant to instill in the survivor.

In addition, the scale of torture practices may at first be unbelievable to practitioners, and then overwhelming. The sociopolitical violence inflicted by millions upon millions adds to the pernicious mistrust of others, as well as emotional flooding, hopelessness, and helplessness. Further, the obscenity of the violence inflicted; the frequent political success of the perpetrators; and the overwhelming scale may all lead to an existential crisis in which one's spiritual faith and concepts of good and evil may be challenged, or even temporarily lost. This spiritual hopelessness also echoes the despair that torture is meant to inflict on its victims.

It is not uncommon for practitioners who are repeatedly exposed to the triple trauma of immigrants and survivors of sociopolitical violence to find themselves, if at first enraged, eventually jaded and apathetic about U.S. policies, procedures, attitudes, and treatment of immigrant populations. Again, this reflects the intended effects of torture on its victims: political apathy and lack of faith that political change is possible.

To offset these effects, it is important to pay particular attention to psychological, spiritual, and emotional self-care. Psychologically, cognitive affirmations of the value of working with torture survivors have been helpful. The mistrust that one experiences for other human beings as the result of a torture narrative is offset by the courage, resilience, and past victories of the survivor. If perpetrators of sociopolitical violence sometimes represent the worst of human nature, perhaps survivors of such violence represent the best.

It is important—psychologically, emotionally, and spiritually—to find ways to participate meaningfully in survivors' successes and to draw from their strengths. As the practitioner inevitably shares the survivor's trauma, it is equally important to share intentionally in the victories, successes, and spiritual connections that survivors demonstrate. The majority of torture survivors cite a strong spiritual connection as central to their survival and their ongoing success. One way of appreciating this spiritual connection and of helping to offset existential crises is through engaging with others and participating in the shared rituals.

Last, doing multicultural work with immigrants from around the world also can be inspiring and rejuvenating. Exposure to a diversity of cultures enriches the practitioner's work and life experience. In the face of difficulties, immigrants' experiences in the host country in a general sense and in their everyday lives simultaneously represent the American ideal of a rich, vibrant, multicultural society, continuing to build hope for the future of our multicultural society as new patterns emerge.

Reflections on Ecological and Empowerment Principles for Transformation at the Community and Sociopolitical Levels

Six ecological principles (Germain 1991; Germain and Gitterman 1995; Miller and Rasco 2004b), together with the empowerment principles that are part of the structure for this volume, provide a framework for community and sociopolitical interventions for work with survivors of torture, flight, and resettlement. Both sets of principles are included because, even though they are similar in many ways, certain aspects of the ecological principles are particularly relevant to work with refugees and torture survivors. In combination, these two sets of principles can increase the options from which workers can choose the most fitting interventions. Given culturally specific knowledge and skills, these principles can be generalized and applied to diverse immigrant communities.

Empowerment principles of building on strengths while diminishing oppressions and working from an awareness of people's needs mirror the first ecological principle: Seek to alter problematic settings, create alternative settings that are better suited to people's needs and capacities, or enhance people's capacity to adapt effectively to existing settings. The specific recommendation for how to do this with refugee families, by the use of culture brokers, coincides with the second empowerment principle, multicultural respect.

The caseworker for refugee families may find that interventions provided by culture brokers are helpful in bridging the gap between the refugee culture and that of the host community. Culture brokers, individuals from the refugee community who have lived in the host culture for an extended time, may have received special training to facilitate cross-cultural understanding. They offer bridges between the two cultures, advocating for newcomers and interpreting cultural meanings to host providers.

The presence of a culture broker was critical to accessing medical help for both Gertrude Wilson and Theresa Davis. Because both women needed testing for sexually transmitted diseases as a result of their torture and dislocation experiences, they were referred to a gynecologist who was skilled in working with tortured women. Even so, both women resisted going to the doctor until a Liberian culture broker, who had herself been a victim and received needed medical treatment, was found. The culture broker was able to provide the women with culturally acceptable explanations of the medical procedures and the importance of having the testing done. The culture broker accompanied Theresa and Gertrude to their medical appointments and assisted the doctor in building a trusting relationship with each woman by articulating questions that Theresa and Gertrude were reluctant to ask. The advocacy of the culture broker made it possible for Theresa and Gertrude to receive the screening and care that they required.

Culture brokers and other professionals may be accessed through a local or regional torture treatment center to address mental health issues associated with torture and trauma. Mutual assistance associations, community organizations run by and for the benefit of refugees and asylees, provide advocacy and supportive social networks to refugees. These refugee-specific services also may provide consultation for non-refugee-oriented organizations needing greater cultural competence to work with increasing numbers of newcomers in their communities.

The empowerment principle of working from an awareness of people's needs is also reflected in the second ecological principle: Address problems that are of concern to community members and include interventions that reflect the priorities of the community.

Before any intervention is designed or planned, it is essential to involve the refugee community in defining issues and priorities. A community is empowered by being asked for its expertise. Focus groups offer one method by which a refugee community can demonstrate its knowledge, priorities, and concerns, preparing members for participation in shaping and carrying out their own meaningful interventions.

An important element of recovery and community integration for Frederick Wilson was an opportunity to exercise leadership in a focus group organized by Lutheran Family Services to talk about successful parenting in the United States. First in the focus group and later at the community elementary school, Frederick articulated Liberian child-rearing practices for his community and the concerns of Liberian parents that they would lose control without physical punishments. In this way, Frederick was able to reclaim his previous role as a community elder in his new home country. As Frederick began to embrace American ideas of discipline in the home, other families followed his lead. His subsequent involvement in teaching newly arrived refugees about parenting in America decreased the number of referrals to child protective services and enhanced parental involvement of Liberian families in the community schools on behalf of the children. He was once again a community leader.

The third ecological principle is particularly relevant for trauma survivors: Whenever possible, prioritize prevention over treatment. It is helpful to remember the social worker's obligation to social justice:

> Social workers pursue social change, particularly with and on behalf of vulnerable and oppressed individuals and groups of people. Social workers' social change efforts are focused primarily on issues of poverty, unemployment, discrimination, and other forms of social injustice. These activities seek to promote sensitivity to and knowledge about oppression and cultural and ethnic diversity. Social workers strive to ensure access to needed information, services, and resources; equality of opportunity; and meaningful participation in decision making for all people.
>
> (NASW 1999:7)

Thus, the social worker has at least four ways in which to frame prevention with this population. The first is to *ensure access to needed information, services, and resources* for immigrants who have survived sociopolitical violence. Access to information can help new refugees adapt and function successfully and also meaningfully participate in decision making in their new environment. Such access helps *meet basic needs* for services and resources such as shelter, food, transportation, financial and social resources, mental health services, and health care, all of which are core factors in the prevention of physical illness, mental health problems, and the potential retraumatization of poverty and deprivation.

The Jefferson, Davis, and Wilson families faced a variety of physical and mental health issues upon their arrival in the United States. Additionally, they needed assistance with their financial and educational concerns. To help them with these challenges, their social workers took the following actions: As refugees, all three families received time-limited cash assistance to help pay their living expenses. Within this time frame, they received bus passes to look for employment and to get their children to school. Classes for refugee families were offered at their apartment complex (for ease of access and child care); among the topics covered were financial management; successful parenting in the United States, including laws about child abuse and parental rights; the local school system; and home management, including instruction about using appliances and safety issues.

The second way to enact prevention is to *raise social awareness* about the needs of immigrants in the host country, combined, thirdly, with *attending to laws and policies* that fail to meet these needs. In some cases, a social worker will be obliged to engage in *political advocacy* to change policies that further retraumatize immigrants upon their arrival in the host country. Examples of retraumatizing policies include the lengthy detention of asylum seekers upon arrival in the host country, denying asylum seekers access to legal work authorization during their asylum-seeking process, and deportation without the opportunity for legal appeal.

Finally, it is important to remember that we, as social workers in the United States, are also part of a global community where torture is still practiced in 132 nations. Insofar as we are able and aware, it is our responsibility to raise our voices about worldwide oppression and advocate for a just world in which torture is no longer practiced.

The empowerment principles of multicultural respect and integrating support from others are visible in both the fourth and the fifth ecological principles. The fourth ecological principle is to incorporate the community's values and beliefs about psychological well-being and distress in community-based interventions.

"People are more likely to use mental health and psychosocial programs that embody their own cultural beliefs and include culturally familiar rituals of healing" (Miller and Rasco 2004:44). To address the symptoms and consequences of torture and trauma, the meaning of these experiences must be understood within the community's culture. Group work is particularly relevant for communities from collectivist cultural backgrounds—i.e., psychoeducational workshops help refugees to normalize the symptoms of trauma and develop strategies to assist themselves and their community. Community meetings provide a venue for sharing in ways that resonate with culturally valued practices.

Because Liberian culture is more community focused than individually based, group interventions, where concerns and problems are raised in the context of a community, are consonant with the values and practices of the refugee families in this case study. Food is central to many community activities. Drinks and snacks for group meetings add an element of cultural comfort to discussions of mental health issues. Rituals such as including music from the culture or lighting symbolic candles facilitate both discussion and recovery.

The fifth ecological principle is to integrate interventions into the existing community settings and activities whenever possible, to enhance participation and long-term sustainability. Participatory and collaborative roles are also a key aspect of the seventh empowerment principle.

One way to build on strengths and diminish oppression in a refugee community is to demonstrate that its culture and experience are valued and respected. *Focusing on the strengths* within a cultural group allows members to reconstruct identities they value, while moving beyond the pain of traumatic experiences of the past. *Collaborating* with the refugee community to create evenings of cultural exchange, celebration, and cross-cultural education builds alliances within and across cultures.

With our case study families, for example, the elementary and middle school administrators and teachers might propose an evening for sharing culture through food, music, and dance. A religious community might be encouraged to invite refugee women such as Annie, Gertrude, and Theresa to share a cooking group where members exchange recipes and favorite dishes. Refugee community members might incorporate cultural rituals and practices as part of traditional American holidays and events.

Finally, the sixth ecological principle is stated as building capacity within the community and focusing on empowerment, helping people achieve greater control over the resources that affect their lives. This principle is closely aligned with the empowerment principles of building on strengths while diminishing oppression, multicultural respect, assisting clients as they empower themselves, equalizing power differentials, and using cooperative roles.

Capacity building, using the strengths of the refugee community to design, plan, implement, and evaluate interventions, not only recognizes but also values the contributions of the refugee community. It assumes that *natural leaders* will emerge within the refugee community. It develops *collaboration* among community resources and the refugee community. It *equalizes power* differentials and encourages cooperation.

Orientation groups introduced the Jeffersons, Davises, and Wilsons to local resources for education, health, social services, legal and mental health programs and invited them to access opportunities, thus achieving greater control over their lives and enhancing the functioning of the community. Culture brokers and other refugee services help refugee community members learn to negotiate the complex system of services, advancing their integration into the larger community and providing transferable skills to other newly arrived immigrants.

Capacity-building approaches have notable advantages over expert-driven strategies. They expand the reach of mental health services by including refugee community members who understand the cultural context and meaning of the traumatic experiences of their communities. Capacity building encourages collaboration with the refugee community, thus ensuring that cultural practices and values will be reflected in interventions (Miller and Rasco 2004:47).

Conclusion and Recommendations

Practitioners can learn from immigrant clients. Having demonstrated remarkable resilience to simply survive and immigrate, these individuals, families, and groups often embrace the challenges of their new homeland—eager to start over, to learn new skills, to define fresh goals, and to build new lives.

Working cooperatively with immigrants, refugees, asylees, and asylum seekers, our efforts reflect the empowerment principles (Lee 2001; Wise 2005). We at Lutheran Family Services recognize the strength demonstrated by immigrants. We work with them, individually, in communities, and as advocates for humane public policies for those who have come to our country in search of freedom and justice. We respect and value efforts to move beyond the pain and oppression they have experienced. We encourage immigrants to make intentional choices to retain the best of their cultural identities and rich histories. We celebrate their cultural contributions to our communities.

We maintain open and ongoing dialogue with our immigrant communities, encouraging them to participate actively and fully in defining their specific needs, setting priorities, and implementing programs that empower them to succeed. As immigrant communities set goals and work toward them, we add our expertise, identifying new options, introducing culturally appropriate strategies, and assisting clients in their efforts to access information and resources. We model the power of working together within immigrant communities and across organizations to facilitate collaboration, networking mutual support.

We work as partners and consultants when appropriate. We recognize the expertise within our immigrant communities to design culturally relevant practices and strategies for meeting goals. Accepting immigrant communities as the experts about their culture and experience helps to equalize power differentials. We work cooperatively with not only immigrant communities but also those whose mission it is to serve these communities. Our shared goals are best realized by working in concert to build strong, inclusive communities where the contributions of diverse groups are recognized and valued.

When working with immigrants and survivors of sociopolitical violence, it is important to assess the *cultural competence of the practitioner and of agencies and systems* involved in the delivery of services to these clients. Individually, practitioners examine the extent of their own cultural competence: awareness of their own cultural assumptions, of the effects of their attitudes about cultural differences in the helping process, of understanding the dynamics of cultural difference, and of knowledge of the specific culture of immigrant clients.

Equally important is the evaluation of the cultural competence of agencies working with immigrants. Diller (1999) suggests that agencies advocate for multiculturalism within organizational systems and engage in research to improve service delivery to clients with culturally diverse backgrounds. Such efforts involve personnel at all levels, from practitioners to administrators, policymakers, boards of directors, and funders.

Finally, for immigrants who have suffered the multiple traumas described in this chapter, practitioners consider *how to choose and balance interventions* that have the greatest likelihood of empowering the survivors of oppression, reducing individual and family suffering, and supporting immigrant clients as they become members of U.S. society. Clearly there is need for both clinical and community interventions to support the strengths of immigrants and to resolve the symptoms and sequelae of torture and trauma.

Of equal importance is the need to address the worldwide practice of torture and other human rights abuses. This focus not only is an ethical obligation for social work practitioners but also has the potential of therapeutic value for those who have already suffered such abuses. Effective mental health interventions and community connection restore hope and purpose. Both the individual and the community triumph over attempts at deliberate and systematic oppression. Torture can, and does, fail. Survivors can and will be victorious.

References

American Psychiatric Association (APA). 2000. *Diagnostic and Statistical Manual of Mental Disorders, Text Revision (DSM-IV-TR)*. 4th ed. Washington, D.C.: Author.
Basoglu, M., J. Jaranson, R. Mollica, and M. Kastrup. 2001. "Torture and Mental Health: A Research Overview." In E. Gerrity, T. M. Keane, and F. Tuma, eds., *The Mental Health Consequences of Torture*, 35–62. New York: Kluwer Academic.
Behnia, B. 2004. "Trust Building from the Perspective of Survivors of War and Torture." *Social Service Review* 78:26–40.

Diller, J. V. 1999. "Towards a Culturally Competent System of Care." In J. V. Diller, ed., *Cultural Diversity: A Primer for the Human Services*, 12–13. Belmont, Calif.: Brooks/Cole, Wadsworth.

Elsass, P. 1997. *Treating Victims of Torture and Violence: Theoretical, Cross-Cultural, and Clinical Implications*. New York: New York University Press.

Engstrom, C. W., and A. Okamura. 2004. "Working with Survivors of Torture: Approaches to Helping." *Families in Society: The Journal of Contemporary Social Services* 85:310–319.

Everstine, D. S., and L. Everstine 1993. *The Trauma Response: Treatment for Emotional Injury*. New York: Norton.

Fabri, M. 2001. "Reconstructing Safety: Adjustments to the Therapeutic Frame in the Treatment of Survivors of Political Torture." *Professional Psychology: Research and Practice* 32:452–457.

Genefke, I., and P. Vesti. 1998. "Diagnosis of Governmental Torture." In J. M. Jaranson and M. K. Popkin, eds., *Caring for Victims of Torture*, 43–60. Washington, D.C.: American Psychiatric Press.

Germain, C. B. 1991. *Human Behavior in the Social Environment: An Ecological View*. New York: Columbia University Press.

Germain, C. B., and A. Gitterman. 1995. "Ecological Perspective." In R. Edwards, ed.-in-chief, *Encyclopedia of Social Work*, 1:816–824. 19th ed. Washington, D.C.: National Association of Social Workers.

Hanscom, K. L. 2001. "Treating Survivors of War Trauma and Torture." *American Psychologist* 56:1032–1039.

Herman, J. 1997. *Trauma and Recovery*. 2nd ed. New York: Basic Books.

Jaranson, J. M. 1995. "Government-Sanctioned Torture: Status of the Rehabilitation Movement." *Transcultural Psychiatry Research Review* 32:253–286.

Jaranson, J. M., and M. K. Popkin, eds. 1998. *Caring for Victims of Torture*. Washington, D.C.: American Psychiatric Press.

Lee, J. A. B. 2001. *The Empowerment Approach to Social Work Practice: Building the Beloved Community*. 2nd ed. New York: Columbia University Press.

Miller, K., and L. Rasco. 2004. "An Ecological Framework for Addressing the Mental Health Needs of Refugee Communities." In K. Miller and L. Rasco, eds., *The Mental Health of Refugees: Ecological Approaches to Healing and Adaptation*, 1–64. Mahwah, N.J.: Lawrence Erlbaum.

National Association of Social Workers (NASW). 1999. *Code of Ethics*. Washington, D.C.: Author.

Ortiz, D. 2001. "The Survivors' Perspective: Voices from the Center." In E. Gerrity, T. M. Keane, and F. Tuma, eds., *The Mental Health Consequences of Torture*, 13–34. New York: Kluwer Academic.

Piwowarczyk, L., A. Moreno, and M. Grodin. 2000. "Health Care of Torture Survivors." *Journal of the American Medical Association* 284 (5): 539–541.

Rasco, L., and K. Miller. 2004. "Challenges and Critical Issues." In K. Miller and L. Rasco, eds., *The Mental Health of Refugees: Ecological Approaches to Healing and Adaptation*, 385–412. Mahwah, N.J.: Lawrence Erlbaum.

Rothschild, B. 2000. *The Body Remembers: The Psychophysiology of Trauma and Trauma Treatment*. New York: Norton.

Saakvitne, K., and L. Pearlman. 1996. *Transforming the Pain: A Workbook on Vicarious Traumatization*. New York: Norton.

Silove, D. 1999. "The Psychosocial Effects of Torture, Mass Human Rights Violations, and Refugee Trauma: Toward an Integrated Conceptual Framework." *Journal of Nervous and Mental Disorders* 187:200–207.

United Nations High Commissioner for Refugees (UNHCR). 1951. *Convention Relating to the Status of Refugees*. New York: United Nations.

——. 1984. *United Nations Convention Against Torture and Other Cruel, Inhuman, and Degrading Treatment or Punishment*. New York: United Nations.

——. 2002. *United Nations Convention Relating to the Status of Refugees*. New York: United Nations.

United Nations Office for the Coordination of Humanitarian Affairs. 2002. *Global IDP Project*. New York: United Nations.

Wise, J. B. 2005. *Empowerment Practice with Families in Distress*. New York: Columbia University Press.

13

Transforming the Trauma of War in Combat Veterans

MEL SINGER

In the late 1980s and early 1990s, Vietnam vets were beginning to stream into the Veterans Health Administration's PTSD programs, both inpatient and outpatient. The following account represents a situation that was not unusual among veterans during that time.

For a number of years following Vietnam, 43-year-old Amory, a highly suc-cessful brick mason, had apparently made a satisfactory adjustment—that is, until his wife threatened to leave him. Her declaration that she wanted a divorce precipitated a crisis in his life. He regressed in all major areas of social functioning—spousal, work, parenting, etc. A series of suicide attempts and hospitalizations thus followed.

Amory had been born into a deeply religious Protestant family that for gen-erations had resided in a small town located in the Pacific Northwest. He had one sibling, an older sister. His father owned the local hardware store, where Amory had worked as a boy. While not wealthy, they had wanted for little. Generally, Amory remembered his childhood as "pretty good."

He had been born a "preemie," three weeks early, but by the time he was a toddler he had apparently caught up developmentally with other kids his age. As he grew older, there were no lingering medical concerns regarding his pre-mature birth. His mother, however, had a tendency to see him as more fragile than other boys his age. Amory remembered her concerns as mildly irritating to him, both in his childhood and in adulthood.

His hometown was neither ethnically nor racially diverse. Growing up, Amory had had very little contact with African Americans, Hispanics, or members of other ethnic groups. It was not until he joined the army that he came in contact with people of color. He adjusted well, however, to his new-found comrades and established close friendships with some of them. He sometimes felt amazed at both how different their lives had been from his and how much alike.

Before his breakdown Amory appeared to have made a good postwar adjustment. He'd married, fathered a child, and developed a successful career in the construction business. If there were signs of post-traumatic stress, such as nightmares, flashbacks, and a "guilty" conscience, no one knew except Amory and his wife. He had lived all those years as an internally divided man, needing to continually muster vast amounts of psychic energy to avoid becoming consumed by the war and all its memories.

Amory appeared to function well for more than fifteen years after the war. News of his breakdown came as a shock to those who knew him. But a closer look into his postwar years revealed a path strewn with red flags. While I never met his ex-wife, Amory's account of their marriage enabled me to piece together a picture of what led to the breakup. Apparently, his wife had "learned to live with" some of his re-experiencing symptoms, such as occasional nightmares, flashbacks, and intrusive recollections. But hyperarousal symptoms, such as exaggerated startle response, hypervigilance, and irritability, probably gave her more trouble. And harder yet were his avoidance symptoms. He could be cold and distant, unable to relate emotionally. Her sense that she was living with a man she didn't know and would probably never know was more than she could bear. She knew he needed help; they needed help, but he wouldn't listen. Feeling at the end of her rope, she told him she wanted a divorce. Amory was shattered.

During his first hospitalization, he had become flooded with war memories, and a diagnosis of severe PTSD was added to his existing diagnosis of major depression with psychotic and suicidal features. When he came to our clinic several years later, he was no longer working and was receiving disability, 100 percent service-connected. He had tried a number of therapy groups, but instead of helping, they had the opposite effect. When I began to see Amory in individual therapy, he was struggling with feelings of guilt.

Amory shoved his hands deep into the pockets of his fatigue jacket as he stared beyond me, over my left shoulder, at my wall calendar and that month's picture of an Indian motorcycle and said, "No one . . . no one could ever know what it's like to have killed innocent people, women and children, even the family dog. We didn't know until it was too late, but that doesn't matter, we still did it. My family could never love me if they knew what happened there."

"You looked for a moment like you were no longer here, but back in Vietnam."

"I guess so . . . I don't belong here . . . I belong there."

The theme of shame and guilt over having killed innocent people, the dissociation from the present, as well as Amory's PTSD symptoms and depression, are shared by other veterans who have been through combat trauma. A discussion of those themes, and the social work responses to help Amory, follows.

Understanding Combat Trauma

One might wish that the painful complexities of war could be captured by a diagnosis and treated with a few well-selected techniques, but that is not the case. In this chapter I hope to broaden the concept of the "trauma of war" beyond PTSD. War takes a toll on the total personality. War, probably more than almost any other traumatic experience, tears at preexisting values and belief systems. In its wake it leaves uncertainty and confusion. Veterans may have to comb through their combat experiences to find new ways to understand the world and their place in it (Frankl 1962). For some this may not be so hard to do; for others it is more difficult. Some wars, and even some experiences within a particular war, may offer more opportunities to establish meaning than others. We know that not all wars are the same.

Many people have deemed World War II "the last good war." The enemy was clearly defined and easily located. Our country was united in its resolve to defeat our foes. Despite all that, many WWII veterans have waited more than fifty years to begin to talk about their experiences. This fact should not be taken to mean, however, that their lives have been without emotional suffering; it means only that they have suffered in silence. Why the silence for all those years? I don't think we have a good answer for that question.

One study, comparing the narratives of WWII veterans with those of Vietnam vets, revealed that when WWII vets did recount their war experiences they tended to emphasize losses, particularly the loss of buddies (Barnes and Harvey 2000). Closely paralleling the loss of comrades, WWII vets often talked about how four long years at war had stolen their youth.

In contrast, Vietnam vets, while similarly stressing the loss of buddies, also emphasized the loss of emotional and psychological functions, in particular the ability to express their feelings, to build trusting relationships, and to be intimate with others. Overall, in this study, Vietnam vets seemed to have more residual anger about their war and to be more likely to talk about its naked brutality, such as its atrocities.

Both groups of veterans still ached for the buddies they saw die, sometimes in their arms. But while WWII vets were showered with gratitude for their patriotism and sacrifice, Vietnam vets were not. A country divided too often scorned the returning soldier instead of the war. While many WWII vets felt they had lost their youth, the Vietnam vets felt they had lost parts of themselves.

WWII vets suffering from "combat fatigue," the equivalent of today's PTSD, seemed to have fewer adjustment problems following that war than Vietnam vets did after their service in Vietnam. In the future we may have to wonder about the relative emotional and psychological toll on veterans from a controversial war versus that from a relatively noncontroversial one. Perhaps the more controversial the war, the more difficulty soldiers have in making satisfactory postwar adjustments.

After WWII the returning soldiers had much to be proud of. A thankful nation showered them with gratitude and "filled" them with pride. Vietnam was almost WWII's direct opposite. Too often I have heard stories about Vietnam vets arriving home alone and sneaking into airport bathrooms to change into civilian clothes, dreading confrontations with antiwar protestors. Whereas WWII vets were filled with pride, the Vietnam vets have had to search out their honor and pride, buried by the war's controversy.

It took a number of years for Vietnam veterans who needed help adjusting to civilian life to find understanding within standard psychiatric settings. Initially, many of their PTSD symptoms were viewed instead as evidence of behavior problems, character disorders, or paranoid schizophrenia (Bloom 2000). Eventually, largely because of political pressure from concerned therapists and veterans' groups, the diagnosis of PTSD was codified and officially added to *DSM-III*, psychiatry's diagnostic manual, in 1980.

The new diagnosis of PTSD was meant to cover a whole host of traumatic conditions. Before long, however, some experts in trauma, among them Judith Herman (1997), pointed out that the new diagnosis was keyed to a single life-threatening event and did not cover victims who had suffered prolonged life-threatening events, such as childhood abuse, sexual and otherwise, often perpetrated by people in positions of trust. Almost without exception, Herman noted, such abuse led to personality changes characterized by "deformations of relatedness and identity" (119). Herman called this syndrome "Complex Post-Traumatic Stress Disorder."

These three criteria of complex PTSD—prolonged life-threatening events, a sense of betrayal by a person or persons deemed to be in positions of trust, and personality changes encompassing deformations of relatedness and identity—also describe the psychological and emotional effects of war that ex-combatants suffer.

In terms of prolonged life-threatening events, a soldier's tour of duty compels him or her to stay in a combat zone until the tour is completed (twelve months for an army infantryman, thirteen months for a marine). Obviously, throughout those months the environment is replete with life-threatening experiences. Soldiers experience betrayal of trust, especially in the wars since WWII, as feeling unnecessarily sacrificed by high command, by the government, and by their country.

One more factor both fits the criterion of personality changes and clearly demarcates war trauma from other forms of complex PTSD. Combat soldiers are not only acted upon but also have been taught to act upon others. In short, they are taught to kill. Such training countermands all previous childhood training not to be cruel, not to hurt or injure others, and, certainly, not to kill. When a soldier kills for the first time the experience is frequently traumatic, especially if he or she is close enough to see the victim die (Grossman 1995; Hedges 2002). After up-close killing, it can be especially unnerving for soldiers to realize that they momentarily felt exhilarated. In reaction, they may be immediately overcome with shame and self-revulsion (Hedges 2002). An even greater degree of shame, guilt, and self-revulsion occurs when they learn they have been involved in the killing of innocents, particularly women and children (Singer 2004).

When the war or the tour of duty is over, when these men and women finally come home, many of them begin to experience PTSD symptoms. But beyond the symptoms there can be lasting personality changes, not unlike those cited by Herman, namely, the distressing alterations in relatedness and identity.

As described in a synopsis of Erich Remarque's classic novel about German soldiers in World War I, *All Quiet on the Western Front*:

> They were a generation of young people, who whatever their level of involvement, loss, or outlook, were fated to shoulder guilt, remorse, trauma and dysfunction. Through loss of ideals and beliefs held sacred by prewar society, survivors unmoored by the safe anchorage usually accorded the young, drifted into despair, disgust and spiritual unrest. Deprived of innocence by nightmarish sounds and sights that they were incapable of articulating to family and friends, they survived on the edge, never quite in tune with the present and hopelessly detached from the future. They were, as Gertrude Stein commented to a war-maimed Ernest Hemingway, a "lost generation."

> (Van Kirk 2001: 21)

Seventy years and three major wars later we seek to provide a safer harbor for our returning warriors.

Combat trauma is thus a variant of complex PTSD. It arises from combat stress manifested over an extended period of time and involving multiple life-threatening stressors, rather than a single life-threatening event of relatively brief duration. Initially, its clinical picture may not seem that different from ordinary PTSD. Both include symptoms from PTSD's three major symptom groups—re-experiencing, hyperarousal, and avoidance. But in addition to the symptoms of PTSD, combat trauma involves prolonged experiences of having been powerless in the face of life-threatening events, as well as the experience of exercising power over others, of learning to kill and killing. Both the many life-threatening events of combat and the experience of killing others may act in concert to produce the "deformations of identity and relatedness" written about by Herman (1997). Using Herman's framework and adding a specifier, we could also categorize combat trauma as "complex post-traumatic stress disorder, combat related."

Responding to Combat Trauma

Self-empowerment among veterans who suffer from war trauma, if it is to occur at all, must be achieved throughout all realms of experience: intrapsychically, interpersonally, socioculturally, and finally, spiritually and philosophically.

RESPONDING AT THE PERSONAL LEVEL

In the personal realm power arises from within and is reflected in a sense of efficacy and overall self-esteem. The symptoms of any psychiatric disorder, including PTSD, can threaten people's sense of efficacy and control over their own mental functioning (Shay 1994). Symptoms, by definition, are painful and almost impossible to control without outside help of one kind or another. Amory's inability to control his anxiety, intrusive thoughts, flashbacks, and various dissociative experiences often left him feeling helpless and ashamed.

Sometimes during our sessions Amory dissociated. And, as much as I could, I called his attention to these experiences, hoping that I could help him to see how easily he moved back and forth between current realities and the past. Whenever this happened, we tried to understand what had just occurred in our session that had possibly triggered the dissociative experience; when it happened in ordinary social venues, however, other people, such as family and friends, were often perplexed and even frightened. My objective here was to enhance Amory's awareness and sense of control with respect to his psychic functioning and social interactions.

It was clear that Amory suffered from war-related PTSD. But in addition to having been a victim of war, he suffered from shame and guilt stemming from war-related experiences in which he had been involved in the killing of innocents. In a session almost a year after the one reported above, the following dialogue ensued:

"Amory, as you and I discussed a few weeks ago, you said you might like to talk with the hospital chaplain about finding a choir to join. Have you had a chance to do that?"

A tense silence followed my question, during which he looked at the floor, rather than at me. After a minute or so he spoke:

"Yes, I thought about it. Sounds nice, doesn't it? Me in a choir once again, singing religious songs, entertaining people, being appreciated . . ."

"And?"

"And that's for someone else, not for me. You know what I did. I don't deserve to stand up there in a choir pretending I'm something I used to be, something I'm not anymore."

"I see. Maybe even the idea that you might do something you enjoy makes you feel worse in some ways, even more undeserving?"

"Maybe so, maybe so."

Amory's wartime sins haunted him; he felt eternally damned and unforgivable. He knew all too well how power could be perverted, and he remained conflicted about whether he deserved to enjoy life.

Ordinarily, empowerment may be defined as the freedom to choose and the ability to make things happen (Wise 2005). But for veterans like Amory, combat experiences expose them to a perversion of power (Hedges 2002). They come home conflicted, afraid to access their personal power. They do not know if they can modulate and focus their power toward their own good and the good of others. Some of them will need considerable help, in the form of group therapy, individual therapy, and couples/family therapy (Flora 2002). The choice of modality depends on the client—we start where he or she is.

In thinking about Amory and the way his life was shattered after his wife asked for a divorce, I am often reminded of a line from the nursery rhyme "Humpty Dumpty": "All the king's horses and all the king's men couldn't put Humpty Dumpty together again." I imagine that this nursery rhyme, like so many others, was probably first an Edwardian political cartoon and became a nursery rhyme only later on. Its survival over the years, however, suggests that it resonates with certain deep anxieties shared by children (and adults). Humpty Dumpty's anxiety relates to falling apart or, as referred to psychiatrically, the annihilation of the self.

Amory virtually fell apart. His Christian upbringing was diametrically opposed to what he had done in the war. He had managed to function during his postwar years by narrowly forcing most of his attention out- ward, onto his work. He couldn't risk having memories and emotions from the war infiltrate his life in the present. But like howling wolves kept at bay only by the campfire's light, his dreams, flashbacks, and intrusive recollections threatened to overtake him.

His defenses against being overwhelmed by the past were organized around keeping parts of himself and his history separate from other parts. His life as a brick mason, husband, and father had to be kept separate from his experiences in the war. These defenses were costly in terms of day-to-day reality. The energy needed to maintain these internal divisions was considerable. He sometimes seemed to other people as though he was not fully present.

Defense mechanisms needed in ordinary life, those that promote rea- sonableness in most of life's endeavors, might not help one survive a war. Under wartime conditions a shift to more-primitive defense mechanisms, such as acting out, displacement, projection, dissociation and splitting, and so on, may better aid the cause of survival (Laufer 1985).

When I first started seeing Amory he was flooded with memories and feelings that he had never talked about before. He was awash in shame and guilt for what he had participated in during the war. His suffering seemed akin to atonement. As our work together progressed, he started a relationship with the hospital's Protestant chaplain, a man with considerable training and experience in working with combat vets. As Amory grieved for his lost innocence and those he had killed during the war, he began, ever so slightly, to think that there still might be a place for him in life. He would always be a man with a past, but he could become a man who now wanted to help others. At one point, later in his treatment, he participated as a brick mason with Habitat for Humanity. Eventually, family relationships were rekindled, as well as some new relationships with his church community.

Fontana and Rosenheck's (2005) study of Vietnam vets who had suffered a lessening of religious faith as a result of their exposure to combat led to a recommendation that veterans consider seeking help from clergy in addition to their primary mental health treatment. The authors reasoned that clergy could be helpful in reestablishing a sense of meaning about life. In Amory's case the hospital's Protestant pastor became involved in his treatment, which later proved invaluable.

Some veterans come back with shattered bodies as well, a trend that is increasing. The number of soldiers saved from death on the battlefield is much greater than in any other war. The number of people needing treatment for combined PTSD and brain injury is also growing. How psychological treatment techniques might need to be modified to help this group remains to be seen. In general, one study has shown that PTSD symptoms are greater when they are associated with a physical injury (Koren et al. 2005). This interrelationship between physical injuries and PTSD will hopefully become better understood as a result of Iraq and Afghanistan.

The reader might wonder if the severity of Amory's regression and his apparently difficult recovery might indicate preexisting trauma and/or psychiatric disorder. At least one study has shown that the prewar existence of borderline personality disorder predicted more variability in postwar PTSD symptoms, beyond that ordinarily predicted by combat exposure (Axelrod, Morgan, and Southwick 2005). Evidently, in this study, combat exposure made for more variability in the borderline personality features, and preexisting borderline personality made for more variability in PTSD symptoms, beyond what might be expected from combat exposure alone. With regard to Amory, there was no evidence that he had a severe personality disorder before the war. There is some indication that he might have felt that he was viewed as less than adequate as an adult male because of having been born prematurely and his mother's perceptions of him. But in the course of his psychotherapy that never seemed to be the case.

As a fragmented person, he had had little emotional efficacy and depleted self-esteem. The grief process facilitated by treatment helped him to work through such painful emotions as shame, guilt, self-hatred, and loss (Singer 2004), which had prevented further integration. Eventually, identity diffusion yielded to identity consolidation. He was now ready to tackle broken connections within the interpersonal realm.

RESPONDING AT THE INTERPERSONAL LEVEL

In the interpersonal realm, empowerment derives from a soldier's connectedness with others. In the war his or her connections are with buddies. Many a veteran will tell you that these were the closest connections to another person or persons they ever had. Nevertheless, as the soldier faces homecoming, connections to his buddies must be pushed from center stage and room made for his immediate family and friends.

More than likely the soldier has been gone for at least a year, perhaps longer. It may take some weeks or even a couple of months after returning home, but sooner or later, the excitement and joy of the reunion settle down and certain realizations dawn on all parties. He or she has changed. They have changed. While the military tries to help soldiers and their families anticipate some of the difficulties often experienced during reunions, problems may still accrue.

Because of the Department of Defense's policy on redeployment, the family may feel uncertain as to whether Mom or Dad is home for good or possibly could be redeployed at any time. Parents may struggle with such issues as the reshuffling of roles and who should have authority over this or that aspect of the family's functioning. Children may experience loyalty conflicts. Usually they want to please both parents but feel safer pleasing the one who has been there the most.

It may be difficult for spouses and other family members to adjust to a vet's PTSD symptoms (the re-experiencing, hyperarousal, and withdrawal). Counseling for couples that organizes treatment around these three symptom clusters has been found to be helpful (Sherman, Zanotti, and Jones 2005). If the spouse comes to understand the symptoms, he or she can help the children in the family understand their veteran-parent's behavior.

Unmarried vets may have an even tougher time. Their connections with their families of origin and whatever friends they had before the war are their mainstay. For single vets, especially if they are younger, the military may have played a larger role in fulfilling emotional needs than for those who are married. Young single vets may be even further removed from establishing their place in the world.

Women veterans may have a different sort of problem. In Iraq and Afghanistan, women are being allowed to assume combat roles. These women are usually eager to show that they can handle combat as well as the men. Therefore, when they come back from a war zone and have symptoms of PTSD, they fear that they will perceived as weak, thus illustrating that "women can't handle combat."

The problems of substance abuse and anger management deserve special attention, as they can have profound effects on interpersonal relationships. A significant number of the vets returning from combat zones will have difficulty managing their anger, and it goes almost without saying that substance abuse diminishes the ability to control anger and elevates unpredictability.

Most often, vets start using substances to self-medicate their PTSD symptoms. They may not want to go to a vets' center, a VA hospital, or some other psychiatric facility where they will have to admit to others that they are having problems. It is much easier to abuse substances. Social work practitioners working with the family must confront this problem, as sensitively as possible. Referrals to programs specializing in anger management and substance abuse may be necessary (Rosen et al. 2001).

In combat, life happens fast and is often marked by tragic finalities. In peacetime, coping usually involves slowing down and putting things in perspective. Information is sought and needs to be carefully weighed. Actions are taken deliberately, not reflexively. If our veteran client had these skills before entering the military, the adjustment to civilian life will be much easier. If he or she did not, however, it will be necessary to learn them for the first time.

The differences between making decisions on the home front versus making decisions in combat will probably have to be pointed out innumerable times. Social workers need to know that repetition is crucial in this kind of work. The veterans and various members of their families need to hear about these issues many times and in many places (van Wormer 1994). Group therapy with other vets is a treatment of choice that proceeds concomitantly with other forms of treatment. Hearing how other vets are struggling to make the transition to home can provide a powerful source of help.

RESPONDING AT THE SOCIAL LEVEL

In the social realm, empowerment derives from meaningful connections with the community and society at large. Returning vets hope to find a society that honors them and lives up to its commitments to provide a variety of services: medical, educational, financial, and vocational. They are entitled to nothing less in their struggle to reintegrate themselves into the larger community. Once they made war, but now they must be helped to make peace.

To be welcomed home, to be thanked for one's courage and sacrifice, to be honored as a warrior and given one's place in the community from this time forth is a deeply emotional and humbling experience that historically has been given form by many cultures through ritual and tradition. Consider the following example:

Sitting alone and isolated from other spectators in the bleacher seats on a hot, dusty day at an Oklahoma fairground, Ron, a one-armed Vietnam vet wearing fatigues and a cap with "Vietnam" written on it, watched as a group of Native Americans, in headdress and other tribal regalia, danced to the sound of drums, bangles, and chanting. The dancers, themselves Vietnam vets, had circled the track a couple of times, but this time they stopped close to where the lone vet was sitting. There they huddled as they busily talked, casting a few glances and gestures toward the stands. One dancer, who may have been the tribal leader, broke from the huddle and started moving in the direction of the stands where the Vietnam vet was sitting. When he reached him he said, "We've seen you sitting here and know you are one of us . . . please, come dance with us." Ron was taken aback and at first didn't know what to say. As soon as he could gather his composure he said, "Yes, yes . . . I'd be honored."

A moment of silence passed, as the two men looked each other in the eye. Finally, the dancer spoke: "No, my friend, it is we who are honored."

That day Ron danced. He danced with his newfound Native American brothers. Years later, when he told me the story, it was clear that that experience had been life-changing for him. He had finally received a warrior's acceptance home.

As a society, we need to think more about how we bring our servicemen and -women home, how we honor them and help them to reintegrate. In many ways Vietnam showed us how *not* to bring combat veterans home

(Shay 2002). Then they came home individually, without the support of the community, and separated from their comrades.

Voice is another aspect of empowerment in the social realm. To a struggling vet, "having been there" and telling the story can be the basis for an authentic authority. It should come as no surprise that those who have been to war frequently are not so eager to commit present generations of young people to new wars. At present a number of Iraqi and Afghanistan vets are planning to run for public office in Washington, D.C., and elsewhere. These men and women are finding their voice within society.

While Amory didn't tout his veteran's status within the church, he didn't deny it either. Parishioners came to know this about him, respected him for it, and welcomed him to the church community. Somewhere along the way he had acquired some cooking skills and was known to make a "mean" chili. Cooking for certain events was a way for him to contribute, while keeping a low profile. It was also a way for people to get to know him, which was beginning to happen.

RESPONDING AT THE SPIRITUAL AND PHILOSOPHICAL LEVEL

In the spiritual and philosophical realm, empowerment derives from the establishment of personal meaning regarding one's experiences throughout life, especially tragic ones. What one has experienced in war can be a challenge to one's faith. Beliefs fundamental to the way people have always lived their lives are often upended by war. War can be the ultimate deconstruction of a belief system. But this does not have to be the end of meaning, belief, and/or faith. It does mean that certain brutal realities must be incorporated into any belief system that was previously in place. With the help of the hospital's chaplain, Amory wrestled with how to integrate his wartime past with his faith. Doing so was not easy, but it did prove to be worthwhile. While he never could totally forgive himself for what he had been a part of during the war, atonement could be a part of his life from this point forward, and in time he came to see that he still had a life to live.

Certainly, most combat vets have seen their share of senseless tragedy. In Nazi Germany's concentration camps, those who survived were often those who wrested small bits of meaning from the void. Though their captors tried to strip the prisoners' daily lives of meaning, some of the captives learned to create it out of almost nothing and to cling to it like a lifeline (Frankl 1962). Helping professionals have long known that people who have deeply held spiritual and philosophical belief systems weather tragedy much better than those without such anchors, and that is true of combat veterans as well (Scurfield 1994). The search for purpose and meaning is a lifelong endeavor.

More than likely Amory had long since thought his search for renewed faith and meaning was over. It usually takes many years of reflection on wartime experiences to shape them with meaning. Work with the chaplain helped him to see that the process wasn't over, but in some ways had just begun.

Vicarious Trauma

A large part of the social worker's job is geared toward helping the vet tell his or her story, no matter how horrible it may be. Inevitably, the story will have an impact on both the teller and the listener. And, if one listens and feels with the vet who is telling the story, it may be hard to avoid becoming secondarily traumatized. Pearlman and Saakvitne (1995), in their discussion of vicarious trauma, remind us that it is our very empathy with the clients that leaves us vulnerable to their trauma.

But how much is too much? If an ordinarily empathic social worker/ therapist finds himself or herself blocking and unable or unwilling to elicit the vet's story, it is a sign that the practitioner's own limits are being reached. This is nothing to be ashamed of; we all have our limits. Contingent upon our personal backgrounds, particular subject material may be more traumatizing to some therapists than to others. Or we may have an unusual amount of stress in our own lives at the time when we are being made privy to certain stories. If we sense that we are having trouble listening to a story, it probably means that we should ask for help from colleagues, usually a supervisor, peers, or consultants. More often than not, with the benefit of such assistance, we are able to make the adjustments needed to help us take better care of ourselves while seeing to it that the vets get the care they need.

Reflections on Empowerment Principles

Building on strengths while diminishing oppressions. Veterans, even those in extreme states of distress such as Amory was when he was first hospitalized, can regain a sense of their own legitimate core strengths. It sometimes takes working through the sense of distorted power that came with learning how to kill, and there may be a period of time when it is the social worker who is "holding" that belief in his or her strengths while the veteran has lost it. When the vet is ready, he or she will also be able to process the oppression that may have come with both betrayal on the battlefield and betrayal upon coming home.

Enacting multicultural respect. Even if client and social worker share many characteristics of the same culture (for example, being white or being male), an attitude of seeing the client's whole life as reflecting his/her culture denotes a respect for his or her uniqueness. In this case, religion and getting reinvolved with church and choir were a part of Amory's culture, and the support of his social worker to do so facilitated this crucial part of his spiritual life.

At the same time, it should be remembered that veterans of color have faced additional burdens from the enduring legacy of racism toward African Americans (Parson 1985) and Hispanics (Ruef, Litz, and Schlenger 2000) and may return with higher levels of combat stress. Ruef et al. review a study that found the prevalence of PTSD to be 27.9 percent among Hispanic vets and 20.6 percent among African American vets, compared to 13.7 percent among white vets.

Working from an awareness of specific needs. The work with Amory incorporated all three levels of needs—individual, interpersonal, and community—in that order. His needs for stabilization and psychological wholeness were prominent in the beginning phases, when he felt as though he was "falling apart." Seeing him begin to reintegrate a sense of self, the social worker could then discern and support Amory's own direction in reconnecting with others and with his church and community.

Assisting clients as they empower themselves. In war, power is ruthlessly and globally applied in the name of survival. In peacetime, power's intent changes from power over others to power from within, aimed at the freedom to choose and the ability to make things happen (Wise 2005). The latter goal for the use of power is life-enhancing. Most combat vets, given time and a supportive social network, are able to put their wartime experiences into perspective and exercise their power on behalf of themselves and others. But others, those who suffer from war trauma, often have trouble taming their use of power and directing it benignly toward the enhancement of their daily lives.

Once combat veterans are home with their families, they may realize how unfamiliar they've become with the day-to-day routines of running a household and raising a family. For most vets their unfamiliarity serves as the impetus to learn how to do things. For others, however, this state of affairs produces frustration and, sometimes, feelings of inadequacy. Such feelings may, in turn, trigger rage and the attempt to force results, as on the battlefield. Needless to say, this rage can have devastating effects on the family.

The social worker joining with such a family must make the case that what worked in war has no place at home. This is a difficult and sensitive task. Hopefully, it can be done under the aegis of an institution, such as the VA, a vets center, or military psychiatry. Many vets understand and usually still have respect for authority. The social worker must remember, however, that for some former soldiers, seeking help is itself tantamount to an admission that one is not handling current problems independently. Bearing this in mind, the social worker will be able to help the vet to work through this issue and forge a treatment alliance. Whereas a sense of power once came from the discharge of unfiltered aggression, it can now come from the exercise of restraint and cultivation of a sense that one can still "make things happen"—life-enhancing things rather than life-destroying things.

Integrating the support needed from others. As described in the responding sections above, depending on the vet's family status, work with vets will involve work with couples, work with a family of origin, connection with other veterans, and ultimately a reconnection with the noncombat community. Not all vets will use each level of support—for example, Amory was not comfortable in a veterans' group setting—but it should be made clear to vets that they have choices.

Equalizing power differentials and using cooperative roles. Throughout the treatment process it is imperative that the social worker avoid operating from a top-down, hierarchical stance. At the same time, social workers do have treatment authority, which they need to understand and learn to use in a collaborative manner. All clients, especially veterans, expect us to wear our authority well and to use it wisely on their behalf. If we have conflicts with regard to our own authority, our veteran clients may lose confidence in the treatment process.

All treatment has a beginning, a middle, and an end, and the social worker may take on different roles at each stage. But what do "beginnings," "middles," and "ends" look like with respect to the treatment of combat vets suffering from war trauma? First, combat vets are struggling to become familiar with life at home. For the social worker, the beginning of treatment is all about establishing a working relationship with the veterans and, frequently, their families. Simultaneously, part of that process entails identifying the issues that will be addressed throughout the course of treatment. Once both of these objectives have been achieved, the beginning phase comes to an end and the middle phase can begin.

The middle phase of treatment is often long and hard, filled with small gains and frequent disappointments. The social worker must be ready to provide realistically based encouragement to help the vet and his or her family overcome this or that obstacle. Over time, positive changes are made and the family reaches a new, more satisfactory level of adjustment. Once it becomes clear that the gains are solid and withstand the test of time and stress, it is likely that the middle phase is ending and the ending phase is beginning. Termination is in the air.

Termination is about the social worker and the client letting go of each other and saying good-bye. If the job has been done well, a unique relationship has been formed. It is interesting to note that years after successful treatment clients have few specific memories about what was said and done during the many months when they met with the social worker. What they do remember, however, is the relationship: "She was somebody we felt comfortable with." "He always kept his word." "She understood." Amid a mixture of sadness over the loss of a "good friend" and the pleasure at having acquired new skills, the relationship comes to an end. It is as it should be.

Conclusion and Recommendations

This chapter examined the effects of war on combat veterans. It suggested that PTSD, as codified in *DSM-III*, does not sufficiently describe the traumatic effects of war upon our soldiers. The psychological and emotional effects of war are not the result of a single life-threatening stressor, but rather result from many such stressors extending over weeks, months, and sometimes years. This is also true of childhood sexual abuse. Indeed, Judith Herman classifies any trauma that results from multiple life-threatening stressors extending over a protracted period of time as "complex PTSD."

War trauma is further differentiated from complex PTSD in general by one factor in particular: a soldier's sworn duty is to kill the enemy. The act of killing, especially for the first time, is traumatizing for most soldiers. The impact of this event upon the soldier is greatly magnified when the victims are not other combatants but innocent people, particularly women and children.

Throughout the chapter the interplay between war's perversion of power and the concept of empowerment is looked at in each of life's major realms of experience: personal, interpersonal, sociocultural, and spiritual and philosophical.

As this chapter is being written, the United States is involved in the "war on terror." Active combat is occurring in two different places at once, Afghanistan and Iraq. As in Vietnam, guerrilla warfare characterizes both of these war zones. There are no frontlines and the enemy is anywhere and everywhere. While precise numbers are hard to obtain, troop levels in Iraq are apparently kept somewhere between 130,000 and 150,000 at any one time. Approximately 18,000 more troops are said to be fighting in Afghanistan. Considering rotations and resupply, as many as 500,000 different troops may have served there.

Since the invasion of Iraq in 2003, more than 3,000 soldiers and marines have been killed in action. More than 20,000 others have been seriously wounded. The Pentagon estimates that more than 2,000 of those may involve brain injuries of varying levels of severity. Other wounds include amputations and various bodily injuries. Women soldiers in Iraq and Afghanistan are beginning to assume combat roles, whereas in Vietnam, 7,500 women served, but none in combat positions. Of that number 8 nurses were killed. In Iraq, 15 percent, or approximately 22,500, of the troops have been women; 48 women soldiers have been killed in action and 300 more wounded. A recent survey shows that at least 17 percent of Iraqi combat vets met the criteria for PTSD, major depression, or generalized anxiety, compared to 11 percent of Afghanistan vets (Hoge et al. 2006).

At this point in time, not many therapists have worked with veterans of the wars in Iraq and Afghanistan, at least not in large numbers or for any length of time. There is much to be learned about this group of vets; their stories are only beginning to be told. Only as men and women combat vets trickle back from these war-torn countries will we realize the full extent of their difficulties. Vietnam, our most recent benchmark, serves as an enduring example of how *not* to bring soldiers home. How much, if at all, our way of bringing home and honoring our vets from current wars has evolved since the Vietnam era remains to be seen.

References

Axelrod, S. R., C. A. Morgan, and S. M. Southwick. 2005. "Symptoms of Post-traumatic Stress Disorder and Borderline Personality Disorder in Veterans of Operation Desert Storm." *American Journal of Psychiatry* 162:270–276.

Barnes, C., and J. H. Harvey. 2000. "Comparison of Narratives of Loss Experiences of World War II and Vietnam Combat Veterans." In J. H. Harvey and B. G. Pauwels, eds., *Posttraumatic Stress Theory, Research, and Application*, 67–82. Philadelphia: Brunner/Mazel.

Bloom, S. L. 2000. "Our Hearts and Our Hopes Are Turned to Peace: Origins of the International Society for Traumatic Stress Studies." In A. Y. Shalev, R. Yehuda, and A. McFarlane, eds., *International Handbook of Human Response to Trauma*, 27–50. New York: Kluwer Academic.

Flora, C. 2002. "Trauma Services to War Veterans." In M. B. Williams and J. F. Sommer, eds., *Simple and Complex Post-traumatic Stress Disorder: Strategies for Comprehensive Treatment in Clinical Practice*, 325–350. Binghamton, N.Y.: Haworth.

Fontana, A., and R. Rosenheck. 2005. "The Role of Loss of Meaning in the Pursuit of Treatment for Posttraumatic Stress Disorder." *Journal of Traumatic Stress* 18:133–136.

Frankl, V. 1962. *Man's Search for Meaning*. Boston: Beacon.

Grossman, D. 1995. *On Killing: The Psychological Cost of Learning to Kill in War and Society*. New York: Little, Brown.

Hedges, C. 2002. *War Is a Force That Gives Us Meaning*. New York: Public Affairs, Perseus Group.

Herman, J. 1997. *Trauma and Recovery*. 2nd ed. New York: Basic Books.

Hoge, C. W., C. A. Castro, S. C. Messer, D. McGurk, D. I. Cotting, and R. L. Koffman. 2006. "Combat Duty in Iraq and Afghanistan, Mental Health Problems, and Barriers to Care." *New England Journal of Medicine* 351:13–22.

Koren, D., D. Norman, A. Cohen, J. Berman, and E. M. Klein. 2005. "The Increased PTSD Risk with Combat-Related Injury: A Matched Comparison Study of Injured and Uninjured Soldiers Experiencing the Same Combat Events." *American Journal of Psychiatry* 162:276–282.

Laufer, R. S. 1985. "War Trauma and Human Development: The Viet Nam Experience." In S. M. Sonnenberg, A. S. Blank, and J. A. Talbott, eds., *The Trauma of War: Stress and Recovery in Viet Nam Veterans*, 32–57. Washington, D.C.: American Psychiatric Press.

Parson, E. R. 1985. "The Intercultural Setting: Encountering Black Viet Nam Veterans." In S. M. Sonnenberg, A. S. Blank, and J. A. Talbott, eds., *The Trauma of War: Stress and Recovery in Viet Nam Veterans*, 360–387. Washington, D.C.: American Psychiatric Press.

Pearlman, L. A., and K. W. Saakvitne. 1995. *Trauma and the Therapist: Countertransference and Vicarious Traumatization in Psychotherapy with Incest Survivors*. New York: Norton.

Rosen, C. S., H. Chow, R. T. Murphy, K. D. Drescher, G. Ramirez, R. Ruddy, and F. Gusman. 2001. "Traumatic Stress Disorder Patients' Readiness to Change Alcohol and Anger Problems." *Psychotherapy* 38:233–244.

Ruef, A. M., B. T. Litz, and W. E. Schlenger. 2000. "Hispanic Ethnicity and Risk for Combat-Related Posttraumatic Stress Disorder." *Cultural Diversity and Ethnic Minority Psychology* 6:235–251.

Scurfield, R. M. 1994. "War-Related Trauma: An Integrative Experiential, Cognitive, and Spiritual Approach. In M. B. Williams and J. F. Sommer, eds., *Handbook of Post-traumatic Therapy*, 179–204. Westport, Conn.: Greenwood.

Shay, J. 1994. *Achilles in Vietnam: Combat Trauma and the Undoing of Character.* New York: Atheneum.

——. 2002. *Odysseus in America: Combat Trauma and the Trials of Homecoming.* New York: Scribner.

Sherman, M., D. K. Zanotti, and D. E. Jones. 2005. "Key Elements in Couples Therapy with Veterans with Combat-Related Posttraumatic Stress Disorder." *Professional Psychology: Research and Practice* 36:626–633.

Singer, M. 2004. "Shame, Guilt, Self-Hatred, and Remorse in the Psychotherapy of Vietnam Combat Veterans Who Committed Atrocities." *American Journal of Psychotherapy* 58:377–385.

Van Kirk, S. 2001. *Remarque's "All Quiet on the Western Front."* New York: Hungry Minds.

van Wormer, K. 1994. "Preparing for War Casualties: Therapy Considerations." *Journal of Teaching in Social Work* 10:149–164.

Wise, J. B. 2005. *Empowerment Practice with Families in Distress.* New York: Columbia University Press.

14

Triumph Over Tragedy
Transformation Through the
Aftermath of Disaster

JANE PARKER AND MICHAEL ZAKOUR

Angelina Batiste, a 39-year-old married mother of three children ages 13, 9, and 6, is just returning to New Orleans after six months of displacement in Texas and Georgia. Angelina and her husband, 37-year-old Harold, are of mixed racial descent, known in the culture as Creole. Her story is best told in a stream-of-consciousness style, drawn from courageous conversations of actual survivors of Hurricane Katrina, considered the worst natural disaster in U.S. history, which struck New Orleans and the Gulf Coast in late August 2005. The authors' own experiences of displacement, threat, and personal losses provide further insights into the potential for post- traumatic growth as individuals and as professionals in the wake of unspeakable tragedy.

Angelina's Story

Oh, God, what have I brought my children home to . . . just look at all this devastation, all the garbage, all the bad images . . . Mamma and Xydeco on the roof, the helicopters coming . . . the rush out of the city. We had to leave Xydeco, the dog, as the emergency rescue policy was people only, no pets. The children were frantic and crying. I was cool and oddly focused. The strain of being airlifted, herded onto buses and then into the Astrodome, later a Red Cross shelter in Baton Rouge, then a kind family member outside Atlanta . . . all of it was just too much for Mamma. She died of a heart attack at Fulton County Hospital in Atlanta within three months. Her child was devastated. But I knew I had to keep going for my children. I had to find Harold. He was being flown in from an offshore oil rig to someplace in Texas. I had to stay cool and focused, or surely we would all die. My energy is almost gone. I have talked with so many people, making application for so many services. We did get some FEMA money, and case management from Catholic Charities . . . but the lines, the waiting, the reports of looting, the grief . . . oh, the grief of so many hundreds in one room was suffocating. Stay cool, stay focused, stay alive, help me dear Jesus . . . over and over I say it. Was it aloud? Where is Harold? He should be here. Aunt Chantal got a call saying he was at a shelter in Atlanta, so I went there looking for him. Put a big sign up and walked through the cots looking for him. Turning a corner coming out of the bathroom, there he was. I lost my cool. Wailing, hugging, and then slapping him . . . bizarre . . . I had never struck him before. Now he is working construction and painting jobs, much quieter and drinking more than usual. We are in a FEMA trailer in New Orleans, near where our house once stood, trying to get the kids in school somewhere, anywhere. What will our lives be from now on? Oh God, help me to stand. Stay cool, stay focused, stay alive. I am cleaning and gutting houses with a crew, getting minimum wage. But it helps. The lady at Catholic Charities tries to counsel me when I go in for service, tells me my reactions are normal. I have not been normal for a long time now, never will be again. I will be better than normal—stronger, more refined, more humble, more realistic. People in the rest of the country have no idea what we have survived . . . the TV makes us look stupid and helpless. If the crying spells would just stop, I could do more. My priest showed up the other day, said the archdiocese was closing our parish church, just no population to support it. I am furious. My whole world, everything that anchored me to my city, got torn away. They will not take my church. It is too soon . . . give people a chance to come home. We in the neighborhood join together and get the decision reversed. Having done all to stand, just keep standing, the Bible says. Stay focused, stay cool, stay alive. Fight back, don't roll over for this . . . I am so tired, dazed, walking as if in a dream . . . but I am awake . . . I am on autopilot . . .

Understanding the Trauma of Natural Disasters

A natural disaster is both the impact of a physical hazard on a community and the societal disruption that occurs. Nonadaptive relationships with the physical environment (such as building on a floodplain or in a fire-prone area) result in widespread disaster, but the disruption may disproportionately affect the segments of the population that are the most vulnerable. Disasters tend to unmask the long-term distributive injustices in a society, such as poverty, by harming vulnerable populations in a very dramatic manner (Oliver-Smith 1999b).

GLOBAL DATA ON DISASTERS

Disasters are increasing in number with the passing of each decade. This increase is related to unprecedented human destruction of the biological and other physical environments. As the earth teeters on the brink of ecological collapse, the increase in natural disasters is a sentinel, warning of large-scale ecological damage and the increasing vulnerability of human society. The tsunami of 2004, killing more than 200,000 people; Hurricane Katrina in 2005, the most destructive natural disaster in U.S. history; and the 2006 Indonesian earthquake are examples of the way natural disasters are increasing at a rate greater than the rate of world population increase. By far the most deadly and destructive of natural disasters are coastal flooding and tropical storms. In Asia, and in U.S. states such as Louisiana, a majority of the population resides along the coast, and these numbers are rapidly increasing. Though coastal regions are rich in natural resources, they are also at risk for severe flooding and wind damage. Societies in which an ever-larger population resides in coastal areas face greater vulnerability to destruction.

Just as resources are inequitably distributed in many societies around the world, so is vulnerability much greater among impoverished populations. Worldwide, these populations disproportionately include children, the elderly, women, people of color, and ethnic minority groups. Because of their high rates of poverty, these populations are more likely to reside on marginal land, which is highly vulnerable to disasters. They lack the household resources, such as insurance and savings, to recover from disaster. They are also less likely to receive aid from disaster-service organizations and disaster-mitigation projects. Their recovery after a disaster is longer and more difficult, and they are more likely to develop severe psychosocial problems as a result of the disaster (Peacock, Morrow, and Gladwin 1997). Families need access to basic sustenance, health care, employment and income, and a safe and predictable environment to ensure the development and well-being of their members (Garbarino and Kostelny 1996). When those needs are not met, looting and physical fighting over scarce resources may surface.

Most individuals and systems are able to respond in an adaptive manner to disaster, and a great deal of aid during a disaster comes from the mass efforts of survivors who help each other before and immediately after the events. A large proportion of people recover psychosocially and economically after disaster as well. However, the percentage of the population suffering from psychiatric symptoms and post-traumatic stress disorder (PTSD) increases by about one-third. About 20 percent of the population will experience mental health problems related to the disaster, and about 2 percent of affected individuals will develop PTSD.

Understanding typical reactions (Myers and Wee 2005) and special issues of certain broadly indicated age groups is necessary for practitioners to be effective. Table 14.1 provides an overview of such reactions and issues for adults in disaster situations.

Children's psychosocial status after a disaster is largely dependent on the functioning of parents and other caretakers, though their prospects for recovery are better in the long term than those of very elderly individuals. This is the case particularly if both parents are present in the household. However, a caregiver's diminished capacity to adequately provide basic needs and security for children can compound the stresses of life in a disaster setting. Overwhelmed by the situation, parents may lapse into ineffective parenting and may be in a poor position to make good decisions for child well-being (Wessells and Monteiro 2004). The resulting impacts on children may include large amounts of time spent unsupervised, leaving them vulnerable to exploitation and abuse and devoid of attention and nurturance from adults.

While adaptations that parents make are often well intended, the side effects can be detrimental (Garbarino, Kostelny, and Dubrow 1991). Parents dealing with their own anger and irritability may develop impatience and a "hair trigger" temper with children or others. Anger may be displaced and directed at family members, resulting in increased levels of domestic violence and child abuse (Elliot 2002). In attempting to adapt to a dangerous post-disaster environment, parents may develop extremely protective patterns of parenting, restricting the child from going outdoors and/or using harsh discipline to protect children from negative forces; such changes in parental behavior may be diametrically opposed to what the children need to resolve their own trauma experience. Children organize the world and make sense of new information through play, which allows them to

Table 14.1.

Adult Reactions to Disaster

General reactions across groups	Heightened anxiety, anger, aggression; shock, grief, mood swings; sadness, depression, loss of sense of control; hyperactivity and restlessness; domestic violence; detachment, isolation, derealization; fatigue, trouble sleeping, gastrointestinal problems, aches and pains; substance abuse, change in eating patterns, change in libido, menstrual irregularities; impaired concentration, memory, problem-solving, time distortion; despair, concern about the future, hopelessness, changes in religious beliefs (strengthening or weakening).
Younger adults	May have greater physical stamina and social networks. May be earning less than older groups, have fewer liquid assets. May be caring for young children during a disaster. May exhibit change in parenting patterns, detaching or overprotecting. May not yet have a deep repertoire of prior mastery over acute traumas.
Middle adults	May be caring for both children and parents or older relatives. May have more economic resources than younger groups. May suffer more material losses and adverse effects. May engage in deeper philosophical questioning, be angry, challenge the worth of their pre-disaster lifestyle.

(Table 14.1 continues next page)

(Table 14.1 *continued)*

Older adults, 60-80 years	May have chronic or acute health issues. May experience acute disappointment over loss of family home, plans for retirement or a life with less stress. May have more difficulty in evacuating or relocating from a disaster area. May have experienced social network losses in close proximity to the disaster. May be able to call upon prior recovery from losses or trauma.
Very elderly adults, 80+ years	In addition to factors for Older Adults, May be more dependent upon others for housing, care, recovery decisions affecting their lives. May be at risk for medical complications or inadequate use of medicines for ongoing conditions. May be more affected by disruption of traditional mail services in terms of being able to receive checks, pay bills, or other transactions. May be at risk for institutionalization in the wake of the disaster.

experience a sense of mastery over imaginary or real frustrations. In "post-traumatic play" children may reenact aspects of their traumatic experience or repeatedly play games based on traumatic events (Elliot 2002; Herman 1997). The enjoyment that typically characterizes ordinary play may be absent, and anxiety and discomfort may surface instead.

Regressive behavior is common among children who are overwhelmed by a crisis. There may be a loss or slowdown in language acquisition, increase in or development of bedwetting, and fears of being left alone. Children may lose the capacity to control aggression and to comfort themselves. Table 14.2 illustrates the potential impact of traumatic events on children by developmental stage (Elliot 2002).

Table 14.2.

Children's Reactions to Disaster

0 to 2.5 years	Crying, clinging, hard to console; separation fears; heightened startle response; disrupted sleep; sudden rigidity; regressive behavior.
2.5 to 6 years	Separation anxiety, focus on pain and needs, feeling overwhelmed; wondering who will take care of them; increased narcissism; decreased empathy; fear of the dark; sleep disturbances, night terrors and sleepwalking; noticeable anxiety and withdrawal; withdrawal from activities previously enjoyed; avoidance of situations/people that remind them of the trauma; repeated questions; magical thinking and self-blame.
6 to 11 years	Fear, anxiety, concern that the critical event may reoccur; behavioral or mood changes; focus on details surrounding the traumatic event; less energy for other activities; loss of enjoyment of previously pleasurable activities; difficulty concentrating; intrusive images; multiple questions; repetition of the traumatic story; rapid fluctuation of emotions; feelings surge at certain stimuli; feeling responsible; having a sense of failure at not stopping the event.
11 to adolescence	More adult reactions mixed with those of a child; may feel need to take on adult responsibilities; may be accurate with this redistribution of roles in some cases; value privacy and independence but may not want to be alone; may spend a lot of time with family near the home; previous sense of invulnerability may be damaged or heightened; may engage in risky behaviors.

In addition to developmental stages, the pre-disaster psychosocial health of the family and child, the duration of displacement or separation, the nature of parental reactions, and the lack of information or protective resources are all factors that can exacerbate the impact of traumatic events on children (Elliot 2002).

Cultural, economic, gender, and spiritual influences must be considered in understanding responses to trauma. Neighborhoods and communities can help survivors, and may recover well after a disaster, depending on the conditions before the disaster occurs. Because disasters are partly caused by longer-term developmental conditions in communities, some local areas are much more vulnerable and will recover more slowly, if at all. Communities with strong local leadership, with access to numerous social service organizations and disaster-service organizations, with a future-oriented culture, and with some level of household wealth and social capital are much more likely to survive and thrive after a disaster. Those neighborhoods with many vulnerable, low-income individuals, which are economically distressed, have few social service organizations, and a low level of social capital may not recover from disaster. These communities are more likely to experience an increased rate of decline, which was already ongoing before the disaster (Peacock et al. 1997).

Responding to Disaster from a Clinical-Community Perspective

MEZZO-LEVEL INTERVENTIONS: MITIGATION, RESPONSE, AND SOCIAL DEVELOPMENT

Numerous prevention and intervention methods in disasters take place at one level and have a positive effect at another. For example, many interventions at the community level, such as neighborhood development, are very helpful for individuals who are trying to restore themselves to pre-disaster functioning. Community interventions that have a positive effect on individual outcomes are usually thought of as preventive. Conversely, rebuilding personal support networks and providing opportunities for survivors to engage in meaningful volunteer work is immediately helpful for individual outcomes, but is also helpful in rebuilding the social infrastructure and social capital of communities. Ideally, these interventions will provide social development resources that will make individuals, populations, organizations, and communities less vulnerable to future disasters. Disaster interventions also have the potential to redress issues of social and distributive injustice that existed before the disaster and that may have created the roots of the disaster (Zakour and Harrell 2003).

If neighborhood development interventions are successful, not only can successful locality development occur, but the psychosocial well-being of residents will improve and the likelihood of severe mental health problems will decrease. Reconstruction of the home is an important predictor of mental health status one year after a disaster occurs. Also, because neighborhoods can foster social support networks for individuals, restoration of the neighborhood can provide needed social support for survivors, particularly those who have lost a loved one. Personal social networks are likely to extend from the neighborhood to the workplace, voluntary associations, and the entire community and region. Since disasters are increasingly regional in scope, they often disrupt the entire social support network of family, relatives, friends, and associates. Helping an entire community to recover will facilitate the rebuilding of these support networks, which are critical for individuals' recovery. Programs that engage disaster survivors as trained disaster volunteers can be useful in rebuilding both the social infrastructure of the community and the social capital and self-esteem of the volunteers themselves (Zakour 2000).

Because many social welfare services are available through the workplace, economic redevelopment of the affected community provides meaningful work, monetary resources, and an array of services for people who have lost their jobs after a disaster. The workplace may be damaged or unemployed individuals may be unable to return to their homes and jobs because of severe physical damage inflicted by the disaster. Additionally, customers of the damaged worksite may have evacuated or relocated out of the immediate area. Economic and social development interventions and jobs programs can help provide households with the resources they need for recovery. If the social service, governmental, and business organizations in the region are highly coordinated, their effectiveness in providing services to people and assisting in social redevelopment will be increased. A well-coordinated network of disaster-relevant and community-based organizations will hasten recovery for the community and will improve the restoration of mental health for individuals. These interorganizational networks represent parts of the community structure, so that improving their coordination is a type of community organization that treats the entire community as the client (Zakour and Harrell 2003).

A critical factor in the recovery of survivors who have lost loved ones is a renewed search for meaning, and a reconsideration of assumptions held before the disaster that are now in shambles. Disasters, particularly if they are associated with loss of life in the families of survivors, present these survivors with a dramatic event that seems to refute meaning and order in the world. There is no sense of fairness or justice in the suffering and death of loved ones during the disaster. Survivors are likely to feel a complete lack of control concerning the death of the loved one. Suddenly assumptions about the safety of the world and the belief that death happens only to very old people when "it is their time," and not to others, are completely shattered. Survivors will not be restored to their previous level of biopsychosocial functioning until they are able to reestablish a new understanding of the world, a new set of realistic assumptions, and a new worldview to fit the reality that they are now facing (Solomon, Greenberg, and Pyszczynski 2004).

For these survivors in particular, a sense of self-esteem and of belonging to a larger social entity, such as a religion, nation, or community of interest, can help provide new meaning and a more realistic worldview. Through cultural consensus about valuable social roles and their successful enactment, survivors can regain a strong sense of self-esteem by successfully filling these roles (Mikilincer, Florian, and Hirschberger 2004). These new roles, which often include providing help to others who have suffered in disasters, can bring heightened self-esteem because they replace roles lost after the death of a loved one. Cultural consensus comes about through membership in a cultural group transcending the individual and can help provide the survivor with a new and realistic worldview (Batson and Stocks 2004). As important as a social network is in the provision of social support, a personal community is also a source of self-esteem and meaning.

Improved self-esteem and greater belongingness are inextricably tied to membership in a cultural group with its own system of meaning and worldview. For survivors, this entire process creates a strong sense of community in which status differentials are reduced after a disaster (Oliver-Smith 1999a). This temporary situation of greatly increased altruism and reduced social hierarchy often involves a meaning and symbol system in which social interaction is like a brotherhood or sisterhood. Such a close community provides a foundation for real social change, which empowers low-income or formerly low-status survivors to create greater distributive justice long after disaster recovery. During this period of enhanced community, community organization can more easily occur, so that power differentials among strata of a community are leveled out. Long-term access to resources, including social services, can be improved for all members of the community.

Reconnecting to the community was extremely important to Angelina. Her references to family, to church, and to neighborhood gave the social worker an insight into the long-standing social supports in her life. Almost as soon as her own family's situation in a FEMA trailer was secure, Angelina asked her social worker about any neighborhood work groups she knew of. Her work of repairing damaged homes reflected both an economic decision and an altruistic one. Such "otherness" and altruism have been shown not only to help victims of trauma to recover but also to actually develop new aspects to character.

MICRO-LEVEL INTERVENTIONS

With individuals, families, and small groups who have been affected by disaster, the social worker engages in crisis intervention to provide immediate emotional and environmental first aid, as well as brief therapy and case management when follow-up after the initial stabilization efforts is possible (Roberts 2005). The social worker began to assure the safety of the Batiste family by working with them to set up FEMA housing and income. She also started to identify schools that were open for the children. During the process she was assessing the functioning of the family and children. Fortunately, the parents of the Batiste children were eventually reunited, and while the children had some anxieties resulting from temporary dislocations, they felt more reassured each day that went by in their new, more permanent location. The worker also assessed the family for any detachment or undue protectiveness of the children by the Batiste parents, knowing that radical shifts in parenting styles are normal in the wake of trauma. In this case, Angelina was very reluctant at first to let the children out of her sight, but once she met the families in the immediate area of their trailer and realized there was a group of children that her children could play with, she felt better about letting them socialize—though always with one parent within sight and hearing distance. The social worker also heard Angelina's reference to Mr. Batiste's drinking more than usual. This is fairly common after a disaster (and is one of the reactions listed in table 14.1), but she made a note to reassess in a few weeks to see if it changed or seemed to become a new pattern.

Finally, the social worker knew that the Batistes—like many post-Katrina families—were still focused on survival tasks. She encouraged an atmosphere of safety in sessions to allow for mourning, expression of anger, and beginning to make meaning (Herman 1997) from the tragedies of the storm and the loss of Mrs. Batiste's mother.

Within brief crisis interventions, a solution-focused approach can help to (a) shift the traumatized person from an affective to a cognitive state, (b) evoke memories of past successes and strengths, and (c) promote hope for and eventually a sense of mastery over what seems unbelievable and unmanageable (DeJong and Berg 2002). Clients may feel empowered in the therapeutic process—be it a few minutes or a few sessions—in that the approach is accepting of intense emotional content and focuses inductively on working collaboratively. Negative emotions during a disaster aftermath and recovery period are viewed as situationally appropriate rather than as symptoms to be eradicated. Normalizing statements such as "You are having a normal reaction to an abnormal event" can alleviate undue self-blame and questioning of one's own psychological strength.

Interventions should be highly specific and goal-oriented, adhering to the criteria of such mechanisms as SMART—specific, measurable, attainable, relevant, and time-bound. Progress is then evaluated with the client, typically through scaling questions and reports of actual behaviors. During a disaster period, goals should be focused on present safety and stabilization, then move to future possibilities. Creative questioning (DeJong and Berg 2002) such as using the miracle question, eliciting exceptions, amplifying "what has worked," and asking the clients their ideas about the meaning of the recent tragedies flow together for a faster, relevant, and powerful course of action. Placing clients in the acknowledged position of being experts in their own lives with a history of successes and a vision for future possibilities may turn the client's self-identity from victim to victor.

Angelina Batiste had the ability to "fight back" with how she thought, spoke, and collaborated within her own neighborhood. For the practitioner to simply observe and remark upon those abilities with Mrs. Batiste was empowering and could even increase her effectiveness in daily responsibilities. Mrs. Batiste was a person of color who happened to live in a flood zone. Her strengths in personality and culture were, in part, what helped her respond to her geographic and economic challenges with perseverance and resilience. She was someone who talked to herself in order to keep going, so her social worker knew she would be a good fit for solution-focused therapy's cognitive approach. According to Ellis (1996), the ability to challenge irrational statements of panic and despair is a cornerstone of positive mental health. Further, Mrs. Batiste's frequent focus on how her reactions were being observed by her children, along with her protectiveness of them and the desire to return them to school as soon as possible, were indicators of her ability to focus on human beings besides herself. As part of educating Angelina about typical reactions among children, the social worker provided information about allowing their children to use play to process what had happened during and in the wake of Katrina. Should their children seem stuck in an unchanging or traumatic pattern of play, Mr. and Mrs. Batiste or other adults would need to process the traumatic events within the play in a manner that demonstrated the child's mastery over the events (Elliot 2002).

The use of solution-focused approaches after a crisis does not imply solving or even defining a problem; it works in the present to identify and amplify clients' strengths and resources (Greene et al. 2005). It takes the clients' worldview as a starting point, and uses respect and a cooperative approach to focus on what steps the client is ready to take to overcome the crisis. Another theoretical fit between crisis intervention and solution-focused therapy is its time-limited nature and the assumption that after a period of disequilibrium, the client will be able to make changes to restore prior functioning or move through crisis to a new sense of meaning.

In dealing with multiple bureaucracies, clients tend to talk about what they would like others to do differently; however, in solution-building, the focus is continually returned to the client, on what will be different about the client when his or her goals are achieved. Goals may relate to methods of individual or group advocacy efforts directed toward said bureaucracies, another method of inviting clients to move from a passive to an assertive stance in the face of trauma. While the practitioner must be careful not to minimize the horrors of disaster and most certainly should allow healthy ventilation within an empathetic atmosphere, to constantly reiterate and dissect problems and weaknesses is disempowering and potentially paralyzing.

Vicarious Trauma in Responding to Disaster

One of the most common threats to the longevity, personal health, employment retention, and effectiveness of the professional helper is that of secondary traumatic stress syndrome (Hoffman 2000; Houtman 1999; Lewis 1994).

Secondary traumatic stress syndrome (STSS) is most commonly understood as the sequelae of physical, cognitive, behavioral, and emotional symptoms experienced by professionals and paraprofessionals who respond to first-line victims of a critical incident or trauma. STSS may also be experienced by clinicians who, in their daily routines and operations, provide psychotherapeutic or case management interventions to acutely traumatized populations (Pearlman and Saakvitne 1995a; Rudolph and Stamm 1999). Such traumatic stress usually manifests itself through the following symptoms: anxiety, fatigue, depression, emotional detachment; increased substance abuse, intrusive thoughts or upsetting dreams, avoidance, hyperarousal and heightened vigilance; diminished affect or interest in activities; irritability; pessimism and a foreboding sense of a shortened life span (Figley 1995:7–8). It may be experienced as a cumulative process from chronic exposure to the trauma of others over time; however, the general public usually thinks of stress reactions as being associated with one overt, identifiable critical incident (Everly and Mitchell 1998). Even the lay helper or the naturally evolved community sage who is always there to help with matters of ordinary life in impoverished and crime-ridden communities can experience secondary traumatic stress syndrome. While the experience of stress as well as recovery from traumatic stress is largely culturally driven, certain events—such as devastating disasters or the sudden death of a family member, close friend, or coworker—seem to be universally defined as a critical incident across cultures (Hobfoll 1998; James and Gilliland 2001; Parad and Parad 1990).

Key helping groups like police officers, health workers, counselors, and certain military personnel are frequently exposed to violence, drug or alcohol intoxication, accidents, illnesses, deaths, and psychosocial disturbances in their daily encounters with those they seek to serve. Such routine strain only compounds the impact on the responder to a major disaster such as Hurricane Katrina. Responders may be survivors of the same disaster as their clients, thus experiencing a double exposure to the stresses of the event. Additionally, these responders may experience personal physical attack or media derision that erodes morale.

Reflections on Principles of Empowerment

In considering the global, local community, and individual impact of natural disasters, Barton's (1969) concept of the "therapeutic community" seems to best capture the authors' commitment to the strengths perspective in holistic clinical-community social work practice. Each of the interventions discussed is strongly influenced by the strengths perspective in social work, which directs social workers toward building on the strengths of clients (Saleebey 1992). Much of disaster response and recovery comes not from professionals but from the strengths of the community itself. Barton (1969) documented the existence of the therapeutic community, in which the community acted as a system providing much support and aid after a disaster. Padgett (2002) described the need for better understanding the strengths of communities and the need for a stronger focus on community interventions for the survivors of disasters and complex emergencies such as 9/11. At the family level, the social worker focused on the Batistes' strengths, and used support, praise, and encouragement as Angelina renegotiated her connections to her community.

SOCIAL CAPITAL, RECIPROCITY, AND DISTRIBUTIVE JUSTICE

Social capital refers to the resources embedded in social networks. Social capital promotes distributive justice through the reciprocity of exchanges. The strengths perspective emphasizes rebuilding and supporting personal, interorganizational, and community social networks. By building on the resources that are already embedded in social networks, the social capital of individuals and households can be better mobilized to help people and communities recover. Substantial relief for disaster survivors can come from their social networks of family, friends, and others.

If these networks can be reconstructed and reconstituted by the efforts of professionals and volunteers, then the prognosis for individuals and neighborhoods improves. The effectiveness of response coordination is increased by the high levels of trust that social capital promotes. Coordinated networks of organizations working in disaster can reduce the physical damage and societal disruption from disaster and begin the relief process in a timely fashion. Timely delivery of relevant mental health services after a disaster is important in preventing PTSD. Because disasters affect systems and networks at all levels, rebuilding and strengthening social networks and social capital are needed for community recovery. Mutual aid approaches to rebuilding these networks and social structures, such as those encouraged by Catholic Charities, are much more acceptable to survivors than services delivered using a medical or deficiency model. The pattern of helping is seen as an act of reciprocal social exchange, rather than as a situation in which resources flow in only one hierarchical direction. Reciprocity and equality in resource exchanges are critical aspects of networks and make social capital accessible to people.

CULTURAL TRANSFORMATION OF WORLDVIEWS AND MEANING

Culturally defined personal and other social networks play an important role not only in recovery but also in providing new meaning in a world that many survivors may not recognize. As previously stated, those survivors who have lost loved ones, homes, and neighborhoods must reconstruct their worldviews to accommodate the new realities that they face. When human beings are unable or unwilling to reconstruct their worldviews, recovery and successful grieving may be severely impaired or delayed. Personal and geographic communities, as well as communities of interest, often are the source for creating new meaning.

Angelina's participation in a neighborhood advocacy group working to reopen their church, her work with a cleanup crew, and her involvement in her children's schools all became avenues for conversation and exchange of ideas on the meaning of corporate and individual losses. Through a process of cultural consensus on the meaning of loss and of the "new normal," individuals are able to rebuild their worldviews and their lives, and to understand loss through a less painful lens. This process of meaning-making can transform the terrible knowledge of loss into terrific wisdom for living, helping the individual and community to triumph over trauma. It can aid helping professionals as well, encouraging them to redouble their efforts on behalf of vulnerable individuals. In this way professionals can draw on all of their strengths to cope with their own losses and yet come through the trauma with even greater strength than before.

EMPOWERMENT OF THE PRACTITIONER AND OTHER RESPONDERS IN DISASTERS

Given the problem of secondary or vicarious traumatic stress, the concerned practitioner logically begins to seek both palliative and preventive measures to assist primary responders. Some possible solutions for responders to disaster are offered below on both the mezzo and micro levels. Much can be done at the workplace level, to ensure safety and communicate the agency's concern and respect for its workers. Even the physical layout of the workplace can communicate a positive message, both to workers and to clients coming for help (Gutheil 1992). Another way to demonstrate concern is attention to the trustworthiness of organizations, which includes clear, consistent policies and practices; ongoing training; financial stewardship; demonstrated support for members; engagement of members in a larger mission; and a moral climate based on shared values (Catherall 1995; Munroe et al. 1995; Pearlman and Saakvitne 1995b; Rudolph and Stamm 1999). Perceptions of trustworthiness in organizations that are involved in responding to emergencies, mass disaster, or chronic serious human difficulties may be a bridge between micro and macro variables in future disaster response.

Zunz (1997, 2001) challenges us to examine our own attention to resiliency for ourselves through curriculum, training, and personal/professional practices. Certain solution-focused activities can empower and strengthen the individual responder not only to survive the work but also to become the "best of class" in that work. While factors of physical hardiness, constitutional temperament, positive social support systems, workplace policies and environment, and preparedness training may be variable, there are certain activities in which the primary or significant responder can participate in a fixed, predictable manner:

1. Establishing and following a written "Resiliency Plan" (Parker 2006)
2. Developing a philosophy of death and suffering in the world
3. Maintaining basically good health habits of sleep, exercise, recreation, nutrition, and routine health maintenance appointments
4. Avoiding unhealthy escape traps like drugs, alcohol, violent media, or toxic conversations
5. Building a social network outside of work
6. Engaging in humor and play, daily if possible
7. Engaging in regular personal meditation, spiritual practice, or corporate worship that is instructive and inspiring
8. Recording and revisiting personal and professional successes regularly
9. Advocating for workplace improvements and technical training to promote performance in response work
10. Encouraging others with your own "lessons learned" in the field as to how to maintain resiliency

Conclusion and Recommendations

As illustrated through the story of the Batiste family and Hurricane Katrina, natural disasters have potentially damaging effects at all levels of the family, the neighborhood, and the community. Because of the wide-ranging effects of natural disasters, interventions need to focus on these multiple levels of disaster impact, ideally in a coordinated case management fashion. Individuals, families, and communities can be vulnerable to disaster, and to counteract this socially produced vulnerability, empowerment approaches are necessary. Unless disaster services practitioners are themselves empowered and consistently resilient, it will be very difficult for them to assist clients in becoming more empowered. The transformation from vulnerability to empowerment is a challenge and an opportunity in natural disasters. Moving from basic survival to achieving empowerment and finally to sharing lessons learned represents the human triumph over the trauma caused by disaster.

References

American Psychiatric Association (APA). 2000. *Diagnostic and Statistical Manual of Mental Disorders, Text Revision* (*DSM-IV-TR*). 4th ed. Washington, D.C.: Author.

Barton, A. H. 1969. *Communities in Disaster*. New York: Anchor Books.

Batson, C. D., and E. L. Stocks. 2004. "Religion: Its Core Psychological Functions." In J. Greenberg, S. L. Koole, and T. Pyszczynski, eds., *Handbook of Experimental Existential Psychology*, 141–155. New York: Guilford.

Catherall, D. 1995. "Preventing Institutional Secondary Traumatic Stress Disorder." In C. Figley, ed., *Compassion Fatigue: Coping with Secondary Traumatic Stress Disorder in Those Who Treat the Traumatized*, 232–247. New York: Brunner/Mazel.

DeJong, P., and I. K. Berg. 2002. *Interviewing for Solutions*. 2nd ed. Pacific Grove, Calif.: Brooks/Cole.

Elliot, T. L. 2002. "Children and Trauma: An Overview of Reactions, Mediating Factors, and Practical Interventions That Can Be Implemented." In .E. Stout and K. Schwab, eds., *The Psychology of Terrorism*, 2:49–73. Westport, Conn.: Praeger.

Ellis, A. 1996. *Better, Deeper, More Enduring Brief Therapy: The Rational Emotive Behavior Therapy Approach*. New York: Brunner/Mazel.

Everly, G. S., and J. T. Mitchell. 1998. *Critical Incident Stress Management: Assisting Individuals in Crisis. A Workbook*. Ellicott City, Md.: International Critical Incident Stress Foundation.

Figley, C. R. 1995. "Compassion Fatigue as Secondary Traumatic Stress Disorder: An Overview." In C. R. Figley, ed., *Compassion Fatigue: Coping with Secondary*

Traumatic Stress Disorder in Those Who Treat the Traumatized, 1–20. New York: Brunner/Mazel.

Garbarino, J., and K. Kostelny. 1996. "What Do We Need to Know to Understand Children in War and Community Violence?" In R. J. Apfel and B. Simon, eds., *Minefields in Their Hearts: The Mental Health of Children in War and Communal Violence*, 33–51. New Haven, Conn.: Yale University Press.

Garbarino, J., K. Kostelny, and N. Dubrow. 1991. "What Children Can Tell Us About Living in Danger." *American Psychologist* 46 (4): 376–383.

Greene, G., M. Lee, R. Trask, and J. Rheinscheld. 2005. "How to Work with Clients' Strengths in Crisis Intervention: A Solution-Focused Approach." *Crisis Intervention Handbook: Assessment, Treatment, and Research*, 64–89. 3rd ed. New York: Oxford University Press.

Herman, J. 1997. *Trauma and Recovery*. 2nd ed. New York: Basic Books.

Hobfoll, S. E. 1998. *Stress, Culture, and Community: The Psychology and Philosophy of Stress*. New York: Plenum.

Hoffman, C. 2000. "Responding to Workplace Trauma." Retrieved March 16, 2007, from the American Academy of Experts in Traumatic Stress Web site: http://www.aaets.org/article106.htm.

Houtman, I. 1999. "The Changing Workplace." *Work, Stress, and Health \ '99: Organization of Work in a Global Economy*. Proceedings of a joint conference of the American Psychological Association and the Centers for Disease Control's National Institute of Occupational Safety and Health. Washington, D.C.: Centers for Disease Control.

James, R. K., and B. E. Gilliland. 2001. *Crisis Intervention Strategies*. 4th ed. Pacific Grove, Calif.: Brooks/Cole.

Lewis, G. W. 1994. *Critical Incident Stress and Trauma in the Workplace: Recognition . . . Response . . . Recovery*. Levittown, Pa.: Accelerated Development.

Mikilincer, M., V. Florian, and G. Hirschberger. 2004. "The Terror of Death and the Quest for Love: An Existential Perspective on Close Relationships." In J. Greenberg, S. L. Koole, and T. Pyszczynski, eds., *Handbook of Experimental Existential Psychology*, 287–384. New York: Guilford.

Munroe, J., J. Shay, L. Fisher, C. Makary, K. Rapperport, and R. Zimering. 1995. "Preventing Compassion Fatigue: A Team Treatment Model." In C. R. Figley, ed., *Compassion Fatigue: Coping with Secondary Traumatic Stress Disorder in Those Who Treat the Traumatized*, 209–231. New York: Brunner/Mazel.

Myers, D., and D. Wee. 2005. *Disaster Mental Health Services*. New York: Brunner-Routledge.

Oliver-Smith, A. 1999a. "The Brotherhood of Pain: Theoretical and Applied Perspectives on Post-Disaster Recovery." In A. Oliver-Smith and S. M. Hoffman, eds., *The Angry Earth: Disaster in Anthropological Perspective*, 156–172. New York: Routledge.

———. 1999b. "What Is a Disaster? Anthropological Perspectives on a Persistent Question." In A. Oliver-Smith and S.M. Hoffman, eds., *The Angry Earth: Disaster in Anthropological Perspective*, 18–34. New York: Routledge.

Padgett, D. 2002. "Social Work Research on Disasters in the Aftermath of the September 11 Tragedy: Reflections from New York City." *Social Work Research* 26 (3): 185–192.

Parad, H., and L. Parad. 1990. "Crisis Intervention: An Introductory Overview." In H. Parad and L. Parad, eds., *Crisis Intervention Book 2: The Practitioner's Sourcebook for Brief Therapy*, 3–66. Milwaukee: Family Service Association of America.

Parker, J. 2006. *Staying Well in Hell: Ten Commandments for Responders*. New Orleans: Tulane University School of Social Work.

Peacock, W. G., B. H. Morrow, and H. Gladwin, eds. 1997. *Hurricane Andrew: Ethnicity, Gender, and the Sociology of Disasters*. New York: Routledge.

Pearlman, L., and K. Saakvitne. 1995a. *Trauma and the Therapist: Countertransference and Vicarious Traumatization in Psychotherapy with Incest Survivors*. New York: Norton.

———. 1995b. "Treating Therapists with Vicarious Traumatization and Secondary Traumatic Stress Disorders." In C. R. Figley, ed., *Compassion Fatigue: Coping with Secondary Traumatic Stress Disorder in Those Who Treat the Traumatized*, 150–177. Levittown, Pa.: Brunner/Mazel.

Roberts, A. 2005. *Crisis Intervention Handbook*. New York: Oxford University Press.

Rudolph, J., and H. Stamm. (1999). "Maximizing Human Capital: Moderating Secondary Traumatic Stress Through Administrative and Policy Action." In H. Stamm, ed., *Secondary Traumatic Stress*, 277–290. Lutherville, Md.: Sidran.

Saleebey, D., ed. 1992. *The Strengths Perspective in Social Work Practice*. New York: Longman.

Solomon, S., J. Greenberg, and T. Pyszczynski. 2004. "The Cultural Animal: Twenty Years of Terror Management Theory and Research." In J. Greenberg, S. L. Koole, and T. Pyszczynski, eds., *Handbook of Experimental Existential Psychology*, 13–34. New York: Guilford.

Wessells, M. G., and C. Monteiro. 2004. "Healing the Wounds Following Protracted Conflict in Angola: A Community-Based Approach to Assisting War-Affected Children." In U. P. Gielen, J. M. Fish, and J. G. Draguns, eds., *Handbook of Culture, Therapy, and Healing*, 321–342. Mahwah, N.J.: Erlbaum.

Wise, J. B. 2005. *Empowerment Practice with Families in Distress*. New York: Columbia University Press.

Zakour, M., ed. 2000. "Disaster and Traumatic Stress Research and Intervention." *Tulane Studies in Social Welfare* 21–22. New Orleans: Tulane University.

Zakour, M., and E. Harrell. 2003. "Access to Disaster Services: Social Work Interventions for Vulnerable Populations." *Journal of Social Service Research* 30 (2): 27–54.

Zimmerman, T. S., R. B. Jacobsen, M. Macintyre, and C. Watson. 1996. "Solution-Focused Parenting Groups: An Empirical Study." *Journal of Systemic Therapies* 15 (4): 12–25.

Zunz, S. 1997. "Resiliency in Human Service Professionals: Do We Practice What We Preach?" *Resiliency in Action* 2 (3): 13–16.

——. 2001. "Building More Resilient Professionals: The Role of Social Work Education." *Arete* 28 (2): 35–45.

Conclusion

Transforming Trauma Through Empowerment and Resilience

MARIAN BUSSEY

Human service professionals face trauma in clients' lives on a daily basis—whether it's the early trauma of an abused child or the sudden and mass trauma of a national terrorist attack. There are physiological changes in a child's brain as a result of trauma, changes that affect adult life. War, terrorist attacks, and violent assaults have lasting effects long after the event itself has ended. We are expanding our understanding of the effects in adulthood of early trauma and, further, the additive effects of adult trauma or disaster layered upon earlier trauma.

Our clients can and do work through these traumas to transform their lives. Our social work interventions, as shown in the chapters of this book, can help to empower clients and build upon their own natural resilience. To do that empowering work, we need to understand the depths of what our clients have endured and to apply a trauma response framework to help them through those depths.

Practitioners and researchers have found a strong connection between the experience of childhood abuse and later risks for physical illnesses, relationship violence, and mental health issues such as depression, anxiety/panic disorder, and substance abuse (Everett and Gallop 2001). There is a gender connection as well; a high percentage of women seen in various systems, such as child protective services, TANF, mental health, substance abuse treatment, and shelters, have experienced trauma, and a number of them live with symptoms that interfere with daily functioning. Not all abused children will have these problems as adults, but their risk is higher.

Some clients live with a chronic state of chaos and crisis. They may feel helpless to change it. Their earlier experiences may have conditioned them to feel comfortable with the chaos. Just as some traumatized children expect, and therefore provoke, angry responses, adults may re-create a similar dynamic (engaging in self-destructive choices or substance abuse). Our job, as helpers, is to recognize that these are life adaptations to earlier traumas (Saakvitne et al. 2000). Knowing that many live with unresolved trauma is a first step toward accepting their choices and adaptations, and increasing the chances that they will engage in the services they need to strengthen their lives.

Many adult clients seek help for their current life issues while still dealing with aftereffects of earlier trauma, including childhood abuse, prior assaults/violence, or historical trauma. This does not mean we always focus on the underlying trauma. That therapeutic choice depends on both the agency context and the individual needs of each client.

Agency context is important because many human service agencies, such as those that provide shelter, job training, or income security, do not have a mandate to treat trauma (i.e., to provide trauma-*focused* services). However, they can create a climate of acceptance for clients by providing trauma-*informed* services. Trauma-informed services, according to Harris and Fallot (2001), involve: recognition of the role trauma plays in clients' lives, assessment of both client and agency dynamics to minimize treatment-sabotaging power struggles, and creation of an atmosphere that supports safety, coping skills, and reconnection to community. Workers in a trauma-informed agency understand the signs of a trauma response or PTSD and can refer clients when needed, assuming that there are low-cost options for trauma-focused treatment. Even if it is not easy to access the trauma-focused treatment that clients need, workers who are informed about trauma and who let clients know they are prepared to hear their stories have taken an important first step.

Some of the case examples discussed in this volume illustrate the power of a trauma-informed agency. The Institute for Family Services (chapter 5) uses gender-specific groups and their knowledge of the trauma of family violence to challenge the power and privilege disparities that promote domestic abuse. Project WISE (chapter 11) focuses on empowering women in poverty, also with an underlying recognition of the dynamics of trauma and oppression in their lives.

Trauma-Focused Treatment and Empowerment

Clients may seek a social worker not to talk about trauma but for other reasons—such as depression, anxiety, or substance use—or they may arrive ready to talk about a trauma. One central question of intervention is to what extent do we help the clients uncover the painful feelings and memories? Even if we use a model, such as Herman's (1997), that moves from establishing safety to remembrance and mourning and then to reconnection, it will be the clients who cue us as to whether or not they are ready to do any verbal remembering and mourning. If they are not ready, we respect their lead.

Some approaches do not require an in-depth processing of traumatic memories. Examples are the mind/body approaches used with an adult survivor of childhood violence (chapter 4), the supportive approach used with a child being bullied (chapter 6), and the workplace debriefing approach used to help an agency grieve a client death (chapter 8). In those cases the intervention was more present-focused. Work with other clients included and even required a direct look at the secrets that they had held in for so long: the treatment of an adolescent who revealed sexual abuse (chapter 2) and the work with the Vietnam veteran who for years had suppressed his memories and tried to go about his life (chapter 13).

Several of the approaches described in this book use an interplay of trauma treatment and a supportive, trauma-informed intervention. The work with an injured child and his mother required both play therapy to process the frightening memories and support for the mother, whose own childhood vulnerabilities arose (chapter 1). When a client revealed sexual molestation at her mental health agency itself, she needed both to talk about the experience and to have the agency act to protect her (chapter 3).

If the trauma has been long-standing, insidious, and discriminatory, the social worker brings a special awareness of intervention at simultaneous levels (personal, interpersonal, and social) to the work. For example, a lesbian client begins treatment with a focus on her current career and relationship issues, but underlying them is a history of threats and danger based on her sexual orientation and that history must also be addressed (chapter 7). Clients from groups that have endured massive attacks upon their very existence, such as Native Americans, benefit from an approach that names this historical trauma and facilitates their grieving both personally and as part of a community (chapter 9).

When the trauma is caused by natural disaster, war, or terrorism, those affected may need individual or group approaches, or both. The power of the group is used to help youth who lost a parent in the tragedy of September 11 (chapter 10). Refugees fleeing from torture and temporary camps use both groups and individual case management to adjust to a new life (chapter 12). When a whole community is swept away by the power of a hurricane, families are helped to regain some sense of normalcy and find meaning in their reconnections with community (chapter 14).

These chapters have referred to a number of trauma specialists and trauma response frameworks (Briere and Scott 2006; Everstine and Everstine 1993; Herman 1997; Saakvitne et al. 2000). Table C.1 synthesizes the phases of trauma-focused intervention with the phases of empowerment work (Wise 2005). The presence of boxes that lead from early stages on the left to final stages on the right does not mean that intervention is a lockstep process. Client and social worker may move several times between different phases or tasks, but overall there is a movement toward a reworking and resolution of the trauma and distress that brought the client to treatment.

The common elements of a trauma-focused intervention, then, are that it establishes safety and a connection/empathy between client and social worker, that it addresses the painful memories and feelings when the client is ready or uses stress-reduction techniques to make it possible for the client to address them, and that it moves toward reconnection with and meaning-making in the client's world.

The final row in the table shows the phases of empowerment work. Within these phases, the social worker has kept in mind all of the principles illustrated throughout the book—always emphasizing strengths and self-empowerment while diminishing oppression, enacting multicultural respect, having an awareness of specific needs, integrating the support needed, and using cooperative roles that have the effect of equalizing power within the relationship.

The empowerment framework includes a deep respect for client resilience. This resilience is the well from which clients draw their strength and find ways to empower their own lives. As stated in the introduction, resilience is not a static, either/or condition. Resilience is a continuum, and

Table C. I.
Common Phases of Trauma Treatment and the Parallel with Empowerment Work

Treatment Phase:	Early	Middle	Late
	Healing Relationship: This is not so much a phase but a necessity in trauma treatment that covers all phases. Herman writes that both therapist and client build a 'collaborative relationship' based on 'persuasion rather than coercion, ideas rather than force, mutuality rather than authoritarian control. These are precisely the beliefs that have been shattered by the traumatic experience' (p. 136).		
Judith Herman *Trauma & Recovery*, 1997	**Safety** • Moving from 'unpredictable danger to reliable safety' • Even before safety comes accurate assessment and 'naming' the trauma (as it is often disguised or hidden) • Somatic safety – no longer being triggered and highly anxious • Providing information • This stage is not rushed – it is important to regain control, predictability (even if client has heard that he/she must pour it all out at once – best to put	**Remembrance & Mourning** • Moving from 'dissociated trauma to acknowledged memory' • The therapist bears 'witness' to the client's story – told in depth so that it can go from an unformed fear to an actual memory with a narrative • Timing – always, both therapist & client are aware of his/her readiness to do this work; it will be hard • Client remembers life before the trauma, remembers what happened and how it felt emotionally and physically, and constructs a **meaning**	**Reconnection** • Moving from 'stigmatized isolation to restored social connection' • Building a new life – even for those who are not moving, there is a quality of being a 'refugee in a new country' • The trauma survivor re-engages with the world – not just to protect self, as he/she did in the safety phase, but to discover or rediscover aspirations, ambitions, power, new friends

(*Continued*)

Table C.1.
(*Continued*)

Treatment Phase	Early	Middle	Late
	brakes on revealing details until client feels safe and stable)	• Mourning – sadness over what was lost, a very difficult stage (one people wish they could skip)	• Some survivors feel a mission to transcend the trauma and take social action/help others
John Briere and Catherine Scott *Principles of Trauma Therapy, 2006*	**Safety, Stability, Psychoeducation, Distress Reduction and Affect Regulation** The client must feel safe, have stability in life and psyche, and learn how to stay within a 'therapeutic window'	**Cognitive and Emotional Interventions** Rather than a tension, these two approaches are both used – to engage a client's cognitive insight and to work through the fear	**Increasing Identity and Relational Functioning** Encouraging self-awareness, repairing attachments, building positive interpersonal relationships
Karen Saakvitne & Laurie Pearlman (who with Gamble & Lev wrote *Risking Connection*, 2000)	The authors use Herman's concepts, and include the importance of holding a 'trauma framework' that sees adaptations clients have made after trauma not as pathology but as ways to survive (adaptations such as substance use, eating disorders, self-mutilation, social isolation), and recognizes the lasting impact of earlier events (does not expect people to just 'get over it'). They present a model, based on a strong therapeutic alliance and on empowerment, that includes: Respect, Information, Connection, and Hope (RICH) They also review seven components of recovery defined by Mary Harvey: authority over the remembering process, integration of memory and affect, affect tolerance, symptom mastery, self-esteem and self-cohesion, safe attachment, and meaning making.		

(*Continued*)

Table C. I.
(*Continued*)

Treatment Phase:	Early	Middle	Late
Louis & Diane Everstine *The Trauma Response*, 1993	**Stabilization** Providing information: education about the normal reactions to traumatic events and about the process of recovery If seen in an emergency room after a physical trauma, client may need calm, directive help	**Psychotherapy** A 'dynamic systems' approach – simultaneously working on a person's feelings and also on his/her interactions with family, work and other systems Begin by strengthening a client's natural defenses, teach ways to lower strong feelings Move into the therapy stage, treating depression, accepting anger, using somatic methods such as relaxation if needed, reframing distortions	
Judith Bula Wise, *Empowerment Practice with Families in Distress*, 2005	**Beginning Phase:** Worker preparation includes self analysis and consideration of family of origin, setting the stage through information-gathering, anticipatory empathy, and meeting the clients to find out their views of what is needed and offering help that will address those needs	**Middle Phase:** A time for the clients to tell their stories. Also a time for providing information, helping to strengthen coping skills, expanding the client's participation with others (support groups, family, etc.). The relationship with the social worker deepens in this phase as the client experiences a cooperative and mutual relationship	**Ending Phase:** In this phase clients deal with feelings about endings (especially if prior endings have been painful and unfinished), identify & consolidate gains, and reunify with the community. It ends with evaluation of achievements.

thus it can be nurtured, through a warm and caring relationship, encouragement, and promotion of self-efficacy (Norman 2000).

Some writers have focused on qualities within resilient individuals. Bonnano (2004), writing about resilience in the face of normal bereavement and with brief stressors, identifies the healing qualities of hardiness, self-enhancement, repressive coping, positive emotion, and laughter. Glicken (2006) identifies, among other capacities, the presence of creativity, satisfaction with work, spirituality, humor, biological makeup, and altruism as important in coping with adversity. Some cautions should be noted in applying the idea of resilient traits to resilience after severe trauma. Glicken's work reminds us that it may take longer to deal with trauma that involves interpersonal violence or assault and to deal with multiple traumas, especially if they happen in rapid succession.

It is more useful to think of resilience in the face of trauma as a process or a journey available to all, and the absence of resilience in the face of adversity as reflecting an early stage of that journey. This developmental nature of resilience is captured in Gitterman's (2001) reflection on its definition: "The process of 'rebounding' and 'returning to prior state' does not suggest that one is incapable of being wounded or injured. Rather, in the face of adversity a person can bend, lose some of his or her power and capability, yet recover and return to [a] prior level of adaptation" (17).

Resilience is also fostered by caring social environments, perhaps never more so than after a trauma. Some of the most important contributions to resilience after trauma actually come from the social environment, specifically from: "a) environments that promote physical and mental health; b) environments that promote normative development; and c) environments that promote social cohesion and the development of social capital" (Lepore and Revenson 2006:32). An example of a resilience-enhancing physical environment would be the healing gardens used in some hospitals to promote connection with nature and reduce the stress of illness. Social support, the presence of a safe listening environment, and the process of therapy itself are also examples of caring social environments. This concept of resilience fits well with a person-in-environment perspective and a process orientation toward recovery after trauma: "Moving the focus away from individuals to the settings they inhabit avoids the trap of 'blaming the victim' for negative circumstances or poor adaptation . . . and may point to more fundamental 'upstream' social-environmental factors that create negative outcomes" (32).

Resilience applies to the social worker as well. Each chapter has described the ways in which our clients' trauma may be felt by the practicing social worker as a form of vicarious trauma or secondary stress. This emphasis is intended to remind us of the need for self-awareness in all trauma work—an awareness that acknowledges the pain we may hear, allows us to bear witness to it, and keeps us mindful of our own needs and our own strengths. As helping professionals, we face the need for periodic self-care and burnout prevention (Skovholt 2001). In addition, as professionals who work with trauma, we face the need to confront the meaning of this work. Vicarious trauma brings about a need for awareness, balance, and connection (Saakvitne and Pearlman 1996). Awareness is the first step—letting ourselves see and name the impact of this work on us. Balance refers both to the interplay between work life and home life and to the inner state that accompanies awareness and unhurried mindfulness. Connection is necessary in this work, especially connection to other trauma professionals, but also connection to significant others, to ourselves, and to what we consider meaningful in the larger world. This last suggestion is a powerful one—though the job of social work itself is based on altruism and a desire to help, those who work with trauma can find meaningful connection in other, community-based projects. "Working together for a common goal or the common good offsets the psychic and spiritual isolation of vicarious traumatization" (Saakvitne and Pearlman 1996:74).

It has been our goal in this book to present a variety of client stories and an explanation of the empowering interventions used by the social workers who engaged in the process of healing with them. This work can be difficult and at times daunting—for the student, the new social work graduate, and the seasoned professional. It can also be profoundly meaningful. We hope these chapters show the resilience and the meaning that emerged from the collaborative work of social workers and clients. We have emphasized the principles of safe and compassionate trauma intervention, the need to respond at all levels (personal, interpersonal, and social), and the need to challenge the often unacknowledged traumas of racism, violence, economic injustice, and poverty. The result is, we hope, a unique reflection on responding to trauma using our deeply felt *social work* values. Bearing witness to the depths of client trauma and tragedy calls upon all our strengths as helpers and as members of the human community. By nurturing our own personal resilience through awareness and balance, maintaining supportive interpersonal connections with loved ones and colleagues, and having the institutional social support that empowers us, we will be prepared to join in the work of this book: transforming trauma through empowerment and resilience.

References

Bonanno, G. A. 2004. "Loss, Trauma, and Human Resilience: Have We Under-estimated the Human Capacity to Thrive After Extremely Aversive Events?" *American Psychologist* 59 (1): 20–28.

Briere, J., and C. Scott. 2006. *Principles of Trauma Therapy: A Guide to Symptoms, Evaluation, and Treatment.* Thousand Oaks, Calif.: Sage.

Everett, B., and R. Gallop. 2001. *The Link Between Childhood Trauma and Mental Illness: Effective Interventions for Mental Health Professionals.* Thousand Oaks, Calif.: Sage.

Everstine, D. S., and L. Everstine. 1993. *The Trauma Response: Treatment for Emotional Injury.* New York: Norton.

Gitterman, A. 2001. "Social Work Practice with Vulnerable and Resilient Populations." In A. Gitterman, ed., *Handbook of Social Work Practice with Vulnerable and Resilient Populations,* 1–36. 2nd ed. New York: Columbia University Press.

Glicken, M. D. 2006. *Learning from Resilient People: Lessons We Can Apply to Counseling and Psychotherapy.* Thousand Oaks, Calif.: Sage.

Harris, M., and R. D. Fallot, eds. 2001. *Using Trauma Theory to Design Service Systems.* San Francisco: Jossey-Bass.

Herman, J. 1997. *Trauma and Recovery.* 2nd ed. New York: Basic Books.

Lepore, S., and T. Revenson. 2006. "Relationships Between Posttraumatic Growth and Resilience: Recovery, Resistance, and Reconfiguration." In L. Calhoun and R. Tedeschi, eds., *Handbook of Posttraumatic Growth: Research and Practice,* 24–46. Mahwah, N.J.: Lawrence Erlbaum.

Norman, E. 2000. "Introduction: The Strengths Perspective and Resiliency Enhancement—A Natural Partnership." In E. Norman, ed., *Resiliency Enhancement: Putting the Strengths Perspective Into Social Work Practice,* 1–18. New York: Columbia University Press.

Saakvitne, K. W., S. Gamble, L. A. Pearlman, and B. T. Lev. 2000. *Risking Connection: A Training Curriculum for Working with Survivors of Childhood Abuse.* Baltimore: Sidran.

Saakvitne, K. W., and L. A. Pearlman. 1996. *Transforming the Pain: A Workbook on Vicarious Traumatization.* New York: Norton.

Skovholt, T. M. 2001. *The Resilient Practitioner.* Needham Heights, Mass.: Allyn and Bacon.

Wise, J. B. 2005. *Empowerment Practice with Families in Distress.* New York: Columbia University Press.

Index

Accountability, Cultural Context Model and, 103, 104, 114, 119–20

Acute stress disorder (ASD), 5, 143; PTSD v., 6

Adolescents: developmental needs of, 37; empowering support for, 47; incest and, 38–41; September 11th trauma group work and, 194–212; sexual abuse and, 35–49; as terrorism survivor, 195–200; traumatic stress and, 36–37

Adult memory trauma: empowerment principles and, 89–92; mind-body approach to, 80–88, 302; trigger for, 84

Adversity, cumulative, mental illness and, 56, 73

African Americans, and PTSD of, 182

Agency grief: CISD for, 172–73; client's death and, 159–73; debriefing for, 162–73; dynamics of, 160–62; empowering support and, 171; empowerment principles and, 170–72; Lattanzi-Licht on, 161; multicultural respect and, 170–71; needs awareness of, 171; power equalization and, 171; psychological intervention and, 167–68; responding to, 162–68; strength/oppression and, 170; victimization sense and, 161

Aggression: bullying and, 125, 127; of males, 101

Alcoholism: historical trauma and, 179–80; Lakota reservations and, 179–80; see also Substance abuse

All Quiet on the Western Front (Remarque), Van Kirk on, 264

Almeida, Rhea, 99, 102, 105

Amnesty International, on torture, 240–41

Anxiety: from bullying, 127; from disasters, 289; insidious trauma and, 146; among LGBT, 145; post-traumatic, 31; poverty and, 222; sexual abuse and, 37

Armendariz, B. A., 187

Art therapy, 31; for assessments, 24; clay as, 25–26; for dog attack, 24–25; painting as, 24–25

ASD; *see* Acute stress disorder
Asian Americans: family identity of, 42; family system structure of, 42–43; social worlds of, 42
Assessment: art therapy for, 24; strengths based, 61, 64–66
Asylee/refugee, 303; application for, 238; immigrants and, 238; international law and, 238; NGOs and, 238–39; oppression of, 240; resources for, 239; torture of, 239
Atwood, G. E., 126
Autonomic nervous system, PTSD and, 80

Barton, A. H., on therapeutic community, 292–93
Bell, H., 41
Bereavement; *see* Traumatic bereavement
Biofeedback, for mind-body approach, 81
Bisson, J., 167, 168
"Boarding school era": Bureau of Indian Affairs and, 178; impact of, 184; of Native history, 178; negative impact of, 181
Bonanno, G. A., 8, 307
Borderline personality disorder, PTSD and, 267–68
Boulton, M. J., 135
Boyd-Franklin, N., 225
Brave Heart, M. Y. H., 187, 190
Briere, J., 305
Broca's area, trauma and, 80
Brom, D., 167
Bullying: aggression and, 125, 127; at Columbine, 128; as complex phenomenon, 128, 137–38; depression/anxiety from, 127; disclosure of, 132; ecological/societal contexts of, 127; empowering support and, 136; empowerment principles and, 133–37; forms of, 132; Fox/Boulton on, 135; impact of, 126, 130, 131; indirect/direct, 126, 127–28, 130; interventions for, 129, 133–34, 135–36, 137; LGBT and, 135; multicultural respect and, 134–35; needs awareness and, 135; Olweus on, 127;

perception of, 127–28, 130, 134; power imbalance in, 125, 136–37; prevalence of, 126; psychological trauma and, 125–26; recognition of, 131–32; repetition of, 129–30; reporting of, 128–29; responding to, 128–32; schools and, 127, 128, 130, 134, 137; studies of, 127; therapist's reaction to, 132–33; trauma of, 125–28; Twemlow/Cohen on, 129; victims/victimizer characteristics of, 126; VT and, 132–33
Bureau of Indian Affairs, 178
Burnout, STS *v.*, 5

Capacity building: ecological principle and, 254; mental health system and, 254–55; results of, 254–55
Carlisle Indian School, 181, 187; Native Americans and, 178
Census Bureau, poverty guidelines and, 218–19
Change the Channel: as group work, 203–4, 210; Webb on, 203–4
Chavkin, W., 221
Child abuse: aftereffects of, 300–301; child protective services and, 38; mental illness and, 300; statistics of, 36
Child protective services: child abuse and, 38; foster care and, 38
Childhood trauma: adult memories of, 78–80; play therapy for, 21; resilience from, 28, 32; transformation of, 15–32; unresolved, 20
Children: disasters and, 282, 284, *285*; poverty and, 219; September 11th trauma group work and, 194–212, 303; as terrorism survivor, 195–200
CISD; *see* Critical incident stress debriefing
CISM; *see* Critical incident stress management
Clients: Cultural Context Model and, 104, 116; death of, 159–73; IFS experience of, 115–20; privacy between, 105–6; *see also* Sexual minority client

177, 183–88; substance abuse and, 177; Takini Network for healing of, 184; understanding of, 177–78; unresolved grief intervention and, 183–90

Historical Trauma and Unresolved Grief Intervention (HTUG), 183–90; activities for, 185; effectiveness of, 186; empowerment principles of, 184; identity and, 185; for life span trauma, 190; parenting skills and, 184, 189

Historical trauma theory: development of, 178–81; emergence of, 178–79; Jewish Holocaust descendants and, 179

HTUG; *see* Historical Trauma and Unresolved Grief Intervention

Hurricane Katrina: memoir on, 279–80; poverty and, 217, 218, 228

Hyperarousal, 248; awareness of, 83; of combat veterans, 260, 265; reduction of, 82–84; relaxation techniques for, 83; talking interventions and, 81; terror and, 57

Hypervigilance, 63, 78, 207

Identity: after war, 261, 263, 265; of Asian Americans, 42; Brave Heart on, 187, 190; Colon/Armendariz on, 187; disasters and, 291; empowerment practice and, 42–43, 189–90; HTUG and, 185; of Lakota, 186–87; verbal abuse and, 156; victimized due to, 146–47

IFS; *see* Institute for Family Services

Immigrants: asylee/refugee and, 238; challenges of, 240; classification of, 238; needs of, 252; political advocacy for, 253; as political topic, 237–38; resettlement of, 244–45; resilience of, 255; resources for, 245, 252; therapists and, 255–56; trauma of, 240–41; triple trauma paradigm and, 242–46; undocumented, 239–40

Incest: adolescents and, 38–41; consequences of, 44; survival skills of, 44–45

Insidious trauma, 142–57; anxiety and, 146; community empowering support

and, 154–55; depression and, 149; empowerment principles and, 149–57; mental health system and, 153–54; National Coalition of Anti-Violence Programs on, 145; need awareness and, 152–53; oppression and, 148; power equalization and, 155; PTSD and, 145–46, 151; responding to, 147–48; role of, 147; self-empowering support and, 153–54; stressors for, 144, 146, 148; symptoms of, 143, 156; understanding of, 143–47; VT and, 148–49

Institute for Family Services (IFS): client's experience at, 115–20; Cultural Context Model by, 103, 120–21; empowering support by, 112–23; empowerment principles at, 113–20; mission of, 113; reflecting teams at, 115; sponsorship program and, 107–8; trauma knowledge of, 301–2; VT and, 112–13

Institutions: captivity and, 59–60; experiences of, 60; learned helplessness in, 56; oppressions in, 55; trust in, lack of, 60; *see also* Mental health center; Mental health system; Oppression, institutional

Intergenerational trauma; *see* Historical trauma

Interpersonal empowerment, 224–25; combat trauma and, 268–70

Intervention: agency grief and, 167–68; for bullying, 129, 133–34, 135–36, 137; crisis, 290–91; debriefing and group, 166; disaster, prevention and, 286, 290, 296; historical trauma and unresolved grief, 183–90; hyperarousal and talking, 81; for post-traumatic stress disorder, 188; strengths-based assessment, safety and, 61, 64–66; for torture, 256; for triple trauma paradigm, 246; *see also* Historical Trauma and Unresolved Grief Intervention

Intrusive thoughts: trauma and, 199; Webb on, 203–4

Iraq War: combat veterans and, 276; enemies of, 276; PTSD and, 276

Native history and, 179, 182; Phase Oriented Treatment strategies for, 185; poverty and, 222, 229; risk of, 16–17; self-medication of, 269; September 11th trauma and, 207; from sexual abuse, 37; symptoms for, 6, 36, 264, 265, 301; torture and, 241; Vietnam veterans and, 262–63; VT and, 148; *see also* Complex Post-Traumatic Stress Disorder

Poverty: in Aberdeen Area, 180; after WWII, 218; anxiety and, 222; children and, 219; class lines and, 228; complex concept of, 217, 221; disaster and, 281; economic guidelines for, 219; education and, 220, 227; employment and, 220; empowering support and, 230–31; empowerment principles and, 226–32; empowerment response to, 223–25; guidelines of, by Census Bureau, 218–19; Hurricane Katrina and, 217, 218, 228; implications of, 232–33; Katz on, 221; Kilty/Segal on, 217; level of, set by Social Security Administration, 218; literature on, 219; mental health and, 221–22; mental illness and, 54, 66, 221; moderate *v.* extreme, 218; multicultural respect and, 227–29; needs awareness and, 229; oppression of, 226–27; Pearce on, 219; power equalization and, 231; Project WISE on, 225–26; PTSD and, 222, 229; racism/sexism and, 220; resources, lack of, and, 220–21; Romero/Chavkin/Wise, P. H./Smith on, 221; Sachs on, 218; Samuelson on, 218; self empowerment and, 229–30; situational *v.* long-term, 222–23; survey of, 218; TANF and, 220, 233; trauma and, 215–33; understanding scope of, 217–23; verbal abuse and, 215–16; victimization and, 222; VT and, 225–26; web of, 219–21, 233; women and, 219

Power: according to hierarchies, 101; of people of color, *108*; domestic abuse and, 99–102; empowerment *v.*, 9,

100; equalization of, 29–30, 45, 62, 91–92, 105, 115, 120, 136–37, 155, 171, 187, 231, 274–75; of gay/lesbian partnerships, *109*; within gay/lesbian relationships, *111*; of heterosexual relationships, *110*; imbalance of, in bullying, 125; influenced by mental illness, 54, 60; of LGBT, 154; men and, 105; misuses of, 100, 101, 102–12, 117; reconnection and, 71; trauma's influence on, 57–58

"Power and Control" Wheels, tactics of, 100

Preflight displacement periods of exposure: experiences of, 242–43; triple trauma paradigm and, 242–43

Privacy: between clients, 105–6; Cultural Context Model and, 104–12; between family members, 106–7; between therapists, 104–5

Privilege: Cultural Context Model and, 104–12; domestic abuse and, 99–102; misuses of, 102–12; removal/ withholding of, 101

Project WISE; *see* Project Women's Initiative for Service and Empowerment

Project Women's Initiative for Service and Empowerment (Project WISE), 217; community empowerment and, 225; programs within, 223–24; public housing development and, 227; roles of, 231–32; self empowerment and, 229–30; target population of, 227; on VT/ poverty, 225–26; Welfare Reform Board and, 229; for women, 223–24, 302

Prolonged life-threatening events, complex PTSD and, 263

Psychiatric disability, women: living with, 54–56; responses to trauma, 56–60; sexual abuse of, 51–52; trauma and, 51–74; victimization of, 52, 62; vulnerability of, 53, 59

Psychological trauma, 4; bullying and, 125–26; disasters and, 282; Stolorow/Atwood on, 126; terror/disconnection of, 222

of, 240; prevention of, 252; PTSD and,
241; trauma of, 236–56, 303; UN on,
241; as unbelievable, 248–49
Torture syndrome, 241–42
Torture trauma treatment: challenges of,
248–49; culture broker and, 250–51;
group work and, 253; multicultural
respect and, 249; needs awareness and,
251; principles of, 246–47; therapists
and, 249
Trauma: brain changes after, 79; Broca's
area and, 80; of bullying, 125–28;
chaos/crisis and, 301; childhood,
15–32; collective reality/consciousness
and, 199; of combat veterans, 259–76;
coping skills for, 65–66, 202; crimes
identified as, 53; dimensions of, 3;
disclosure of, 62, 64; disconnection
and, 60–61; empowerment practice
for, 308; fight-or-flight response to,
79; Herman on, 275; IFS knowledge
of, 301–2; of immigrants, 240–41;
intergenerational massive group,
177, 182–83; intrusive thoughts and,
199; meaning/reasoning for, 1, 82,
87–88; memory retriggering from,
20, 26; multicultural respect and,
66–67; Myers on, 200; parental
distress to, 17; person's response to,
2–3; physiological response to, 78;
political action against, 72; poverty
and, 215–33; power influenced by,
57–58; processing of, 84–87; resilience
from, 3, 307; resource teams for, 48;
sense of self and, 58–59; shock of, 19;
of torture/flight/resettlement, 236–56,
303; transformation by, 7, 144; triple
trauma paradigm and, 242–46; by
trusting people, 44; of victimization,
53–54; of war, 259–76; of women
with psychiatric disabilities, 51–74;
women's responses to, 56–60;
see also Adult memory trauma;
Collective trauma; Combat trauma;
Disaster trauma; Historical trauma;

Insidious trauma; Physical trauma;
Psychological trauma; September
11th trauma; Social trauma; Vicarious
trauma
Trauma naming, safety and, 61, 62–63
Trauma recovery: education and,
247; reconnection and, 70–72;
remembrance/mourning and, 67–70,
304–5; safety and, 61–67; stages of, 60
Trauma response, 6–7; captivity as, 59–60;
depression and, 143; disconnection
as, 58–59; empowerment and, 60–71;
Herman on, 56–60, 82; hypervigilance
as, 63; psychological responses and, 247;
terror and, 57–58
Trauma treatment: approaches to,
302; EMDR for, 85–86, 90–91;
empowerment and, 302–3, 304–6,
307–8; healing process for, 7, 82, 84–87,
92–93; HTUG, 183–90; hyperarousal
reduction, 82–84; van der Kolk, B.,
on, 208; lack of cohesion in, 37, 40;
mental health systems and, 301; open
communication regarding, 155–56;
safety/control in, 247, 304–5; SE for,
86; stabilization and, 306; stages of,
82; therapists skill and, 85; trauma
meaning/reasoning and, 82, 87–88; VT
and, 88–89
Trauma-informed services, Harris/Fallot
on, 301
Traumatic bereavement: Neria/Litz on,
161; traumatic grief v., 161
Traumatic grief: Jacobs on, 161; September
11th trauma and, 207; traumatic
bereavement v., 161
Traumatic stress, adolescents and, 36–37
Treatment providers, high turnover rate
of, 48
Triple trauma paradigm, 242–46; flight
and, 243–44; immigrants and, 242–46;
interventions for, 246; preflight
displacement periods of exposure,
242–43; psychological effects of,